KNOCK FOR KNOCK

Keith Rawlings

British Library Cataloguing In Publication Data
A Record of this Publication is available
from the British Library

ISBN 1846854873
978-1-84685-487-3

First Published 2007 by

Exposure Publishing, an imprint of Diggory Press,
Three Rivers, Minions, Liskeard, Cornwall, PL14 5LE, UK
WWW.DIGGORYPRESS.COM

About the Author

Keith Rawlings was born in 1940 and joined the Insurance Industry in his early twenties. He is married with two children and two grandchildren.

In 1969 he set up his own Insurance Broking Company and husbanded it to become one of the largest independent firms in the South East.

He has served on the Boards of several Public Companies (with interests ranging from overseas plantations, property and corporate finance).

He has also served as a non-executive on the Boards of an NHS Trust and a College of Further Education.

Whereas *Knock for Knock* is not an autobiography, some of the characters, and some of the incidents, do bear a passing resemblance to true life.

Chapter One

Tim must have yawned, although he could not be sure.

"Yer 'eart's not in it, is it?" suggested Bill Warrington in his gruff east-ender's voice. "Yer, bored, ain't cha?"

Bill was absolutely, one hundred percent spot on. Tim had been and Inspector with the Universal Insurance Company for seven long years now, and, to tell the truth, he was much more than bored. He was utterly, completely and balls-breakingly bored stiff.

He had joined the Company as a lad, keen and eager, when he was barely twenty years old – back in 1963. It was now 1970 and he felt that, in his social life, in his sex life and in his business life, he had missed out in a big way – a very big way. Ordinary would be the most exciting word to describe his life today.

Even living through the 'swinging sixties' he'd missed out – the years simply hadn't swung for him, and it still depressed him.

Everything he did now seemed repetitive. The excitement and nervous anticipation that he had felt when he was promoted seven years ago, when he first went out 'on the road', had long since evaporated. In fact, today he was not just bored; he was, as his old granddad would say, truly pissed off.

It was over a month since Colin Cooper, a fifty-year old going on sixty-year old Insurance Broker, had arranged this afternoon's appointment. He had been asked to carry out a routine annual review of Warrington's insurances. He and Colin carried out the same review every January with dear old Bill Warrington, the founder and Managing Director of one of the town's largest and most successful heavy engineering Companies. Every year it was the same old thing – Colin would act like God's gift to the Insurance Industry while Tim would be the poodle who would answer all the technical questions, make all the notes and generally ensure that Colin did not make too big a cock-up of the event. Cooper got the glory (and the commission) whilst Tim did all the work – and for peanuts.

Many had been the times when Colin would guarantee unequivocally that Warrington's were covered for this contingency or that unlikely event. Tim would then have to politely intervene, with a word of caution, to point out that that this was not necessarily the case. He then had to explain the true scope (and limitations) of Warrington's current insurance protection. In fact, Tim would have far preferred to carry out the meeting with Bill on his own, without the embarrassment of having Colin around. Provided, of course, that Tim had had the time to fully prepare for the meeting.

And that is how it should have been today; except that Colin had phoned only half an hour before the time that they were due to meet to ask Tim to go on alone because "something very urgent had cropped up." The fact that Tim had passed Colin's Mercedes travelling rapidly towards the Golf Course, in the opposite direction as he was dutifully driving to Warrington's did nothing to improve his mood.

The real problem was, of course, that Colin had all the papers needed for the meeting, together with the Agenda itself, so Tim would now have to stumble through the meeting the best way he could without any supporting data or information.

The fact that this was the fourth annual review with Bill Warrington meant that, at least he knew most of the answers, and at least he was pretty sure that he could get through fairly well unscathed.

"You're bored out of your mind, ain't cha?" Bill repeated, having noticed that Tim had a glazed, far-away look in his misted eyes.

"Of course not Bill. It's just that I had a latish night and then the baby woke up half a dozen times. Teething problems again I'm afraid. How Mary manages to get up so many times and still look as fresh as she does in the morning, I'll never know. I'm sorry; nothing could be further from the truth. Now where were we? That's it, your latest Stock Declaration, what was the total value at the end of December?"

"Bugger the Stock valuation. I don't know why we go through this effin' charade every year. You should be able to insure me for what I want without asking so many bloody fool questions. It's always the bloody same thing, more or less. Can't you just do what you think is right and drop me a line confirming what yer've done? I'd feel much 'appier leaving it to you rather that having that la di dah prat Cooper sticking his bloody nose into things what he certainly don't understand."

"I'm sorry you feel that way about Colin. He's looked after your Insurances for at least ten years now and I've always thought that you and he got on well. He always does a professional job".

"That's crap, and you know it. He ponces in 'ere with 'is bleeding bow tie an' 'is patent leather brief case, gets in the way and leaves you to do all the work. Ten year's ago it was a different story I'll give yer that. He was young and 'ungry and keen to get our business. Over the last few years 'e's got too bloody fat and too effin' idle. 'E's a tosser an' you know it. I've a good mind to change Brokers. Who'd you recommend?"

"I really couldn't answer that, Bill. Colin has seen fit to pass 100% of your insurances to the Universal and I do have to respect his decision. I'm sure you agree that it would be quite unprofessional for me to go around recommending another firm".

"That's another thing. Don't get me wrong mate. I like dealing with you and I am sure that we're in good 'ands with the Universal. But I thought that an Insurance Broker was meant to actually broke the business – not just stick it all with one Company. It seems to me that you might be the best for our Fire Insurance, you might be the best for our Liability Insurance, and you might be the best for our bloody Motor Insurance but you sure as 'ell can't be the best for all of 'em! Why doesn't Cooper spread it around a little? I'll tell you why. He's too bloody lazy and he thinks that I'm a soft touch and I that won't rock the boat. Well I'm tellin' you, things 'ave got to change. I'll always give you first refusal for old time's sake, but I want to be sure that I'm paying the absolute rock bottom for all our Insurances, not just bits and pieces of it. You tell Cooper to get off his arse and do some work for a change".

Thanks Colin, Tim thought to himself. Where are you when I need you?

"I will certainly go through everything with Colin first thing tomorrow. In fact, having said that, it might be possible that another Company might be able to shave a pound or two off here and there, but we're giving you a package so, with the swings and roundabouts you've got a pretty good deal. And besides, we've handled your insurances for so many years now that you know we'd always give you the benefit of the doubt if you were to have a borderline claim."

"I'm not so sure about that – I wouldn't trust the Universal to give me a 'undred grand if they didn't 'ave to. Why don't you act as my Insurance Broker? I'm bloody sure you'd make a better job of it than Cooper. I said that you was bored. What you need is a change in life. You'll never make dough working for the Universal. Why don't you start up on your own? Start your own effin' firm. I'm sure you'd make a bloody fortune.

"I always remember, it was about twenty years ago when I was chief engineer at 'aywards and I fell out with the boss in a big way. 'e told me that I was making a balls up of a job and I told him that if he thought he could do it any better, 'e could fuckin' well take off 'is jacket and try. I even showed him how to start the lathe. 'e told me that if 'e got any more lip from me I could fuck off. I told 'im that I'd had enough and 'e could stick his effin' job where the monkey kept 'is nuts and I fucked off there and then. Did my Missus give me 'ell when I got 'ome? She damn near brained me.

"Mind you, it was the best thing I ever done. The following morning I walked round to Smith's Bakeries – it was Smiths wot I was making a Bread Roll carrier system for - for their ovens and that sort of thing. I told 'im what 'ad 'appened and I told him that 'aywards was trying to cut corners and was making a roller that would, in my opinion, wear out in one year flat, if it even lasted that long. Give old Smith his due, 'e said, "see that empty workshop at the back? 'ow much would it cost to tool it up so that you could do all our work 'ere on the premises wivout botherin' about 'aywards? 'e said that, as soon as I 'ad them all fixed up, it was OK for me to go round looking for more work for meself from other Companies, which is exactly what I did.

"I told him that a couple of grand should do it. 'He said fair enough, I'll lend you the money, you get it sorted.' And there I was, two weeks later, two grand in me 'and, an' I was away.

"That was twenty years ago, and look at me now. I employ a 'undred machinists, and an army of office staff. I've got the Roller and the missus 'as her Merc. We live in a lovely 'ouse and both me kids are at Cheveney Court at two grand a term each. Five years later, I give old man Smith a cheque for twenty grand, 'e give me back 'is share sustificates and we was both as 'appy as Larry. That's the way to do business. You back someone what you 'as faith in, give 'em their 'ead and sit back and wait. A good bloke'll never let you down or, if 'e does, 'e'll 'ave damn near died in the trying.

"'ow much do we pay you a year?" asked Bill, seemingly with an inexplicable change of direction.

"Well, with everything in, I reckon we're looking at £90,000 a year, give or take".

"And 'ow much does that greedy bugger Cooper get 'is sticky fingers on then?"

"I am not sure that I can tell you that," replied Tim. "I really think that you should ask Colin. It would be quite unprofessional if I were.........."

"Bollocks. All I want to know is what rate of commission the Universal pays its middlemen. You tell me the rate and I can soon work out the effin' figure. I may not 'ave got any "O" levels, but I know "ow many two's make four".

"Well, I suppose that the average rate of commission would be about 14%".

"Fourteen percent! Do you mean that that thievin' bastard is skimming off nearly fourteen grand a year from me for doin' bugger-all an' leaving all the work to you? That's daylight bloody robbery that is".

"I wouldn't say that," defended Tim. "Coopers have a ton of overheads to be able to give you the standards of service you need. I am sure that their actual profit is not that great."

"Bollocks. If you started your own Office, 'ow much would it cost to get set up?"

"Well, funnily enough, I do have some idea. Between you and me, I've been thinking of leaving and starting my own Company, but I just don't have the capital. With two kids under five it's....."

"ow much?" interrupted Bill. "It can't cost much to run a frigging office. It's not like 'ere where you need a factory and 'undreds of thousands of pounds worth of bloody tools and machinery".

"Well, there'd be rent and rates of about two thousand pounds a year. A secretary at three thousand, a leased car at one thousand, I'd need five thousand myself to cover Mary and the kids etc and say two thousand for stationery and odds and sods – say thirteen thousand pounds a year".

"That's it then. You start your Office and take over my business and you're onto a grand's profit in your first year before you get out of bed. Couldn't be simpler. When do we start?"

"That's very kind, very kind indeed and I would love to have a go," replied a stunned Tim, his heart skipping several beats. "I would, of course, have to speak to Colin first. It wouldn't be very fair to pinch his business without giving him a chance. I would also have to speak to my Office – find out what my restrictive covenants say. And I would also have to talk it over with Mary. It would be quite a momentous decision to take. Despite your generous, your very generous offer, there would be quite a few risks involved. I feel sure I could make it work, but even Colin Cooper faced some risks when he started."

"Bollocks to Cooper and bollocks to the Universal. You go an' talk it over with your Missus and if she thinks it's a good idea, just give me a call tomorrer and we'll get everything sorted. I'll 'ave 25% of the business for getting you started and you go out and make us both an effin' fortune. Old Smithy got me started and I'll do the same for you".

"I just don't know what to say Bill. This sounds like just the sort of thing I've been waiting for. If we can get it started, and I'm damn sure I can, I won't let you down. I'll go home, speak to Mary and then put some figures together. I'll be on the phone first thing tomorrow".

And with that Tim, with trembling fingers, shuffled his papers together, scooped them haphazardly into his briefcase and departed – post haste. Reviewing Warrington's insurances now seemed a pretty low priority. He couldn't wait to get home.

Chapter Two

The Lion Public Hostelry was situated in the least salubrious district in Town. It was a shabby Pub at the best of times, and this was not the best of times. At three-thirty on this wintry afternoon, it was about as shabby as it was possible to be without, that is, being closed down by the local Health and Safety standards office.

The television above the bar was turned up to full volume – what was showing no one had the slightest idea. One listless down and out (a decrepit patron), was playing the one-armed bandit, shovelling his dole money in as fast as he could, cussing loudly at the world at large and the proprietor in particular, whenever he lost. Cheering hoarsely whenever he won. The cussing out-stripped the cheering by about ten to one.

Every now and then the cacophony of sound was heightened by the raucous shrill of the winning bells. Thankfully, he would run out of money soon.

The atmosphere reeked of stale beer and cigarette smoke. The visibility was down to virtually zero; everything was obscured by an all-pervasive smog of dense, choking, swirling cigarette smoke. It was impossible to see one end of the room from the other.

The clientele were well used to this scarcity of oxygen, the noxious fumes and the drunken, incoherent conversations of their fellow denizens, for this was their regular mid-day haunt. Mid-day normally lasted from eleven in the morning to four in the afternoon. This pub was seedy. The barman was mean and seedy. The barmaid was fat, mean and seedy. The clientele were idle, mean and seedy.

This was, however, Joe Hendry's element. This was where he was at home. In the Lion, he was a success, a man who had the world at his feet. A man who dealt in high finance and who could teach those poor suckers around him how to make a bob or two. He was, in essence, a veritable Robin Hood. That is, if it were not for the fact that, whereas he endeavoured to take from the "rich", he somehow overlooked the bit about giving to the poor. How he did it, or what exactly his business was, they never did understand – but then, there was not too much that they were even capable of understanding.

In fact, Joe Hendry's 'profession' was selling double-glazing. To his fellow drinkers he described himself as a building surveyor and something to do with 'Environmental Improvement' – or, to his fellow drinkers, "the bloke what does up 'ouses and makes a mint from them toffs what've got more money than bloody sense."

At this moment in time, Joe was leaning on the Bar, an elbow in a puddle of stale beer, expounding to his companion how, last night, he had encouraged an elderly lady to part with most of her savings and how he had made a few grand in "commission" in the process. All for fixing her windows which, truth to tell, would have seen her out, no trouble at all – not that she knew that. He had knocked on her door that morning and told the old biddy that he had noticed dry rot in her downstairs windows. So charming had he been, that she had invited him in for a cup of tea. Being as he was in a good mood and had plenty of time, he offered to carry out a free survey of all her windows there and then, absolutely no charge and no obligation. 'Trust me luv.'

She was so grateful that he had drawn her attention to all the problems that she had been unaware of. Hardly a window in the house was free from infestation, he had assured her and, unless she acted soon, she would be faced with the virtual certainty of having to re-build the house within a matter of months. How it had stood up so long was a bleedin' miracle, Joe had told her.

Fortunately for her, Joe was in a position to help, and provided she promised not to let on to his bosses, he could get the job done quick and clean - for cash and at half the price the Company would normally charge. In fact, if she could get him a grand by that evening, he could get the boys to earmark all the materials from a load that was coming in from Holland first thing next morning. This was a real favour but, unless she kept schtumm, no way could he deliver.

Seven o'clock that evening, round he went, on the dot and there and then, with a cuppa in one hand and an envelope in the other, she delivered the goods. Sweet as a nut. Of course, he wanted to get right out and down to the pub, but there were some easy pickings here so half an hour or so with the old bag was time well spent. So sit down, turn on the charm, act the Prodigal and there was plenty more where that came from. He checked all the measurements again, pointed out one or two more spots that needed attention that he hadn't noticed that morning and sat down with his calculator and acted the Surveyor.

After ten minutes humming and harring, he reckoned that the list price for replacing the ten windows and two doors would be six grand give or take a bit, but today was her lucky day, five grand cash and the job would be done.

He had to admit that the old biddy blanched a bit at that so he tapped away at his calculator a bit more (God knows what numbers he was hitting) and, with a heartfelt sigh said, "OK love, seeing as its you, and its cash and I want you to be nice and warm for the winter (hypotherapy or whatever it's called is a terrible killer, he added), I'll knock them all out for four and a half grand. God knows what my boss will say, but that's my problem. You leave him to me."

"That's really most decent of you," she says. "I don't want to get you into any trouble though. Are you really quite sure?"

"Put it this way, I say's. I'm a man who's as good as his word and if I say I'll do it for four and a half grand, I'll do it for four and a half. If I've got it wrong, I'll just let them take it out of my commission"

"I couldn't possibly let you do that she say's. "Let's call it four thousand seven hundred and fifty, just to be on the safe side. Will that be alright with you?"

"I could hardly believe my luck, Joe tells his audience. "So out with the old forms, signature on the line and I'm off. Change the four seven fifty to three seven fifty for the Office when she's not looking, all going to be paid in cash anyway, and we're off. Candy from kids. A grand in the back pocket – good day's work, no problem".

"I don't know how you do it Joe," said Ted Bushell, admiringly. Ted hadn't held down a proper job for more than six month's at a time in his whole life and he relied totally on the State and, Maggie, his long-suffering wife of twenty years, for his drinking and his betting money. He was totally overawed by this Captain of industry that stood before him. The fact that his wealth emanated largely from crooked deals only enhanced Joe's standing and Ted's admiration in equal measure.

"I only wish there was some way I could make a bob or two without, of course, Maggie getting to hear of it. Or, worse still, those bloody dole people. They're bastards they are. Just when you make a little bit on the side, they come over all heavy like and start threatening to turn off the tap. Where the hell they think we can get the cash from if they freeze up, God only knows."

"There is a way that might work," mused Joe. He always felt quietly benevolent and expansive in front of such an admiring audience. "One of the hardest parts of our job is getting the punters interested in the first place. Once I've got my foot in the door, I can sell them anything - like water off a duck's back.

"There are several ways of getting them interested, but I just don't have the time. What you could do is to pose as a Builder and knock on a few doors and spin the old biddies a line."

"What do yer mean, tell them they need a good shagging and offer them me services like?" suggested Ted.

"With a face and a gut like yours, you'd have no bloody chance at all, you'd be broke overnight," laughed Joe. "No, you say that you have been doing some work on a house down the street and managed to save them a fortune by putting them in touch with a specialist who can install the latest thermal insulation windows at a knock down price. You say that there's nothing in it for you, but you were so impressed by the standard of their work that you just had to knock them up to tell them. You say you were just passing and you couldn't help seeing that their windows had the same problem. If they leave them as they are any longer, you tell 'em, they're going to have real problems that will cost them thousands to sort out if they don't act sharpish.

"You don't give them a chance to think, just give them my card and say that Joe Hendry will pop round one evening, in his spare time as he would be working for cash, so as to save them the tax and the Company's forty percent profit.

"If you do your job properly, they'll think that I will be doing them one hell of a favour to spend so much of my own time helping them. I'll give you two hundred quid, cash, for each job I pull off."

"Two hundred quid! That's a fucking fortune. What 'appens if they tell me to fuck off?" queried Ted expressing a not unreasonable thought.

"You simply ask them if they are likely to change their mind in the foreseeable future. That usually makes them laugh and you can have another go. If they still say fuck off, then fuck off - no point in wasting time. There's always another punter next door."

Pyramid selling in those days was in its infancy. Joe Hendry's little pyramid selling scam was about to take off.

Chapter Three

Tim had intended to go back to his Office and dictate his notes of the meeting and his memos to he departments. These were the usual part and parcel of the job of reviewing Warrington's Insurances – a time-consuming and boring, albeit essential, chore. There was no way that he could be bothered with this chore on this occasion however. His mind was in turmoil. He had been thinking of getting out and starting on his own for years but there was never any time or never any opportunity to think about it.

More importantly, his fantasies always came to an abrupt end when he started thinking about where the cash would come from, how he could support Mary and the kids, and what would he do if the whole thing went belly up? There was no way that the Universal would ever take him back. If he left now, he would have burnt his boats completely - and thrown away the rescue craft in the process.

But Bill's offer was just what he needed. He reckoned that he could survive on five thousand a year and, with Bill's own business, he would have almost fourteen thousand pounds to cover expenses before he even got started. He could think of a few friends that would probably transfer their personal insurances to him - that would bring in a few quid. Then there were some of the Universal's other clients with whom he got on particularly well with. They just might want to give him a chance and let him handle their insurances if he was on his own and independent.

He would have to sit down and write out a list of probables and possibles and see what it all added up to. To see whether he would have a fighting chance of making a success of Harrisons, the Insurance brokers. The very thought of seeing his own name on the letter heading sent a shiver of anticipation (and apprehension) up his spine.

But first things first. Mary had to be persuaded. If she said 'no', then no it would be. He couldn't face the risk of starting a new business if he didn't have Mary's one hundred percent support behind him. Besides, she could be useful in doing a bit of typing and admin when the kids were at school. She also had a few useful friends, or her father did, who might be persuaded to come on board as clients.

However, first things first. Tim pulled up outside the Florists, jumped out and ran into the shop. He had not realised that there was such a bewildering choice. Mary did all that sort of thing usually and, as far as he was concerned, flowers were flowers. He was only ever vaguely aware that Mary had often put a few flowers out around the house, or that she had changed them from time to time.

"What do I buy the perfect wife with the perfect husband who is about to throw in his job and put the whole family's finances in grave danger?" he asked the young, pretty, blue-eyed shop assistant.

"Well, if things are that dodgy, I would suggest plastic flowers so that she will still have something when the roof falls in, or Lily's are always popular at funerals," Polly, suggested with a conspiratorial smile. "On the other hand, a dozen red roses never fail."

"Red roses it will be then. Red roses for a blue lady. Wrap them up. How much will that be?"

Tim blanched at the reply and gave serious consideration to amending the order to half a dozen. On second thoughts, he reasoned the primroses didn't look too bad either. No, in for a penny. This was the time for the grand gesture. He loved Mary dearly, and, after eight years of marriage, perhaps it was about time that he bought her flowers - for the first time in his life (that is, if you overlooked the impossibly expensive bouquet that he had had to stump up for at their wedding).

Next stop, the off-licence. Neither Tim nor Mary were big drinkers. They couldn't afford to be. But tonight would be different.

"Champagne my man," intoned Tim theatrically, as he confronted the young assistant in the off-licence. "A bottle of your best if you please."

"I can recommend the Dom Perignon at eighteen pounds a bottle or the '66 Bollinger is very good value at seventeen pounds ten shillings," came the reply.

"Christ," exclaimed Tim, "I was thinking of something nearer a fiver."

"Well we do have quite a good sparkling wine at four pounds two and sixpence. Frankly you (and he rather disdainfully emphasised the 'you') might well not tell the difference."

Feeling slightly deflated, Tim accepted this wise counsel and settled for the compromise. 'What the hell was the difference between Champagne and sparkling wine anyway?' he reasoned.

He then drove home, far too quickly, parked the car in the drive and sprinted up the path to the front door. Unlocking the front door and calling a cheery 'I'm home', Tim was immediately tackled around the legs by an excited three-year old. He suffered the risk of tinnitus from the ear-piercing screams from the teething one-year old and a 'what on earth are you doing back at this time, its only five o'clock,' from his overwrought, but smiling, wife.

This was not the ideal time to discuss their immediate, and extremely perilous, future, felt Tim. Disentangling himself from the adoring Becky, and before Mary had seen his 'booty', Tim quietly opened the downstairs toilet door, ran a little water in the washbasin and stuffed a dozen red roses and the bottle of wine therein.

The next hour and a half was devoted entirely to amusing Becky, comforting the six month-old Tom and generally helping to maintain a sense of sanity despite the all-pervading chaos. Tim began to have serious reservations as to why he had arrived home so early and made a mental note to take the six o'clock watershed as the earliest time to arrive home in the future. He had absolutely no idea how Mary managed to cope with this torment every day and still have the supper ready by seven every evening. This woman's a wonder he told himself, not for the first time.

At last, six-forty five pm, and peace once more descended on 34 Cherry Avenue. Stories read and both kids sleeping peacefully, Tim experienced the utter bliss of children too tired to make a sound. Perhaps it was worth the torture to be able to enjoy the calm after the storm, he mused.

Mary, hair awry, was bending over a fat-spitting frying pan when Tim entered the kitchen clutching his trophies, one dozen red roses and one bottle of highly commended sparkling French wine.

"Darling," exclaimed Mary as she turned to see such beneficence. "What have I done to deserve this? It's not my birthday, not the kids', not yours, not our Anniversary. Or have you been a naughty boy? Come here, let me kiss you. I can always tell by a kiss whether you have been up to something."

Tim readily succumbed to this scientific test and, if the length and intimacy of the contact was anything to go by, judged that he had passed the test (and with colours flying).

"No, to all of the above," gasped Tim as soon as he was free to breath again, flowers in one hand and wine in the other. "Apart from telling you that I quite like you, perhaps quite love you, I thought that this would be as good a way as any to tell you that, tomorrow, I shall resign from the Universal, the fountain of all our wealth and the current pillar of our financial security."

"Resign! How exciting! What a wonderful idea," was the unexpected response.

"Wonderful?" echoed Tim. "I thought you'd be horrified."

"I am assuming, of course," demurred Mary, "that you do have something else in mind that might enable me to live in the manner to which I hope, one day, to become accustomed. I didn't give up five grand a year at Lloyds Bank to be married to a pauper who would reduce me to penury in eight years flat. I am assuming, dearest husband, that you are about to tell me that you have been head-hunted by a Multi-National who wants to give you twenty grand a year, a Mercedes and a Villa in the South of France."

"Not quite," admitted Tim. "Or at least, not yet. You know how I've always thought that I would like to set up on my own. Well, now's the time. Bill Warrington, you remember old Bill, you've met him at the firm's day at the County Show a few times, he's come up with the proverbial offer that I don't think I can refuse."

"Fantastic. Now open the wine. Put the flowers in that jug on the window-ledge, let me finish cooking and tell me all about it."

Fifteen minutes later, bangers and mash in front of them, a half-emptied bottle of fine wine to hand and the sweet smell of a dozen roses assailing their nostrils, Tim began to fill in the details and, in the process, start formulating his own business plan.

"The great thing is," said Tim, "that the commission from the business that Bill's putting on a plate is worth about fourteen thousand pounds a year. I reckon that rent and rates, I must pop into Claverton's tomorrow to see what they've got, will cost about two to two and a half thousand pounds a year. A good secretary should cost about three thousand, a car another thousand, fees another two thousand, light heat and power a thousand and all the other bits and pieces can't come to more than another thousand. That leaves four or five thousand for me. I don't see how I can go wrong."

"I think you've forgotten the cost of equipment, furniture, bank charges and whatever you think things will cost, try doubling them for a start," reasoned Mary. "In my experience, nothing is as cheap as you think it will be. Unless you intend to sit on soap boxes and write with a quill pen, I'm afraid you're going to have to go out and wheel in a few more clients than just dear old Warrington's."

"Don't I know it? The one thing that I've been good at with the Universal, is pulling in the business. I know that it will be different representing my own little company rather than a household name, but I am sure that I can do it. In fact, since my heart will be in it, I have no doubt but that I shall be a bloody sight better - it can't fail."

"I totally agree darling, the sooner you get started, the better. I was thinking, Bob Lyons, you know, that friend of my father's who runs the printing business. I am sure that, if Daddy told him that his beloved daughter's old man was stepping out on his own, he'll give you a chance. He's always had a soft spot for me."

"If I remember aright, I think he's also got a hard spot for you. I'll never forget how he drooled over you when he got you on the dance floor at our wedding. He's nothing but a dirty old man."

"You're probably right, but there's nothing wrong with a rich dirty old man, particularly if some of his money comes in your direction. Put him on your list of potential clients. If Warrington's is worth that much, Lyons has got to be worth at least half as much."

"I was thinking," mused Tim, "I would have thought that people like Bob, Graham, Peter and even old George would let me have a go at their business. I'm sure that I would be able to save them all a bob or two and between them, I reckon their accounts would be worth another thousand or so. It soon adds up. I must make sure that I rent an office big enough to allow for expansion. I would imagine that, if I put it to him, Graham at the Office wouldn't mind coming in with me, once I got started. He looks after a tidy few clients and I would be surprised if they wouldn't follow him too."

"I admire your enthusiasm and I am sure that you're right, but aren't you getting a little ahead of yourself? What about the Universal, will they let you go or will they tie you down with hopeless covenants? Is there any chance of them insisting on you taking six month's gardening leave? Not that that would be a bad thing, the lawn's a disgrace and the vegetable patch hasn't seen anything but weeds for the last two years. And another thing, what about Colin Cooper? He may be a bit past his sell-by date, but sure as eggs are eggs, he won't take kindly to you pinching his best client. He will be down on the Universal – and you - like a ton of bricks screaming for your head on a platter. Old Roy Brown might be a very good branch manager, and a good friend, but he's not one to stick his head above the parapet, not when the proverbial's about to hit the fan."

"The sweet voice of reason as usual. I thought being a Mum had blunted your business sense but I see that there are still a few grey cells knocking around. Actually, Colin Cooper won't have a leg to stand on. He's taken old Bill Warrington for granted far too long and he knows it. The fact that it was Bill himself who came up with the idea won't make Colin's argument look too bright and I am sure that Roy will support me - especially if I leave most of the business with the Universal for the first year or so. He can always tell Head Office that Cooper's were bound to lose the business sooner or later and that, by backing me, they stand to keep most of it - at least for the foreseeable future. No, I don't think that there will be any insurmountable problems on that score.

"The covenants could be another matter. I haven't read my contract of employment for over five years, but I'm pretty sure that I am not allowed to canvass clients of the Company for a period of at least one year. On the other hand, I haven't canvassed Warrington's, it's they who have canvassed me!"

And so the discussion went on until midnight, when Tim and Mary, retired happily to bed. But it was sometime before they were able to sleep - after all, Mary had to say thank you for her flowers.

Chapter Four

"Come in," mumbled Roy Brown without looking up from a file of papers in which he was obviously totally engrossed. "You're making the place untidy."

Tim had been hovering in the open doorway for a full minute trying to attract Roy's attention. He was trying to judge his mood and had little desire to engage in what might be an extremely difficult conversation if Roy was in his "don't waste my time, I'm far too busy" mode.

Roy Brown had been the Local Branch Manager for the Universal for over twenty years and was looking forward to a cosy retirement within the next five years - probably much sooner, if he could negotiate a satisfactory redundancy package.

When, fifteen years ago, he had realised that his chances of promotion had disappeared (that prat Bigginswood had seen to that), he had accepted his circumstances with equanimity and had settled for a quiet life with as few complications as possible. In consequence, he was a good Branch Manager in that he was always fair to his staff (things were much more peaceful that way) but remained sufficiently conscientious to ensure that the Branch always met its budgets. He had, of course, mastered the art of ensuring that the budgets he set himself were never too demanding to meet with relative ease.

As it happened that morning, Roy was in one of his expansive moods, though he seemed rather more interested in sorting out the problem in front of him than starting up a new line of conversation with Tim.

"Look, what I don't understand Tim, is why the Loss Adjusters – Turners in this case - are recommending that we turn down Warrington's fire claim. I mean, they've been insured with us for donkey's years and, as far as I know, old Colin Cooper always makes sure that their cover is up to date. They've got a claim here for a the best part of a hundred grand, and Turner's are saying we needn't, or more precisely, we shouldn't, pay it."

"What!" exclaimed Tim, "turn down a claim of Warrington's' for a hundred thousand pounds - we can't do that! Bill Warrington might be an easy-going guy, but he is not going to take kindly to a repudiated claim for any amount, let alone a small fortune. He'll blow his stack."

The very last thing that Tim could contemplate at this particular time would be to be the bearer bad news, let alone, such appalling news. Just when his entire future may rest upon Warrington's' largesse, this would not be just bad news; this would be catastrophic news.

"What an earth can they be driving at? Warrington's are one of my best clients; we can't turn a claim of theirs down, we just can't. What grounds are Turners suggesting for such madness?"

"Well, I haven't been through the file word for word, but it appears that Warrington's have been doing some paint spraying in a booth next to the welding shop and that a spark misdirected itself and, whoosh, up she went.

"Fifty thousand pounds of workshop, twenty thousand pounds of machinery, twenty thousand pounds of customer's goods and some odds and ends for loss of profits. It's amazing where the money goes, but that's what it is going to cost."

"But that was ages ago. I thought that claim had been paid two or three month's ago. Bill never mentioned it when I saw him yesterday."

"Ah, yesterday, he wouldn't have known then that Turners had come up with this little problem. What Turners have pointed out is that there is a warranty under their Policy specifically excluding any welding work within ten metres of any painting work."

"But that's ridiculous," exclaimed Tim. "Colin said that he had sent one of his own Risk Manager down to survey the place. He charges enough for one of those surveys and, at last renewal, he had given a glowing report to the effect that everything was hunky dory and that absolutely no risk improvements were needed. If they didn't spot that welding and spraying were being carried out in contravention to one of the Policy conditions, then it's down to them. I'm not having Warrington's penalised by Cooper's negligence. They've got Professional Indemnity Insurance. They will have to pick up the tab."

"Hold hard there. You don't want to upset Warrington's. I can sympathise with that, but neither do I want to upset Coopers. They give us a ton of business every year – they always have done - and the last thing that I want, is a bust up with them. Its hard enough to meet our budgets without upsetting one of our major producers."

Tim could feel the euphoria of the night before evaporating mist in a hot sun. He was here to explain to Roy that he wanted to leave the firm on good terms and that he was to be backed by one of their largest clients (who, it seemed, the Universal was about to upset in spades) and to pinch business from Coopers (who the Universal wanted to treat with kid gloves). Things were beginning to look pretty black. Something would have to give but it wasn't looking as if the Universal would be doing the giving.

"Can I take the file and look through it to see if I can come up with a way round the problem? If we want to be fair to both Warrington's and to Coopers, there must be a middle way where everyone could be happy."

"Be my guest," smiled Roy with obvious relief, handing the file across the desk to Tim. "With only a year or two to go before I depart to greener pastures, anything for a quiet life. Now, what was it that you wanted to see me about?"

"If you're busy, it can wait, nothing urgent." Tim was not at all sure that he had picked the perfect time for a heart to heart on this particular subject.

"Nonsense," said Roy. "Let's get on with it. What's your problem?"

"No problem, actually, " said Tim, sinking resignedly into the visitor's chair. "You know that I've often thought about leaving the Company and setting up on my own. Well...."

"Stuff and nonsense Tim. You're bloody well placed here. They're going to get rid of me sooner or later, preferably the former, and there's no doubt that you'll walk straight into my job. Head Office has as much as said so. You know all the clients, well all the ones that matter and, though I shouldn't say it to your face, you're popular with the rest of the staff here and popular with the clients. You're a natural for the job. How old are you, thirty one, thirty two?"

"Twenty seven actually, but...."

"But nothing. At, say thirty, you'll be a Branch Manager, on five grand a year, plus a car and plus a damn good pension. What more could you want? No, you forget these crazy ideas. You speak to Mary - she'll tell you that you're on to a damn good thing here and that you'd be crazy to give it all up on some madcap gamble."

"Actually, I have spoken to Mary and she thinks that I should take this opportunity. It's not such a gamble and I really think that........."

"Opportunity? What opportunity? Don't tell me that you've been looking for a job behind my back. After all the things I've done for you........"

"Its nothing like that Roy. I was with Bill Warrington yesterday and he was moaning about the lack of service that he was getting from Coopers and that I seemed to be doing all the work whilst Colin creamed off all the commission for doing sweet F A. Well, he suggested that I should set up on my own and that he would finance me from the commission that he would have been paying to Coopers."

"Sweet Jesus Christ!" cried Roy, uncharacteristically (for he was not one to use bad language). This was all too much for him. "You walk in here telling me that you want to waltz off with one of our largest clients and, at the same time, kick our largest Insurance Brokers in the balls. And you expect me to say 'thanks a million'. Just what Planet are you coming from? Let me know who else you want to bounce into touch. You must think that I've gone soft in the head. You've got covenants let me remind you, and the Universal is not in the habit of kissing them goodbye. Just one false move and they, and I, will be down on you like a ton of bricks."

This conversation was not going the way that Tim had intended.

"I tell you what. I'll look through this file and see what I can come up with, and when I've done that, I'll come back again and perhaps we can have another chat and see if there's some way in which we can all get what we want."

"You do that. Come and see me at ten o'clock tomorrow and we'll talk the whole thing through." Roy knew in his heart of hearts that he had no right to stymie Tim's ambitions. He was all too well aware that he had wanted to do the same thing himself, but the time never seemed right, or Margaret, his wife, couldn't see the reasons for taking any unnecessary risks. Tim was a good chap and, although he would do well with the Universal, he knew, if he was being totally honest, that he could do far better for himself on 'the other side'.

"Bring a cup of coffee with you, when you come," he added, to signal a modest softening in his attitude. "Provided that you can sort out Warrington's claim, keep Colin Cooper happy, I might be prepared to listened to this harebrained scheme of yours. But, pigs might fly," he added, rather less encouragingly.

Chapter Five

Back at his desk, Tim reflected that things could not have gone much worse. His first priority was to try to find a way in which he could persuade Turners, the Loss Adjusters, that they should not be recommending repudiation of the claim. He did not fancy asking Bill Warrington to back him if, on day one, he had to be the bearer of tidings to the effect that he was about to be one hundred thousand pounds worse off than he had thought he was. It was a touch too coincidental, Tim mused, that Bill had actually hinted during their conversation yesterday that this could happen - that the Universal would be quite capable of reneging on a one hundred thousand pound claim. Bill was a wily old bird; was he covering himself by putting Tim in the position that he simply had to get the claim paid? Was the offer of setting him up as a broker simply a smoke screen to get his claim paid?

He pored through the file but, try as he might, he could not fault Turner's logic. There was a copy of the offending Warranty – 'no spraying within ten metres of welding operations.' That warranty was not put there to invite a claim for burning down the paint shop and a one hundred thousand pound loss by wielding a blowtorch around inflammable material. It was fair, it was clear, and the Universal were not likely to roll over when there had been such a specific breach of warranty. Tim remembered from his examination days, a breach of warranty meant that the contract of Insurance was void - there were no ifs and no buts. The Universal had no need to pay up. And with one hundred thousand pounds at stake, who could blame them?

But did Warrington's know that they had such a warranty? Not that ignorance would be an excuse - but it might make things easier to argue if it could be proved that Coopers had not told their client about the dangers of welding near a spray shop. Furthermore, only twelve month's earlier, they themselves had given Warrington's a 'clean bill of health'. It would help if Tim wanted to shift responsibility from Warrington's to Coopers though he was now fully aware that Roy would fight any suggestion that Coopers should pay. Roy saw Coopers as a safe way of ensuring his budgets were met until the day he could happily retire.

Even if he could shift the blame, Bill Warrington would not be in the mood to support a new venture of Tim's if he had problems of his own – a hundred thousand problems to be precise.

In any event, if they had to fight Cooper's Professional Indemnity Insurers, the whole process would be expensive and might take years, and they would be the years during which Bill Warrington's offer would remain 'on the shelf'.

It might be fair to sue Coopers, but it would make no commercial sense for the Universal to draw swords against one of their biggest sources of new business. If Roy was to have an easy ride to retirement, he needed Coopers.

Mind you, thought Tim, if things go the way they should, the Universal would be getting a lot more business from Harrisons than ever it did from Coopers.

Firstly, he decided, he must go and take a look at the scene of the fire.

He picked up the phone and called John Whiting, Warrington's foreman. After a friendly chat with their receptionist, and a two-minute wait whilst John was tracked down, John himself came on the line.

"Watcha mate. What can I be doing for you?"

"John, glad you're there. If I came round straight away, would you have a couple of minutes to show me something?"

"As long as its not Cilla's tits, she's fussy that way (Cilla, the voluptuous receptionist, was clearly still within earshot), I'll show you anything you want. Meet me in the canteen at ten thirty, I'll be going for my cuppa about then."

"Great, see you then." Tim tidied up a couple of jobs that were cluttering his desk, strolled down to his car and within twenty minutes he was sitting opposite John across a plastic table, both with Styrofoam cups full of something steaming, weak and watery.

"You know that bloody awful fire in the paint shop a few months ago?" started Tim. "Well, I just wanted to find out a bit more as to how it happened."

"Gawd. I thought that was all done and dusted. I 'ad a bloke round last week asking a lot of tomfool questions about that. Nosey bloody parker he was an' all. Didn't take to him a bit. Here, don't say that you buggers are not going to pay for it. I always knew you was greedy buggers - take money off the firm every year and then, soon as we want some back, it's 'sorry mate, you 'aven't done this or that or some other bloody thing so we're not paying'. I know your sort."

"We're not all like that. Certainly not the Universal. No, there's no problem. I just want to check out things for myself," Peter affirmed with an assurance he did not feel.

"Well, its old Fred you want to see. He's the stupid fucker who started the fire. Damn near killed 'isself. It was a miracle there was no one in the paint shop at the time. If there 'ad've been, then they wouldn't be wiv us no more. Christ what a bang."

Five minutes later, they were standing in the workshop with Fred. Fred, white haired, stooped back and with ancient wire-framed glasses perched on the end of his nose, looked more like an out of work school teacher than an experienced welder.

After the usual introductory banter and good-natured mutual insults, Tim asked,

"So can you tell me what you were doing and how the spark managed to get out from your workshop and into the paint shop? I know there's nothing left of the paint shop now - thanks to you - but the walls of this building looked pretty sound. I can't see how a fire could have spread."

"Nor me mate. I was just finishing a job here, minding me own business when there was this almighty explosion and I looks out the door and it looked as if it was bleedin' fireworks night again. Bloody great flames, twenty feet high they must have been, but I'm telling you, there was no way a spark got out of here into there. No way at all. I've bin doin' this job long enough to know that you don't fuck about wiv oxy-acetylene. In any case, I always rests those two sheets of asbestos up against that wall just in case a spark gets onto the woodwork and catches fire and fries me up. I know we shouldn't still be using sheet asbestos, but it's the best thing I know for stopping fires from getting out of 'and."

"Asbestos? No-one said anything about asbestos," Tim's hopes soared. "Anyway, if the fire didn't start from here, how did it start? Have you any ideas Fred?"

"No doubt about it. Some stupid fucker left a fag end lying around and won't own up. Don't blame 'em mind you. Must 'ave cost a fortune to put back everything what was burnt. No point in admitting you started a fire unless you 'ave to. No bloody medals for that sort of thing. Just so long they don't think it was anyfing to do with me."

"Well, I hope not, but John here reckons you tried to burn the whole factory down just so you could have an extra week's holiday. Only joking, but thanks a lot," said Tim, turning to leave. "You've both been most helpful. I'd better be getting along and leave you two, to sort out who caused the fire and then get back to work so you can make Bill Warrington a wealthy man."

"Bit late for that ain't it?" replied John. "He's already worth more than the bleedin' Bank of England. Mind you, 'e's earned it so I hope 'e enjoys it. Bye fer now, see you later."

On his way back to the Office, Tim felt that things were looking decidedly brighter. Firstly, it might not have been the welding that caused the fire. Not that that would nullify the warranty, but it would give the Universal less of a reason to repudiate - possibly make an ex gratia payment. More to the point, however, he seemed to recall that the warranty said something to the effect that it did not apply should there be a fireproof wall. Not that a timber wall would be construed as 'fireproof', but two sheets of asbestos - that was a different matter.

Back in the office, he dialled Jane Newman, the manageress of their Fire Department.

"Jane, Tim here," he began. "Would two sheets of asbestos constitute a fireproof wall?"

"Yes," came the answer without hesitation. "Why do you ask?"

"Thanks. Question two," Tim replied, ignoring her query. "Does the welding warranty apply if there is a fireproof wall between the welding booth and anything else."

"No," came the equally emphatic response. "Why do you ask?"

"You know that Turners have pointed out that we should repudiate Warrington's fire claim because of the breach of warranty. Well, old Fred, who was doing the welding, tells me that he always puts two sheets of asbestos up against the wall whenever he is doing any welding work. I've seen the sheets there - he's a careful old cove and he knows what he's doing."

"Well, apart from the fact that he shouldn't still have sheets of asbestos lying around, then Warrington's claim must be OK. Do you want me to speak to Turners and tell them that we're happy with things and that they can now go on and agree final settlement?"

"Many thanks. That's exactly what I want you to do. You're wonderful."

"I know that, you know that, just make sure that Roy knows that when its time for my salary rises."

"Leave it to me, though he might not like another hundred grand creeping on to his claims budget," laughed Tim. Hurdle number one was out of the way and he was now actually looking forward to coffee with Roy tomorrow.

Chapter Six

Joe Hendry was thinking that the deal he had struck with Ted might work out quite a bit better than he had first thought. Ted, admittedly was a bit of a rough diamond, a bit thick and he was not too worried about keeping to the straight and narrow. His great virtue from Joe's point of view was, however, his hunger to make a quid or two regardless of the ethics of the case. Ethics were not what drove Joe Hendry.

Two hundred pounds to Ted was, as he had said himself, a small fortune, and Joe reckoned that he would work like a dingbat to make that kind of money. Don't worry about the morality; Ted didn't even know the meaning of the word.

For every customer that Ted could produce, Joe reckoned that he could make at least another grand – one thousand lovely smackers a go. As with most of Joe's transactions, the taxman would remain blissfully unaware. Not a bad little earner thought Joe.

Nor would it end there. There were dozen's of 'Teds' out there and he would be able to sponge off the lot of them. No reason why Ted himself should not find a few of them and hand them a slice of his own commission. There was a gravy train out there and Joe had only just started it rolling.

Coincidentally, as Joe was pondering his good fortune, Ted was knocking on the door of number 16, Acacia Avenue making his first 'cold call'.

The door opened to reveal a burly, six-footer, shirtsleeves rolled up, newspaper in one hand and a mouthful of supper in the early stages of mastication.

"Well?" demanded the occupant, spitting globules of undigested food in Ted's general direction and very clearly displeased with the interruption and intrusion on his time.

"Good evening Guv," responded Ted civilly. "I couldn't help noticing that some of your windows is showing signs of rot – rising damp as we calls it in the trade. Nasty business if its not treated soonest. Can cost a fortune if it gets a 'old. It just so happens that my old aunt had just the same thing and she got this........"

"There's bugger-all wrong with my winders. Now piss off," came the unpromising response.

"I was just passing and I thought that you might........"

"Can't you understand plain fucking English? I'm happy with what we've got and if we ever want double glazing, I wouldn't come to a prat like you."

With that, Ted found himself confronting a closed door and a very positive feeling that further discussion on the subject would be pointless.

Ted's next two visits were equally unsatisfactory though, on those occasions the repartee had not been quite so bruising. He had began to have second thoughts about his chosen new career, but perhaps he was beginning to get the hang of it now – at least, no further doors had actually been slammed in his face.

Number 27 Acacia Avenue looked a little more hopeful. He noticed through a gap in the net curtains that the resident of number 27 was a slightly built lady of advancing years. Remembering Joe's tale of riches from little old ladies, he knocked on the door with a feeling of greater optimism.

"Yes, can I help?" came the timid voice from a narrow gap in the door, carefully restricted by the security chain.

"Well Madam," replied Ted in his most courteous tone. "I fink its more a case of what I can do for you. I was just passing and I couldn't help noticing your winders. 'ave you noticed they've got rot, rising damp as we calls it in the trade?"

"Just a minute," and Ted listened to the rattle of the chain being removed. The door opened to reveal a rather sprightly little lady, not quite as old as Ted had surmised. Probably early sixties and very smartly dressed for Acacia Avenue, Ted had to concede.

"Show me what you mean, young man. I know that the paint is peeling a bit, but I'm sure that there's no rot."

Mrs Hampshire, for that was the lady's name, escorted Ted across the narrow lawn to the front window. He then stood before it, gazing intently at the woodwork.

Ted had to admit that the windows did, in fact, look to be in remarkably good condition but, since such an admission would be unlikely to lead to a sale, he wrinkled his brow, scratched his head and, with an impression of as much wisdom as he could muster, informed his potential customer,

"Well, superficiously, there ain't a lot wrong to the untrained eye, but, if you looks in the corners 'ere, you sees a bit of rot and rust." Ted produced a pocketknife and began to dig into the putty, which, not surprisingly, flaked away in chunks.

"Steady young man," exclaimed Mrs Hampshire. "You're ruining my window. If you keep on like that, there'll be nothing left."

"Nothing ter worry about missus," comforted Ted. "I've bin doin' this for years and I knows what I'm about. No, what yer need is a visit from an expert. That's why I popped in when I saw the problem what you've got 'ere and there. Now this mate of mine, Joe Hendry, 'e's the one who you ought to see about this. There ain't nothing wot he don't know about winders. If you like, I could give him a bell and get 'im to pop round ternight and give yer all the dope yer need to know. Won't cost yer nothink to listen to 'im and I can promise yer, it'll give yer the peace of mind wot yer need. It could be, with the rot wot I've seen meself, you might 'ave to "ave all yer winders done."

"And how much do you think that would cost Mr, Mr what is your name? My name is Mrs Hampshire, by the way."

"Bushell. Ted Bushell at yer service. 'Fraid I couldn't give yer any idea now of what it'd cost cos I don't know how much needs doin'. It's only when you gets an expert around that yer can tell wots wot. Wot I do know, is that Joe can do the best price in town. 'e seems to be able to get 'old of everything cheaper than wot any of the other firms seem to do. How about if I get him round about six o'clock ternight?"

"That's very kind of you, Mr Bushell. If it's not too much trouble, that would be fine. I'm not making any promises though. I'm not made of money and if it's going to be too expensive, no matter how much it might need doing, I just won't be able to have it done. Please tell Mr Hendry that I don't want to waste his time, so if he thinks I won't be able to afford it, do tell him not to bother. But I'm quite happy to have the benefit of his professional opinion if it's free."

"No trouble at all Mrs H. Ted's a professional 'an 'e'll only tell yer sumfink needs doin' if it really does need doin'. If you 'ave the work done, Ted only uses the best materials in the world but 'e 'as a way of getting' everyfink done cheap like. Yer'll be in good 'ands with Joe, I can promise yer that."

So with a shake of hands and a cheery wave, Joe made his departure. It being almost four thirty in the afternoon Joe considered it about time that he should adjourn to the Lion. He deserved a pint he told himself, after all that graft. Thirsty work, that was. Ted just hoped that Joe would appreciate his labours and that he would be able to get the old biddy to buy some windows. If this came off, he congratulated himself; he had become a salesman and well on his way to more than a few bob's worth of commission. Easy work, he told himself. Two hundred quid would come in handy just now.

At the Lion, whilst his beer was settling, he cadged a few coins off a mate and strolled over to the payphone to give Joe a call. After only a few rings, he was pleasantly surprised to hear Joe's voice.

"Hendry here, Joe Hendry, specialist property improvement surveyor. How can I help you?"

"Cor, luv-a-duck, Joe. Yer don't 'alf sound posh Joe. 'Ere, it's Ted. I've got yer a punter. No kidding. A little old lady wot's got piles of dough and wot wants 'er 'hole bleedin 'ouse fixed up. Can yer see 'er tonight, about six o'clock?"

"Well done Ted. Sure I can see her. What's her name and where does she live?"

Ted provided the information while Joe jotted it down.

"That's excellent. Now, how much does she really need doing and what did you tell her it would cost?"

"S'far as I could tell, 'er winders looked OK, but I got me knife out and digged about a bit and told 'er that she needs the 'ole 'ouse doin'. She wasn't totally convinced, but I'm sure you can spin 'er a line and convince 'er that the bleedin' 'ouse'll fall arse over tit unless you and yer boys gets in there sharpish."

"OK, that's fine. I'll pop in to see her tonight and I'll let you know how I got on. Will you be at the Lion tomorrow about lunchtime?"

"Does a duck? I'll be there. Bring plenty of cash. I fink I've earned it."

"Let's hope you have. See you then, Bye."

The Hendry machine was rolling.

Chapter Seven

At ten o'clock precisely, Tim tapped on Roy Brown's semi-opened door with a cup of coffee in one hand and a few handwritten sheets of paper in the other.

"Come in, come in," called Roy. "Come in and sit down. I see you've got your coffee already. Give Marilyn a shout would you, and ask her to bring me in a cup of my usual."

Tim did as bid, strolled across the room, pulled out the 'client chair' sat down and crossed his legs.

"Good of you to see me," began Tim. "I'm sorry if what I had to say yesterday came as a shock. To tell the truth, everything seems to be moving rather faster than I expected."

"Not at all, not at all." Roy seemed to have mellowed slightly since his initial outburst yesterday. "I've been thinking quite a lot about what you said and I have to say that it probably makes a great deal of sense. The last thing I want to see is a first rate young chap like you to leave the firm. I still think that the Universal has a great deal to offer you and that you would do very well – far better than me I'm sure – were you to stay, but, and I say this advisedly, if you set up on your own, you'd probably do better still. Far, far better."

Tim surprised but pleasantly surprised, was encouraged by this change of view. He allowed himself an inward smile as he took another sip of his coffee. At that point, Marilyn tapped on the door and, without waiting fro a response, entered with Roy's coffee.

"And what do you make of this, Marilyn?" Roy started. "This stupid young bugger wants to leave the Universal and set up on his own. What do you think of that? He wants to throw all of this away," waving his arms around expansively taking in every inch of his twelve by twelve office, "and he wants to start his own firm. The mad fool will be bust in his first twelve months, don't you think?"

"Not at all, he'll make a fortune. Best thing in the world you could do Tim," came the not unexpected response. "Got any good jobs going? The pay here's peanuts and, when Roy here leaves in the next year or so, when they pension him off that is, they'll probably want to dump me at the same time."

"No chance of that Marilyn," interjected Roy. "You're here till you're the same age as me. Now cut the crap. It's bad enough to be losing one member of staff without my secretary mutinying at the same time. Any more of that and I'll have you keel-hauled."

"Seriously Tim, if you do go, we'll all be very sorry but, rest assured, we'll all be rooting for you. Go on, you go for it."

"Thanks a million, Marilyn," moaned Roy. "Not only a prospective mutiny, but now I've got my loyal secretary encouraging my key man to leave us. That's treason, that is."

With that, Marilyn withdrew and, drawing his chair to his desk, Roy announced, "Right, down to business.

"As I've already said, I think that what you're proposing makes sense. In fact, I only wish that a similar opportunity had come my way when I was about your age. It did, as a matter of fact. But what with one thing and another, Margaret mainly, I let it slip. Still, no good harping on about what might have been. Let's look at what we've got.

"I have three main problems. Number one, your contract and your covenants. It's no good you starting out if the Universal are going to hound you from pillar to post. Your life would be a bloody misery.

"Number two, Bill Warrington. I can't sit idly by and watch you take one of our largest clients away from us. Head Office would crucify me, to say nothing of you buggering up my budgets.

"And number three, Colin Cooper. He'll go ape-shit if he sees you taking his largest client with you and with us doing damn-all about it. You can see that, can't you Tim? I know Warringtons is important to you, but you're going to have to do it without them. I'm sorry, but that's how it's got to be. You leave Warringtons alone, and you go with my complete blessing. Take them away from us, and I'll be forced to do everything in my power to stop you – if only to appease Colin Cooper. In any case, I'm sure you will do perfectly well without them – you've got enough other contacts of your own, I know."

Not half as many as I need, thought Tim. Warrington's was the key, the crucial part of all his plans. Without Bill Warrington behind him, he would not be risking it – not now, anyway.

" Can we take point two first?" suggested Tim. "If, and I emphasise the 'if', if Bill Warrington decides to appoint my new firm as his Broker, then I would undertake to keep his Insurances with the Universal – or at least the overwhelming majority - for a period of, say, at least two years. In that way, the Company will lose nothing."

"That's out for starters," replied Bob. "How can you call yourself a Broker if you're not going to broke the bloody business?"

"No problem, Colin's been doing that for years. I have already answered that with Bill and I've told him that, although he could save a bob or two by shopping around a bit, he's got a package with us and, what with the swings and round-a-bouts, he's well off where he is. Particularly now that we're going to pay his claim in full, he can see the advantage in that."

"Pay his claim! The last I heard, we were putting the boot in and I would be saving £100,000 on my claims budget. What the hell has happened now?"

Tim explained what he'd been able to discover about the alleged breach of warranty and was pleased to see that Roy was visibly relieved. He had not been looking forward to having to be face an irate client on this particular issue – particularly one as blunt as Warrington. Cordial relations with clients were far more important to him than a blip on his claims statistics, especially with only months to go before a peaceful retirement.

"It may be," continued Tim, "that I will have to offer him a modest saving here and there, but I can achieve that by giving him a little extra cover – delete the odd exclusion and that sort of thing – and I would be prepared to take a lower commission on some of his business so that we can get him a better deal overall without the Universal suffering too much. We pay Coopers a profit commission and I would be quite happy to waive that for a year or two – that could save the Universal a thousand or two. I will give you my firm promise that the Universal would keep at least ninety percent of Warrington's business for at least two, maybe three, years."

"That's OK with me, I'll be retired by then," affirmed a relieved Roy Smith. "Now, what about Colin Cooper? You won't be keeping him happy for five minutes, let alone two or three years."

"What about him?" queried Tim. "Colin hasn't given us any new business for about three years now. You look at the figures. All he's interested in is getting people like me to do all the work whilst he's out on the golf course. I wouldn't go out of my way to stand on Colin's toes, Warrington's excepted, but he's no bloody use to us any more. The Universal will, I can assure you, get far more business out of Harrison and Co than anything that they're likely to get from that out-dated dead-beat."

"Probably a fair point," conceded Bob. "I must say that I've been meaning to pop in to see Colin and ask him why the well seems to have dried up lately. Pity I don't play golf; I might have seen a bit more of him if I had.

"Thirdly though, what have you got to say about your covenants? I checked them this morning and I can inform you that you are not allowed to work in any other Insurance Office within a radius of five miles of this Office (or any other Universal Branch Office) for at least two years. Furthermore, you cannot join a firm that takes over the business of a client of ours for a period of twelve months and neither can you poach any of our staff for a similar period. Quite frankly, you're buggered"

"As to the last point, the only staff I would wish to poach from the Universal would be you and Marilyn and neither of you become available for about thirteen months........"

"You're joking, of course. I'm going to retire and put my feet up. Marilyn might be a different story, I admit."

"Not at all," replied Tim. "I have no idea whether I will even be able to afford to employ any staff at all by the end of my first year. If I do, I would love you to join me. You've just said that you don't play golf. You'll be bored out of your mind sitting around at home. If you worked at Harrison's, it needn't be full time, you would keep your hand in, keep interested, and you may even be able to persuade a few other clients to see the light and come on board."

"Got it all worked out then," said Roy. "We'll see about that when the time comes. You offering me a job is not going to persuade the Universal to let you swipe all of their business, of that I can assure you. They take a dim view of bribery and corruption. I've seen them in action before. You remember how they screwed old Tom Forsby to the floor when he tried to do the same sort of thing......"

"That was completely different," interrupted Tim. "Tom was a bloody fool. He wrote to half a dozen clients suggesting that they change Insurers before he had even handed in his notice! Of course the Universal went bananas and it served him right. In the event, he had to join the "National" and not one of his prospective clients wanted anything to do with him. I don't know what he's up to now, but, if anything, there's a lesson to be learned there, and I think I've learned it.

"No, the difference with my proposition is that, if the Universal plays ball with me and releases me from my undertakings and covenants, I will guarantee, absolutely guarantee, that, by the end of three years, my account with the Company will be far greater than the amount of business that I already handle for them. I might want a favour from you from time to time in shaving a rate here and there to give me a competitive edge, but the Company will not lose by it, I give you my word."

"That's good enough for me, but whether it will be good enough for our lords and masters, we'll just have to see. I'll give Mike Hardy a call, he's our best bet, and I'll probably pop up to Head Office to talk it through with him. With a bit of luck, I'll be able to see him on Wednesday or Thursday, and I'll let you know the score as soon as I get back."

Tim could not help but notice the 'we' in Roy's summing up and it gave him heart. Much encouraged, and much relieved, he thanked Roy for his time and, collecting his cup and saucer, withdrew to consider his next move.

As he passed Marilyn's desk, she winked and, whispered sotto voce, "good luck and don't forget the job."

....

Friday seemed to take weeks to arrive. Tim felt that he was 'treading water'. He was conscientious enough to keep at his job, as diligently as he could, but his heart was no longer in it. He was busting to get started.

Every time he sat in front of a client now, he could not help wondering whether the client would remain a 'Universal' client or would he soon become a 'Harrison and Co' client? He could not rid himself of the feeling that he was wasting valuable time. He seemed to be killing time, when he should be working flat out on his own Company. Mary was patient, but every evening he returned home he was greeted by the same question – "Well?" To which his answer was always – "not yet".

The sense of frustration was becoming unbearable. He had already written his letter of resignation and was just waiting for Roy's green light.

At last, at eleven thirty on Monday morning, Marilyn called him, "Would you pop up and see Roy please. I think he's got some news for you. Good luck Tim," she added.

With his heart in his mouth, Tim leaped up the stairs to Roy's office three at a time, tapped on the door and walked straight in.

"Well?" he echoed Mary's regular query.

"Well what?" echoed Roy. "What sort of a question is that?"

"I think you know 'what'," replied Tim. "What did Mike Hardy have to say?"

"Oh that," said Roy dismissively, obviously enjoying the tension and Tim's anxiety to know where he stood. "Mike agrees with me that you would be a bloody fool and that there is no way that he would do anything that would endanger our relationship with Warringtons," he said bluntly.

"Oh," said Tim, crestfallen. "But didn't you tell him that I guaranteed to keep the account with the Universal? Surely that would count for something?"

"Precisely that," confirmed Roy. "He felt that, if the account were to continue to be serviced by Cooper and Smythe, for whom he has very little respect, we would probably lose it anyway. He made the point that it was a miracle that we had kept it for as long as we have done and a wonder that one of the Nationals had not moved in and swiped it from Coopers and, consequently, from us. He inclined to the view that possibly, only possibly you'll understand, the main reason for the account staying with us was something to do with your own abilities. I tried to disabuse him of that notion, of course, but for some reason, Mike Hardy seems to hold you in pretty high regard.

"In a nutshell, he says that he will be very disappointed to see you go but felt, like you, that the Universal will probably get more business by supporting you as a free agent than by employing you as a frustrated Inspector.

"In short, and subject to an appropriate exchange of letters, you may leave with his blessing and without any of the tiresome covenants that might otherwise have restricted you.

"He wishes you well, and the same goes for me. It's a bit early, but lets go to the Pub and have a quick one to celebrate."

Tim sighed an enormous sigh of relief. "I can't tell you how relieved I am to hear all of that," he said. "How very kind and thanks, thanks a million for your hand in this. Yes, let's go and have a drink – on me of course. I can assure you that I have enjoyed all my years here, but I'm sure looking forward to being your ex-employee. And your future employer perhaps?" he added with a wink.

Chapter Eight

At six o'clock, on the dot, Joe strolled briskly down the front path of number 27 Acacia Avenue and knocked sharply on the front door. After a short while, he heard the rattling of the door chain and the front door opened a few inches to reveal the sprightly Mrs Eileen Hampshire.

"Who are you young man?" enquired the elderly resident peering through the gap.

"Joe Hendry, madam," responded the salesman civilly, adding, "Joe Hendry of International Surveyors at your service." There was, of course, no such firm, but Joe was not one to let facts stand in the way of a sale. He believed that this particular title sounded better that 'Everbright Double Glazing Ltd'. "I believe that my colleague, Mr Bushell visited you earlier today. He has expressed some concern about the safety of your structure. I am calling to see if there is any way in which I might be of assistance to you."

The door closed slightly, as Mrs Hampshire removed the chain, and opened fully as she ushered Joe in.

"I really don't know what all this fuss is about," said Mrs Hampshire. "My son looked over the property only two or three weeks ago and could see nothing wrong. Still, if you disagree, I would be interested to hear what you have to say, though I don't want to waste your time. I'm sure that you must be a very busy man."

Joe adopted his warmest professional smile and enquired, with a nonchalant lift of an eyebrow,

"Never too busy to assist a lady in distress. You mention your son. I am delighted to hear that. It is always a good thing to have a second opinion. We often find, however, that the layman misses little structural deficiencies, which the trained eye of we professionals will spot immediately. What, out of interest, is your son's profession may I ask?"

"Actually, he's a Structural Surveyor. He's done very well really. He's the senior partner of Grays and Tompkins, you must have heard of them in your business. I believe that they're the second largest firm of Surveyors in the country."

This information indicated a change of tack. However, Joe was never one to be fazed by the opinion of an expert. He simply shifted tack and pronounced,

"Excellent. That means that one of my worries has been answered before I start. There is definitely no major defect then, or else your son would have spotted it. I will only have to concern myself with the latent possibilities. Penetration, ambient temperature, moisture movement and all that sort of thing. I apologise if I'm being a little technical but that's my training. Structural integrity (he'd read that somewhere) is my passion. Now can we have a look at one or two windows please, and then I can give you some idea of how we might be able to help – if, of course, any help is needed.

"Mr Bushell's a very good man, one of the best, and I'm sure that he would not have called me in unless he was very concerned."

With a "follow me please," Mrs Hampshire escorted Joe down the narrow hallway into a light and spacious living room. Joe could not help but be impressed by the quality of the furniture, leather upholstery, a very fine Regency side table and a stunning collection of paintings. Sure as hell there were no prints on these walls, mused Joe. Nothing but originals, and worth a few grand, of that he was certain. Joe had a feeling that Ted might have struck gold on his very first assignment.

"Hmm," muttered Joe, "peering closely at the surrounds of the window frame. "I think I can see what Ted spotted. Let's take a closer look."

With that, Joe took a gadget from his pocket, switched it on, and pointed it in random directions at various sections of the window. The gadget was, in fact, an old-fashioned exposure meter that his father had liked to use when taking photographs with his old 35mm camera. In the current circumstances, it had absolutely no relevance whatsoever, but Joe always felt that his punters were impressed by technology and impressing punters was his strength.

With a worried frown, Joe asked Mrs Hampshire if she wouldn't mind if he took a look at the outside and followed her out into the garden in silence. Joe was a great believer in the psychology of silence. It helped raise the tension and, the greater the tension, the more likely the sale.

Outside, Joe silently inspected the window frame minutely, flashed his exposure meter a few more times and placed his ear to the window pane.

"What on earth are you doing now?" asked Mrs Hampshire. "Surely you can't hear anything?"

"You'd be surprised Mrs Hampshire. The trained ear can detect a host of problems. I'm listening for what we in the trade call 'muffle'. If I can detect muffle, then I know that something needs doing."

"And can you?"

Joe smiled. "I'm pleased to say that you have no muffle. That is, not yet. With properties of this age, there is always a possibility, and we should keep and eye, or perhaps I should say, an 'ear', on it. No, no great problem there, but I'm a bit worried by the stability and by heat penetration. If you would just give me a few moments."

With that, Joe took out his steel rule and started measuring the window, jotting down the measurements carefully on his clipboard. He then took out his calculator and spent an aimless two or three moments tapping in random numbers and jotting down equally random figures, interspersed with the occasional 'tut tut' and "oh dear, what have we got here?"

After about five minutes, he looked up thoughtfully and said, "should we go and sit down somewhere and I can then go through my findings with you."

"Can I get you a cup of coffee Mr Hendry?"

"I'd love one Mrs Hampshire. That's very kind of you. White with three sugars if you don't mind." Joe savoured the customary wave of euphoria that he always experienced when he felt that he had 'cracked it'. He followed his customer down the garden path (rather appropriately, he thought) and through the back door into her kitchen. It was, Joe had to admit, a particularly attractive kitchen furnished tastefully with a pine dresser, a pine table and four sturdy pine chairs.

"What a beautiful kitchen," admired Joe. Making a customer feel good was an important part of the sales strategy. In any case, on this occasion, it happened to be true.

"Well, thank you very much. I do try to keep everything in shape. Though, at my age, it gets increasingly more difficult. Now, sit yourself down," ordered Mrs Hampshire. "I'll just get the kettle going whilst you finish your calculations. It all looks very complicated I must say."

With a resigned shrug of his shoulders as if to say, 'where would the world be without professionals such as we', Joe busied himself with more disjointed jottings whilst the lady of the house completed her preparations. After a few minutes, she laid the tray down, complete with two fine bone china cups and saucers, a sugar bowl, cream jug and a half-filled cafetaire, on the table between them.

"Help yourself to milk or cream and sugar, please," she said, pouring the coffee.

With a dash of cream and three spoonfuls of sugar, Joe stirred his coffee, sat back and pronounced,

"Well, the tests show that the frames are generally in good order but there is a slight danger of latency which could mean that you are storing up problems for the future. The heat transference problems are a cause for immediate concern, however. You might be surprised to know that, for every three ergs of heat you generate through your central heating, two and a half ergs escape through your windows. That alone is putting something like forty per cent on your heating bill every year. In the summer, of course – if we ever have a summer - the reverse is the case and you will get about one erg of heat coming through (one erg more that is, than you need for comfort). It comes straight through your window from the sun up there in the sky and can cause you to be uncomfortably hot in the summer and, of course, far too cold in the winter.

"Now, if you were to install energized, double thickness transparencies" (Joe had long since learned that the term 'double glazing' was a turn off), "then we could eliminate ninety nine point five per cent of all of your heat loss. If, at the same time, we replaced the old-fashioned wooden window frames with ultra light, double-strength polymers, we could overcome any possibility of 'muffle' and your windows would last you a lifetime. Forget latency, no more worry, no more heat loss, no more maintenance. Furthermore, the quality of my firm's work, coupled with our lifetime guarantee, would put thousands of pounds on the value of your property, should you ever want to sell it, that is."

"That all sounds very nice, but how much is this all likely to cost? I told your Mr Bushell that I'm not made of money."

"Not anywhere as much as you would think," smiled Joe. "At first glance, I'd say that there is ten thousand pounds worth of work here (it was always good strategy to start with a 'frightener') but I'd have to look around the whole house and take a few measurements before I could give you a better idea."

"Ten thousand pounds! I couldn't possibly afford that. That's quite out of the question."

"Don't worry about that Mrs Hampshire," reassured Joe. "That's the sort of figure our competitors would expect to charge you. There are far too many crooked profiteers out there I am embarrassed to say. No, let me take the measurements and let's see if we can come up with something that would fit the bill. Do you mind if I have a little wander around with my tape measure?"

Twenty minutes later, Joe returned to the kitchen and sat down whilst Mrs Hampshire topped up his coffee. Very laboriously, he checked through his measurements. This time he employed his calculator more purposefully for he had to make certain that he overcharged within acceptable limits.

If he was honest – but honesty was not one of Joe's natural tendencies - in his opinion, none of the windows needed replacing yet. But that sort of opinion was not, of course, even remotely relevant to him today. If every window were to be replaced, he reckoned that he could have the work carried out for a little less than three thousand pounds, including his forty per cent commission – a grand to him, after squaring Ted Bushell. However, if he could get away with it, he could make some real money here, over the top.

"Well, as I said before, I reckon that the going rate to replace every window with the best state of the art materials, would be something in the region of ten grand. However, if we are careful, and if I squeeze the firm to the bone – I would take a smaller commission myself, of course, because I want to help – we would be looking at a price nearer half that figure. Say six thousand pounds."

"Six thousand!" echoed Mrs Hampshire. "Where do you think that I could get that sort of money from?"

"To be honest, Mrs Hampshire, if you don't have the work done now, I would estimate that you could be looking at a bill in the region of three times that amount in only two or three years from now. If you take into account the amount you will save on heating bills, the protection of your property and its increase in value, you will actually be making a profit. As to being able to find the money, have you ever thought of a second Mortgage? We have a link with a first class Mortgage Broker who would, I am sure, have no trouble in raising six grand for you on this house. It must be worth not a penny less that seventy grand at the very least, if my reputation is worth anything."

"A mortgage at my age, young man? I'm far too old for anything like that. My husband, Cyril bless his heart, paid off our mortgage the day he retired – that was twenty years ago, and he swore that we would never be in debt again. And that's the way I want it to be. Do you think that I should get a quote from another firm and see if it could be done a little cheaper? Somewhere nearer a figure that I might be able to afford?"

Joe, an experienced campaigner, acknowledged both the threat and the opportunity. He noted that Mrs Hampshire had now come to accept (however erroneously) that the work really was a necessity; it was just a question of cost.

"Well, if it can be kept strictly between you and I," smiled Joe confidentially, "there is something more that I could do if you could pay part in cash. This is not something that a firm of our standing would normally even consider, but I would like to help you and I honestly feel that this work needs doing sooner rather than later so as to save you big problems in the future. If push became shove, how much cash do you think you could lay your hands on?"

"I've only got about one thousand pounds in the bank, about six thousand in the Building Society, a few premium bonds and a few Stocks and Shares that Cyril used to dabble with – I've no idea how much they're worth."

"H'mm, let me have another look at the figures," said Joe thoughtfully. "If we take into account a saving in VAT, a saving in Corporation Tax and cash discounts that I might be able to wangle out of our suppliers, I might be able to do something. I could possibly get some of our men to work in their spare time for a little cash; that would keep the price down even lower. Yes, if you were to pay the whole amount up front, and say nothing to anyone about our 'arrangement', I could get the whole job done for five grand. Five grand on the nose."

"Well now you are getting down to something that I might be able to afford," responded Mrs Hampshire. But isn't that all a bit illegal? Paying cash and all that sort of thing. What if you got caught out? I wouldn't want you to get into trouble on my account."

"Don't give it a moment's thought, Mrs H," reassured Joe. "If it's strictly between the two of us, I shan't worry a bit. I can sort everything out and you'll still get the Company's ten-year guarantee. The only thing is, we've just taken delivery of some materials for another job I'm doing and I would have to slip the suppliers the cash tomorrow if I am going to be able to get it done at this sort of price. The other Customer won't worry because he's just gone on a three-week holiday and I'll be able to get some replacement stuff in before he gets back. What it all boils down to is, that I will have to give the Supplier two and a half grand tomorrow if I am going to have a chance. There's just been a ten per cent price rise on Polymers, and if I leave it even a week, I won't be able to get round that one.

"Would you be able to get two thousand five hundred quid by, say, lunch time tomorrow? We could accept a cheque for the balance."

"I could do, but I don't have a car and I usually wait until my son or daughter-in-law have the time to drive me when I want to go down town. I suppose I could get a taxi, but they're so expensive these days."

"Not a problem, Mrs H," said Joe, taking out his diary and skimming through half a dozen empty pages. I see I have an eleven o'clock appointment just around the corner from here tomorrow. It shouldn't take more that an hour, and then I'm free until about two. It would be my pleasure to drive you down town. I could wait outside the Building Society whilst you draw the cash and drive you back home – a full chauffeur service. In any event, I am sure that you wouldn't want to be walking about with all that cash on you. You can't be too careful these days." Joe was desperate to keep her son and daughter-in-law out of the equation.

"That's really very kind of you Mr Hendry. If it's not too much trouble, that would be marvellous. Oh, you wouldn't mind, would you, if I just popped into Tesco's on the way down. I would only be a couple of minutes. There are one or two things I need and I was wondering how I might be able to get them. It really would be a great help if you wouldn't mind."

"Not at all," replied Joe expansively. He wouldn't mind waiting all afternoon for the profit he was going to pocket on this one. "No trouble at all. Now if you would just put your signature on this order form, I'll do all the paper work for you. Let's see, may I have your full name?"

Joe ran through all the questions filling in the answers as Mrs Hampshire provided them.

"Now," explained Joe. "I'm going to leave the amount for the job blank for the time being. You and I know that the price is five grand, but the firm does not. They think that it will be six thousand or more, so I will have to do a bit of work with my people in the Office. I'll leave the actual details of the work blank too, just for the time being. Don't worry about a thing, everything will be all squared up. But I don't want to raise any red herrings just now – just when we're looking at a ten per cent price increase on Polymers. So if you'll just sign here and here, and initial here, here and here."

Joe reached across with the form and handed Mrs Hampshire his ball point (a replica Mont Blanc) and indicated the various spaces.

Mrs Hampshire dutifully signed where shown and handed the form back to the much-relieved Joe Hendry.

"There, I think that's everything. I'll look forward to seeing you tomorrow at about twelve then. Thanks for the coffee and, may I say, it's a real pleasure to do business with you."

"Thank you Mr Hendry," smiled the good lady. "And thank you for being so helpful and so kind. Mum's the word so far as the tax man is concerned," she added, winking and tapping the side of her nose.

Joe, his work for the day complete, headed for his favourite hostelry.

....

The next morning Joe overslept, which wasn't so surprising since, on arrival at the Lion yesterday evening he felt it appropriate to entertain his good mate Ted Bushell. Ted had only been there an hour or so and, as soon as Joe had been able to regale him with the story of the pliable Mrs Hampshire, a drink or two by way of celebration seemed to be more than justified.

A customary late night had ensued and it was just by chance that the Milkman woke him – an unusual occurrence in itself. Except that he, the milkman, had to be a little more determined to raise him this time as Joe was now six weeks in arrears. The incessant ringing of the bell proved effective in bringing Joe to life, and through a dense mist, he was able to stagger downstairs, deal with the frustrated tradesman and crawl back to his dishevelled bed. Fortunately for Joe, in so doing, he knocked over his alarm clock and, on picking it up, noticed to his horror that it had just turned 11 o'clock. An alarm bell stirred in his befuddled brain.

"Jesus," he exclaimed. "Mrs Hampshire! Jesus Christ!"

With that, Joe shot into the bathroom and in less than ten minutes he had shaved (more or less), washed under his armpits, brushed his teeth and attended to the calls of nature. Dragging open drawers, banging open cupboards and searching behind chairs, he was more or less able to get dressed and prepare himself to face the world, all within a further ten minutes.

Feeling like death warmed up, he staggered down to his car and eventually managed, with unsteady fingers, to insert the ignition keys in the correct aperture. Reversing gingerly out of his drive, he set out on his mission to relieve Mrs Hampshire of two thousand five hundred pounds.

Joe congratulated himself that he arrived in Acacia Avenue only a quarter of an hour late and, with a cheerful smile, which totally belied his actual condition, he greeted an impatient Mrs Hampshire with:

"Top of the morning Mrs H. Lovely morning. I'm so sorry I've run a little late. There's so much going on at the moment, we're all run off our feet. I've just agreed another three installations this morning and I'll be doing the same again after lunch. The world's gone mad. Mind you, I'm not complaining. I always like to keep busy and it seems that all discerning house-owners in this area are beating a track to our door. Quality counts I always say and the word soon gets around. Now are we ready, your carriage awaits?"

"Well, I was beginning to think that you had forgotten me. But now you're here, let's go. Don't forget, I want to pop into Tesco's first."

"No trouble at all," smiled Joe as he held the car door open to let his customer in.

After about thirty minutes sitting in his stifling car outside Tesco's, waiting for Mrs Hampshire to complete her purchases, Joe was reconsidering the virtues of offering to act as a taxi, but, puffing and panting, the good lady eventually arrived. Joe helped her store about a dozen bulging polythene bags in the boot of his car.

"Grandchildren coming for tea this weekend," explained Mrs Hampshire. "Thank you so much; now let's get to the Century and draw out my money."

This was much more to Joe's liking and, some twenty minutes later, they were standing in front of the Cashier with Mrs Hampshire clutching her passbook.

"I would like to withdraw two thousand five hundred pounds," she said, importantly.

"May I see your passbook please," replied the pretty young cashier. She flicked through the pages and, with an apologetic smile said, "I'm awfully sorry Mrs Hampshire, but with this type of account you have to give a month's notice. I can only let you have one thousand pounds now. I can give you a withdrawal slip, and if you will sign it, we can let you have the other fifteen hundred pounds in one month. I am so sorry, but will that be alright?"

"Oh dear. What do you think Mr Hendry. Would your firm mind waiting a month for the balance?"

In view of the nature of this transaction, Joe was reluctant to wait another five minutes, let alone a whole month. However, a discussion such as this in front of a Building Society cashier was definitely to be avoided and so he said,

"That could present a bit of a problem but, leave it to me and I will think of something."

The business was duly completed and Joe and his customer, with fifty twenty-pound notes in her handbag, withdrew to his car.

"I've been thinking," mused Joe. This could work out to your advantage. If I take the thousand cash now, and you give me a cheque for one thousand five hundred pounds made payable to C and D Plastics – they're the firm that supplies the Polymers – and at the same time make out a cheque for five hundred pounds to my Firm, then I'll wait for the other two thousand pounds cash and you will have saved all the bother of getting out the cash now. You see, by paying the supplier direct, and I'd be only too pleased to arrange that for you, we will get round the Firm's commission – they can afford it, don't you worry."

"That all seems rather complicated. Are you sure everything will be all right? I don't want you getting into trouble on my behalf and I certainly don't want anything to go wrong. You can't be too careful these days."

"I couldn't agree with you more. Don't you worry about a thing, Mrs H, leave it all to me. That's what I am here for – to make your life easier. You're going to have the best workmanship in town and all done for at a fraction of the normal cost."

"If you're sure everything will be above board," said Mrs Hampshire, rifling through her handbag and passing her chequebook and the little plastic wallet containing one thousand pounds to Joe. "You write out the cheques, and I'll sign them. It's all too much for me, this high finance."

The temptation for Joe to make a mistake in his favour was very great indeed, but after further thought, he felt that discretion would be the better part of valour and, against his better judgement, filled in the amounts correctly and as agreed.

To his great relief, she signed the cheques and allowed Joe to drive her back home. He deposited her as quickly as possible and drove to his Office for the first time in two weeks. He had some fast talking to do with C and D Plastics and something of a work of art to perform on the order forms, but he was confident that he would clear fifteen hundred cash on this deal plus, of course, his legitimate commission on a three thousand five hundred pound job. Not a bad two day's work.

His hangover, he noticed, seemed to have passed.

Chapter Nine

The next few days were a whirlwind of activity for Tim. He had another meeting with Bill Warrington to check on his commitment, and to update him as to the present state of play with the Universal. He met with his Accountants to draw up some form of a Business Plan.

He spent hours with his Solicitors drawing up contracts of employment, Memorandum and Articles of Association, discussing terms of leases and, it seemed, a never-ending assortment of other issues.

He spent a morning with John Barlow, his Estate Agent and good friend, looking at particulars of dozens of offices for rent and he then trudged round the town looking at every one that seemed to have the amount of space he thought he would need at the sort of rent he thought he could afford.

He devoted much time to his Bank Manager discussing overdraft limits, office accounts, client accounts, payroll and a host of related issues.

He also visited the Employment exchange. A very efficient, but matronly, lady listened to Tim's wish list of the qualities required in the perfect secretary and said, without hesitation, "I know just the young lady you need. She used to worked for a local Insurance Company, let me see." The redoubtable Mrs Thomas then shuffled through a box of cards and, with a triumphant smile, held one aloft. She then strolled over to a rusting filing cabinet and extracted a thin dossier.

"Eureka!" she exclaimed. "Miss Janet Bligh. A very attractive, well-spoken young lady who, until only a week ago, worked as a secretary for a firm called Cooper and Smythe. Perhaps you know of them?"

"Know of them? Indeed I do." Tim's heart gave a leap. He could not believe his luck. To be offered the chance of taking on a secretary from the 'enemy' camp would be a real coup – all other things being equal of course.

"Why, do you think, she left them? Do you have that sort of information?" he asked.

"Well," whispered Mrs Thomas conspiratorially, leaning forward so that no one could hear. "Between you and me, and I really shouldn't be saying this, but between you and me, I think that their Mr Cooper was getting a little too fresh for this young lady. She didn't say as much. She just said that the job was not what she expected. But here, take a look at her CV. I really think that she is just the person you are looking for. Would you like me to give her a call and arrange for you to meet with her?"

"Please do," was the unhesitating reply. After the most cursory glance at her CV he handed Mrs Thomas his card and asked, "Could you call me back at this number and say that any time this Wednesday for a chat will be fine with me."

This, the good lady promised to do.

His next visit was to the local Ford agents to negotiate the leasing of a modest car and then to the local office equipment specialists to talk desks, chairs, typewriters, photocopiers, paper clips and the like.

That afternoon, Tim enjoyed a working lunch with Sandy Bartholomew whom Bob Lyons, Mary's father's friend, had passed him on to. Lyons happened to be the largest firm of printers in the area and was, particularly in view of Bob Lyon's 'paternal' interest in Mary, a most important prospective Client.

Tim studied a whole range of the ways of displaying the Logo Harrison Insurance Services Ltd, the colour it should be and how letters, compliment slips, invoices, visiting cards and a plethora of stationery should be styled. After exhausting the combined talents of himself and Sandy, Tim hit on the only logical solution. "I'm taking the whole lot home and I'm going to let Mary decide."

On arriving home, Tim found a quiet moment to phone British Telecom and to learn about waiting lists. He phoned his Accountant, his Solicitor and then his Bank Manager to check on progress. He felt as if he had called just about everyone listed in the local telephone directory.

That evening, after the kids had been bathed, read to and tucked in, Tim opened a bottle of wine and, with a deep sigh, sank back in his armchair and confessed to his wife,

"God, I'm knackered. I had no idea that there was so much to do. I thought that I had to do was just walk into an office, open the doors and let the business pour in. Instead of that, you've got to be head cook and bottle washer for every flaming thing. Here, take a look at these ideas from Sandy. Which do we go for?"

Settling herself comfortably on the floor, leaning against Tim's legs, Mary scanned through the wad of doodles and jottings, extracting one for closer scrutiny, rejecting it and moving on.

"If it were that simple, darling, everyone would be doing it." Then, with a cry of success, she selected one particular sheet of paper. She held it at arm's length, peered closely at it and laying I back on the floor, announced,

"I think that you should have this logo, with this style of print and I would have everything done in black. Colours are for trades, black and white for professions," she said decisively. "Now let's have supper and we'll have an early night. Aren't you seeing Roy tomorrow to find out what the Company are going to do about you? You'd better be bright eyed and bushy tailed for that. You haven't agreed anything yet and might well have a battle on your hands. You'd better get all the sleep you can."

As it happened, an early night did not mean more sleep but Tim did not complain, far from it.

....

"Come in," called Roy to Tim as he tapped on the open door. "How's my ex-employee today, then?"

"I never thought I'd hope to hear those words from you Roy," laughed Tim, as he settled down in his usual chair facing Roy's desk. "Is everything OK then?"

"Everything's OK, just as we agreed with Mike Hardy. You'll just have to sign this letter, and I'll do the same. Mind you, they said that they'd have my guts for garters if you don't guarantee to give the Universal more business each year than you get us at present. No problem, I told them."

"I agree. I can't see why I shouldn't give the Universal the lion's share of everything I do. That is, of course, on the assumption that you knock twenty percent off your rates on everything I ask you to quote for."

"Nuts to that, but let's get down to brass tacks. Which of our Clients do you think will follow you? Let's agree who you intend to talk to and then, if I agree, I will give you chance to get the business provided that you do your best to leave the majority with us. If we agree a plan of action, we're not likely to fall out with each other. In short, if I scratch your back, I'll expect you to do the same."

After two cups of coffee, they had agreed their strategy. Tim ended the meeting feeling that he had the basis for a very good first year. At the same time, Roy let with the feeling that he would have a peaceful last year or so with his target being largely met by the sweat and toil of his protégée, as he now liked to think of Tim.

....

And so it happened that six weeks to the day following Tim's fateful talk with Bill Warrington, Harrison Insurance Services Ltd was born - in a tiny second floor office in a modern office block situated on the outskirts of the town. He shared his floor with a small firm of Architects and a self-employed graphic artist.

He shared his office with the bubbly and delightful Miss Janet Bligh, who had passed every test he had set her with flying colours at his one and only meeting before he offered her the job without a moment's hesitation.

Tim's first few days were a frenzy of activity. A priority was to call all the Insurance Companies that he would want to use and to open Agencies with them. Most were only too pleased to give him what he wanted, but one or two were stuffy and demanded personal financial guarantees. These could 'get stuffed' – Tim was taking enough risks without putting his house and his family on the line.

Janet seemed to know just what had to be done without Tim's telling. She set up diary systems, she organised invoice procedures. She installed a filing system and she treated any visiting Insurance Company representatives as if they were minor royalty. Not one Inspector left without a cup of tea or a cup of coffee and not one left without the strongest desire to see more of the alluring Miss Bligh. Every one of them would do whatever was necessary get their own Employer to support this thriving and exciting new Company.

It was some days before Tim felt that he was prepared enough to start the real work – the task of trying to get some clients. He had to start making a few phone calls and make some appointments. It all seemed so easy a week or two ago, but now came the crunch. Would he be successful, or would he fall flat on his face?

His first call was to Bob Lyons.

"Bob, Tim Harrison here," he began as soon as he was put through. "I'm glad to say that Harrison Insurance Services is now up and running and ready for business. We've got the smartest stationery in town thanks to you, we have Agencies with all the Insurance Companies that matter and we have the brightest staff on the planet but, to date we only have one client. I thought that I'd give you the opportunity of being my second. When would you like me to call and see you and tell you why we should now be your Brokers?"

"Saucy young bugger, aren't you?" drawled Bob Lyons. "Just because we've done your stationery is no reason why we should place our insurances with you. Now if it was Mary who was asking, then I might be able to be a little more encouraging."

"I'm quite happy to get Mary to set up the meeting, and even run it, but I have to tell you that, lovely as she is, she knows bugger-all about insurance. I think that you'd be better off with me."

"You may be right," laughed Bob. "I wondered how long it would take you to call me. Come and see me after lunch tomorrow and we'll see what we can do. I'll get Tom Lacey, our FD, to be there – he's the only one here that knows anything about our Insurances. Is tomorrow OK for you?"

"Tomorrow's fine. I'll be there at two thirty on the dot. And many thanks, and I'm looking forward to seeing you then. Bye for now."

That, thought Tim, was extremely encouraging. If only it would always be as easy as this.

....

"Right its crunch time Janet. Having dealt with a friend of the family, who shall I phone next? Who is to be the third new client – excluding Warringtons and Lyons of course – of the firm of Harrisons Insurance Services Limited? Who shall the lucky person be?"

"No problem," replied Janet as she handed Tim a sheaf of papers. "Take these."

On the top of each sheet was typed the name of a Company, the address, the telephone number, the Managing Director's name and a series of boxes and columns.

"I have made a list of all the clients you discussed with Roy Brown at the Universal, all the friends whose names you have mentioned from time to time and I've added one or two names of Companies who, I know for certain, are pretty pissed off with Cooper's. I thought that they might come in handy, and these boxes are spaces where you can insert our own notes – which person you need to speak to, who they're insured with, how much they pay, when their insurances are due for renewal and all that sort of thing. I hope you find it useful."

"Janet, you're wonderful."

"I know that," she agreed. "Just you get in enough business to make sure that you can afford to keep me."

With that, Tim started the laborious task of phoning and making appointments whenever he could. He was not entirely unsuccessful.

The following day, at two thirty precisely, Tim was ushered into Bob Lyon's spectacular office, an office which boasted a vast antique partner's desk, several fine leather-upholstered occasional chairs and a Board Table with chairs for twelve people.

Tom Lacey was already occupying one such chair and had, before him, a stack of files and computer printouts.

"Come in, come in, dear boy," greeted Bob Lyons effusively, rising from his own chair and moving towards Tim with outstretched hand. "How are you and how's the delectable Mrs Harrison?"

"Good to see you Bob. We're both fine thanks and Mary sends her love."

"I'd rather she delivered it personally but, I suppose I'll have to make do with second best," this with a resigned sigh. "Now meet Tom. He's our FD. Been here over twenty years haven't you Tom? Nothing he doesn't know about our business and he'll tell you anything you need to know, won't you Tom?"

Tom rose and shook hands with Tim. He was a shortish man, rather slightly built, with receding hair topping a studious face. "Glad to meet you Tim. I'll be pleased to let you know whatever you need to know."

They sat down and Tim ran through the preliminaries. He ascertained their turnover, the type of work they did, the type of machinery they used and, much to the point, with whom they were already insured and how much they were paying them.

"The one problem we have Tim," said Tom Lacey, "is that all our Insurances are under a three year long term agreement with about two years to go, so I don't think that, with the best will in the world, we can do anything until then. We can't possibly break that agreement so I think that you will have to be patient for a couple of years."

Tim was ready for that one.

"That's not a problem," he said. "Your agreement is with the Insurance Company, not with your Broker. Subject to a few minor issues, you are free to change Brokers even if you ma not be free to switch Insurance Companies."

"Does that mean," interjected Bob Lyons, "that, if we wanted to, we could appoint you as our Broker and you would simply carry on with the same policies for the balance of the three years?"

"Precisely that," confirmed Tim.

"And do you think that you could give us the same service that Boltons are currently giving us? They are a very large firm as you know."

"I'm absolutely certain that I can more than match the service. It's not the size of the firm that matters. It's the quality of the people with whom you'll be dealing. I can assure you that with me, you'll always be dealing with their top man and they don't come any better than him.

"Furthermore, when you want to see someone from Boltons, you have to wait for them to trot down from London, whereas I'm here, right on your doorstep. With me you'll not only get service with a smile, but you'll get it instantly."

"Lippy little bugger isn't he Tom, but I like the cut of his jib," smiled Bob. "What do you think, Tom, should we give him a chance or should we tell him to bugger off for a couple of years and see if he's still in business by then?"

"Well Bob, you're right to say that Boltons are big – they're enormous, they're. We'd be taking a chance that Tim here doesn't go down the tubes just when we might need a bit of clout. And I certainly would not be impressed if Tim here could only match their service. He'd have to do better than that if we were to switch.

"Over the last few years, Bolton's service has deteriorated. We pay them about fifty thousand pounds a year and, yet, whenever we need anything urgent, you'd think that we've asked them for the crown jewels. As it happens, I'd like to kick them into touch and let them realise that they can't take everything for granted. If Tim here is as good as his word, we can't do any worse than we do at present. But will Tim still be here in twelve month's time and will he be able to give us a better deal than we get from Boltons?"

Tim spent the next half hour explaining precisely what how would handle their account, precisely what is own resources were and precisely why they would be better off with him than Boltons. He must have pressed the right buttons for, without warning, Bob cut in and announced,

"Well that's done then Tim. You've just got your second client. Now I've got to slip away and I'll leave it to you and Tom to sort out the details. I look forward to many years of happy dealings with you, but if I find that we have any trouble with a claim, or if you let us down in any way, I'll screw your balls to the floor. Is that understood?"

"That's fine by me. I can't tell you how grateful I am for your decision and I promise that I'll not let you down. You can rely on that."

"Good enough for me," replied Bob. They shook hands and whilst Bob tidied up his desk and made his departure, Tim started the laborious process of finalising the paper work with Tom. They waited whilst Tom's Secretary typed out the letter of appointment and, one hour later, Tim was driving happily back to his office to break the marvellous news to Janet. His mood could fairly be described as euphoric. His first new client had only taken him only two days to find.

....

Twelve months later, Harrisons was becoming a minor force in the Insurance world. Insurance Companies were vying with each other to entertain Tim out to lunch and to convince him that they, rather than their competitors, were the people he should be using.

Janet's original lists had soon been superseded by longer lists, and Client files now took up an ever-increasing amount of space in the modest battery of filing cabinets. Not a bad first year, thought Tim.

....

"'Ow's fings going then?" enquired Bill Warrington, as they met to consider his Firm's annual review.

"'ave I made a good investment or what? I've been looking forward to me dividend for mumfs. Told me missus she should be able to afford that fur coat she's always wanted. I tell you wot though, if you 'and't sorted out that bleedin' fire claim before you got started 'ere, I'd've 'ad your guts for garters and none of this would've 'appened. You did a good job there an' it showed me that I was backing a good 'un", he added with an expansive wave around Tim's limited office space.

"That's good of you to say so Bill – I was only doing my job. As for Martha's fur coat, I don't think she should go quite that far yet. That is, if you're expecting to pay for it from your dividend. Might be able to afford a plastic Mac from Woolworths though," suggested Tim generously.

"The truth is, though, we've had a fantastic first year. We thought we'd do about twenty thousand in year one, including your business. In fact, it's nearer forty thousand. Mark you, the expenses are far higher that we ever could have imagined but I reckon we should make a profit of about five grand or a bit more. Not bad for the first year, don't you think? We might even be able to run to a pair of shoes for Martha."

"She's got all the bleedin' shoes she needs – enough to last 'er a lifetime. No, not that ain't bad at all young man. You keep yer 'ead down and we'll all be eatin' caviar and drinkin' champagne next year. You just keep at it."

They spent the next twenty minutes or so reviewing Warrington's Insurances – a job that used to take half an afternoon in Cooper's days and then chewed the cud over Harrison's first year and its immediate prospects.

It was a cheerful and morale-boosting discussion. And in that spirit, so ended Harrison's first Annual General Meeting.

Chapter Ten

For Joe Hendry, the last twelve months had not gone quite so smoothly. He had, to be fair, been more than pleased with Ted's first customer, Mrs Hampshire. She had been a great success and, adding everything together, he reckoned that he had netted a cool thousand pounds on that deal alone. To his great satisfaction, this success had spurred Ted to move into his own top gear.

All would have been well if Joe had heard no further from Mrs Hampshire. The trouble started when Joe received a call from an extremely irate Mr Hampshire, who turned out to be the son of his very good customer. He was accusing Everbright Double Glazing Ltd of every type of chicanery known to man. In this, it must be said, he had a point.

It transpired that he was decidedly unhappy that his aged Mother had been ripped off and twisted out of every cent she had diligently saved, for a double-glazing job that was totally and utterly unnecessary.

"Leave it to me," said Joe to the fuming Mr Hampshire with a confidence that he certainly did not feel. "Obviously there's been some misunderstanding here. As you can see, we have done a first class job for Mrs Hampshire – I do recall, for sure, that the windows needed replacing as a matter of urgency. I will investigate and call you back."

What did not help his case was the fact that the Mr Hampshire he was confronted with was a firebrand Solicitor and the brother of the Mr Hampshire, the partner of Grays and Tompkins, the well-known national firm of surveyors. It absolutely apparent that the Hampshires knew exactly what they were talking about and that matters would not be allowed to quietly die down.

He decided to call George Haskins, his MD and confront him with the problem – a problem shared was the buck passed on as far as he was concerned.

"What the fuck were you playing at?" was George's immediate and unpromising response to Joe's preliminary explanation.

"Well, I reckoned that, by the time Ted and I had scratched around in the putty, the windows could have done with a bit of a smartening up. I offered her a good price. I used the old one about the prices going up unless she got in a bit sharpish, but we all do that. I took her deposit in cash just to make sure we didn't get landed with a bummer. All straight and above board. I'll soon get it sorted."

"You do that," demanded George Haskins. "We've already been in the press for this sort of thing far too many times for comfort. If it gets any worse, we'll have to change the Company name again and that'll make Tom Cummings scream blue murder. I don't care how you do it, but just you make sure that this Hampshire bastard doesn't take us to Court. One more Court case, and we'll be paying more in legal fees than we do in wages."

"OK, George. I'll speak to Mrs Hampshire and you won't hear any more. Trust me."

Back in his own office, Joe had time to ponder. "Christ," he thought. "How the hell do I get out of this one? I could have sworn that the old biddy would have kept her mouth shut about the cash – she didn't want to drop me in it. There's no trusting some people. You do people a favour and this is how they pay you back." Not for the first time, Joe concluded that the World was not a fair place.

Having considered the matter from every angle, and after a good deal of head scratching, Joe decided to bite the bullet and telephone the good lady. He was mildly surprised that the response to his cheery 'hello' was a rather frosty one. And that was putting it mildly. After some five minutes of rambling explanation, excuse and prevarication, he judged that Mrs Hampshire was slightly mollified. Sufficiently, in any case, to agree to see him the following evening at seven.

Little did Joe realise that this was the time that her son, the structural surveyor of repute, had agreed with his Mother that he could be at 27 Acacia Avenue. Indeed, he would be there. John Hampshire was very keen to meet Joe Hendry.

To say the meeting went smoothly would have been an exaggeration. Joe found himself having to explain 'muffle'", explain why he used an old fashioned exposure meter for checking windows and to defend his opinion that the work was even necessary at all.

After a thirty minute grilling, the like of which he had never been through in his life – nor ever wished to experience again - Joe found himself soundly back footed.

By the end of the grilling, Joe realising that discretion was the better part of valour, found himself facing the appalling prospect of having to agree to refund five hundred pounds. 'Refund' was a word that had never before featured in Joe's vocabulary and he was not enjoying the experience at all.

The five hundred pounds had to be in cash and on the table "by lunchtime tomorrow" or a Solicitor's letter (George Hampshire's) would be on Everbright's doormat first thing Monday morning.

In the event, the money was on the kitchen table next morning and Joe, a very chastened Joe, had learned several valuable lessons.

Firstly, never screw an old lady if she has a son in a similar business. Secondly, never pay a couple of hundred quid to Ted until the dust has had time to settle. (Joe had already witnessed a large chunk of Ted's commission disappearing over the Bar at the Lion and knew that there was no way that it was ever going to see the light of day again). In future, it would be half down and the other half in six to twelve month's.

Thirdly, always take more than fifty percent in cash – if you ever have to give it back, you want to keep the taxman out of the equation.

Being philosophical or, more accurately, having been forced to be philosophical, Joe accepted his loss and treated it as part of his learning curve. Time to move on, he told himself. Indeed, events were to prove this to be sound and practical philosophy and a lesson well learned.

As for Ted, he had absolutely no qualms over the morality of his devious selling practices. It was all water off a duck's back as far as he was concerned. His only worry was the possible harmful effect on his faltering cash flow.

In consequence, Ted redoubled his efforts, and started to get a surprisingly steady flow of 'punters' for Joe to work his charm upon. Ted was beginning to bring in two or three 'leads' every week and Joe, for his part, was converting a good fifty percent of these into firm orders.

Of course, some of the deals had to be 'kosher' and, on these, Joe was only able to earn his legitimate commission. Even so, every third or fourth enquiry offered an opportunity for a 'cash' element – and Joe was always prepared to 'make an exception to his normally inviolate rule' and find a way of accommodating the tax adverse customer (and, of course, his own back pocket).

Much to Joe's surprise, Ted was getting quite good at his job and, much to Ted's own surprise, he was actually beginning to enjoy the challenge of arranging a deal. He had even bought himself a blazer and would often be seen resplendent therein, sometimes with a clean shirt and a reasonably well knotted, and occasionally matching, tie.

It was at one of their evening discussions at the Lion, that Ted suggested to Joe that he was wondering whether he might get old Cedric, a fellow patron, to try his hand at getting in a few punters. A sort of sub-agent.

"Old Cedric," affirmed Ted, "is always one to shoot a line. There ain't a dirty story told wot Cedric 'asn't already 'eard. I'm bloody sure 'e'd go a bomb on the doorstep. Course, we'd 'ave to toff 'im up a bit. 'E normally looks a bloody shambles, but I'd get 'im along to Oxfam or somewhere and find 'im something cheap wot don't look too bad. Wotcha think?"

"Sounds a bloody good idea to me. I tell you what. You have a word with him, and if you think he might be able to bring in a few punters, take him round with you one evening so that he can see what you do. Give him a lesson so as to speak."

"Staff training sort of fing? I always wanted ter be a Manager. I tell you wot though. If 'e's any good, I'm not giving 'im my two 'undred knicker. You'll 'ave to cough up a bit more yerself."

The man's even becoming a businessman admitted Joe to himself, ruefully. Still, he couldn't complain if Ted was going to bring in more sales. The more punters, the more profit for Joe.

"OK," agreed Joe. "You're a hard bastard. I do all the selling and you get a couple of hundred smackers for virtually bugger-all. But I'm a fair man and, to help you out, I'll make a sacrifice. I'll up your commission to two hundred and fifty quid a go and if you give Cedric half of that, you'll both be on to a bloody good thing. Of course, I'll have to drop from pints to halves, but that's my problem."

"Well that's all fine but, I've been finking. You give me two 'undred and fifty quid wevver it's a two thousand pound job or a ten thousand pound job. I was talking to a bloke in 'ere the uvver day wot was in the same line of business as us. When I told 'im wot you paid me, 'e said I could come an' work for 'im and 'e'd give me twenty percent of whatever he got an' I'd end up earning double wot you give me. I told 'im to take a running but I fink you can afford to pay me more. Specially if old Cedric starts pullin' 'em in."

This was the type of conversation that Joe thoroughly disliked – it went against his nature. It always hurt badly when he had to give some of his own cash away. But things were beginning to look up, he conceded, and he had no wish to rock the boat. The fact that Ted was becoming a negotiator, bloody nuisance that it was now, could prove to be an asset if Joe were to develop some of the other plans he had in mind.

"Not only are you a hard bastard, but you're also a shifty bastard," Joe informed Ted. "I'll tell you what I'll do. I'll give you three hundred quid per punter that signs up and you give half of that to any that Cedric pulls in. We'll keep a score, and as soon as you have brought in ten Customers between you, I'll raise this to three hundred and fifty quid and, once you get over twenty in any one year, I'll also give you a ten percent over-rider. How's that? Seem fair to you?"

"Done," responded Ted. "So long as the ten percent is retrispective, or whatever the word is. When we've got twenty punters, me and Cedric between us, you gimme ten percent of the 'ole year's earnin's. OK?"

"Bugger," thought Joe. "OK, you win," he said, reluctantly.

And so, the sales force was taking shape.

Chapter Eleven

Tim felt that it was about time that he took Roy Brown, his old Branch Manager, out to lunch. It had been over a year since he had left and he had a great deal to discuss and even more to be grateful for.

"So, how's it all going?" said Roy as he sat back to enjoy the rather fine Pouilly Fuisse that Tim had splashed out on.

They were seated at a corner table of their favourite Italian Restaurant – La Taverna. Tim had become something of a regular there over the last few months. Notwithstanding his desperate workload, Tim had decided that it was occasionally worth succumbing to the constant invitations from Branch Managers and Insurance Company Inspectors for a "bite to eat". He found that La Taverna could get him in and out within an hour and that this was a pretty good investment of his time.

It never ceased to amaze him how many favours he could wangle out of a mildly inebriated Insurance Company Inspector or his Manager over a glass of reasonable wine, even if the latter were paying.

If he was after a block of business and he needed someone to shave a few percent off a rate to give him an edge over the competition, then one hour over lunch was the time and place to do it.

"You've been going about a year now so you should have a pretty good idea whether you're likely to be broke by Christmas or a millionaire by Easter," opined Roy.

"Neither," laughed Tim. "I had hoped to be at a break-even position by the year end but, with the way things are, I seem to have cleared about four or five thousand pounds profit. Not bad in year one, and that's after paying myself a little more than you mean buggers at the Universal ever did."

"Not bad at all," agreed Roy. "But then I always knew you would. What about expansion plans? Anything on the horizon?"

"Well that's why I wanted to have a talk with you. Let's order first and then I'll tell you what I have in mind."

Luigi was hovering over them with his scrappy note-book at the ready. Tim had not even looked at the menu but ordered without hesitation. "Melon, followed by liver, underdone, new potatoes and broccoli, for a change Luigi, and be fast about it."

"Meester 'arisson, you always hava the sama. I gotta kitchen full of things you've neffer even tried. Whya you not be more adventurous for a change? I'va gotta beautiful salmon which you oughta try."

"You know I don't trust anything coming out of your kitchen that I've not tried before. Salmonella is rife out there. It's a miracle I've survived as long as I have. Now just cut the cackle, get your backside in gear and get on with it you Italian nutcase," Tim responded good-naturedly.

"And I'll have exactly the same, Luigi," added Roy.

As Luigi, sighing deeply, dutifully waddled off to his kitchen, Tim took another sip of wine, pulled his chair closer to the table and said,

"Yes, the problem is not the getting of the business, but the managing of it. Janet's marvellous – an absolute gem. Nothing's too much trouble for her, the clients love her and the Inspectors think she's gorgeous – which she is, by the way.

"What I need, though, is someone who is technically competent, someone who knows all the policy conditions, the exclusions, what the competitors are offering and all that sort of thing. I need someone who can run the office whilst I'm out seeing clients – or, more importantly, prospective clients"

"Don't look at me," rejoined Roy. "I may know the business inside out but I haven't read a Policy document for over twenty years. I have as much idea of the detail of what we cover as does our post clerk."

"I wasn't thinking of you. Well not until you retire, that is. No, the person that I would like to take on is your Graham Wiltshier. I keep in touch with him almost daily, in fact he deals with the lion's share of my business, bearing in mind that I have kept my side of the bargain and supported the Universal whenever I can."

"I'm well aware of that Tim. Your account has grown exponentially – more than made up for the drop in support we seem to have been experiencing from Coopers. Mind you, the other Managers in town that I still talk to all seem to be experiencing the same thing – I think that Coopers are going backwards fast."

"I'm sure that's the case. But, back to Graham. I would ask him direct but I fully appreciate how important he is to you, and the last thing I want to do is to make your life more difficult, especially as you only have about six month's to go before you hang up your brief case."

Their conversation was interrupted by the arrival of Luigi, complete with two dishes of a rather ripe looking ogen melon.

"Shall I putta the Port in meester 'arrison?"

"Don't be a tiresome old wop Luigi. You know I've got work to do this afternoon. Back to your kitchen, there's a good chap and let those who have to work, carry on in a relatively sober state."

"I have to admit," continued Roy, after tasting and approving his melon. "I can't wait to get out of the Universal. Things are nothing like they used to be. I can't even make a decision to blow my nose without signing something in triplicate. As to Graham, I seem to have been over similar ground with you about twelve month's ago. It seems to me, that if Graham joined you, the Universal would get even more business. Graham's very solid and if he feels that he can get the deals and the service that he wants out of us, and I'm sure that we can deliver on that, he'll support us all he can.

"In truth, I can only see good in it for us if Graham were to join you. If you're sure that you can give him reasonable job security – he's got two kids too, you know – I'm all for it. Go on; you give him a call and make him an offer. I'll deal with Head Office and I'm sure that there's someone lurking about somewhere in the Company who we can promote to take Graham's place."

"Thanks for that Roy. I really do appreciate it. I'll give him a call this afternoon. Now, I'm also looking for someone with a bit of experience who might be able to lend me a hand and persuade the occasional client to shift his business in my direction. Ideally, a newly retired Branch Manager should fit the bill. You don't know anyone like that do you?"

They were interrupted by Luigi's assistant, Gina, clearing away their empty dishes. A delightful young Italian girl who happened to be Luigi's favourite 'niece'. Tim and Roy sat back contentedly to watch Gina at work. As she completed her chores and withdrew, Roy agreed,

"There are quite a few old codgers being put out to grass now, so it shouldn't be too difficult to find someone in their early dotage that might be able to bring a breath of wisdom to your burgeoning empire. Mrs Brown thinks that I ought to apply for something like that. I think she's already started having nightmares at the thought of having me around all day in six or even month's time. Must say that the feeling's mutual".

"Precisely," replied Tim. "With all the early retirement packages going on at the moment, I'm surprised that you've stayed as long as you have. That's the second reason for having lunch together today. I would love you to join me as soon as you retire - six months from now would great since it would give me time to save up for another desk and chair."

"Sure is. I retire on the first of August and I can't wait. I'm slightly flattered that you still think I've got some useful life left in me and I shall be delighted to come aboard. To tell the truth, ever since we had our first little discussion, just over a year ago, I fancied the idea of joining you and your project one day. To be honest, I have a feeling that I might be able to be of some use. There are a good few clients who could do with a better Broker than the one they have at the moment and I would have thought that the right word at the right time might just pay dividends. I'd certainly like to give it a try. You appreciate though, don't you, that I would not do anything that would be the least bit injurious to the Universal. Apart from my loyalty to them, they will be paying me my pension!"

"I would expect nothing less. No, with Graham, you and me – and hopefully Marilyn would come along too – the Universal will never have had it so good. We'll be giving them so much business, they won't know what to do with it."

"I know that Marilyn would jump at the opportunity. The only thing is, though, her kids are growing up and I know that she wants to be round more when they get back from school. Ideally, she would like to work a couple of days a week and, possibly, drop down to one day a week during school holidays."

"That would be ideal. If you were working here as often as is necessary, an arrangement like that with Marilyn would ensure that you get just about all the back up you're likely to need, just when you need it. That's settled then. The day you get the boot, is the day you start with me. Let's drink to it."

They continued lunch companionably, discussing opportunities, remuneration packages and the prospects for Insurance Broking in general, until it was time for Tim to sign the bill and for them to get up and go.

"You give Graham a call, then," said Roy, "and tell him to pop in and see me. If he's keen, I'll tell him what a great opportunity he's being offered. If all goes well, I'll give Mike Hardy at Head Office a call and smooth things over so that Graham can leave with as little fuss as possible. In any case, as an inside man, I can't think that he would be pinching any clients, although, I dare say, there will be quite a few who would be happy to deal with you if they realise that you've got Graham working for you."

"That's great Roy, and thanks for everything you've done – and will be doing. I'll call you tomorrow. Bye for now."

And with that, Tim strolled back to his office to share the glad tidings with Janet.

Harrison's looked as if it would be starting year two in an expansive mode.

....

"Hi Graham, it's Tim," he announced once he had been put through. "How're things going?"

"Hello Tim, good to hear from you. Not too bad. Rushed off my feet as always. Bit of bad news though. Did you hear that Morrison's have just gone bust? The Receiver was appointed this morning. It looks as if we could be in for a bad debt of about twenty grand – well, not us, but for Coopers. They're the Brokers and it's them that will have extended the credit. Mind you, knowing Colin Cooper, he'll wriggle like the snake he is and try to land the bad debt on us. Knowing how soft our lords and masters are, I'm sure that we will pick up some of it. I don't suppose Roy is going to be too pleased either – it will bugger up this year's budget."

"I had no idea. I would have thought that Morrison's were as strong as the Bank of England. I bet that their trouble is connected with one of their overseas customers going down the tubes. I know that we tried to sell them Credit Insurance a few years ago, but they always thought that it was too expensive; don't suppose that they'd think so now.

"I shouldn't worry about Roy's budgets though, he's only got six month's to go and I doubt that that will affect his pension. Bit of a bugger for Coopers though. Couldn't happen to a nicer firm," Tim observed wryly. "Anyway, enough of other people's problems. I've got one of my own. I'm absolutely inundated with work – you know that the technical stuff has never been my forte – and I desperately need someone good who can take over the reins. Know of anyone good by any chance?"

"It depends on how much you want to pay him, or her. I do know a good chap, but he wouldn't come cheap."

"What's this good chap earning now," asked Tim.

"Three thousand four hundred a year, plus a non-contributory pension and a cheap mortgage," came the immediate reply.

"I'm too small to bugger about with cheap mortgages, but would five thousand a year and ten percent into a pension be of any interest to your friend?" suggested Tim.

"When do I start?" laughed Graham.

"Well, if you toddle in to see Roy and give him one month's notice, how does four weeks from next Monday strike you?"

"Done. But what do you think Roy is going to say? There's a hell of a lot on at the moment and it might not be fair to leave him in the S H one T."

"Just go and see what he has to say. I'm sure you're not as indispensable as you would like to think you are. The Universal will be able to lay their hands on someone who'll be twice as good as you at half the price. No problem at all."

"Thanks for the vote of confidence! Right you are, Tim, I'll see Roy as soon as I can and give you a call tomorrow, when I've talked things over with Sue. I think that my dependants ought to be involved in the fact that their breadwinner is about to jack in a perfectly good and secure job in favour of joining a back street bucket shop like yours."

"Thank you too! I'll speak to you tomorrow. Sleep well and my love to Sue."

Four weeks later, Graham became the third employee of Harrison Insurance Services Limited.

Chapter Twelve

As the months went by, Joe Hendry had reason to be fairly well satisfied with the performance of his little team. He still spent many evenings wasting his time calling on hopeless cases, but the percentage of 'hits' was improving and his bank balance was taking on a healthier hue.

The only cloud on the horizon was a Mr and Mrs Perkins who seemed hell bent on making trouble for him.

Cedric had done a good job and convinced them that there was essential work to be done on their windows and Joe had found it surprisingly easy to get them to sign up for a five thousand pound job. As was often the case, he had got his good friend, Trevor Watkins, to fix up a slightly dodgy second mortgage to cover the cost.

Joe had told the Perkins that the interest rate on the mortgage was a giveaway at only one percent a month and Mr Perkins had remarked how cheap that was – "how can they do it for the price?" he had asked. It had seemed an irrelevance to Joe to explain, at the time, that one percent a month worked out a rate considerably in excess of twelve percent per year, and that this compared somewhat unfavourably with the going rate of nearer six percent per year available from most banks or building societies.

Apart from that, in view of the Perkins's ages, the fact that there was a real prospect of him being made redundant in the near future, and the inflated price that he would be paying for his windows, no self-respecting Building Society would have touched this particular proposition with the proverbial barge pole. Joe, with his 'professional connections' was clearly doing the Perkins a considerable favour in arranging this finance for him – or so Joe thought.

What was it to Joe if the Customer couldn't understand plain English and simple finance? It was hardly Joe's role to explain to the punter that, what he was signing up for could very easily bring about his financial ruin. Where was the mileage in that?

In fact, the mortgage was being provided from private funds put up by Trevor's uncle who had, not unreasonably Joe thought, insisted on one or two additional clauses. Nothing particularly onerous, of course – just a doubling of the rate of interest if there was a failure to meet even one month's instalment and foreclosure with penalties if there should be a three month failure to pay.

The problem was, that Mr Perkins had been made redundant - the day after he had signed the agreement. He had immediately called Joe and asked him to cancel the contract.

Naturally, Joe was sympathetic but told him that cancellation was quite impossible – after all, Joe stood to make just over fifteen hundred quid on the deal – plus a small 'back-hander' from his good friend Trevor. No self-respecting businessman could be expected to kiss that sort of deal goodbye.

Mr Perkins seemed unnaturally distraught so, to help out, Joe took a personal interest in seeing that the work was carried out promptly. That way, he got his commission more quickly and reduced the risk of the Perkins' appealing to George Haskin's better nature and getting the whole job cancelled. Not that there was much risk of that occurring since, so far as anyone one could discern, George was completely devoid of a better nature.

When the Perkins' first instalment fell due, not surprisingly, the standing order bounced. George Watkins phoned Joe to warn him of this little problem and Joe took the trouble to call round and see Mr Perkins personally to explain the facts of life.

Joe found the entire meeting rather distasteful since Mrs Perkins was in tears for the duration and Mr Perkins ended by calling Joe every name under the sun, and then a few more. Joe felt that Mr Perkins had been unnecessarily abusive. Joe concluded the meeting in as conciliatory manner as he could, by pointing out that, if further payments were not made, then the Finance Company would have no alternative but to foreclose and insist that the house be sold under their feet.

Joe tried to comfort them by pointing out that, if this were the case, and then there should be some small cash surplus left. In any event, Joe advised them, with brand new Everbright windows, the Estate Agents should have no difficulty in getting a good price for the house.

Joe reported back to George that he had sorted things out and was confident that the Perkins would now find some way of clearing up the arrears. He congratulated himself on a job well done.

Unfortunately, from there, matters began to go down hill. Mr and Mrs Perkins took their story to the Local Press who had, for reasons best known to themselves, decided to make an issue of the case.

The Headline the following week read "Double Dealing by Double Glazing Company". The article went on to describe how an unscrupulous salesman had allegedly convinced a couple of elderly Pensioners to have work carried out on their house that was entirely unnecessary – they published a synopsis of a report from a firm of Chartered Surveyors (Grays and Tompkins as it happened) who confirmed this to have been the case, and that they had experienced a similar situation with this particular firm in the past.

The article went on to say that the salesman who had persuaded the Perkins to sign up for the work had introduced them to a finance scheme that could only be described as usurious. Furthermore, the salesman had allegedly misrepresented this as being a special rate of interest of only one per cent when the true rate was in excess of twelve per cent a year – almost double the rate currently obtainable from the High Street Banks and Building Societies.

The Reporter stated that he had endeavoured to get a response from the Managing Director of Everbright Windows but he had only succeeded in eliciting a "no comment."

The following week's commentary was even more damaging and George Haskins felt compelled to call Joe in for a meeting.

Joe accordingly attended the following morning at nine o'clock – an unearthly hour in Joe's book – and was rather startled to see that the Everbright's owner, Tom Cummings, was sitting comfortably behind George's desk, puffing on his customary oversize cigar.

"What the bloody hell's been going on with you and this fellow Perkins?" was Tom's peremptory welcome. "As if I haven't got enough on my plate without the bleeding Echo breathing down my neck. Just what the fuck have you been up to?"

"I really have no idea what all the fuss is about Tom. I surveyed their windows myself and, although there wasn't much wrong with them, I was able to persuade them that they wouldn't last forever. They even agreed that they didn't look too good and that they were hoping to have them painted later that year. The old codger had a bad back and couldn't do it himself so I pointed out that we were doing them a favour. Taking all the bother away for them and all that sort of thing. You know as well as I do, that if you don't get the punters to believe that they've got problems, you won't be selling them any double-glazing."

"I know that, but according to that bleeding firm of tossers that calls themselves Chartered Surveyors, there was nothing wrong with those windows at all. For Chrissakes, you've got to be a bit bloody careful; there's got to be something wrong with them before you sell them a new set. Anyway, what's all this about the finance deal? How come you've got yourself mixed up with that? Are you on some sort of back-hander that George and I don't know anything about?"

"A friend of mine, Trevor Watkins, runs a bloody good Mortgage Company – MoneySure Financial Services they call themselves. You know how hard it is to get a second mortgage for double-glazing these days, especially when the punter hasn't really got any credit-worthiness for the loan. Well, these blokes get money from what they call 'private sources' and they're good for almost anything, even County Court Judgement cases. I always use them when the punter has no hope of raising the cash any other way."

"That's all well and good," cut in George Haskins. "But their rate of interest is double what you can get anywhere else. How do you get the punters to pay?" The rights and wrongs of the case clearly took second (if any) place to the opportunities to make money in George's mind. If there was a good scam about, George wanted to be in on it.

"It's easy," replied Joe. "You just tell them that you've got this fantastic deal, only available to Everbright (because of the quality of our work and all that crap) where the rate is only one percent, and they jump at it. They're all too thick to understand what the real rate is. I just tell them what the actual monthly payment is – I usually spread it over twenty years to make it look cheap - and they sign up straight away, candy from kids. You'd laugh if you saw what some of them pay. I had a chap who signed up for a four thousand pound job and, when I worked out the figures when I got home that night, I calculated that he would actually be coughing up over twenty thousand pounds by the time he was through. Those finance boys are making a fucking fortune. You ought to try it Tom, it'd be a doddle."

"Perhaps I should," mused Tom, the plight of the Perkins continuing to take a back seat in all of their thinking for the moment.

"Well, it seems that you've done everything by the book. I'll just tell the Echo to fuck off and mind their own business and the whole thing'll die down in a few weeks. Serve the Perkins right, if they lose their house, making all this fuss and buggering up my day." Tom Cummings was a reasonable man.

But die down it did not.

The reporting became even more virulent, the threatened Solicitor's letters started arriving and Everbright Windows received visits from the Trades Description officers, the Inland Revenue and the dreaded VAT man.

This did not bother Joe unduly, but Ted and Cedric started reporting that, as soon as they mentioned the name 'Everbright', doors started closing and the punters immediately lost interest. It really was amazing how everyone seemed to believe what he or she had read in the papers, Joe thought.

To his chagrin, matters continued to deteriorate and, for the first time since his team started operations, Joe found himself with no appointments to follow up at all for an entire week.

Joe was now thoroughly brassed off. He decided it was time for him to fix a meeting with George Haskins and express his concerns. No appointments meant no commission and, as ever, this was an extremely worrying issue for Joe. When they eventually met, George admitted that his other Salesmen were experiencing the same problems and that something would have to be done, and done fast. A further meeting with Tom Cummings was called for the following day.

At nine o'clock the following morning, Tom Cummings appeared. He was not in a good mood.

"Look at these fucking figures George," was his opening shot. "Just what the fuck's going on? I leave you to run the fucking business and at the rate things have been going over the last month, we might as well all have shut up shop and gone home." There was never too much doubt as to whether or not Tom was happy or unhappy on any given day.

"It's these bloody Perkin's people, Tom. It's they who are fucking everything up. We've got a real problem with them," explained George. "We're getting it in the neck from every direction and with the publicity we're getting now, I don't see things improving. I can't see any alternative but to do another 'Plan B'. We've been going almost three years with the same name – that's not bad for us or for anyone else in this business."

"For Chrissakes!" retorted Tom. "It's alright for you. You just sit there and pick up your wages. I've got all the bother of fixing up a new fucking Company, Solicitors Fees, Accountant's fees – those bastards charge a fucking fortune when they can see someone with their backs to the wall. And that's not counting a few grand in bad debts that we're bound to pick up."

"What's 'Plan B'?" interjected Joe.

"Nothing much really," said George. "Me and Tom have done it several times. You have to in this business. All we do, when things get too hot, is wind the old Company up, walk away from it's debts and bad publicity and start another one the next day. All the problems go out the door with the old Company and the new one's as clean as a whistle. Nothing to it, everyone does it. It saves a lot of fucking about.

"And the best thing is, we keep the same salesman and they get a better hearing from the punters because they slag off that shower of shits called Everbright. 'Wouldn't be associated with a firm like that for all the tea in China', they say. Works a treat, every time."

"That's what you say, you don't have the fucking costs," groaned Tom, but brightening a little, he added, "as it happens though, I registered 'Castle Windows' a few years ago. I was talking to another Accountant, I met at some meeting or other – I think old Bill, and Stillwells themselves, are getting a bit past it – and he recommended that we form a Company in the Channel Islands. Bloody good tax fiddle, even though it costs a bit more to get it started. The good thing is that me and my missus' names don't appear anyway because we use Directors over there in Jersey, so no one over here will ever connect Everbright with Castle."

"What's more," continued Tom, "I bought a shell Company that was formed in 1955, so we can put in all our brochures and publicity guff that we have been going for over twenty years. All good stuff." Tom looked around the room for approval and not noticing any discernible reaction from either George or Joe, made up his mind.

"OK, we'll go for it. Now you try and get as much cash out of the Company as you can over the next two weeks, settle up a few of those phoney bad debts we've been owing some 'friends' just in case we need to keep something out of the taxman's hands. Make sure you take the overdraft up to the absolute maximum, and I'll get any credit balances transferred to the National Bank of Jersey. Let's wind up Everbright three weeks from now."

"Looks like we'll all be working for Castle Windows next month," observed George wryly. "I hope they pay well!"

Tom suggested that Joe should now "bugger off" so that he and George could get down to business and sort out the details. This Joe did and decided to hold a 'board meeting' of his own at the Lion as soon as possible.

On the way over to the Lion, Joe decided to call in to see Trevor Watkins, his friendly Mortgage Broker, to see what was happening to his commission on the Perkins' job, which despite the traumas of the case, Joe felt he had more than adequately earned. He would also hint that there might be some changes to be made in the future and test the water for a clever little scheme that was already gestating in his devious mind.

....

Over a cup of coffee at MoneySure Financial Services, Joe explained what bastards the Perkins were and how he had done everything in his power to help them. Notwithstanding this, it did seem that the ungrateful bastards would not be meeting their obligations. "There's really no helping some people," Joe opined.

"Anyway," concluded Joe. "You'll still get your money in full because they will have to sell the house and there's more than enough equity in that to cover the loan. So I take it you'll be seeing me straight then, Trev?"

"I would love to say 'yes' Joe, but I'm afraid it's not that simple," responded Trevor. "I have no idea whether we'll get all, or even any, of our money back. I can tell you that my uncle's well and truly pissed off that we seem to have got roped into all these stories in the Echo. He thinks, and so do I, that all this will rub off on us and that we too will get a bad name. And, with a slur on our reputation, then where will our business come from?"

"Don't you worry about that. My boss, Tom Cummings – you must have heard of Tom – he's a brilliant financial guy. He's got plans to get us up and running as an offshore Company. We've formed a Company in the Channel Islands that's already been going for over twenty years.

"When Tom, George and me get our hands on it, things'll really start to happen. It will be huge, and I'll be giving you more work than you'll be able to handle. I'm sure that you'll have to take on more staff to cope with what we'll be sending you. Now what about my cheque?"

"I'll tell you what I'll do," said Trevor, beginning to believe that there may be a germ of truth in what Joe was telling him. He had no wish to turn his back on what may be substantial potential commissions.

"We'll see how things go over the next few weeks, and if we look as if we are going to get our money, I'll give you a hundred quid then and the rest in about a year, or sooner if we get paid in full. Is that OK? I can't say fairer than that."

"It will have to do, you're a tight bastard you are," agreed Joe, with his customary ill grace. "Here, I've been thinking. I've been watching how you operate and it seems to me that you have an easier time than me and my men in earning a few bob. You blokes make a pile of money. I've got a sales team – and it's going to get bigger – and I would have thought that me and my chaps could make more money selling insurance than double-glazing. What do you think?"

"Well, we make our money from interest charges on loans, secured and unsecured. Our people need to have a sound knowledge of the financial markets to be able to secure the best possible deals for our clients," began Trevor.

"That's bollocks," interjected Joe. "As far as I can see, all you do is to get your Uncle or some of his buddies to ante up the dough as soon as we can find you a punter who is too daft to understand what you're selling him."

"That's nonsense, and you know it," rejoined Trevor, the flush of his cheeks indicating either wrath or embarrassment – but probably both. "It's true that there are occasions when we can satisfy our client's needs by means of private finance, but in the majority of cases, we have to know our market so that we can get the best rate that's going. Furthermore, we also need to have a detailed knowledge of the Life Assurance Industry. That is because the only other way that we can make money is by selling Endowment Policies."

"What the hell are 'Endowment Policies'?" rejoined Joe.

"Simple," explained Trevor. "The Life Assured, or 'punter' as you would call him, takes out a Policy with an Insurance Company for a fixed term, and the Company agrees to pay back the Sum Assured selected should he die before the end of that term. If he survives, then he will get back the Sum Assured plus profits, or 'Bonuses', as they are called.

"For example, you could agree to pay the Insurance Company fifty quid a month for twenty years and they will pay you fifteen thousand pounds if you die before the end of the twenty years and, perhaps, twenty five thousand pounds if you live to the end of the twenty years.

"If the punter takes out a mortgage for, let us say, fifteen grand, he only pays interest to the lender who waits twenty years for his money – unless, of course, the punter dies first and then he gets his money back on the nail."

"But why the hell should anyone lending money want to wait twenty years to get it back," asked Joe. "Surely they want to get their hands back on it as quickly as possible?"

"Not at all. Don't forget that they are in the business of lending money and if they've got a good customer, then it saves them all the hassle of starting again with a new punter, filling in forms, setting up records and all that crap. In any case, they usually charge a higher rate for what's called an 'interest only' Mortgage – commonly another half a percent or so, so they're not doing too badly."

"So what's in it for you?" asked Joe, getting to the nub of the matter.

"We get paid two percent of the Sum Assured," answered Trevor. "In this case, we would have earned three hundred pounds plus, of course, a fee for arranging the Mortgage and a small retainer from the Mortgage Company."

"Three hundred quid!" exclaimed Joe. "That's half of what the punter pays each year. How the hell do you get away with that?"

"We only get that in the first year – usually within a month of the policy being taken out. After that we only get about thirty pounds a year. Still," he added with a smile, "for doing nothing, I have to admit that the thirty pounds here and thirty pounds there, soon adds up. Not bad business really."

"That's not the end of it though," Trevor continued. "If we were a little unscrupulous, which we are most certainly not, we wouldn't sell our clients 'With Profits' policies, we would sell them 'Non Profit' policies. In that case, our commission would be nearly as half as much again but.........."

"Why the hell don't you do that then?" interrupted Joe, not unreasonably. "What's the point in earning less for selling the same thing?"

"Well, that's just it," continued Tony. "It's not the same thing. True, the punter - or, at least, his wife – would get the twenty grand, instead of the fifteen, if he died within the twenty years, but at the end of the term, he would only get the twenty grand instead of possibly, say, twenty five thousand, or even more if the profits turn out to be better than expected.

"There is, I believe, an Insurance Company out there that is literally buying that sort of business and is paying Brokers three percent for the same thing. You just imagine that. They're paying six hundred pounds for a Policy that we would only earn three hundred pounds on – and we would be doing a better job for the client.

"We wouldn't, of course, have anything to do with a Company like that. More than our reputation's worth."

"Of course," agreed Joe, without the slightest understanding as to how a sensible chap like Trevor would turn away the chance of earning double. "Who is this Company that's paying three per cent? Just in case anyone tries to sell me one of it's policies," he added, hurriedly.

"Lifesave or Lifeboat or something like that," replied Trevor airily. "I really can't remember. Anyway, that's enough of a lesson on Life Assurance and mortgages for a day. I've got work to do."

"OK and many thanks for playing fair with the Perkins business, because I've worked my nuts off on that case. I can see that it has not been the most straightforward on for you. I'll expect my hundred quid any day now and look forward to seeing the rest when it comes. Cheerio for now."

And, with that Joe bid his farewell and returned to his car. He had a lot to think about – six hundred quid just for sticking a punter into a Life Policy (who probably ought to have one anyway); this sounded too good to be true. He must get in touch with Lifesave or whatever they're called as soon as possible. He simply could not begin to understand Trevor's reluctance to use a Company which, so clearly, had the salesman's best interests at heart – especially in the light of the rather dodgy mortgages that he fixed up using his Uncle's money. He never seemed to lose him any sleep over that sort of deal and yet the majority of those mortgages got called in before their time.

There was no accounting for some people, mused Joe. Time for his "Board Meeting", he felt. He was feeling thirsty and was looking forward to his meeting at the Lion.

Chapter Thirteen

Tim was sitting at his desk poring over a mountain of paper work. Shirtsleeves rolled up, collar undone, window wide open and he was still sweating like a pig. Five years had gone by since he had left the Universal. Never in his wildest dreams did he think that a workload could mount up like it did. Since he had started Harrisons, the working days had grown longer and the stresses considerably greater. But, he had to admit, he was loving it.

Even with Graham Wiltshier, Roy Brown and the redoubtable Janet working flat out, there were never enough hours in the day to get everything done. The business was rolling in and Tim had no wish to apply the brakes.

Still, it worried him sometimes that, with the pressure that they were all working under, mistakes were liable to occur – and mistakes in this business could be disastrously expensive, even ruinous.

Only recently, he had heard of a small firm of Lloyds Brokers who had failed to place a Public Liability insurance in force for a major client, in the mistaken belief that the present cover had another month to go before expiry. The clients, a national firm of Architects, had found themselves without Insurance just at the time when a multi-million pound lawsuit appeared on their doorstep. They lost their case and had only one course of action open to them to save their firm.

They sued the Broker. They were successful, and recovered their entire losses - plus costs. As a result, the Brokers went into liquidation and all it's Directors were held personally liable and all became personally bankrupt – a nightmare scenario.

Tim had his own Professional Indemnity insurance of course, but would it be enough to bale him out if the rhubarb hit the fan?

The phone rang. It was his benefactor, Bill Warrington.

"Watcha mate. How's fings me old china?" came the cheerful greeting.

"Going like a bomb Bill," smiled Tim. No matter how much pressure he was under, a chat with Bill always cheered Tim up.

"Too much work and not enough time to do it in, but there's always a chance we'll be able to pay you a dividend at the end of the year."

"I should bloody well 'ope so. I was telling the Missus last night, I don't fink I need to work no more. Me boy, young Tim, he'll bring 'ome the bacon I said. Let's 'ave a bleedin' 'oliday then, was all she said. I've got a feelin' it won't be Majorca no more. She's got it in to 'er 'ead that she wants to go on one of them la di dah cruises or somethin'. Suppose we'll 'ave to though, she's been a good old girl an' she deserves a 'oliday nar and then."

"It'd do you both good," laughed Tim. "I don't know why you don't go away more often. You've got your sons running the business and I'm doing my best to make you a little pocket money. Why don't you just take yourselves off somewhere nice and have a good time? I would if I were you and," he added ruefully, "if I had the time. Anyway, enough of your leisure-time, I've got work to do. What can I do for you?"

"I've just 'ad a letter from those stuck up bastards Hayter and Goddard, they calls themselves. You know, those toffee-nosed gits who run our pension scheme. They want to put up their bleedin' fees again. They now want ten thousand pounds a year just for runnin' our poxy pension scheme. Its all with the Universal anyway and I was thinkin', if you're my Insurance Broker, why the 'ell aren't you doin' it for me. I'm sure you wouldn't charge a poor old bloke like me anything like ten bleedin' grand just for shufflin' around bits of a paper."

"Well it's a thought," said Tim. "At present, we don't handle Life Assurance or Pensions and all that sort of thing, but I've been thinking that we should. I had in mind approaching Chris Johnson at the Universal and seeing if he would like to join us to set up a financial services division. He's a bloody good chap and would certainly fit in. I'll have a word with him. How long have I got?"

"It's the fifteenth of July today, and the scheme's due for renewal at the end of August, so you've got yerself six weeks. More than enough for a fast mover like you. Now get yer arse into gear an' get it sorted. OK then? I'll leave it to yer."

"Right," said Tim. "I'll get back to you within two or three days. Bye for now."

All thought of dealing with the piles of papers in front of him vanished. That would have to wait. Expansion was Tim's adrenalin. He always knew that he would have to set up a Financial Services division one day, but never had the time to get the project started. Now dear old Bill, as he had done once before, had kicked him into action. He dialled the number of his old Office, the Universal.

"Tim Harrison here," he informed the telephonist. "Could you put me through to Chris Johnson please?"

After about thirty seconds, a voice announced, "Ashbridge knocking shop. May I take your name, number and knicker size and we'll deal with you in a moment."

"Hi Chris, Tim here. Can we talk pensions for a minute, if you're not too busy with your extra-mural activities?"

"Tim! Christ! I'm sorry. I thought you were Jonno calling from downstairs. I'm terribly sorry. How are you, you old bugger?"

"Not bad, not bad at all," replied Tim, pleased to have got Chris on the hop. "Here, do you deal with Warrington's Pension Scheme, or is it handled by Edinburgh? I seem to remember that that's where Hayter and Goddard place their business."

"As a matter of fact, the business passes through our Edinburgh Office but we do all the work here. Bloody liberty, if you ask me, we do all the work, and there's a ton of it, and those idle bastards north of the border, get all the credit. It's because Bill Warrington insists that the Ashbridge branch deals with his scheme so that, if anything goes wrong, he can get in his car and blow out our brains personally. Strong supporter of local business is our Bill. I only wish that Head Office would agree that those who give the local service get the credit for it. Still, I always enjoy my annual skirmish with Bill. He's one of the good guys."

"You can say that again," agreed Tim. "Listen, Bill has suggested that I should take over his Pension and all the other bits and pieces but, as you know, I know bugger-all about pensions and I'd only make a cock of it if I took it on. How would you like to come and join me. Set up Harrison's Financial Services. You'd be the MD, of course (in fact, you'd be the only member of staff to start with) and you could have a crack at all the Financial Services work for all of our clients. How does that seem to you?"

"Would there be a salary, by any chance, or would you want me working for love?" enquired Chris. "It's just that you're such a mean bastard and, judging by the way you've grown, you can't be paying much to the workers. Assuming that there would be an honest crust for the hired hand I would have to say that, quite seriously, Tim, I'm flattered. You'd be a bastard to work for, but I can't think of any reason why I want to stay here. So, all things considered, why not?"

Tim's heart leapt. He quite thought that he would have a battle trying to persuade Chris to leave the security of the Universal and join a relatively risky operation like his. Although he would never admit it, especially to Mary, it would always be within the realms of possibility for him to go down the tubes at any time; especially if he expanded too quickly.

"That's fantastic Chris," exclaimed Tim. "Can you get round for coffee about ten or eleven tomorrow and we'll discuss how we can make all this work? We'll have to work quickly, though. Bill's schemes all fall due in about six weeks' time and we'll need the fees and commission from that to cover your costs."

"No problem," responded Chris. "I'll be there. Looking forward to it. Bye till then."

....

Tim looked up to see Janet standing over him with a rather worried look on her face. "Why the frown?" he asked. "It can't be serious. Listen, I've got the most fantastic news. Bill just asked me to take over his Pension scheme that, according to him, is worth about ten grand a year in fees. As you know, I haven't the foggiest idea how to run a pension scheme – so I phoned up our old mate Chris Johnson. Guess what? He's going to join us, set up a Financial Services division, and off we go! Piece of cake."

Noticing that Janet's face did not light up with her usual enthusiasm, he asked, "You don't look convinced Janet. What's the problem?"

"It's not anything to do with Chris. That's wonderful," agreed Janet, "but I'm afraid I think that we've got a bit of a problem here. I'm sorry to be the bearer of bad news, appalling news I'm afraid, but you remember that Bill Sykes recently bought a rather expensive Jaguar and we transferred the insurance from his Citroen to the Jaguar?"

"Of course I do. What's the problem?"

"Well, you probably remember that he asked you to extend the list of named drivers to include his son, Peter – who had just passed his twenty first birthday. "You said that there would be an extra premium and that they might have to pay the first two or three hundred pounds themselves, but that you'd get it fixed."

"Bugger," cried Tim. "I completely forgot. No problem. Give me the papers. I'll do it straight away. I'm sure the 'Car and General' will agree. They'll OK us to issue a cover note today. I'll have a word with old Bert Green – he's always very helpful. What's the problem? You still don't look so sure, have you already asked him? Are the buggers being difficult?"

"I'm afraid it's too late Tim. It's much more serious than that. Bill's just phoned in, whilst you were on the phone to Chris, with the most terrible news. Peter was involved in a head-on collision this morning. In the Jaguar. Peter's dead, his girl friend in the passenger seat is very badly injured, probably paralysed from the waist down, the car's a write off and so is the car he hit."

The colour drained from Tim's face. The euphoria of only a few moments ago completely evaporated. He felt as if he had been kicked in the stomach by a horse. Tim sat back, stunned.

He held his head in his hands and slumped over his desk.

"Poor Bill. Poor Wynne," he groaned. "What have I done? I know I've been far too stretched lately. I knew that something terrible could happen. But this! This is so sad, so appallingly bloody unfair. Peter has gone. God knows how his girl friend is. What about the passengers in the other car? Were they hurt too?"

"I don't think so Tim. They were in one of those 'Jeep' type things and, as far as I know, they were only badly shaken. I should imagine that their vehicle is a write-off though, judging by the extent of the damage to Peter's car."

Janet walked round the desk and put an arm around Tim to try to comfort him. Tim was almost sobbing now.

"All this, all this carnage, and I've got to tell Bill that he wasn't even insured. I can't do it Janet. I just can't do it. We're finished of course. Bill will sue us for every penny he can and I won't blame him. He can have everything. Everything we've worked for is his, and I don't give a damn. I cannot conceive the heartbreak of losing a son. Of losing Peter. He was a lovely chap. He was going to take over Bill's business in due course. It's just all too terrible. Too bloody terrible."

"I know, Tim," said Janet, realising that she would have to try being the stronger of the two this time. "But we've got to do something. Bill has asked for the cover note as he's got to take it to the Police tomorrow. What are we going to do Tim? We can't just sit here letting events take over. We've got to do something."

"I know, I know. But at the moment I just can't think straight. Here, let me have all the paperwork to do with Bill's Motor Insurance and everything to do with his Firm's insurances and anything that we've got for the family. I'll go through everything and see what I can come up with, but God knows what – this is a total, tragic, bloody appalling, disaster."

Janet handed Tim the files she was holding and went off to find everything else that he had asked for.

Tim checked the number on the file and dialled Bill's home number. What he was going to say, he had no idea. He had never been involved in anything so tragic in the past: let alone something so disastrous from both his own and his client's point of view.

"Oh hello, can I speak to Mr or Mrs Sykes please?" he asked of the lady who had picked up the phone.

"I'm Bill's mother, " she said. "I am afraid that Bill won't be able to come to the phone just now. I'm afraid that something terrible has happened and Bill is unavailable. Who shall I say has called?" her voice breaking with emotion.

"I know Mrs Sykes. I've already heard the terrible news. It's Tim Harrison. Apart from being a friend, a close family friend, I'm also Bill's Insurance Broker and I want to tell him not to worry about this side of things. I'll see to everything. Could you please tell Bill and Wynne that I am so terribly upset and so sorry to hear of Peter's accident. My heart goes out to them both, and to you and to the whole family.

"I won't say anything more now, no words can help at this time, but please tell Bill not to worry about the Insurance. I'll deal with everything. I'll go down to see the Police tomorrow and I'll sort all that side out for him. I'm so, so sorry, so very sorry." Tim's voice was also breaking with emotion and he knew that he could not hold back his own tears if he stayed on the phone a moment longer.

"That's very kind of you, Mr Harrison. I'll tell Bill. I'm sure he'll be relieved that this is one thing he will not have to bother about. He's got enough on his plate at the moment, I know...............her voice broke down and, after a long pause, Tim gently replaced the receiver.

Tim sat back. Oh God, what was he going to do now? Janet placed the papers on Tim's desk and said, "why don't you take all that lot and go home and see what you can come up with? It's six o'clock now anyway and there's nothing you can do here. I'll tidy up your desk and deal with anything urgent; you go home, have a stiff gin and I'm sure you'll come up with something. You always do."

"You're a wonderful girl Janet. I don't know what I'd do without you. Thanks, I'll take your advice. Perhaps Mary will come up with something. You never know." He was just clutching at straws, but this time, Tim could see no hope, no hope at all.

Tim shuffled up his papers with a heavy heart. Until now, much as he loved Mary and the kids, he finished his day's work with a feeling of dread, worried how he was going to face them with this devastating news. The drama of this evening's events, coming so soon after the excitement of starting a new division for his rapidly expanding Company hit him like a ton of bricks. He had never felt so low, so utterly beaten, and so full of foreboding.

He grieved for his friend's loss and he saw no solution in sight for himself or his Company.

What would tomorrow bring?

Chapter Fourteen

Joe arrived at the Lion a little later than usual and was not, therefore, surprised to find Ted and Cedric already propping up the bar and well into their second pints.

"You look pleased with yourself," greeted Ted, "'ad a good day on the 'orses 'ave you?"

Joe ordered a pint for himself and two halves for his sales force. In response to the expressions on their faces resultant from the offer of half measures, Joe said,

"You both look as if you've had enough to drink already. I've got business to discuss. Bring your glasses over here and let's have a bit of a chat. There have been a few developments."

They followed Joe to a corner table where Joe removed the half empty glasses left by previous patrons, still standing in their own pools of stale beer. He found a couple of cardboard beer mats and sponged as much of the excess fluid off the table as he could. He then pulled out a chair and sat down. To ask the barman to perform such a task would, as Joe well knew, be a waste of breath.

"There, that's better. We can hear ourselves talk over here. Now, as you know, that Perkins bloke has been a bit bad for business."

"You can bloody say that again," interrupted Cedric. "I aint 'ad one punter want to see yer in the last three weeks. If this goes on any longer, I'm jacking it in. I tell yer, I don't want no bleedin' punter tellin' me I'm a crook before I've even got through the door." To be called a crook anytime thereafter was of no concern to either Cedric or Ted. Once the 'lead' had been established, nothing else was of any consequence to them.

"All that's in hand, lads. Me, George and Tom have had a meeting and we've agreed that things have got too hot for Everbright Windows and so we're going to wind the Company up." Joe always felt that a bit of poetic licence in the matter of management hierarchy was in the best interests of staff relationships. 'We' always sounded better than 'they' in this context.

"We've formed a new Company called Castle Windows which will take over in a couple of weeks. We've decided to base it in the Channel Islands – a bloody good tax fiddle – and all the new brochures will be up and running in about ten day's time. Everbright will cease to exist, so when you see punters now, you will be able to tell them that Everbright were a bunch of twisters and thieving bastards and you would have nothing to do with them. You could see trouble coming and you got out before everything went pear-shaped. It'll be a piece of cake.

"But, I've also been giving some thought to another little scam that could make us a ton of dosh," continued Joe pleased that he now had their complete attention.

"You know how some of the punters can't afford to pay for their windows up front?" Ted and Cedric were both nodding; they could never understand how Joe persuaded seemingly broke couples to lash out a few thousand quid on second-rate double-glazing but, then again, this was no concern of theirs.

"Well what I do then is to fix them up with a mortgage. I use my old mate Trevor Watkins at MoneySure Financial Services and he gives me a few quid for the introduction. What I didn't realise was that he was also selling them Life Insurance Policies and making a bloody fortune in the process. Now, half of the people we see could be flogged a Policy and we, instead of Trevor, should be doing that selling and making the extra dosh for ourselves.

"He calls them Endowment Policies and the Punter pays so much a month and gets his money back, plus some, a few years later.

"All you have to do, is tell the punter that if he saves, say twenty quid a month, not only will he make a fucking fortune, but he can pay off his mortgage and, if he kicks the bucket, his old lady will have enough money to keep the house and home going. He can't lose, so selling this sort of thing will be a piece of piss. And the best thing is, the Insurance Company gives us most of the first year's subs for our work. What do you think of that, boys?"

Joe settled back, took a swig from his glass and, with a raised eyebrow, invited questions.

"Well, I dunno," started Ted. "High finance and all that sort of thing was never me strong point. I can get them interested in winders and all that, but saving money, that's somefink else.

"I tell you what though," he added, brightening somewhat. "Me nephew, Jimmy Smith, now he's a clever little bleeder. He's just left school wiv a 'andful of sustificates an', do you know what, no rotten bastard'll give 'im a bleedin' job. Now 'e could sell them high finance fings. I could get 'im on the road and show 'im the ropes an' then let 'im loose on the money fing. Bloody sure 'e could sell condoms to a nunnery could our Jimmy."

"Fine," said Joe. "You get him down here one evening and I'll interview him and see if I can sort something out for him. What about you Cedric? Reckon you could sell these endowments policies?"

"Not a bleedin' chance mate, but like Ted 'ere, me Missus' sister's boy Fred, 'es in the same boat. I shouldn't be surprised if there's a lot of 'em about now. Bin out of school a year or so an' no bleedin' job. Loungin' around doin' bugger all. I'm bloody sure he'd jump at somethin' like this if it was put to 'im proper. I'll 'ave a word wiv me Missus when I get 'ome tonight. So when do we start sellin' this Castle Winders stuff? 'less I earn a few quid soon, me Missus' goin' ter go round the bleedin' bend."

"As I said, give me a couple of weeks and we'll be all set. So I'll get you sorted on the windows job and I'll see Jimmy and Fred, and anyone else you can think of, to get this finance thing going. Can you both get them to give me a call soon, preferably tomorrow, so that I can start the ball rolling?"

They both reckoned that they would be able to get through to their budding tycoons within the next twenty four hours and promised that Joe would hear from them soon.

There was little more to be said on the subject, but it was not until well past eleven that they eventually left the Lion and made their way to their respective homes.

....

The next morning saw Joe up surprisingly early and on the phone. His first call was to Directory Enquiries. No, there was no number listed for Life Save Insurance, Life Sure, Life Guard or any other permutation that Joe could think of – at least, not in the Greater London District.

Joe was stumped. He could start with any Insurance Company he could find advertising in the daily papers, but there was no point in doing business with a company that was not going to pay the highest commission going. Joe meant to get to the top and that meant starting at the top. Only the best was good enough for Joe. The possibility that this was not likely to be the best for his 'clients' never even entered his head. It was simply not a factor to be taken into consideration. If you don't look after number one yourself, no one else was likely to step in to help, reckoned Joe Hendry.

Adverts – it suddenly dawned on him. No good looking at adverts in the papers. If this Company was offering such a good deal, they would be advertising in the Trade Press. His first port of call was W H Smiths whereat he enquired of the girl at the pay desk what would be the best selling Life Assurance journal.

"Haven't the faintest idea," came the helpful reply. "I'm new here. But if you go down that aisle," she pointed vaguely in a general direction, "you'll find all sorts of technical stuff. Bloody boring if you ask me. Don't understand why anyone reads all that junk."

Not that was any likelihood of her ever reading anything, thought Joe. He did not envisage her as a potential member of his sales force.

He wandered down the indicated aisle and browsed through a medley of dull but informative magazines. He was about to give up when he spotted a drab-looking periodical entitled "The Policy". Flicking through the pages, he felt sure that this would serve his purpose well enough and he completed his purchase. The girl made it clear that she felt he was wasting his money, but what did she care?

On returning home, Joe thumbed carefully through the magazine. He never ceased to be surprised how much crap could be written about so many subjects about which he knew absolutely nothing, and about which he had absolutely no wish to become better acquainted. Nevertheless, there were quite a number of Insurance Company advertisements extolling the virtues of their own wares and suggesting that any half-intelligent salesman who would care to join them could earn at least ten thousand a year, plus car, plus benefits and, all of that, in double quick time.

He was interested. Ten grand for starters was no mean salary and if this was from the average Company, what couldn't he and his team do with a Company offering more or less double the commission that everyone else was paying?

Suddenly he spotted it. There it was, on the inside back page, an advert enticing "Smart young men with ambition". "Very Generous Packages" were offered for the right people by Life and Equity International Ltd".

Applicants were invited to call George Wellbeloved, the Director of Marketing, anytime between nine and five any weekday.

It was eleven thirty and Joe picked up the phone and dialled. Joe was about to enter another world.

Chapter Fifteen

"Mary, I'm home," called Tim, as he unlocked the front door. In less than a minute he was virtually thrown to the floor by the impact of his two over-excited and exuberant offspring.

"Not now darlings," Tim managed to blurt out as he gently extricated himself from beneath the scrimmage. "Daddy's got a headache and wants to talk to Mummy quietly for a bit. Just go back in the garden and play for a little while will you? Please."

Sensing Tim's dark mood, the children did as they were bid, reluctantly withdrew and peace reigned once more.

"What's the trouble darling?" asked Mary. "You look terrible. Here, let me fix you a gin and tonic, you look as if you could do with one."

As she busied herself with the drinks, Tim explained the tragedy that had befallen the Sykes and the disaster that was about to befall them.

"I can't believe it," cried Mary. "Peter was such a lovely boy – his whole life in front of him. It's too much to take in. How must Bill and Wynne be feeling? And Peter's girl friend. How awful, the poor thing. I just hope that her injuries are nothing like as bad as they seem.

"As for us, we've got nothing to worry about. If things are as black you seem to think they are, what have we lost? You can get another job, and I can go back to work. It won't be that bad – certainly nothing in comparison with the Syke's, the poor things. I can't imagine how they must be feeling. If anything happened to Becky and Tom, I just don't know..........." she left the words hanging in the air.

"I wish I could see it your way, darling. In the first place, because of me, the Sykes' position is already worse. I've only got Professional Indemnity Insurance for one hundred thousand pounds – that's all I could afford, or all I thought I needed. The claim for Peter could be for more than that alone. If his girl friend is completely paralysed, her claim could be many times more. Then there's the car, it's a write off, the third party's car probably the same and God knows how badly injured the driver and his passengers will be. They'll claim for everything they can.

"If the Company can't afford it, we'll be paying off debt for the rest of our lives. I've let you and the kids down so badly, so terribly badly....." Tim choked back the tears.

Mary put her arms around him and held him tightly. "Now just calm down darling. You go in the other room and go through all those papers you've brought back. I'm sure you'll come up with something; there must be some way out of this, some way to help the Sykes. If there is, I know you'll find it."

Tim's confidence was at its lowest ebb. There was no way he would be able to extricate himself from this mess, no way of softening Bill and Wynne's terrible blow. Their suffering must be intolerable and the news that he would have to impart to them could only make matters worse, much worse.

He knew that there was nothing he could do but, even so, he would look through the files, do as Janet had suggested, and just try to see if there was anything at all that might make a desperate situation even fractionally better. If there was any way at all in which he could persuade the Insurance Company to help, then it was his duty to find it. But, in his heart of hearts, he knew that no Insurance Company was going to lay itself open to claims of this magnitude - unless they absolutely had to. Charitable Institutions they certainly were not.

He took a sip of his gin and tonic and immediately felt guilty. He could sit back and enjoy a drink, but what could Bill and Wynne do – just sit and suffer? They had left it to him to deal with the Police and he had absolutely no idea what he was going to tell them tomorrow.

He turned to the papers and opened a tattered file marked "Motor Fleet Insurance" and began to study it, mechanically. There were pages and pages of endorsements, mostly notifying the Insurance Company that a particular vehicle had been sold and replaced by another. A larger capacity vehicle led to an additional premium, and a smaller one, to a rebate. Boring and irrelevant, but he must keep reading.

There was an endorsement headed "Driving other cars extension" and his heart skipped a beat. Could it be that Employees could drive one of the firm's vehicles and still be covered? Could it be that Peter was, after all, insured to drive the Jaguar? That would be the answer to most of his problems.

He searched for the paper work that would show him that anyone would be insured to drive the Jaguar, knowing in his heart of hearts that the reverse was far more likely to be the case. Insurance Companies were averse to letting youngsters drive high performance cars, and with good reason Tim dolefully reflected.

He searched for the endorsement showing when the Jaguar had been added to the fleet, but despite looking at every page since January, when Bill had bought the car; there was absolutely no mention of it. "Christ," thought Tim, "don't say that we didn't even tell the Insurers that Bill had even bought the bloody car!" Things were going from bad to worse. But, surely, they could not get any worse?

This cannot be right, he thought. Then it occurred to him that the Jaguar was Bill's private car and perhaps they had insured it in Bill's name, rather that the Company's. Bill was, Tim recalled, a stickler for doing the 'right thing'. Even though it was his firm, he did not believe that it was right that his employees should see the boss getting the firm to buy him a luxury car (and insuring it) whilst the staff had to accept whatever they were given. Nor would he have approved of fiddling the tax man by getting the firm to pay his premium for him. Bill was remarkably straight about some things – a rare quality these days.

Tim searched the pile of folders for a file that he knew must exist. He found it. A file marked "Private Car Insurance – W Sykes". There it was. Tim leafed through it, hoping for inspiration, fearing and expecting disappointment. Right at the top of the file was a copy of the endorsement noting the cancellation of the Insurance on the Ford Granada and its replacement by Jaguar XJ 6, registration number WAS 123 – additional premium thirty-nine pounds. What endorsements were attaching? There on the bottom of the endorsement were the words 'Named and Approved drivers as per Policy'. Who were the named and approved drivers? Was there, by chance, any hope that Peter was a named driver?

He searched back through the file and eventually found the endorsement that had been attaching for the three and a half years since Bill had bought his Granada.

There was a list of named and approved drivers; he read 'The insurance on this vehicle applies only when the vehicle is being driven by W A Sykes, Mrs W D Sykes and C G Brown.' Tim remembered that Bill had always been happy to restrict the driving to himself and Wynne (and take the ten per cent discount) but that they had decided to include Colin Brown, their gardener, some years ago, since he often volunteered to drive them to lunches or dinners when, it could be assumed, they would have had a drink or two.

Mary came quietly into the room, carrying a tray containing two cups of coffee and a plate of biscuits.

"Any luck, darling? I've given the kids their supper, bathed them and tucked them into bed. I told them that you had a headache but that you'd pop in to give them a kiss when you're ready for bed. They can clearly sense that something's wrong and they've settled down with the minimum of fuss. They are darlings."

"Thanks, Mary," replied Tim, reaching out to take the coffee that Mary had handed him. "They're good kids – it makes me realise just how appalling the Sykes' loss really is. Thanks for the coffee too – I couldn't eat a thing. In answer to your question, no, I'm afraid that I've read every word on every file and I can find nothing that could be any help at all.

"I thought for a minute that I might have cracked it when it looked as if their Fleet Insurance Policy covered any employee whilst driving another car. They don't have that cover unfortunately. If they did, that would have solved almost everything, except for the damage to the car itself. At least things would have been OK with the Police and all the third party claims would have been paid in full. I'd willingly find the money myself to buy Bill a new Jaguar if I could have sorted everything else out."

"It's a pity Peter wasn't driving his old banger instead of his Dad's car, then," said Mary. "At least that wouldn't have cost so much. I doubt whether that old thing could have been worth more than a hundred pounds. Probably a danger on the roads as it is."

"What old Banger?" Tim almost shouted. "Peter didn't have a car of his own did he? I've looked through every file and there's no mention of any Insurance in his own name."

"I'm sure he had his own car. I think Wynne told me that Peter had earned a few hundred pounds, farming or something like that, and he went straight out and bought an old jalopy without telling them a thing. Wynne was horrified that he bought such a 'death-trap' but Bill was quite chuffed that his eighteen year-old son had had the initiative to go out, earn his own cash and then buy himself a car. Showed he had what it takes, he said. Why, what difference does that make? Does it make any difference at all? You look quite animated at last."

"Any difference?" echoed Tim. "Any difference? It would make all the difference in the world, or it could do. If Peter was insured to drive his own car, he was almost certainly covered to drive any other vehicle 'not belonging

71

to him or not hired to him under a hire purchase agreement.' As the endorsement goes." After reading all the files he had brought back, Tim could not get out of the habit of quoting the jargon, as opposed to plain English.

"In other words, if and only if, Peter had a Policy in his own name, not only would he have been legally insured to drive his father's car, but he would also have been insured for all the third party claims. The damage to the Jaguar would still not have been covered, but everything else would have been. How do we find out at this hour if he had a Policy? I'm sure we didn't issue one – it would have been in these files if we had."

Tim looked at his watch, it was already after ten and he did not feel that he could phone Graham, who was the one person who might have known. Janet, though, was another matter. She wouldn't mind what time of the day or night Tim phoned her, especially with something as important as this.

Tim looked up her number while Mary poured him another coffee, dialled and waited.

"Ashbridge sixty six, seventy six, ninety four," came the chirpy reply.

"Janet, Tim here. Look, I'm sorry to be calling you so late. Bloody liberty I know, but do you know if we ever insured a car in Peter Sykes' own name? An old banger apparently."

"That's OK, Tim, any time," replied Janet. "Let me think." She paused, Tim's heart was hammering, hoping, hoping against all the odds that salvation was in sight. "No Tim, I don't think so. I usually deal with everything from Bill Sykes. I get on very well with Mr Sykes's secretary, Pam, and I'm sure that she has never asked us to insure anything for Peter. I suppose it's always possible that Peter insured a car himself though, to be honest, I wouldn't think so; the Sykes do everything with us. Mr Sykes is always saying that you take all the worry out of insurance for him and his firm and he couldn't cope with Insurance were it not for you. Very loyal, I'm sure he wouldn't deal with anyone else. I'm sorry Tim, is that bad news?"

The news hit Tim like a sledgehammer, but all he said was, "I'm afraid it is Janet. Never mind, it was worth a try. I'm clutching at straws. I'll be in early tomorrow. Perhaps you, Graham and I can get together and see what we can do about this mess. It's absolutely bloody and I don't mind telling you, I don't think Harrison's has much of a future right now. Not that that's particularly relevant when you consider the state poor old Bill and Wynne must be in now. Sorry to trouble you. You go off and have a good night's sleep and I'll see you about eight thirty tomorrow. Bye for now."

"Bye Tim. I'm so sorry I was no help. Let's all sleep on it. Goodnight."

Tim replaced the receiver and turned to Mary. Janet's quite right darling, let's sleep on it.

There was nothing else they could do.

Chapter Sixteen

The following morning, Joe received two phone calls. The first was from Ted who announced, "I've just spoken to me nephew Jimmy. 'e's over the moon about wot I told him about workin' for you. I told him that 'e would 'ave to mug up on a bit of 'igh finance an' that sort of fing an' 'e would then 'ave to sell it to the punters. I told 'im that you'd set everyfing up an' all 'e would 'ave to do is to explain all this 'igh fallutin' stuff and then 'e'd get a wedge of dough for 'is trouble. "Lead me to 'im" is wot 'e said. I told him to be at the Lion seven firty an' you'd tell 'im wot's wot. Is that OK wiv you Joe, cos I can't get 'old of 'im till this evenin' cos 'e's gone to some school or somefing? I fort he was done wiv all that sort of thing but he just laps up this edication sort of fing. 's beyond me, all this learnin'. Dunno wot they sees in it."

"Perfect," replied Joe. "Just the ticket. I'll be there. I suggest that you leave Jimmy and me alone for an hour or so, just so I can explain everything properly to him. I'll buy you a drink when we've finished and tell you all about."

Joe did not want his discussions with Jimmy interrupted by homilies from dear old Ted. If anyone could deter an aspiring Financial Salesman, that man would be Ted Bushell. Besides, Joe had a feeling that the commission deal he would be forced to agree with young Jimmy might be a little more generous than the arrangement he had with Ted for arranging double glazing appointments. The last thing he needed was a request for more commission from Cedric and Ted.

"Rightcha are," affirmed Ted. "I'll see yer later." And, with that, he rang off.

About half an hour later, Joe took a call from Cedric who had received a similar reaction from his nephew, Fred Barker. Freddy Barker, it transpired, had done well at school, better at College but, after two wasted years, could still find no one who wanted to hire his skills. It was agreed that Cedric would ensure that Fred would also be at the Lion at seven-thirty sharp.

Then Joe had to make a call himself. He looked up the number of Life and Equity International Ltd and dialled it.

"Life and Equity International Ltd, Clarissa speaking, how may I help you?" came the monotone response, with no pause for breath.

"Mr Wellbeloved, please," replied Joe. "Mr George Wellbeloved."

"And whom may I say is calling please," came the cut diamond response.

"Mr Hendry, Mr Joseph Hendry, could you please put me through now," Joe had already tired of this conversation with a Dalek.

"Representing whom, Mr Hendry?" Clarissa was not going to break her routine for anyone, certainly not for a Mr Joseph Hendry who, to her, sounded like a 'bit of rough'.

This flawed him. What was he meant to say? Would it look feeble if he was just plain old Joe Hendry, or would he score better if he represented a Company? Joe thought quickly and it came to him in a flash. "Will you please tell Mr Wellbeloved that it is Mr Joseph Hendry of Castle Finance, and would you please put me through right away? I'm a very busy man."

"Of course, Mr Hendry. Please hold," came the clipped response.

Joe waited a couple of minutes, wondering whether to ring off or not, when a deep, cultured voice came on the line.

"George Wellbeloved here. What may I do for you Mr Hendry? I understand that you represent Castle Finance."

"That's right. My company is involved in marketing and I noticed your advertisement in The Policy the other day. I thought that perhaps we might be able to do business together."

"I do hope so Mr Hendry. And what particular line does your Company specialise in at this moment in time?"

"Well, we're in the construction industry. Thermal insulation I think you'd call it."

"Double glazing, do you mean?" asked Wellbeloved helpfully, hitting the nail firmly on its head.

"Well sort of," Joe was forced to admit. "I have a specialist sales force and we have recently been moving into the field of finance – mortgages and all that sort of thing. We have a joint venture relationship with a well respected firm of Financiers and it seems to me that it would be a natural progression for us to move into the fields of investment and family protection more directly ourselves."

"Endowment Policies, you mean?" asked the ever-helpful Mr Wellbeloved. "Well, I think that we can help you there. We offer a very wide range of Life Assurance products, something to meet every need, so as to speak. Tell me Mr Hendry, what is the current size of your sales force?"

"At present, we have four trained salesmen," Joe was forced to admit – the slight exaggeration in numbers and training rolling fluidly off his tongue, "but we have plans to take on a further ten this year and build up to fifty by the end of next year." Joe never had any problem with wild forecasts; far more impressive than the unvarnished truth.

"Perhaps we should arrange to meet," suggested Mr Wellbeloved, his interest now moderately heightened. Although he had heard it all before, many times. "I have my diary before me. Let's see, how would you be placed tomorrow week at about 10.30 am?"

"I think that, if I were to transfer my team to your Company, I would need to move a little more quickly than that Mr Wellbeloved. But before we go on, may I ask you one or two questions?"

"Assuredly, Mr Hendry. Please fire away."

"Firstly, I understand that you issue both 'Non Profits' and 'With Profits' Policies – Endowment Policies I mean," Joe added, hurriedly checking the notes he had made following his meeting with Trevor Watkins. " Which do you prefer?"

"I'm sorry, I'm not sure I quite understand you. How do you mean, "prefer"? I mean, they both fulfil entirely different purposes. If I were to want maximum protection for my family, I would prefer the 'Non-Profit' version, but if I were looking for the greater investment opportunity, I'd go for the 'With Profits" version. Does that answer your question Mr Hendry?"

"Not quite, Mr Wellbeloved. What I need to know is which pays the highest commission and how much will that be. You'll appreciate, my salesmen are my biggest asset and I need to look after their best interests."

"Oh, I see," replied Mr Wellbeloved, understanding perfectly his caller's priorities. "Well, as we are a relatively new Company, with lower overheads than many of our competitors, we like to pass on these economies to our friends, those who support us. Whereas most of our competitors pay their Brokers two per cent of the sum assured, we pay three percent. It seems to be that the majority of our Brokers prefer our Non Profit products because the sums assured tend to be a little higher and that means the commission is correspondingly higher.

"In a typical example, a client paying a premium of twenty pounds a month to us will permit the Broker to reap a reward of about two hundred to two hundred and twenty pounds compared to the one hundred to one hundred and fifty pounds that they would probably receive from our competitors. As I say, Mr Hendry, we like to look after our own."

This was, to Joe, the perfect marriage of business ethics and priorities; on the one hand, Life and Equity International had little interest in their clients' value for money and on the other hand, Joe could simply not understand why his future competitors could conceive of working for less than the maximum 'bung' available. But, apparently, some did and that was their funeral.

"One other thing, Mr Wellbeloved, or might I call you George?"

"Of course Joe, I hope that we can look forward to a very happy mutual business relationship. What else was it you wanted to ask?"

"I understand that Companies such as yours offer training courses. I have a couple of extremely bright young chaps who are keen to learn everything they can about our business. We instruct them as to the basics of course – in house so as to speak – but I feel sure that they would benefit from any instruction that a firm of your standing would be able to give them."

"Of course. Of course we do Joe. We run sales training courses at our Swindon Head Office every month. In fact, one starts next Monday. If you give me the young men's names, I am sure that I would be able to fit them in. I can tell you that, after just one week at one of our sales courses, our people will be able to sell coal to Newcastle and, even, condoms to the Pope."

Since Joe only knew his 'salesmen's' Christian names, he deemed it imprudent to divulge anything further at this stage.

"Let me have a word with them and see how their diaries are fixed, and I'll give you a call, if I can persuade them to join your course. I'll do my best of course. I've always been a great believer that the better trained our people are, the better the service that they will give to the public – always an important principle with me. Now when can we get together to discuss our agreement? The sooner the better as far as I am concerned."

"I couldn't agree more, Joe. It's a pleasure to deal with a fellow professional. Now, how about ten thirty tomorrow morning? I see that I have a cancellation then."

"Fine, George, I'll be there and, at the same time, I'll be able to let you know whether my team will be OK for the training course. It's been a pleasure talking to you. Goodbye for now."

"My pleasure too, Joe. I shall look forward to seeing you tomorrow. Goodbye."

At seven thirty precisely, Joe strolled into the Lion and spotted a young man at the bar, smartly dressed in cavalry trousers, blue blazer and muted woollen tie, drinking what appeared to be a tomato juice.

Joe went up to him, with an outstretched hand and a welcoming smile said, "Hello, you must be Fred Barker, Cedric's nephew. How do you do. I'm Joe Hendry. Call me Joe. Now what are you drinking?"

Taking Joe's hand and shaking it firmly, the youth replies, "actually, no. I'm Jimmy Smith. I believe you know my uncle Ted. He told me to come and meet you this evening and that you might have something interesting to tell me. If you've got a job to offer me, the answer's 'yes'. I haven't had a proper job since I left college – only part-time in pubs, cafes and shops – and I'm bored out of my mind. I'd do almost anything – anything legal that is - to get something to occupy my mind."

"Well Jimmy, this could be your lucky day. Now what's that you're drinking? A Bloody Mary? Let me get you another and we'll drift over to that corner and have a chat."

"No, actually it's just a tomato juice. Another one would be fine. Thank you very much," Jimmy said, downing the last of his drink and handing the glass to Joe. Pointing to the corner of the bar, he added, "Over there? I'll go over and bag us a seat."

Joe completed the transaction at the bar and, carrying the tomato juice and a pint of bitter, he joined Jimmy at the table, which had already been wiped tolerably dry by Jimmy with a towel that he had found from somewhere.

"Now, where to start?" began Joe. "Oh, just a minute." Joe looked up and spotted another young man walking up to the bar, looking about him, and obviously searching for someone. "I think that must be my other guest. Just hold on a tick."

This time, his future salesman was rather more conventionally dressed. Conventionally, that is, for this part of the world. Fred Barker, with a rather pale spotty face, was dressed in a well-worn pair of blue jeans, an off-white sweatshirt and sporting a trio of cheap silver earrings in his left ear (thankfully, Joe observed, none in his nose or, so far as he could tell, in other parts of his anatomy).

With that, Joe walked briskly across the room, again with hand outstretched, offering it to the newcomer and saying, "Hi, you look as though you might be Fred. Cedric's young nephew. How are you?"

Taking Joe's hand, with a rather tentative grasp, Fred replied, "That's right. Cedric told me to come along and see you tonight. Something about a job or something like that."

"You can say that again," confirmed Joe. "Now you pop across there and introduce yourself to Jimmy and I'll bring your drink over. What are you having?"

"A pint of bitter mate, cheers."

Joe returned two minutes later to the table, bearing the second pint. Sitting down, he remarked, "Good, I see that you've introduced yourselves. Cheers, he added as he raised his glass to them both."

"Cheers," responded Jimmy. Fred simply took a silent, and sullen, sip of his beer.

"Now, to business," announced Joe cheerily. "I don't know if you know much about Life Assurance. It's the big thing nowadays. Everyone has to have a Policy and there's an effing fortune to be made for those who can sell them.

"As you know from Ted and Cedric, I run a Company (again, a minor exaggeration would not go amiss) that supplies thermal Insulation to the retail trade. We've decided to expand the business and we're now going to base it off-shore – there's big tax advantages there – and I'm expanding my side of the business into financial services. OK so far?"

Jimmy nodded; Fred took another swig of his beer.

"Well, because we supply the top end of the market, it always pays to supply the best. Some of our punters have to raise a mortgage to pay for the work we do. I have arranged a finance facility where the punter borrows all he needs and pays back the cash in a very clever way with something called an Endowment Policy. They're wonderful things these, because in this way, if the punter dies, his old lady gets the mortgage paid off and everyone's happy.

"So it's an extra service that we're offering to our punters. They can't lose. Now dear old Ted and Cedric, they're ace at getting punters interested in seeing me so that I can fix them up with the windows, but I need someone who can go in after me and wrap up the finance bit. This is where you two gentlemen come in. Any questions so far?"

"Yes," said Jimmy immediately. "How many Companies will you represent for these Endowment Policies?"

"Christ, one's enough!" laughed Joe. "If you have more than one you would only confuse the punter. Besides, the more business you do with one company, the more commission you can screw out of them. I've set up a deal with Life and Equity International, one of the Country's leading Companies, which means that I can pay you a very good screw for every Policy you sell......."

"Are they strong financially, do they have a good free asset ratio, and what's their past investment performance like?" cut in Jimmy.

"Christ, how the hell should I know? What's all that got to do with it? Have you taken a bleeding course in Life Assurance or something?"

"Well, when I knew I was seeing you about Life Assurance this evening, I went to the Library and read a few books on the subject. I read that it is important to deal with a Company that pays out well – it's far better for the client to know that he is going to get the best possible return."

"Take it from me sunshine," replied a bemused Joe Hendry, "it's what they pay out us that's important. The punter can look after himself, I always say. Let me assure you, Life and Equity are one of the best."

"Sounds about right to me," was the first contribution from Fred.

"That's right, Fred," confirmed a relieved Joe. "Now, take it from me. Life and Equity are a top company, the dog's bollocks in fact. They know how to look after the people who bring in the business, and that's you and me. Now, I've managed to wangle you both places on their training course next week. If you spend a week with them at their place in Swindon – all expenses paid – there's nothing that you won't know about the business and you'll be well on you ways to making your first few grand."

"Sounds good to me," said Jimmy. "I would like to get it from the horse's mouth. I've always felt that you can only sell something if you really understand it and really believe in it. I've nothing on next week, count me in."

"Sounds OK to me too," agreed Fred. "I could do with a week's holiday. Wonder if they train birds as well. Might be able to pull one if they do."

And so the first steps had been taken in forging the young men's future careers in the financial services Industry. The conversation drifted onto other topics until an hour or so later, they were joined by their uncles, Ted and Cedric. It was going to be a long evening – not for Jimmy however, who excused himself after his third tomato juice.

Chapter Seventeen

Tim arose very early. In fact he had not slept at all. The night had been a never-ending torture and he had gone through every possible permutation as to how he might resolve his predicament. All had been rejected as unworkable and useless. Over-riding his own problems was the desperate realisation that his good friends, Bill and Wynne, would never live their carefree life again – and, though they did not know it yet, it was he who was about to make their situation infinitely worse than it already appeared.

Mary followed him downstairs and made him a cup of coffee; food was quite beyond him. Even five-year old Becky appreciated that something quite dreadful had happened. It was something that she could not understand, but she knew that it was worrying her father deeply. Still in her nightclothes, with her Teddy clutched tightly to her, she came downstairs into the kitchen and cuddled up on to his lap with a soft "I love you Daddy."

Tim could have cried, not for his own grief, but for the love of his family that he was now about to financially ruin. He must not let them down, but he was about to.

Pulling himself together, he kissed Becky fondly, told her to go and give Tom a kiss from him (Tom never appeared before eight o'clock) and then drew his arms tightly around Mary.

"Well, off to another day's sweat and toil," he declared. "See you all tonight."

"Good luck darling. You'll think of something, I know you will," whispered Mary as she held him close.

At seven thirty, Tim unlocked the door of his Office and strode to his desk. He dumped the files on the desk and went to switch on the percolator for his first coffee fix, when the door opened immediately again and in walked Janet.

"I thought I'd find you here," she observed. Taking the cup from him she added, "Let me do that, you go back to your desk and I'll bring you a cup in a mo. Did you find anything last night that might help?"

"Nothing, nothing at all," replied Tim gloomily. "I did think for a moment that we might have been able to confirm that Peter was covered under the Firm's 'driving other cars extension' but, sadly, no luck there. Tell me, as I said over the phone, Mary was adamant that Peter had an old banger that he must have had insured. I don't remember anything like that, but are you absolutely certain that we didn't insure one for him? I suppose that Mary could be mistaken and that he was simply borrowing a friend's car."

"Let me get your coffee and I'll look through the files again. I think it's very unlikely. As far as I know, we insure everything for the Sykes family and their firm. I suppose it's always possible that Graham might have done something, but I doubt it because I would have had to process it and I can't remember anything at all."

Tim returned gloomily to his Office and started the painstaking task of re-reading all the files, cover to cover.

Five minutes later, Janet entered his office and placed his cup of coffee on his desk.

"I've had a look through all the index cards and all the papers on Graham's desk, and I'm sorry to say, I've found nothing. There is definitely no Policy in Peter's name. We can check with Graham when he comes in, but I wouldn't hold out any hope. I'm sorry Tim, but there it is."

Just then, they both turned as they heard the sound of the main door opening and closing. Moments later, in strode Graham looking at his watch.

"Good God," he exclaimed. "Can't any of you sleep? It's not yet eight o'clock and it's all hands to the tiller. Any luck Tim?"

"None at all," replied Tim. "The only thing is, Mary seems to think that Peter had an old banger which he must have insured, but neither Janet nor I can find any trace. You don't know anything about it do you?"

"Indeed I do," came the heart-jerking and quite unexpected response. "Last year, Peter went out and bought a beaten up old car – with the money he'd earned working for old Tom Bailey. He bought himself a really clapped out old Mini. He knew that his parents would have been dead set against him buying such a heap that he asked the chap who he bought it from to continue the Insurance under his own Policy – that way, Peter would not have had to involve Bill and Wynne until after he had done the deal.

"The young chap he bought it from was insured with the Winchester and General and they simply agreed to transfer the cover to Peter. I was speaking to Peter about it only about six weeks ago and he gave me a letter of authority transferring the Policy through to our Agency. I don't suppose it's got on to our records yet, but I'm sure it's all OK."

"Does the W & G Policy include the 'driving other cars' extension?" Tim shot back, realising a small glimmer of hope for the first time in the last fifteen hours.

"I can't think why not," replied Graham. "Let me go and take a look at the file."

Whilst Tim sipped his coffee nervously awaiting Graham's return, he explained to Janet the possible implications of this latest item of news. If the Policy did, in fact include this cover, then Peter would have been legally entitled to drive his father's Jaguar and, indeed, any other car for that matter. Furthermore, he would have been insured for all the third party liabilities that arose. There would have been no cover for the damage to the Jaguar, but so what in the light of the potential implications? Particularly relevant, would be the fact that they would be in no trouble with the Police.

"Bugger," said Graham as he re-entered Tim's office and both Tim's and Janet's hearts fell. There's nothing on the file yet and I can't find a copy of the cover note. I did everything in a bit of a rush, as is always the case here, and I can't find what I want. I'm sure that everything's OK, but I can't be absolutely sure until I can get through to the W & G. They don't open until nine."

Simultaneously, they all looked at their watches. Eight fifteen. Another forty five minutes. The waiting would be unbearable.

They sat together in morbid silence, interspersed with desultory conversation and cups of coffee. They made abortive attempts to phone through and were rewarded with an answer phone proclaiming, in a cheery voice, the W & G's hours of business.

80

At the fourth attempt, success, a human voice. Tim snatched the phone from Janet.

"Hello, it's Tim Harrison of Harrison's, could you put me through to the Motor Department please. Thank you, I'll hold...............Ah, Motor Department?...........Oh, when will he be in?.........Oh, is there anyone else who could help?.............Well, can I speak to the Manager (Bill held his hand over the mouthpiece and mouthed "what's the bloody Manager's name?" To which Graham confidently mouthed "Keith Waterman").......Peter Waterman please......Oh, sorry, Keith Waterman............yes, I'll hold.........Ah. Mr Waterman, Keith, its Tim Harrison here of Harrison's. We're just looking into a matter involving a private car insurance with you for one of our mutual clients, a Peter Sykes. I wonder if you could help me."

There was a brief pause as Tim listened to what Keith Waterman was saying.

"No, I'm afraid I don't have the Policy number. The Policy has only just been transferred to our Agency and we're still awaiting the documentation. I would just like to make absolutely sure that this Policy contains the usual 'driving other car's extension'.........Yes, I quite understand............I'd be most grateful, as soon as you possibly can, please, it is rather urgent. Yes thank you very much. Goodbye." With that, he put the phone down and lent back in his chair, arms stretched behind him, supporting his head.

"Bit of a bugger," Tim reported. "Bob Jones in the Motor department has the day off today and the Manager has no idea about any detail but will get someone to check and phone back as soon as possible. I'm afraid that there is nothing more that we can do but wait. Let's try and get back to work. God knows, we've got enough to catch up with."

They each returned to their desks to continue with their daily labours, but none of their hearts were in it. If only the phone would ring.

It did, of course. Many times. And with each ring their adrenalin pumped, their blood pressures rose - only to be wasted as yet another tedious routine matter required their attention.

At ten o'clock, Janet buzzed through to Tim with the news that she had Chris Johnson in the Office to see him.

"Christ! I completely forgot. With all this drama about Peter Sykes, it totally slipped my mind that Chris was coming in this morning. The way things are at right now, we won't even have a Company, let alone a Life and Pensions division. I'd better see him though, and explain. Please send him in."

A moment later, Chris breezed in with a cheery smile and a, "how's things me old China? On your way to your second million yet?"

"I'm afraid that nothing could be further from the truth right now. I'm afraid that you've come at a bad time Chris." Tim started to explain the dire predicament that they were now facing.

The door burst open and Janet announced, "Sorry to interrupt Tim, but I've got the W & G on the phone, Mr Waterman."

"Put him through right away. Sorry Chris, but this is quite important." Tim flicked the loudspeaker button so that Janet and Graham, who were now standing in the doorway, could hear the conversation.

"Hello Keith. Thanks for coming back so quickly. What's the position re Peter Sykes?"

"You're quite right Tim," answered Keith Waterman. "The Policy was transferred to your agency three weeks ago. It's a Third Party Fire and Theft Policy numbered R245783, due on the 3rd September, and covering a 1961 Morris Mini, Registration number WYX 436. Does that tell you what you want to know?"

"Almost Keith. But can you just confirm whether it includes the 'driving other cars' extension?"

"Just a minute, Tim." They could hear a mumbled conversation behind Keith's hand – he was clearly referring, on what was to him an inconsequential technical detail, to someone who had a considerably better grasp of Policy wordings than he.

"Yes, Tim, it does. I'm told that all our Policies have that extension. Why, does that help you?"

Tim's relief was palpable. Graham's fist shot in the air in a victory salute and Janet was crying. Chris felt privileged for being a witness to such an outpouring of triumphant relief.

"As a matter of fact it does," continued Tim in as calm a voice as he could manage. I'm terribly sorry to have to tell you that Peter, whilst driving his father's car yesterday, killed himself in an appalling accident. The car was written off, Peter's passenger was seriously injured and a third party vehicle was also badly damaged – I'm afraid I have no information as to whether the passengers of that car were hurt. Peter was not insured to drive his Father's car so I am very sorry to have to report this, but it looks as if you will have a fairly expensive claim to deal with under your Policy."

"I'm so sorry to hear of your client's death, a tragedy, Please pass on my condolences to his family. As to the cost, that is what we are here for. I will inform my claims department and leave it to you to liaise with them in the usual way."

Tim was deeply touched by the man's professionalism and, right then, would have gladly transferred his entire account to the W &G.

"That's most kind of you, Keith. I'll certainly pass on your message. Just one other thing, a small favour I have to ask of you. The Police will want to see Peter's Certificate of Insurance. Would you mind having one ready, or a duplicate, if I ask my Secretary to pop round in about half an hour? As you will appreciate, I'm reluctant to trouble the family for trivia at a time like this."

"Think nothing of it, Tim. I'll have a duplicate at our counter for your Secretary to pick up in the next ten minutes. Goodbye, and thank you for your continued support. We must have lunch sometime."

Tim sat back, smiling for the first time in what seemed a lifetime.

"There we are then," he addressed the three of them. "We're off the hook. Peter was legally insured, thank God." Turning to Janet, he added, "Would you mind popping around to the W&G as soon as possible Janet and picking up that Cover Note so that I can take it round to the Police and explain the situation to them? All the third party losses are covered and we will claim for the damage to the Jaguar under our Professional Indemnity insurance. What's the excess under our Policy Graham?"

"Five thousand pounds," came the immediate reply. We will have to pay out five grand which will hit this year's profits fairly hard but, under all the circumstances Tim, I should reckon that you will think that's a fairly cheap let off."

"You can say that again!" admitted Tim, then turning to Chris. "I think that I can think straight enough now to talk about our Life and Pensions Division. Fancy a coffee? Or perhaps we should ask Janet to nip out and get us a bottle of champagne."

"Coffee will be just fine thanks. I am delighted to have been here to have witnessed the salvation of Harrisons – fat chance of a decent job here if that load of proverbial had hit the fan."

"You can say that again. Before we go on, I must just give Mary a call. She's been worried sick by all of this. She didn't say too much, but I think the thought of the whole Company going down the tubes was affecting her very badly."

He rang his home number and, to his frustration, he listened to his own voice on the answer phone advising him that Tim and Mary were unable to come to the phone at that moment. He obeyed his own instruction and duly left a précis of the glad tidings.

Turning back to Chris, who was now relaxing with his coffee, he said, "Good, that's done. Now down to business.

"As you know, Warrington's Pension Scheme falls due for renewal in about four or five week's time and Bill wants me to take it over. I understand that we could earn about ten grand a year out of handling it. How much profit out of that we could make, I have no idea, but I would like to give it a go, if only to prove to Bill that we are up to it. What do you think?"

"Piece of cake Tim," Chris replied coinfidently. "I have my own computer programme that would deal with the administration. We will need to employ a Consulting Actuary – I would get Wells and Dean to do it – but they would charge a lot less than the firm that Hayter and Goddard are using, so we could show Bill a saving of about a couple of thousand a year there."

"You mean," interjected Tim, "that Warringtons are paying more that the ten thousand a year that Bill thinks he is paying? Bill was sure that ten grand covered everything."

"Not at all," replied Chris. "If you ask me, Hayters are a little shifty in the way that they charge their clients. They may send out an invoice for ten thousand a year, but they get the Actuaries to invoice the client direct for their work, so that it doesn't necessarily get aggregated with their own fee.

"They take a 'servicing fee' of fifteen percent from the Actuaries so Hayters pick up another one or two thousand there. That's not all though, the Investment Managers are making a charge of one per cent a year on the value of the Pension Fund and they rebate another 'management fee' to Hayters – anything between a quarter and a half of one per cent. They also take their full commission on the Group Life and Health Insurances. All in all, I reckon that Hayters are earning upwards of twenty thousand a year out of Warringtons. Not bad, don't you think?"

"Bloody hell," exclaimed Tim. "That's daylight bloody robbery! Bill will go spare when he hears this. More to the point, are you going to come on board – I can't do it without you."

"At the risk of negotiating myself out of a fantastic salary package, the answer's 'Yes'. I can start in four weeks but I can deal with all the detail surreptitiously while I'm working out my notice at the Universal. They won't want to lose this scheme."

"What are you earning at the moment Chris?" asked Tim. They carried on chatting for about half an hour, after which Chris got up and bid his farewells.

Both men were more than satisfied with their discussions and a new chapter in Harrison's progress was about to unfold.

Tim picked up the phone and dialled Bill Warrington's number. After a while, the familiar rasping voice was on the line, "Wot's up then mate. Doubled me divi already 'ave you?"

"Not quite Bill," replied Tim. "I've got some good news and some bad news, very bad news, I'm afraid."

Tim related in detail the tragedy of Peter Sykes' death and it's implications for the firm.

"That's bloody awful," commiserated Bill when he had listened attentively to the saga. "I like the Sykes. They're a straight couple. I'll drop 'em both a line an' tell em 'ow sorry me an' Martha are. It's a bleedin' shame. Lovely bloke was young Peter. Still, you did the right thing about the Insurance. Five grand's nothin' to pay for a disaster like that. Wot it does tell me, me old mate, is that you've got to get some more staff in there an' quick.

"Don't bother about the profits – they'll come along in time. We don't want any more balls ups like that. You make sure you've got someone there who can check wot's wot. Anyway, you said there was some good news, wot's that?"

"You're right," agreed Tim. "We're all working like dingbats here. I'll start looking for a junior straight away – I know Janet and Graham will be relieved. Yes, there is good news. I've taken on Chris Johnson to head up a new Financial Services Division and, in the process, we're going to save Warrington's about ten thousand pounds a year."

"Ten grand!" echoed Bill. "That's all we're paying. I want you do a good job an' there's no way you can do that if you ain't chargin' nothing."

Tim explained the Hayter and Goddard's charging structure and the way that Harrisons would be charging for their services.

"The thieving bastards!" exploded Bill. "You wait till I get my 'ands on that little ponce Maynard wot la di dah's round 'ere a couple of times a year an' bleeds us dry. Wot's more, Robinsons use Hayters. I'll give old 'arry a bell an' tell 'im 'ow 'e's bein' robbed. 'e'll be on to you in to time. I'll get you a few more customers. You leave it to me."

"That's great Bill. I should have you on commission, but I suppose you'll get your reward at dividend time," laughed Tim and, in this cheerful mood, they bade each other their farewells.

....

Three days later, the mood was much more sombre. Mary wore a black dress, black leather boots and a black hat with a veil concealing her face. It was just as well for her beautiful face was marred by her now puffy, swollen, reddened eyes – Mary could simply not stop the tears flowing freely down her face.

She and Tim had stood at the graveside together as the men in black had lowered Peter's coffin slowly into the ground. Wynne and Bill stood side by side, arms around each other, trying to comfort each another. But their attempts were futile. Their misery was total and their bodies shuddered as they tried desperately to hold back the tears.

After the service, Tim went up to Bill, put his arm around his shoulder and commiserated as best he could. Bill turned, with a ghostly smile on his lips and mouthed "thanks for everything you've done" but there was no sound. Tim took his hand and shook it and added, "If there's anything, anything I can do, just call me." There was nothing more that either he or Mary could do so they silently withdrew. There would be no wake, the sadness was too all-consuming.

Mary made her farewells to Wynne but, again, there were no words, only tears.

As they drove away in silence, wrapped in their own thoughts, it was brought home to Tim and Mary that there was nothing in their lives that could ever be as important to them as their own well-being and that of their own children.

Chapter Eighteen

George Wellbeloved was an unattractive man. He was dressed smartly in a dark grey suit with a regimental tie, even the 'Savile Row' tailoring failed to hide his burgeoning belly. The bags under his eyes and the fine purple criss-crosses on his bulbous nose were the obvious tell tale signs of his excessive love of pink gins – a hangover from his military days. In the army, he had risen to the dizzy heights, at the age of thirty-seven, of Major. He had not been a successful soldier though he would be the last man to admit it.

His only redeeming feature was his voice. George had cultivated a rich, aristocratic accent that seemed to convey an impression of calm confidence and control. George exuded an air of superiority that demanded respect. Sadly, beneath this outer veneer lay a limited intelligence and a complete inability to admit to, or to acknowledge, his failings – which were manifold.

"Good to meet you old boy," he greeted Joe effusively, grasping his hand in both of his own and giving it a firm and vigorous shake.

"Sit down old boy and I'll pour us a cup of coffee. Sugar and milk?" George busied himself with a tray already laid out with a glass cafetaire, two bone china coffee cups and saucers, sugar bowl, cream jug and a small plate of expensive-looking biscuits.

"There, help yourself," he added as he placed the tray on the desk and resumed his seat behind it. "Now, how about your sales team? Are we going to have the pleasure of their Company next week? I do hope so."

"Yes," responded Joe, taking a sip of his coffee. "I had a word with them last night and I'm pleased to say that they can both make it. They had a few meetings planned, of course, but I persuaded them that this was an opportunity not to be missed. They're both good chaps and I'm sure that they'll learn a thing or two with you."

"Splendid, splendid," affirmed Wellbeloved, reaching for his note-book. "Now let's have a note of their names and a few other details – their ages, their experience in the Industry, all that sort of thing."

"There's Mr James Smith and Mr Frederick Barker," answered Joe. "I don't have their exact dates of birth with me now, they're both about twenty or twenty one. So far as their experience is concerned, I think it would be best for them to give you their personal details when they arrive at your Course – I would like them to speak for themselves. What I can say, however, is that they both fully understand the need for people to take out as much life assurance as they can afford and that they are more than keen to get started. They can see a great future for themselves in Castle Finance. I've had my eye on both of them for some time now. If I'm any judge of character, and I believe I am, they're winners all right."

"Capital, capital," enthused George. "Now let's get round to the Agency Agreement."

George produced a neat plastic folder with a series of documents outlining the do's and don'ts of the Company's Agency Agreement. Within fifteen minutes, Castle Finance was an approved Intermediary, representing the mighty Life and Equity International Ltd, and all set to market their products to the unsuspecting public. The fact that Joe would earn excessive commissions in the process, only served to reassure him that he had definitely selected the right Company with which to do business. The additional fact that the mighty L&E had not even troubled to check whether Castle Finance even existed (which, at that time, it did not) was a significant plus,

One week later, Jimmy and Freddy duly attended their courses, the former completing his with distinction, the latter without.

Joe decided that a debriefing was in order and duly summoned his team to a meeting – not in the usual good offices of the Lion but, in recognition of the importance of the occasion, at the Taj Mahal, the rather grandly, but inappropriately, named local Indian Restaurant.

After they had ordered and were sipping their drinks, Joe enquired, "Well, how was it? What did you both learn?"

"I found it fascinating," enthused Jimmy. "I'm a bit worried about the Company's solvency margins, but they have some very clever ideas and the type of product they're majoring in does seem to have a ready market. Judging by the results of some of their representatives, the one's that came to give their views of the market, the Company is very well accepted and seems to be doing remarkably well. I see no reason why we should not do quite well selling their products. Don't you agree Freddy?" he said, turning to his colleague.

"S'alright I suppose," admitted Freddy. "What I liked was the amount of dosh they said we could earn. They told us how to stick to a patter and, if the punter tries to get a bit too clever, you shut 'em up and keep going."

"How do they tell you to do that?" enquired Joe, his interest piqued. It seemed that he, too, might pick up a tip or two here.

"You tell them all about stocks and shares, at least all that the Company wants them to know about. You say 'do you have a good understanding of the stock market?' and they nearly always say 'no idea mate' so you give them the spiel. If, on the other hand, they say 'yes', then you say 'then, of course, you will know....' and carry on and give them the same bloody spiel.

"They also have a bloody good way getting the punter's interest. Apparently everyone's bored stiff about Life Assurance so you say 'like me, you probably think that life assurance is as boring as hell, but have you thought of looking at life assurance as an investment?'. They're full of ideas of how to get the punter turned on. It seems like a piece of piss and we just coin in the cash."

"And how did they explain the commission terms?" Joe was naturally concerned that perhaps they had been a little too enlightened in this direction. If they knew what he was earning, they might start getting too greedy. Open management was not Joe's style. After all, this was his gravy train, not theirs.

"They didn't give any detail," cut in Jimmy (to Joe's obvious relief). "They said that the percentages were between the Company and you, but the blokes that they wheeled in were all on at least a grand a month. Most of them had got friends in to work for them too and they got a percentage of what they pulled in on top. One of them had twenty blokes working for him. I thought that, as soon as I'd got the hang of it, I'd get a couple of my mates to have a go. They could all do with the dough."

"Me too," added Freddy. "I've got dozens of mates who would like to give it a go."

"Fine," said Joe, warming to the theme. "I'll tell you what I'll do. Seeing as you'll be the first in my team, for every twenty pound a month policy you sell, I'll give you a fiver a month for the first year. If the punter cancels his policy in the first year, you have to give it all back, if he cancels in the second year, you give me half back and, in the third year, a quarter. Of course, you won't have to give me any cash, like as not. If it became necessary, I would simply deduct it from what I owe you for the next month."

"That's fair enough for a starter," said Freddy. "But what if we keep piling it in and we get our mates to do a bit as well. We'd have to pay them and I'd want to make a bit on what they do – that's the whole idea of getting them in on the deal."

Freddy was not as thick as he looked, Joe observed wryly. Jimmy, the bright one, would have gone along with the deal on almost any terms. He just wanted the job. Joe consulted his pad – he had worked out a few figures in advance, but now he had to take into account sub-agents, something that he had overlooked. He had worked out that, if the boys sold five policies a month, easily achievable he thought, they would each earn about three and a half grand in a year and he would pick up about nine grand. Acceptable terms he thought and a fair reward for all his ground work. But now he was looking at wider horizons and perhaps he could afford to be more generous.

"OK, I'll tell you what I'm prepared to do," he said expansively. "Once you've reached a sales rate of five policies a month, I'll put your commission up to six quid a month and, for every Policy that one of your mates sells, I'll throw in another quid from my own pocket. There won't be much left in it for me, but I can see you're keen and I'd like to give you and your pals a chance. No-one did that for me but, what the hell, why not?"

"That's very fair Joe," agreed Jimmy. "I think I could do alright on that basis. What do you think Freddy?" Receiving a non-committal nod and a shrug of his shoulders from his friend, he added, "So when do we start?"

"I've got a list of all the punters that we've sold windows to in the last three years. I've also included the names of the punters that other salesman have dealt with, not just my own, and I want you to start with them.

"Whatever you do, don't mention the name 'Everbright'. All you need to say is that you are aware that they have recently had improvements carried out to their homes and you realise that this could mean that they might appreciate some independent financial advice. Tell them that you are associated with Castle Windows – an international firm that's been going for over twenty years – and that your company has recently set up a financial services division to assist careful home owners. Then you go into the spiel that you were taught last week. Piece of cake."

Joe handed them each a list of names and addresses – about a hundred each. He then reached into his brief case and took out two thick folders. These are the Company's brochures. They're just like the ones you saw at your course, but we've had them over-printed so that all you see is the name of Castle Financial Services Ltd. The name of Life and Equity International appears in very small print at the bottom of the back page. We don't want the punters going direct to the Company and cutting us out. In the packs are all the forms you need. Now let's finish this curry and get over to the Lion for a proper drink. I can't stand this bloody foreign crap."

As the weeks went by, even Joe was amazed at the speed with which the two of them fell into a routine. Within six weeks, both of them were selling an average of six policies a month and both of them were already talking to a few friends, three of whom had signed up for L & E's training course.

The only problem was that whereas they were selling the same number of policies each, the commission from Jimmy's business was some thirty percent less than the commission Freddy was earning. He took this up with his friend George Wellbeloved at L & E who promised to look into it and get back to him.

An hour later, George was back on the phone. "The thing is old boy, young Jimmy is selling only 'With Profits' Policies, whereas all of Freddy's are 'Non Profits'. As I explained to you, and we made it very clear on the course, the sum insured on 'With Profits' Policies is much lower and so too is the commission in consequence. As I told you, we pay a percentage of the Sum Assured, not the premium."

"What the bloody hell is Jimmy doing then?" retorted Joe, as much to himself as to George. "I'll get the young bugger in tomorrow and explain the facts of life to him. I'm paying them both the same commission per twenty pounds a month of premium they collect. I'd forgotten that I wouldn't be getting the same commission from you. He needs a good talking to, does young James."

A week earlier Joe, could see that there was a much more profitable future in selling Life assurance than flogging his guts out with double glazing. He therefore rented a small one room office, over an Accountant's Office, in Ashbridge High Street. It was to this domain that Joe summoned his errant salesman.

"Now just what are you playing at Jimmy?" began Joe. "I'm giving you a bloody good commission and you're going around selling policies that earn about three-quarters of the one's that Freddy's selling. Surely you can see that there's no future in that?"

"Not at all Joe," replied Jimmy calmly. "You see, the 'With Profits' angle means that the client gets a better deal. With the 'Non-Profit' Policy, at the end of the term, he only gets back about what he's paid in. With the 'With Profits' contract, he will probably get a great deal more – it's a far better deal for the client."

"Bugger the client," retorted Joe. "We're not in business for the bloody client. We're in business for ourselves. Lesson number one. If you keep on selling that crap, then I'm going to have to cut your commission by twenty five percent. I'm not running a charity here."

And in the end, that's what he did. Joe made his margin, Jimmy earned enough by his standards and Jimmy slept at nights.

Twelve months later, Joe was forced to take over the two adjoining offices on his floor. He took on two secretaries and he even had to give in to the idea of taking on a part time book-keeper (though the idea of the tax man getting too involved had been anathema to him). He now employed thirty salesmen and was already grossing commissions in excess of a hundred thousand pounds a year.

A further year went by and he 'sold' his double-glazing interests to Ted and Cedric who had, themselves, metamorphosed into tolerably astute businessmen (Ted had even taken elocution lessons). The deal that Joe had suggested suited them all. Rather than charge Ted and Cedric for the 'goodwill' (something of a misnomer in this instance) of his business, Joe agreed to take ten percent of their gross commissions for the next five years and to act as a 'Consultant' should his services ever be required – which they were not.

Twelve months after moving into his expanded offices, Joe received an unexpected visitor. His secretary, a tarty blonde by the name of Samantha, poked her head round the door and announced, "I've got a bloke here says he'd like a word. Says you know him. Tom Cummings he says he is. Shall I send him in?"

"Bloody hell Sam. Tom owns the firm I used to work for. Send him in. Get him a coffee will you. One for me too."

"Fucking hell Joe, you've come a long way in a short time," greeted a smiling Tom Cummings.

"Come in Tom, take a pew. How are you? Good to see you. How are Ted and Cedric doing? Still pulling it in?"

"You should know you old bastard. I know you're taking ten percent off everything they earn. You're a crafty bastard you are. Now what's all this you're doing here? Seems like I've missed a trick. I hear you're making a bloody sight more out of this scam than I am out of mine, and I've been in the game over twenty years."

Samantha brought their coffee in and they both lounged back, enjoying the warmth of renewed friendship and the feeling that there may be a chance for each of them to make money out of their reunion.

Joe gave Tom a brief outline of the conversations that he had had with Trevor Watkins of MoneySure Finance and how he had spotted that Trevor had been missing a trick or two. He gave himself full credit for the fact that he had found a way of earning almost three times as much as Trevor for selling the same thing – well, almost the same.

"The thing is Tom," confided Joe at the end of his summation. "I'm earning a fucking fortune just sitting back and letting these young lads sell a load of crap and, what's more, getting their mates to do the same as well. What I should be doing is the same sort of thing but in other towns. The trouble is, I don't have the capital or the time to start up other operations.

"Now, it seems to me that you've got both, or you can get hold of the people to run some other offices. What about some sort of partnership?" Joe was thinking out loud but he could smell a deal here.

"Exactly what I was thinking Joe me old mate. Castle Windows is becoming a bit of a bore. I could do the same as you did with Ted and Cedric. I could hand the whole thing over to George Haskins and take ten or twenty percent a year whilst he has all the hassle. Yes, I think you've got a bloody marvellous scam going here and I wouldn't mind a bit of it myself. Let me think on it and I'll give you a bell in a day or two."

After Tom had left, Joe could not help but indulge in a little self-congratulation. After all those years of grafting for a miserable bastard like Tom Cummings, here he was, talking about becoming a partner in his own business. Yes, he Joe Hendry had come a long way in a short time. He certainly had what it takes to be a success in these days. The mid-seventies was the time when everything was happening for the thrusting entrepreneur – and that was precisely what Joe had become.

His reverie was rudely disturbed when an irate Freddy Barker burst into his office.

"Here, what's all this Joe?" greeted Freddy. "That old bastard Sid has just knocked nearly twelve hundred quid of this month's commission." He was referring to Joe's new part-time bookkeeper, Sydney Banks. Having grudgingly concede that he needed a bookkeeper, Joe left this side of the business entirely to Sid (he still kept his own 'books' as well, of course). "He says it's all to do with claw back or something. What the bloody hell's he talking about?"

"I've no idea Fred. Calm down. Let's get him in and explain. Sam," Joe called out. "Get Sid to come in for a minute will you?"

Sydney Banks, a stooped sixty-five year old, had been 'retired' from the National Bank of Wales where he had spent his last ten years as a senior cashier at the Ashbridge High Street Branch. In actual fact, he had been made redundant at the age of sixty and, to supplement his meagre pension, he'd been looking for a job ever since. He was well qualified to handle the bookkeeping requirements of Castle Finance but this was probably the extreme limit of his abilities.

"Come in Sid. Take a chair," said Joe invitingly. "Now what's all this about? Freddy says you knocked over a grand off his commissions this month. Why have you done that?"

"It's because the L & E have clawed back the commission on Policies he sold that have lapsed. If you remember, if a Policy lapses in the first twelve month's, the Company reclaims seventy-five percent of what they've paid us, fifty percent in the second year and twenty-five percent in the third year.

"Under our sales agreement, we claim back all of the commission we have paid to the Sales Consultant for a lapse in the first year and a further, smaller, amount as time goes by.

"I'm afraid that quite a few of the Policies that Freddy and his team have sold have lapsed and it looks as if there will be some fairly heavy claw backs to come in the following months."

"Christ," exploded Freddy, "does that mean that you're going to take even more off me? You can't do that! I need at least two grand a month to live. The HP on my new motor costs me two hundred a month on its own. What the bloody hell are the L & E doing letting these Policies lapse. You've got to get them sorted Joe. This is bloody ridiculous."

"That's not the half of it Fred," put in Joe. "If you're having your commission clawed back, what about me? I can't run the bloody company if half the turnover is running down the drain. I'm going to have a word with George Wellbeloved and find out just the fuck's going on. Now you both bugger off and let me get on with it."

When they had both left, Joe picked up the phone and got through to George Wellbeloved.

"We seem to have hit a bit of a problem George," announced Joe, without preamble. "It seems that your people are lapsing our punter's policies and then coming back to us for a refund of the commission. Let me tell you straight George, I'm not having that. How do you expect me to run a Company if you keep taking back pretty well everything that you have paid us? We give you a hell of a lot of business and if you're going to start poncing around like that, we'll soon find someone else. Don't you worry about that."

"Calm down old boy," replied George. "I can tell you that the lapse ratio on some of your business has been causing some concern with my own head office people. However, let me look into it and get back to you when I have the facts and figures. Why don't I get the data and pop down to see you tomorrow? It's about time we got together again. How about twelve noon and we could then nip out for a bite of lunch? How does that seem?"

Slightly mollified, Joe agreed to this and left matters to be ironed out on the following day.

....

At twelve noon on the dot the next day, Samantha announced George's arrival and, after the preliminaries, George pulled out a sheaf of computer print-outs and announced, "Right, down to business. It seems that Freddy Barker is your most prolific producer by far, but to date, thirty percent of the policies that he has put on the books, have lapsed."

"Why don't you bloody well tell us then, or at least write to the punter and tell him to keep the policy going?"

"We do, old boy, but do remember that the first thing we know about a policy going off is when the bank reject the direct debit mandate. It can take up to eight weeks before we realise that there might be a problem and then we send out a polite letter suggesting that there may have been a banking error and recommending that they should reinstate the direct debit. Sometimes, that's all there is to it.

"Unfortunately, it looks as if young Freddy – and his team, for that matter – have been overselling. In other words, they have persuaded the client to take out a policy for a rather higher premium than he or she can actually afford. On top of that, when the client finds out that there is no surrender value to his Policy at all– and never likely to be in the first five years - most of them just cut their losses and pack the policy in."

"Well, why for God's sake don't you offer them a surrender value or whatever you call it? You make enough profit. If you let them know that there would be something to come after, say three years, at least they'd keep the bleeding thing going long enough for us to hang on to our commission. If you want Castle Finance to keep giving you all this business, you'll have to come up with something better than what's happening now."

"I wish we could old boy. The trouble is that we don't make enough profit. If you sell a Policy at twenty pounds a month, that's two hundred and forty pounds a year to us, we give you roughly two hundred and ten pounds. We then have to buy the Life Assurance, cover our expenses and hope to generate a profit. I'm afraid that, unless the Policy runs three years, we make a loss; and there's not much profit in it even then.

"Taking into account Freddy's team's track record, we calculate that his final lapse ratio will be in the region of seventy to seventy five percent. Apart from the fact that we are all likely to be losers, if I were you, I would stop paying him any commission at all until things get on a more even keel."

"He'd kill me if I did that!" exclaimed Joe. "He's up to his ears in debt as it is and I think he's been giving advance payments to some of his team so any reduction in his income will screw him up completely. There's got to be some other way."

"The interesting thing is that we also had a look at Jimmy's lapse ratio. Do you know what his is?"

"A bloody sight better I hope, or I'll soon be out of business."

"Well, actually old boy, it's nil. It seems that every Policy that Jimmy and his team have sold has stayed in force so far, and we see no reason to believe that this will change. The main reason for this is that all the Policies he and his friends have sold are on a 'With Profits' basis, and none appear to have been pitched at a level of premium higher than that that which the client can afford.

"I know that Jimmy's commissions appear to be running at only about sixty percent of those generated by Freddy, but the end result is chalk and cheese – Jimmy's stick whilst Freddy's lapse.

"My advice is that you either get rid of Freddy and his team as soon as possible, or you ask Jimmy to become their Manager and retrain them along his lines. Now let's go and get some lunch and talk it over."

Unusually for Joe, lunch was a sobering experience. George Wellbeloved may be an overblown, intemperate lounge lizard, but he had bought home to Joe the gravity of his situation. All the time he had been greedily watching young Fred and his mates bring in signed proposals by the barrow load, he had actually been losing money.

All the time he had been tolerating Jimmy's smaller barrow load but, at least he was making money (albeit, not as much as he would have liked).

He shouted out to Samantha. "Is that young bastard Jimmy in? If so, send him in here pronto, will you?"

"He's in the bog at the moment," came the cultured reply. "I'll tell him to pop in as soon as he's washed his hands."

A few moments later, with a tap on the door, Jimmy entered. Joe had to admit that he looked the part these days. Jimmy had taken to wearing grey suits with a clean, crisp white shirt fresh each day. His ensemble was completed with a modestly patterned blue tie – every inch the young businessman, Joe conceded.

"You wanted to see me boss?"

"Yes, come in Jimmy, draw up a chair. There's something I want to go through with you.

"Now I know that we haven't always seen eye to eye with the business you've been writing and I know that I've had a tendency to ram Fred's production rate down your throat. Well, the thing is, I've just been having lunch with George Wellbeloved and he's been pointing out the facts of life. It seems that you've been right and I've been wrong. I want to apologise."

"That's very kind of you Joe," replied Jimmy, clearly delighted, if not a little surprised, by praise from such an unlikely source. "I've only been doing what seems right. I always like to think, what would I want to put my own money in if I were the client sitting opposite me?

"Whilst we're on the subject, I've been thinking Joe, I really do think that we should not be putting all our eggs in one basket. The Life and Equity are all well and good, but don't you think that we should be representing more than one company? Giving clients a better choice, in other words."

"Now for Christ's sake, hold on Jimmy," snapped Joe. "Our job is to make a living, bugger the clients. If we go to any other Company, they'll only give us two percent commission. With the Life and Equity, we're on to three percent – that kind of commission doesn't grow on trees!

"No, if you can get the punters to part with their cash and get the buggers to keep the policies in force for at least three years, then that's all you've got to do. If they pack up then, then it's their lookout, not ours. Let's forget all these damn fool ideas of giving the punter a better deal. I earn little enough with these fucking With Profits Policies as it is. If only Fred could make his bloody policies stick, we'd be in clover.

"What I want you to do is to have a word with Fred and tell him how to sell With Profits Policies instead of this Non Profit crap so that we can keep some of the bloody commission when he earns it – at the moment, it comes in one month and goes straight out the next.

"I'll have him in tomorrow morning and tell him what he's got to do, and then you spend an hour or so with him to get him put straight. Is that a deal?"

"I'll be only too pleased to see him Joe," replied Jimmy, "but I rather think he's not going to like it. He can't see the point of earning a hundred quid when, for the same amount of work, he could earn two hundred, or even two fifty. I'll have a go, and I still think you should consider another Agency as well, someone like the Universal, perhaps."

"For God's sake, give it a rest. Just you leave all that to me. I'll get Fred to see you. About ten tomorrow morning. Is that OK for you?"

"Fine, Joe. Bye for now."

Joe sighed exasperatedly and started jotting down a few notes to remind himself of the ground that he would have to cover tomorrow with Fred.

"Sam!" he called. "Make sure that young bastard Fred is in my office at nine o'clock tomorrow morning first thing, and tell him not to be late or I'll have his guts for garters." Castle Financial Services Ltd always handled it's affairs in a professional manner.

Then an idea occurred to him. He reached for the phone and dialled the number for his new best friend Tom Cummings.

Chapter Nineteen

By nine o'clock the next day, Joe was sitting at his desk enjoying his first cup of coffee of the day. Except that he wasn't enjoying it.

Sydney had left him the latest monthly figures and they did not make cheerful reading. Until only a few days ago he had only been interested in the top line. He figured that, if there was enough commission coming in, then because he had screwed his sales force down so hard, then the bottom line should take care of itself. He figured that, as long as the commission rolled in, he was making a profit, and a pretty good one at that.

But now, for the very first time, he was taking note of the dreaded word 'clawback' and here it was in front of him, in startling clarity.

Last month, Fred and his team had produced commissions totalling £5,000. He had paid Fred £1,500 and Fred had paid roughly three hundred of this to his 'agents'. Joe reckoned that the £3,500 that he kept for himself was a fair remuneration for setting the whole thing up – after all, he had rent and rates and he had to pay for Samantha and, now, Sydney. He would be lucky to take home £2,500 of that himself.

The trouble was, however, clawbacks for the month had reached an incredible £3,000. He was actually making a loss on Fred's business – a loss of almost £500 a month! And it was getting worse.

Six months ago, when Fred's commissions had first started coming through the door, Joe noticed that he had earned just over a thousand pounds in a month and that this figure had been steadily climbing. At this time the clawbacks were nil because none of the punters had cancelled their policies - yet.

In the intervening period, the clawbacks had risen from a relatively modest £50 in one month to the current £3,000 every month. Old Wellbeloved was right – most of Fred's business went off the books almost as soon as it was went on.

On the other hand, Jimmy's figures were running at the order of one to two thousand pounds a month. Jimmy was earning about £800 a month and giving about £200 to £300 to his Agents.

In other words Jimmy was keeping £500 to £600 per month and Fred would be owing up to £1,000 a month – and at the same time, he would be costing Joe a fortune.

Joe looked up to see Fred lounging against the doorpost. "Come in and sit down," he growled.

"Have you sorted out the bleedin' Life and effin' Equity," began Fred. "I hope you've told the buggers where they get off and start paying me my commissions – I'm nearly broke."

"The way you've been going on, you bloody fool, I'll be broke too," retorted Joe to his surprised salesman. "Do you realise that almost all of that crap you've been selling gets cancelled within the first three month's? Not only does the punter lose all his money, but the Life and Equity immediately reclaim all the commission that they had paid us. So I pay you, and then I've got to give it back – it's a bloody farce.

"Now the only thing that we can do, is to make sure that you and your blokes get out there and sell twice as much business as you lazy bastards have been selling up to now. But, the difference is, it's all got to be With Profits business, no more of this Non Profits crap.

"I'm sorry to have to admit it, but Jimmy was right all along. Do you know, not one of his policies has been cancelled? He might not earn as much as you in the beginning, but at least his business sticks and, from now on, yours has got to do the same."

"There's no point in selling that With Profits garbage Joe," whined Fred. "You've said it yourself, there's no commission in it. How do you expect me and my mates to make a living if we're only going to earn half the bleedin' commission we earn now?"

"But you are not earning it you silly bugger. It all lapses. There's going to be no argument Fred. I want you to go and see Jimmy now and you're going to listen to what he says and you're going to sell what he sells, and that's all there is to it."

"Christ!" retorted Fred. "Listen to that wanker? No way. Let me have a go at the Life and Equity. Even if the policies don't run for long, at least they keep the premiums for a few months. Why don't they just give us that? That would be something. At least me and the boys would be earning a few bob."

"Don't be a damned fool. They're not running a bloody charity, just to keep you and your mates in beer money. I've been through all that and it won't work. Now stop fucking about. Go and see Jimmy and you do just what he tells you. Either that, or you can fuck off now and I'll sue you for every penny of commission that you owe me and you'll never work in this industry again. Have you got that?"

A very chastened Fred Barker sloped off for his first lesson on the sound (or relatively sound) techniques of selling of Life Assurance.

Left in peace for a moment, Joe wandered in to discuss the accounts with Sydney. It was clear that he was going to have to pull the wool over the Bank's eyes to give them all some breathing space. But, at least, he was looking forward to keeping his appointment with Tom Cummings. That meeting could turn out to be profitable – very profitable.

Chapter Twenty

Tim was poring over a set of figures when he looked up to see that Graham Wiltshier had walked into his room.

"Come and take a look at these," invited Tim. "They're the provisional management accounts for our first five years. It looks as if we're going to finish this year with a turnover of just about two hundred and twenty five thousand and a profit of almost twenty five grand. If we hadn't had to pay out five grand towards the P I claim on Bill Syke's car, we'd have made about twelve and a half percent on Turnover – about what I had been budgeting."

"Not at all bad Tim," agreed Graham. "I'm hoping to make us a bit more today. We've quoted for Bristows as you know, and Charles Foreman, their F D, has promised me that we'll get their decision this afternoon. If we get it, we'll earn about ten or eleven thousand."

"That's terrific Graham, what are we up against?"

"Last year, Cooper's charged them a shade under ninety thousand. As far as I can tell, they're quoting about the same as last year, so I've assumed that I've got to get somewhere around the eighty thousand mark to have a fair chance – they've been with Coopers for over twenty years and I don't think that Charles will switch for a two bit saving. I was having some trouble finding a market – their liability premiums are a problem because they export so much to the States.

"I was on the verge of giving up when the Merchant's Mutual came back with an unbelievably low premium provided that we give them the Fire and Loss of Profits business as well.

"That could have been a problem because those covers are with the L & M under a three year agreement and we would not be able to break that. However, the L & M wrote to Coopers last week saying that they were increasing their premiums across the board by ten percent. That means that the Agreement is over, of course, and I can switch the material damage cover to the Merchants."

"God job, Graham. Sounds like a deal to me. You look worried though – what's the problem?"

"It's just the relationship with the L & M that worries me. For very good reasons, like difficulty in getting them to pay their claims for example, we don't use the L & M much. On the other hand, Coopers seem to pass about seventy five percent of their business to them and I would not be surprised if they pulled a fast one at the last moment. I've put a hell of a lot of work into getting this account, and although I like fair competition, I wouldn't want us to lose out through dirty work at the cross roads. There's not a great deal we can do about it now, but I just thought that I'd let you know."

"OK Graham, just let me know when Charles Foreman calls. Best of luck."

Tim returned to studying his accounts only to find Chris hovering around in the doorway, trying to attract his attention.

"How's things Chris? Come in. Drag up a chair and let's have a coffee. Janet!" called Tim.

"Yes sir?" answered Janet as she responded to her master's call. "Coffee for two, I suppose. I'm just the under-paid waitress around here these days."

"Got it in one. Now look sharp about it, there's a good girl, you know you love it," pointed out Tim good-naturedly.

Tim showed Chris the figures and they discussed them at some length.

Over their coffee, Chris said, "I'm glad the figures are looking pretty good because it's about an increase in our overheads that I want to talk to you about. As you know, I spend all my time on group schemes and there is absolutely no time left for anything else.

"On the other hand, there is an enormous amount of business being done out there with private clients – family protection, mortgage repayments, regular investments, bonds, unit trusts and pensions and all that sort of thing. I really think that it's about time that we took someone on to deal with that end of the market."

"Do you have anyone in mind?" enquired Tim."

"Not really," admitted Chris. "But there is a firm out there, frankly a rather shifty operation if you ask me, who is placing quite spectacular amounts of business with the Life and Equity. I don't know how they do it, but all the other Company Inspectors keep telling me that they're making an absolute fortune.

"Frankly, I don't know why anyone would want to do business with the L & E. They look pretty shaky to me and, although I'm sure they won't go to bust – the Insurance Industry wouldn't allow it – I can't see them paying out much in the way of bonuses under their With Profits contracts."

"Who is this firm and why are they placing so much with the L & E?" asked Tim.

"They're a firm called Castle Finance and I can only assume that they've negotiated some fancy commission deal with the L & E. They are not registered, they're not members of any of the professional bodies but they do seem to employ a hell of a lot of salesmen."

"Well let's keep an eye on them and, in the meantime, why don't you put and advert in The Policy for a Life Assurance Consultant? I agree entirely that we should not be missing out. In any case, it's a natural progression of the service we should be giving to our clients. You go ahead," instructed Tim.

The afternoon was proceeding fairly routinely when Graham entered Tim's office looking rather dejected.

"What's up, Graham? You look as if you've found a quid and lost a fiver."

"That's about right Tim. I've just had Charles Foreman on the line and he has told me that Coopers had originally quoted ninety thousand to our eighty, and when he told them that he would be transferring to us, they asked for another hour and then came back with a couple of thousand pounds improvement on our figure and told him that our quotation would not stand up.

"I immediately gave the L & M a call and they said that, due to pressure from Coopers, their Head Office had agreed to waive the across the board increase and they would, consequently, not allow their Long Term Agreement to be broken. I'm afraid that we're buggered Tim, because the Merchant Mutual will only take the Liability cover if they have the Fire and Profits covers too. Since most of our savings were under the Liability policies, and we can't place one without the other, we're up the creek."

"Who do we deal with at the Merchants?" asked Tim. "Let me give him a call. I might be able to put a little pressure on them to help us out if they think that there is more to come. I could offer them the Robinsons account when it comes up."

Graham passed over the file, pointing out the names and the numbers of the people they were dealing with, and Tim dialled the number shown.

In a few minutes, he was through to Tony Burroughs, the chief Liability Underwriter.

"Tony, hello. This is Tim Harrison of Harrisons. You know you've given us a good quotation for Bristows? We would like to give you the business, but we have a problem with your terms – apparently you're insisting on the Fire and Profits Insurance too."

"Absolutely, Tim," came the firm reply. "United States liability cover is extremely high risk at the moment and most Companies are running a mile from it. Our Head Office will only let us underwrite it if we 'buy' the business by taking on some good quality home-based business.

"As you know, over the years we've been traditionally a Liability specialist, but the board have decided to expand their book of business in the UK. The last thing that they want is more 'unattached' high risk US business. I'm sorry, but that's the way it is. Why, what's the problem? Aren't our terms for the Fire and Profits any good? Graham told me that we were within shouting distance of the L & M's terms and that they were waiving their LTA."

"That was the case, Tony, but the buggers have just agreed to reduce their current premiums to last year's terms and so the LTA stays. I'm afraid there's not much we can do and if we leave everything until next year, I think that the FD will have lost interest and we might have to wait another three years before we can get a crack at the business again.

"What if we were to guarantee to you we would transfer the Fire and Profits to you at the first renewal? Would your Head Office take a flyer on the basis that they'd get the business as soon as the LTA expires?"

"I don't know, Tim. It's worth a try but I really can't hold out much hope. The losses in the States have been terrifying and we are taking a bit of a 'punt' that things are about to turn around. The punt will only be worth our while if we can make some decent profits on some good quality UK business. Let me have a word with them and I'll give Graham a call back. I would very much like to build up an account with Harrisons. We've only just started a relationship with you and I think that there's a lot of potential there for us. I'll certainly do my best. Bye for now."

Again, there was nothing to do but to wait and Tim returned to work on other matters. In particular, he was intrigued that a firm of Life Assurance brokers that he'd never heard of seemed to be doing so spectacularly well. He decided to give his old friend at the Universal, Tony Abbott, a call and find out what he could.

"Tony, it's Tim here," he said as soon as he had got through. "You know as much as anyone about what's going on in the Life Assurance field. What do you know about a firm called Castle Finance?"

"Thanks for the compliment. I never knew that you saw me as a guru, but that is exactly what I am of course. How are things going with you? Is Chris behaving himself and earning his keep? I saw that you took over Warrington's schemes – Hayter's were well and truly pissed off, I can tell you."

"Yes, yes and good, in that order," replied Tim. "Actually, the Group Scheme business is going like a bomb. Chris was saying, however, that we should be getting into the Individual market. It was he who was telling me about Castle Finance. I'm interested in them. What do you know about them?"

"A bunch of shysters," came the immediate response. "A chap by the name of Joe Hendry runs it. In my view he's a bit of a low life and, as far as I know, he has absolutely no qualifications in Financial Services, or anything else, for that matter. He seems to take on out of work kids and get them to sell absolute crap on a high commission basis. He gives all his business to the Life and Equity. They're a very small Company with no track record and a name for handing out top rates of commission. If they're still in business in ten years, I'd be surprised. How they ever persuade people to buy such crap is a mystery to me. Why, does that tell you what you want to know?"

"Yes, very interesting. Thanks Tony, you've been a great help. Food for thought indeed. I'll be in touch. Cheers for now."

"As he put the phone down, Graham came rushing into the room. "We've done it, we've cracked it," he cried gleefully. "Good old Tony Burroughs persuaded his Head Office to see the light. They said that, provided that we guarantee to offer them the Fire and Profits at the first renewal, they would make an exception and take the Liability on it's own for twelve months. I phoned Charles Foreman at Bristows and it took him thirty seconds to make up his mind and give us the OK.

"He said that he had been pretty pissed off with the service that he had been getting from Cooper and Smythe's lately. He felt that they were being taken for granted just because they had not gone out to tender for the last twenty years. He certainly didn't like the feeling that the only time Colin Cooper made a real effort – and then slightly under-handed at that – was when he realised that he was about to lose the Account."

"One up for us this time Tim, but I think that we must learn a lesson here ourselves. I hope that we are never likely to become as complacent as that, but with the pressure of work, I think we must take on another Account Executive, and soon."

"Couldn't agree more," affirmed Tim, feeling more that usually expansive with another ten thousand pounds a year commission on the books. "The rate the business is coming in at the moment, I think that the bottom line can look after itself for a while. I know Bill Warrington would rather see us properly staffed and retaining our Clients rather than the other way around. You go ahead and start advertising."

Harrison's was growing; Tim could not help but enjoy a quiet feeling of personal pride.

There was a tap at the door and Chris stood there with a cup of coffee in his hand. "Got half a minute, Tim?" he asked, and strolled in without waiting for an answer.

"For you Tobes, I've got the whole afternoon," replied Tim expansively. "Heard the news? We've just got Bristows. Good old Graham. He's done a fantastic job and shown a clean pair of heels to Coopers. Makes it count double, I always think, when we pinch something from those old buggers. Draw up a chair, oh you have. What can I do for you me old salt?"

"Yes, I knew as soon as I saw Graham prancing across the office that he must have done it. Wonderful news – he deserves it - and I should imagine that I will have plenty of scope to have a crack at their Pensions business. That'd be worth a grand or two to us on its own.

"What I wanted to chat to you about is the idea we punted around some time ago that we should expand our Financial Services division to include Personal Financial Services. There's a ton of business out there and I simply haven't got the time nor, I confess, the expertise to deal with it.

"I've been talking to Tony Abbott, my old mucker at the Universal. To be frank, I took the liberty of sounding him out and, on the right terms, He'd be very keen. What's more, he'd be very good for us. He's highly respected by the other Insurance Companies and the clients love him. Wouldn't be a bit surprised if some of them didn't follow him here."

"Well there's a coincidence," exclaimed Tim. "I was only speaking to him an hour ago. I wanted to find out something about a Company called Castle Finance and the Life and Equity International. He was very friendly and very helpful, but I thought that there was something odd about the way he answered. I bet he thought that I'd called him to offer him a job. No wonder he sounded a bit odd.

"As far as I'm concerned, it's entirely up to you Chris. I like the chap, I like him a lot, and if you think that he's the right man for us, then you go ahead. I'm happy to leave it entirely up to you to decide and, within reason, you offer him what you think he's worth."

"That's great Tim, and thanks. I'll give him a call right now. I think you'll find he's got one or two ideas that would be worth listening to so I'll fix a time when you're going to be around. If the interview goes well and he accepts the job, I'll bring him in to see you and we'll have a chat about his other ideas. See what you think."

"Fine by me Chris, keep me posted."

Back at his desk, Chris called Tony Abbott and arranged for him to pop in at noon the next day. Both men were eager to meet.

Chapter Twenty-One

The Day and Night Club was one of the seedier nightspots of Soho. The décor was tired and the strippers were tired – and long past their 'sell-by' date.

The lack of lighting helped, of course. In fact, the girl currently gyrating on the small dimly lit stage looked quite attractive from where the three businessmen were sitting. She was in the process of grinding herself around a stainless steel pole, and thrusting her pelvis provocatively against it. She leant back to unhitch her G-string, legs akimbo, displaying her sex to the world, whilst the three gentlemen fantasized as to the pleasures were they to take the place of the pole.

Seraphim, for that was the lady's rather unlikely name, appeared to be performing her writhing solely for the benefit of these three. It was as if they were the only men in the room.

The threesome comprised Tom Cummings, a long-standing member of this elite establishment, and his two guests. Joe Hendry was obviously enjoying the show and was even finding the 'Champagne Cocktail', now that he was on his third, to be almost palatable. It was the third member of the group, however, who seemed to be enjoying himself the most.

George Wellbeloved, curiously enough, (man of the world that he purported to be) had never been to a Strip Club or 'Clip Joint', as he believed this was known as, in his life. He was finding it an extraordinary experience. Mrs Wellbeloved, like her husband, was a stone or two overweight. She was unattractive – some would even say 'ugly' - and she practised a strong aversion to doing 'it'. The sex act as, performed between Mr and Mrs Wellbeloved, was an infrequent occurrence and, on the very rare occasions that it did occur, was accompanied by considerable huffing, puffing, sweating and general discomfort. It was not a pretty sight. In fact, Mr Wellbeloved's sexual gratification usually involved only himself and a top-shelf magazine.

Seraphim had now discarded her G-string and was in the process of engaging her clitoris intimate sexual contact with the pole. Her voluminous breasts flapped comfortably either side of the pole as she eased herself slowly and seductively, up and down. She was either a tolerably good actress, or this particular exercise was, in truth, giving her obvious and visible pleasure.

The effect on George Wellbeloved was rather more dramatic. If she didn't stop soon, George feared, he was in dire danger of ejaculating in his pants. He had not been as excited since a fresh young third former had climbed into his bed one night at boarding school and offered him his bottom. The charge for this service had been a mere twenty Benson and Hedges – a price that he had been more than willing to pay.

At long last, Seraphim stood back from her pole, revealing herself in all her glory. Her audience, George apart, broke into desultory applause and feeble cries of 'more'. George's applause was considerably more enthusiastic.

"Wow!" exclaimed a panting Wellbeloved as Seraphim gathered up her discarded clothes and disappeared backstage. "Tom, that was fantastic. I have to thank you for this invitation tonight. I'd heard of these places, but in my circles, one never seems to have had the opportunity to get actually get there. What I wouldn't do to Miss Seraphim if I had the chance!"

"All things are possible," smiled Tom. "There'll be another one on in about half an hour. What about another drink?" he asked, waving to the nearby scantily dressed waitress.

"Three more Champagne cocktails Lolita, if you don't mind. It's amazing what they can do with Dubonnet and Coca Cola," he confided to his guests.

"Now, as we were saying George," continued Tom. "Joe tells me that your Company are being a little mean about the rate of commission that you're paying us. Notwithstanding the paltry rates that you pay us, you then seem to want it all back again, just because your Company can't persuade the punters to keep their policies in force."

"It's not exactly like that Tom," spluttered George, taken aback by this rather distorted version of his Company's commission arrangements. "What's been happening is......"

"Of course it's not George," agreed Tom kindly. "We're not getting at you personally, but we do think that, with all the support that you're getting from Joe here and his people, perhaps there might be room to put the rate up a tad. How about from three percent to, shall we say, four percent? That's not unreasonable is it?"

"Four percent! You must be joking. We don't even..........."

"I'm sure you don't," continued Tom. "And then we thought that perhaps, just now and then, you could get your people to make a teeny 'mistake' and overlook that one or two policies of ours have lapsed. Why don't you just continue paying our commission? I'm sure that you'd agree that that would make a lot of sense. After all, we have a business to run and, if you want our support, well, you'll have to earn it. Ah, here we are, our cocktails."

Tom ran his fingers up Lolita's inner thigh in a proprietorial way and gave her bottom a gentle squeeze. He was rewarded with a smile and a wink for his efforts and an "anything else I can do for you Mr C? Nothing would be too much trouble for a gentleman like you sir" (with knowing emphasis on the 'nothing').

"Not tonight Josephine," Tom thanked her, and gave her a gentle pat on the bottom.

George turned to Joe for support. "You know the score Joe, don't you? You're in the business. I'd love to help if I could, you know I would, but we're already running at a loss with the business you're giving us now. Our only hope is that we'll recoup in the years ahead."

"I'm sure you will George. That's why we thought that you just might like to be a little more generous to us," replied Joe helpfully. "Now I'm off to the Gents to make myself comfortable before the lovely Seraphim comes back for her last performance."

After Joe had left, Tom took a long swig of his 'Cocktail' and turned to George.

"That's enough of business for this evening George old lad. Let's enjoy ourselves. If I'm not much mistaken, I'd say that you've taken a bit of a shine to the lovely Seraphim. Would you like me to invite her over for a drink when she's completed her performance? She's a lovely lady, and as I've been a member here for many, many years. I'm sure she'd oblige."

George could hardly believe his ears. "What, get her over here dressed just as she is when she finishes? In the starkers? Would she do that? Could you arrange that? That would be fantastic," he spluttered.

"No trouble at all George. I've known Seraphim for at least three or four years now. As I said, she's a lovely lady. She's classy - not a prostitute, of course. Not like most of them are here. But if she likes someone, then she's not above showing him backstage. She has her own dressing room – all the regulars do – and if she should fancy a little kiss and cuddle as sometimes happens, well where's the harm in that?"

"You're joking aren't you? Five minutes alone with that lady and I'd make all her dreams come true." George, as is the case with most men, was confident that, given the opportunity, he was an irresistible stud.

"I'm sure you would," laughed Tom, as Joe returned to the table. "Ah, here's the lady now, let's see what she's got for us this time."

Seraphim was simply the most gorgeous young thing that George had ever set eyes on in his life. He was completely besotted. She moved like an angel and removed her clothes, one by one and oh so slowly, with such grace and dignity. And, all this time, she was looking at him. Only him. George's mouth was dry. Despite copious draughts of his cocktail, he was temporarily incapable of speech. His hands were trembling, his stomach was churning and his mind was in turmoil. Could it be that this vision of loveliness was going to join them at this table and even allow him backstage to do.... anything? His thoughts were in a turmoil of erotic anticipation.

As Joe had returned, unnoticed by the enraptured George, he had nodded to Tom as he sat down, giving him a sly wink.

As her performance concluded, Seraphim, naked as the day she was born, stood proudly erect with her arms in the air, acknowledging the applause. She stooped to pick up her flimsy shawl and draped it casually around her shoulders. By clasping it around her, she barely concealed her charms.

To George's amazement, she sidled erotically past the other seated members, deftly avoiding their grasping hands, until she stood in front of the open-mouthed George.

"Hi," she breathed. "Aren't you even going to offer a poor working girl a drink then? Mind if I join you gentlemen?" she sighed as she settled on George's lap.

"Ssssorry dddear," stammered George, tongue-tied and bereft of all reasoning. He turned to the waiting Lolita, who had followed Seraphim across the floor. "Champagne pppppplease."

"Would that be a bottle sir, or just a glass for the lady?"

"A bbbottle, of course, my dear." He smiled at Seraphim, or attempted to smile – just what expression his face was set in, he had no idea. His facial muscles were on strike.

"That's very kind of you George old man," said Tom smoothly, and turning to the departing Lolita, "that'll be the Bollinger, of course. My friend wouldn't want Seraphim to die of indigestion with your usual old rubbish."

"Of course," agreed George feebly, all thoughts of economic good sense now out of the window.

As they waited, George found himself at a loss as to what to do with his hands. Here he was, with the most beautiful creature in the world sitting on his lap, virtually stark naked, and he didn't know what to do. Even at this close range, George was oblivious of the sagging breast line, the stretch marks, the cellulite and the pungent whiffs of body odour. George was hooked.

He settled for one hand on her left thigh and the other loosely around her waist. But movement only appeared to arouse the lady. She wriggled her bottom suggestively and whispered in his ear, sotto voce, "You're a big man aren't you? If you don't tell it to lie down, I'll have to give it a little smack."

The effect on George was to produce the biggest erection of his life. Please, he prayed to his unruly member, don't let me down now. He dropped his hands, terrified that he might easily disgrace himself there and then.

At last, Lolita arrived with the uncorked bottle of Bollinger. George realised it would be poor form to ask for another bottle, this time to have the bottle uncorked in front of them. In any event, he was quite beyond caring whether he was being offered vintage champagne or Coca Cola. His mind, like his hand, was on other things.

"Would you like to taste it sir?" asked Lolita, splashing some into the nearest glass regardless. George lifted the glass, held it to the light, raised it gently to his nostrils, savoured the bouquet and tasted it. Rolling it around his tongue and, reckoning that it tasted more like Asti Spumanti than Bollinger, pronounced, with some gravitas, to his amused audience, "excellent, you may pour it, young lady."

"That'll be seventy five pounds please sir," announced Lolita to an open-mouthed George. Fumbling for his wallet, George found that he had two fifty pound notes and handed these hesitantly to Lolita who removed them with a flourish and a "Coo, thank you very much sir, you are kind."

George's horror at being so professionally deprived of several days' salary was immediately forgotten when Seraphim again whispered to him. "Why don't we leave these gentlemen to themselves for a bit? I'd like to show you backstage and, perhaps you'd like to see my dressing room. I think we would enjoy our champagne better there. How would you like to see how we work and how we get ready for our shows?"

To his acute embarrassment, George's voice failed him completely this time. He simply took Seraphim's proffered hand and, in a delirious trance, followed her lamely where she led. He held her hand as close to his crotch as possible; not for erotic reasons, but for concealment of his uncontrolled excitement.

"Don't worry George, me old lad," said Tom to his departing back. "Joe and I will finish off your Bolly, enjoy the show and wait until you've had your grand tour. Have fun. We'll still be here."

Seraphim's dingy dressing room, contained nothing more than a cheap dressing table (fully equipped with pots and potions, all of which were a complete mystery to George), an upright chair and a well-worn rug, about six foot by three. To George though, it was like heaven.

Without a word, Seraphim let her shawl slide to the ground, as she put her hand on hs crotch and gently stroked his rampant organ.

"Here," she whispered. "It's dark in there. Let's give Big John here a little air. With that, she slid her hands down to his waist, unzipped his flies and, with a practised tug, pulled off his belt and let his trousers drop to the floor. Next, she slid his underpants rapidly in the same direction.

To his complete amazement, Seraphim dropped to her knees and, with one hand on his cock, the other around his balls, she slowly swallowed the one almost as far as the other, looking up into his eyes all the time.

It was too much for him. The thought of Mrs Wellbeloved even touching this part of his anatomy was unimaginable. But to suck it! George couldn't help himself. With one gigantic tremor, he came. In one mind-blowing orgasm he was sated. With a yell of sheer ecstasy that might have been heard around the entire building, he had experienced the greatest (and fastest) orgasm of his life.

Even the very experienced Seraphim was startled by the force of his ejaculation. She fought valiantly, and professionally, not to choke and, thereby detract from the magic of the moment.

"That was fantastic," she murmured. "What a man. You've made me so horny. It's my turn now."

And with that, and with one sweep of her arms, she brushed the potions off the dressing table onto the floor. She leant back on the table, legs wide apart. She then drew the befuddled George to her by pulling firmly on his tie. With one hand on his head, she gently forced him to lower himself to a kneeling position. Opening her legs still wider, she pressed her fingers to her vagina and said, "Now lick that. This is going to be the best meal you've had in your whole life. I want you to eat me, suck me, fuck me until I can take no more."

A bewildered George did as he was told. His very first experience of fellatio. Nevertheless, after only a few moments, he was startled and disappointed to hear her command, seemingly without any warning, "Right, that's enough. Time to go. Off you go to your friends, I've got another show in ten minutes. Even the inexperienced George Wellbeloved was puzzled that she could have reached her own orgasm so quickly and, so quietly. He was confused as to whether he should be proud of his prowess and efficiency or disappointed by her unseemly haste.

It did seem to be a rather peremptory dismissal to George, but then, he was a complete novice in these matters. Not to worry, he comforted himself, he had had a night that he would never forget.

And that was certainly to prove true.

On rejoining his friends, eagerly awaiting news of his back stage experiences, he revelled in the glory that he was now a man of the world, one of the boys. Still on cloud nine, George found it difficult to report the precise details of his tryst with the compliant Seraphim, it had all happened so quickly, but both Tom and Joe seemed very understanding and reassuringly pleased that he had had such a good time. For the first time in his life, George felt the true warmth of male comradeship.

A little while later, a completely sated George was relieved when Tom announced, "Time to go" as he settled his account. George was intrigued to note that the doorman handed Tom a large sealed envelope as he left. He assumed that this might be a souvenir of a memorable evening.

Despite himself, George was impressed that an establishment such as this was so efficient. He was very much looking forward to his next visit for he understood that, by virtue of this first visit, he had fulfilled the exacting entry requirements to become a privileged member in his own right.

As Tom and Joe dropped him off from their taxi at the station, he was intrigued when Tom handed him the envelope that he had been given at the Club.

"Glad you enjoyed it George. A little souvenir – a little light reading for you – to enjoy on your journey home. Have a good trip."

George sat on the platform bench waiting for the late train and with half an hour to wait, tore open the envelope, fascinated to know what Tom had given him. Perhaps, he hoped, there might be a selection of souvenir photographs of the delectable Seraphim. He was absolutely right.

Inside, there was a roughly scribbled note from Tom, which simply said, "Don't forget, 4% commission and a few 'mistakes' to improve our cash flow – Good luck and we all had a great evening. Must to it again soon, Tom".

Enclosed was a selection of grained photographs depicting George Wellbeloved, some with his member in Seraphim's mouth and others with his face in Seraphim's crotch.

His heart stopped beating. He felt physically sick.

Chapter Twnety-Two

Chris Johnson was just about to enjoy his second cup of coffee of the day when the receptionist rang to announce that Tony Abbott had had arrive.

"Send him straight up Tina, he knows the way. Oh, and if its not too much trouble, could you please ask him if he'd like a coffee and, if so, you couldn't possibly do the honours could you?"

"Not at all. Your wish is my command. I'm here to serve sir," came the cheery response.

"Thanks Tina, your devotion to duty will be richly rewarded, in heaven, if not on earth."

"I was afraid of that!" laughed Tina. "I'll be with you in a mo."

Chris looked up. "Come in, come in Chris. How's things at my place of previous employment then?"

"Not bad," replied Chris. "Everything's pretty much the same, though there's far too much crap to deal with and we're all having to specialise – a bloody bore if you ask me. Oh thanks a million Tina," he said to the smiling girl as she passed him a cup of coffee.

"Is that all sir?" she asked as she performed a mock curtsey to Chris. "Anything else that I can be at your beck and call for?"

"No, just run along and play with your phones, there's a good girl."

"That's what I've always liked about this place," observed Chris. "You're so friendly and informal, unlike the Universal – it's OK, I suppose, and everyone gets on well enough, but there's no real spirit there. People come in, do their job, and at five o'clock sharp, its down tools and head for the hills."

"Well you don't get that here," chuckled Chris. "Come six o'clock, most of us are still here hard at it and, if there's a rush on, it's not unusual to see the lights still burning after seven. Saturday mornings are pretty busy too. A holiday camp it sure ain't.

"Anyway, having put you off, let's talk about what we've got in mind. As you might agree, I know all I need to know about group business but I know bugger all about the personal financial services side. I'm sure we're missing a trick, or several come to that, and I'd like to offer you the job of building up a new division for us. What do you think?"

"You couldn't have asked at a better time," replied Chris. "As I've said, I'm bored stiff with what I'm doing now and I feel that I need a new challenge. It would be good for me and it would be good for Jean. She's always on at me to get out of the rut, but you know how it is? One day rolls into another, into a week, into a month and into a year and I never seem to have the time to look for another opportunity. You tell me how much you can pay me, and I'll tell you what I can do for you."

"What are you on at the moment Chris?"

"Nowhere enough," came the jaundiced reply. "I actually earn just a tad over ten thousand a year, plus a non-contributory pension and a low cost mortgage. As a package, it must be worth just over twelve grand a year. I get the use of a pool car for business use only, though they tell me that I might be getting a firm's car some time next year. That's about it – not much for the supreme professional that I am, is it?"

"Seems to me you're overpaid, a lazy tyke like you," observed Tony dryly, "but we're not the sort to take advantage of a chap when he's down and out. We're still too small to be able to run a pension scheme and cheap mortgages and all that sort of thing. What I have in mind is a salary of fifteen thousand a year to begin with plus a car – you'll need that to chase around to get all the business that we'll expect from you. After the first year, we should be able to see how your Division is doing and I'd be happy for you to take ten percent of the profit of your division as a permanent bonus – a sort of carrot and a stick. How does that seem to you, Chris?"

With a huge grin, Chris leant over Tony's desk with outstretched hand. "Put it there Tone me old boy. When do I start?"

"As I recall, you have to give one month's notice. It's the first of June today; how does Monday July the first grab you?"

"Great, just great. Now do you want to hear about one or two ideas that I've been mulling over since we spoke on the telephone. I've had time to put a few facts and figures together and it all looks pretty exciting to me."

"Precisely, I told Tim that you would have some thoughts and he's expecting us now. Let's stroll across to his office."

Tim was running over a few memos and notes with the lovely Janet leaning over his shoulder as Tony and Chris strolled in. He looked up and smiled broadly when he saw Chris.

"Watcha me old mate, Chris, How's things with you? Janet, be an angel and rustle up a coffee for us would you?"

"None for me Janet, thanks," said Chris. "I've just had one with Tony and I don't want to spend the morning on the loo. In answer to your question, things are just great Tim. Tony's been telling me that you seem to be doing pretty well yourself since you left the old firm."

"Can't complain," admitted Tim. "Bloody hard work, but well worth the effort. Now, what about you? Has Tony persuaded you that you'd be better off with us than with the Universal? If so, can you make us a profit or would it be an act of charity if we were to take you on?"

"I think we've reached a workable agreement," interjected Tony. "If he's a success, he'll get paid; if he's a liability, he's out on his neck in two minutes flat."

"Seems eminently fair to me. When are you going to start? I'm happy with Tony's suggestion of the first of July. What I would like to talk over with you, though, are my plans as to how we can make this really pay."

"Fire away Chris, the floor is all yours."

"Well," began Chris, "I reckon that I can be pretty well self-supporting. There are enough clients that I am already dealing with who would almost certainly follow me here. At a rough guess, I would expect the annual commissions from my clients to roll in at about twenty thousand a year – that's if at least three quarters of the main ones come across, and I've no reason to suspect that they won't.

"Then there are my own professional connections. There are two firms of Accountants and one firm of Solicitors that give almost all their Life and Pensions business to the Universal, and a few that give us drips and drabs.

"Although they get commission for this, I know that some of them feel slightly guilty that they are not necessarily giving their clients the best possible advice. It's all well and good to say that the Universal is one of the strongest financial Institutions in the country with a pretty good track record for investment performance and all that sort of thing, but that's not always enough.

"By supporting us rather than going straight to the Company, they know that I can do a better job for them. Brokers get a higher commission than Accountants, so if I give them, say half of what we earn, they won't be much worse off financially. As they'll do all the groundwork, I'll be only too pleased to work for half commission.

"I've worked out a few figures based on the support that I already receive from these firms. Here, take a look." He handed Tim and Tony a schedule of figures.

"At a conservative guess, I reckon that we'd bring in another ten thousand a year from professional connections. Furthermore, there are quite a few other firms, including an Estate Agent or two, who could be pretty useful if properly handled."

"All seems pretty good to me," agreed Tim. "What do you think Tony?"

"I'm a hundred percent behind Chris. I don't think that we can go wrong. At this rate, Chris would be contributing some twenty plus thousand to our overhead. And at that rate, we might even turn a profit," he winked at Tim. "But that's not all, is it Chris?"

"Not quite. I think that this would be only the beginning,"

Tim leaned forward. This was the sort of conversation that he relished.

"There are one or two Brokers out there," continued Chris, "who are making an absolute fortune in what is known as 'Direct Selling'.

"They appoint a sales Manager who goes around the Country appointing sub-agents to sell a particular form of Life Assurance. They usually negotiate pretty juicy commission deals and these enable them to pay the sub-agents quite well and still leave the Sales Manager with a very good income. The company is also left with a whacking slice if some of the deals are to be believed.

"What usually happens is that the sub-agent finds a few cronies to sell to and he gives them a few quid from his own commission. Generally speaking, the 'sub sub-agent' is only good enough to flog a few policies to his close friends and family and the turnover in agents is exceptionally high. That doesn't matter if enough mud sticks to the wall and they keep raking in the sub-agents. It's a question of throwing enough mud against the wall and hoping that some sticks".

"This is just pyramid selling isn't it?" interjected Tim. "It's the sort of thing double-glazing firms get into isn't it Tony? Do we really want to be in on this kind of thing?"

"You're right, of course," agreed Tony, "but I think Chris intends to be rather more professional, don't you Chris?"

"Precisely," replied Chris. "I've outlined the way things are working out there at the moment. What I would have in mind is that we set up a separate

Company – just in case it doesn't work and we got tarred with the wrong brush – and employed a completely different class of salesmen to the type you normally find out there.

"You see; the average direct-selling salesman is interested in one thing, and one thing only - his commission.

"That's the average, but there are quite a few out there who have become very professional and who are worried at the way they see their business going. The more cowboys there are, the more likely that someone will clamp down on their type of business and then they'll all be out of a job.

"I have in mind taking on one very professional man and paying him by salary rather than commission. He would have the task of taking on only those Agents that he believes will sell good quality business and business that sticks. Most of these operations give one hundred percent of their business to one Company and one Company alone – the one that pays them the most commission.

"In consequence, much of their business 'goes off' or lapses – sometimes as much as seventy five percent or even more, and the Agent is faced with a clawback of his commission.

"Very frequently, the sub-agent – one of the agent's buddies, has buggered off by now and the Broker has to go cap in hand to try and do a deal. Not a happy state of affairs all round.

"Our great strength would be that we would negotiate generous, but fair, commission terms with a panel of three Insurers – each with its own specialities. In this way, although the agent will earn less commission per policy sold, he should be able to sell far more business since, with a choice of product providers, he is more likely to be able to offer what the client actually wants and needs. Furthermore, the business sold will be good quality business and should stick – hence, fewer or no clawbacks."

"And do you have anyone in mind as Manager of such and operation?" asked Tim.

"As a matter of fact, I do. There's a pretty shitty outfit called Castle Finance."

"I've heard of them," interjected Tim. "Surely you're not suggesting that we get tied up with that bunch of shysters are you?"

"Not at all!" confirmed Chris. "They really are a shower. They're one of those 'Brokers' that place all their business with one Company. I must confess, I don't know how they do it. They seem to have old George Wellbeloved totally under their thumb. Not only do they get four percent commission (two percent is the norm) but they also seem to be able to laugh off a pretty high percentage of their clawbacks.

In my opinion, the Life and Equity is heading South pretty damn fast and, if they go, it will all be down to Castle Finance and the fact that George seems to be licking their arses, if you'll pardon the expression. It's a mystery to me, but there it is.

"No, the person who I have in mind is one of their salesmen. A chap called Jimmy Smith. He's undoubtedly their best salesman and he came to see me a few weeks ago – completely off the record. He seems a very likeable guy and it was he who confided that Castle Finance is making a huge mistake by selling only the Life and Equity. He does his best by only selling their With Profits policies but, quite frankly, they are a load of crap too.

He was asking me whether the Universal might be able to offer Castle a higher commission than we normally pay, in the hope that he might be able to persuade his boss to let him and his team sell at least a proportion of his business from a more reputable Company. When I told him that the absolute maximum that we could go to would be two and a half percent, he realised that he would be banging his head against a brick wall with his boss.

"In my view, if we were to offer Jimmy Smith a basic salary of ten thousand pounds a year, plus a modest profit incentive, he would join us like a shot. I would be very surprised if he, and the team that would follow him, did not make us at least another ten thousand pounds profit a year – and that would only be for starters."

"I think I'm beginning to like this," said Tim. "Once you've got your feet under the table with us Tony, why don't you and Chris put your heads together and get this Jimmy Smith over for a chat. I'm entirely happy to leave the whole thing to you two. Just keep me in the picture, and thanks Chris for coming in and welcome to Harrisons. I'm sure we're not going to regret this change in your career."

With that, Tony and Chris withdrew to finalise the formalities of Chris's new contract.

....

Six months later, it was Chris Abbott's chance to sit in the boss's chair.

He had called Jimmy Smith 'out of the blue'.

"Jimmy," Chris began, "you will remember the conversation we had about a year ago when you came to see me at the Universal to see if we could become one of Castle's providers?"

"Sure do Mr Abbott. I wish you had said 'yes' at the time because I don't like the way things are going here. All our eggs in one basket and, on the grapevine, I hear that the old L & E has a bucket full of problems. God knows where we go if they go down the tubes. Anyway, I was told that you had left the Universal. What are you doing nowadays?"

"Absolutely right Jimmy," confirmed Tony. "I left the Universal six months ago to set up a Personal Financial Services division here at Harrisons. Glad to say that it is going like a train. Definitely made the right decision this time. That's the reason for the call Jimmy. How about you and I having another chat sometime?"

Not only was Jimmy very enthusiastic about such an invitation, but five weeks later, he had left Castle Finance, and joined Harrisons – along with six of his best salesmen. He was the new chief executive of Direct Investments Ltd.

Joe Hendry went ballistic on hearing the news. Tom Cummings was only slightly more reserved but the damage had been done. War had been declared between Harrisons and themselves and he would patiently await his time. Retribution would, he assured Joe, be very sweet.

Chapter Twenty-Three

It was now Nineteen Seventy Six and it was just over six years now since Tim had opened the doors of Harrison Insurance Services. He was looking forward to this afternoon's regular monthly Board Meeting.

Graham Wiltshier and Chris Johnson were now full Directors, Roy Brown still came in now and then as a Non-Executive Director and Tim was particularly pleased that Bill Warrington had agreed to come on the Board as their non-executive Chairman.

As Tim was finishing his sandwich and running through his board papers, Janet appeared at the door to announce that Bill and Roy had arrived and were waiting in the Board Room (a rather grand title since, in point of fact, it was simply a meeting room with a few extra chairs for occasions such as this).

His heart still gave an involuntary lurch when Janet stood silhouetted in the doorway. Hers was a figure to die for with a slender waist, long graceful legs and a perfect bust. An elfin-like face crowned by shoulder length blonde hair completed the picture – a work of art in Tim's view. Why she had never married was a mystery, although Tim was aware, that she had had a string of relationships.

Tim was sure that, were it not for Mary, he would have made a pass at her long before now. Janet would always have this effect on him he knew it. It worried him sometimes. Enough of this, he told himself and, as so often in the past, forced himself to pull himself together.

"Right, Janet," he said. "Lead me to them. Have you told Graham and Chris that we're ready?"

"Sure have boss, they're all there. Give 'em hell."

As soon as they had exchanged their usual pleasantries, Bill called the meeting to order and, in his customary peremptory manner, announced, "Apologies for absence – none, minutes of last meeting – taken as read, matters arising – none, Chief Executive's report – over to you Tim."

"Thank you Mr Chairman. I'll make this as brief as possible as I have one very important matter I want to bring up. It has only just arisen, so it will not be on your Board Papers.

"We have just completed, as you know, our first six years' trading. Although I do not, of course, have the audited accounts as yet, I do have the management figures and it looks as if we will have made a profit before tax for the last twelve months of a little over fifty thousand pounds – well above the budget that we had set ourselves for our current three-year plan. Counting the executive directors here present, we employ twenty one staff and arrangements are well in hand for our move to Albion House in the High Street within the next six weeks.

"Our Life and Pensions Division, under Chris, has been remarkably successful.

"You will recall that, about a ago, Chris appointed Tony Abbott from my old Company, sorry (smiling at Graham and Roy) our old Company, to build up a Personal Financial Planning operation. I'm delighted to say that this has been a run-away success. Between Chris, Tony and their staff, we have generated a further fifteen thousand pounds profit to our bottom line.

"Our subsidiary Company, 'Direct Investments Ltd', very ably headed up by James Smith, now employs twelve self-employed agents and is currently grossing commissions in excess of two hundred thousand pounds a year and making a contribution to profits of a further twenty five thousand pounds a year. Of course, this is a rather volatile market and I think it only fair to say that we cannot anticipate this rate of growth for the indefinite future. Nevertheless, 'make hay whilst the sun shines,' I say."

This was greeted with "hear hears".

"I don't know why the Financial Services Division puts up with passengers like our General Business friends. They have twice as many staff and only make half the profit we do. We'd be far better off without them," observed Chris controversially.

"Bollocks," replied Tim graciously. "You know you wouldn't have any clients at all if you didn't feed off the General Account. However, despite your uncharitable comment, congratulations and many thanks."

"P'raps you'd minute that an' pass on the Board's thanks to your team, Chris. Well done mate," added Bill Warrington.

"Continuing," continued Tim, "apart from that terrible incident with the Peter Sykes debacle, we have made no claims under our Professional Indemnity Insurance and none are anticipated.

"We have lost only one major Client in the last year – Castle Windows – and that was through no fault of our own; they simply went into receivership. I have to report that I am disappointed that our credit control was a little lax and, at one time, it did look as if we would have a substantial bad debt."

"Why didn't you?" asked Bill. I 'eard that they'd gone darn the tubes for about a 'undred grand."

"We can thank Tim for that," said Graham. "Castle did, in fact, owe us about six month's premium – about ten thousand pounds. The Bank pulled the rug, as is their wont, and there was nothing left for the trade creditors. Under normal circumstances we'd have had to write the lot off, but old silver tongue here, (pointing to Tim) sweet-talked the Insurers into writing off all the arrears themselves.

"He persuaded them to back-date the cancellation to the last renewal date, leaving us with a nil balance. We have off course, lost a fairly valuable client – about three grand a year commission – but, c'est la vie, there are worse things at sea."

"Well done Tim," added Bill. "Anyfink else?"

"Yes. We have taken on three clients in the last year where the brokerage has exceeded five thousand pounds and we are in discussions with another three similar-sized firms. We are, as I believe you all know, quoting for the Sunbury International plc account. We are facing intense competition, but if we are successful, it will move us into another league."

"What's the total commission for Sunbury?" cut in Roy Brown.

"The brokerage would be enormous – over two hundred thousand pounds, but for an account like this, we will have to rebate all of our commission and quote a fee. Graham and I reckon that we should quote about one hundred thousand a year for it."

There then followed a detailed discussion as to the pros and cons of fees versus commission, how many additional staff they would have to take on if they were successful in obtaining the account and what other services they would have to tack on. In the light of this, they revisited the management figures and discussed a realistic budget for the next twelve months.

Eventually, Bill drew a halt to the general discussions by announcing, "Well, Tim, you've got the Board's full support for doing whatever it takes to get Sunbury on board. We'll look forward to seein' the revised budget when you know whether you've been successful or not. Good luck, now wot's this special item you wanted to raise?"

"You, especially you Bill, will recall that, when I started Harrisons, I had a bit of a run in with Colin Cooper of Cooper and Smythe. Whereas I was definitely a pain in their arse – we've taken quite a few of their better clients – they still remain a force to be reckoned with. Probably due to our initial friction, they always seem to be quoting against us whenever they can. When they feel that they are losing the battle, they quote some bloody stupid premium just to make life difficult for us."

"Wot does that mean?" interjected Bill. "If them bastards can quote a lower premium, then don't that mean that you 'aven't done your job properly. I'd be pretty pissed off if I found that you was chargin' me more than the other bloke."

"It's not quite as simple as that Bill," replied Tim. "For a start, the cheapest is not always the best. The other side might be using a Company that is a bit dodgy or, more likely, one that is not giving quite the same cover as we're giving; it's like comparing apples with pears. Even then, it's sometimes possible to give a 'desk quotation'."

"Wot the 'ells a 'desk quotation'?" fired back Bill. "Are you selling the bleedin' furniture now?"

"No Bill. If, for example, I knew that you had been quoted fifty thousand pounds for your insurances, I could say that I would do it for, say, forty five thousand, knowing that I would probably not have to prove it. You would come back to me and say that Coopers can do the same thing for forty five thousand and what the hell am I playing at? I would then have to run around the market trying to get favours out of the Insurers in an effort to chip a bit off here and a bit off there. I would know that whatever favours I might get this year on that basis, will almost certainly be clawed back next year – so you would probably be no better off in the long run.

"If, on the other hand, you put Coopers to the test and got them to put up a written quotation, they would probably try to fiddle things to give the impression that they had saved you five grand.

"They can do this in a number of ways. They can say that your turnover and estimates of your wages are lower than expected so you would be charged a lower premium at the beginning. By the time the real figures are declared a year later, and the additional premium is due, it's too late. They can do the same thing with Stock and Motor Fleet declarations or they can simply ask an Insurance Company Underwriting clerk to 'make a mistake'. In other words, to simply charge the wrong premium, a lower premium, in return for a favour."

"What do you mean, 'a favour'?" asked Bill.

"Well, I have known Colin Cooper to take an Underwriter and his wife out for a night on the town or to a first division football match, depending on the Underwriter's fancy. Nothing too excessive or too 'close to the wind' but, in my view, it's a trifle unethical. In return, he would expect the Underwriter to reduce his original quotation – he would exert moral (or, more accurately immoral, pressure on the Underwriter).

"Anyway, all that is by the by. Colin phoned me this morning to say that he is getting too old for all this sort of thing and is thinking of retiring. He was wondering whether we would be prepared to buy his business."

"In view of wot you've just told us, I wouldn't touch 'em with a barge pole," observed Bill.

"Not so fast," rejoined Roy. "Despite these little foibles, Coopers is essentially a sound business. Colin's father started it over forty years ago and although, during Colin's stewardship it has declined somewhat, I should think that they still make a decent profit and have still retained some pretty useful clients. At the right price, it could make a lot of sense. The businesses are complementary and I would have thought that their client bank could prove fertile ground for you, Chris."

"Without a doubt," agreed Chris. "When I was with the Universal, we did quite a lot of business with Coopers and I would love to be able to get some of their clients over to us, those that we have not taken already," he laughed. "Did Colin give any idea as to what sort of price he'd be looking for Tim?"

"Not exactly," responded Tim, "but he did say that the most important thing for him would be his future income. I would have thought that it would be possible to work out some sort of package where we would have to pay relatively little up front, but guarantee him an income for a number of years – either deferred payment or a consultancy agreement or a combination of the two. What do you think, Roy, you've seen this sort of deal done?"

"Yes, I have, several times," confirmed Roy. "I think that the going price for a good Insurance Brokerage nowadays is about two times gross income. However, I've never liked that yardstick. I much prefer to value the business on a multiple of its profits – say somewhere between seven and ten times it's pre-tax profits.

"Of course, much depends on whether the firm is growing or contracting, the quality of its clients and the value of its assets, if it has any. Clearly, a Company owning its own building would be worth more than one with a short-term lease. There are so many aspects and we would need to see at least the last three years accounts together with the current year's management accounts.

"I suggest that Tim and I have a meeting with Colin Cooper and get some idea of what his business is worth. Once we've done that, we can set up another Board Meeting to see where we go from there, but in principle, I think that we should go for it. I'll write you out a 'shopping list' of all the things we will need to see and perhaps you, Tim, could set up a meeting with Colin. I can be free almost any time."

"Is that agreed gen'lemen?" enquired Bill. There being nods of approval around the table, Bill announced, "alright gen'lemen. That's agreed. There bein' no further business, I declare the meetin' closed. Thanks all for comin'."

Tim and Roy went into Tim's office and continued work on what they would require from Colin Cooper and to plan their strategy for the negotiations ahead. The whole thing was giving Tim a "buzz" he had not experienced since he started his Company.

He could not stop himself from reflecting that, in his early days with the Universal, he had held Colin Cooper and his firm in some kind of awe. They were responsible for a large part of the business he had to handle and he had to play his cards pretty carefully to ensure that the Universal got their fair share of the Cooper and Smythe cake. He had never enjoyed being subservient but it was what he had been paid for.

And now, only six years later, he was planning to take the firm over. Exciting times, indeed.

Chapter Twenty-Four

It was June the first nine hundred and seventy six. Joe Hendry was lounging back in his plush new executive chair reviewing the happenings of the last five or six years.

On balance, he had cause for satisfaction but, he had to admit, he had made one or two mistakes on the way. Perhaps his biggest mistake was to marry that stupid bitch Samantha.

Until then, he had been happy with his bachelor existence. Whenever he had felt the need for a little extra-curricular excitement, he had popped into Shirley's massage parlour.

Of course, when the money had started rolling in, he had graduated to The Wilton Club in Baker Street. At a hundred quid a time for the services they offered it was not cheap, but God, it was worth it. Joe reckoned to visit the Club at least once or twice a month and Madame Trudeau (real name, Irene Brown, he had discovered by chance) always found him the type of girl he wanted. His current preference was a lovely young Thai girl (or two) and Madame seemed to have an endless supply of such young ladies fitting the description and only too pleased and willing to oblige. Apart from the one hundred to Madame Trudeau, he usually stuffed a twenty pound note in the girl's pocket on the way out. Worth every penny on his return visit he had learned.

Why on earth had he got himself tied up with Samantha? Agreed, she was pretty in a dumb blonde sort of way, and she was certainly eager to please – 'was' being the operative word.

After two years of marriage, her moods, her insistence of smoking in bed, her intelligence level (only marginally, he concluded, above that of a plant) and her complete inability to understand any of the current affairs of the day, was driving him insane.

Joe had taken to re-visiting his Club and was already a regular every Wednesday afternoon, and Saturdays if he could get away with it.

His second regret, and how it rankled, was to lose his best salesman Jimmy Smith, to those bastards 'Direct Investments'. He had always felt that Jimmy had made too much of wanting to place all of their business with the Life and Equity but, with the benefit of hindsight, he had to agree that Jimmy had had a point.

Still, although they lost Jimmy and one or two of his agents, he had been able to blame it all on George Wellbeloved and, with him well under their thumb by now, a little 'hike' in their commission soon narrowed the gap satisfactorily enough.

His third great regret had been to allow that idle sod Tom Cummings too large a share of his cake.

Tom had suggested that he should invest fifty thousand pounds cash in the business and use money to embark on a rapid and spectacular expansion programme.

Thinking back, it seemed at the time to have been a great idea to have accepted the fifty thousand pound cheque from Tom for a fifty-one percent stake in his business. After all, at that time, his business was pretty insignificant and it took a considerable leap of faith to believe that it could have prospered as it had done.

True, the money had allowed them to open offices in twenty of the largest cities in the UK. Joe had worked all hours God made in building up the operation. He would place adverts in the local press of each target town, promising riches beyond the dreams of avarice to the 'right' person who wished to make a career in selling financial services.

He would hire a room in a local hotel for a couple of days and hold a seminar for his eager applicants the following morning. He would explain, in glowing terms, the opportunities available in this 'dynamic industry'. He would then arrange appointments over the next twenty four hours to interview each attendee and sign up those that had any hope at all of being able to bring in a punter or two.

They were then offered a place on the 'Company's Training Course' – three days with the L & E at their head office and, naturally, all at the L & E's expense. If they showed any promise, they were enrolled as 'Appointed Representatives' of Castle Finance and let loose to sell the Company's high commission products.

At the very least, Joe found, they could be relied upon to bring in their father, their brother or one or two close friends as clients. If they fell by the wayside after that, who cared? There were plenty more where they came from and the L & E was picking up virtually all the costs.

By now, the firm employed twenty Branch Managers around the country who each controlled a sales force of up to thirty agents – all of them self-employed and remunerated solely on commission. If they failed to produce, they went short – not Joe.

Between them, they now grossed commissions from the Life and Equity of over six hundred and fifty thousand pounds a year. Joe was confident that they would be hitting the million pounds a year mark by the end of the current year.

Joe was raking in almost one hundred thousand pounds a year for himself and now considered that he could take his place as one of the Industry's 'high fliers'. After all his efforts, it stuck in his craw that that greedy bastard Tom Cummings was screwing him for fifty grand a year for doing sweet bugger-all – and owned more than half his Company.

Joe would have to deal with this situation before too long and before Tom got the impression that the Company had become his personal money-box.

On the plus side, Joe had been pleasantly surprised to find how Fred Barker had turned out. Ever since Fred had allowed Jimmy to lead him into more profitable sales methods, he seemed to have become a reformed character and had taken a far more responsible attitude towards the business. On Jimmy's departure, Joe had gritted his teeth and decided to appoint Fred as Group Sales Manager on a fairly hefty salary plus a commission deal on the entire sales force's turnover. His decision had paid off handsomely.

All in all, things were looking pretty good and he was again giving serious thought to trading in his Jag for a second hand Roller. He felt that such a car was more appropriate to his newly acquired status of an 'Icon' in the Financial Services Industry.

He was quietly congratulating himself on his success, when the phone rang. It was George Wellbeloved. Joe had noticed that, since they had developed their 'arrangement', things had not gone too badly for George either. With Castle Finance now contributing almost a third of the Life and Equity's new business income, George had become the Company's blue-eyed boy, had risen to become a main Board Director and had traded in his Ford Cortina for a very smart new Granada Ghia.

He wondered what George could be calling him for now. Their day-to-day contact had been limited of late, due partly to the embarrassment George always felt when they met and partly due to the fact that most contact between the two companies now was between the L & E staff and Fred or, occasionally, their respective Finance Directors.

"Hello George, what can I do for you old friend?" began Joe cordially.

"Bad news, Joe, I'm afraid. In fact appalling news," answered George in and uncharacteristically dead pan voice. Joe's pulse rate rose perceptibly as he sensed the fear in George's voice. "We've just had the Department of Trade and Industry in and they're closing us down."

"They're what!" exploded Joe. "What the fucking hell are you talking about? They can't just close you down!"

"I'm afraid they can, and they have. We've failed the regulatory Solvency Tests. Our free asset ratio is way below the market norm, and as from this minute, we are unable to take on any new business. They're carrying out further investigations to see what effect this will have on our existing Policyholders...."

"Fuck the policyholders!" shouted Joe. "What about us? I've got a business to run here and you think you can just call me up and tell me there's nothing you can do. Let me remind you sunshine, we have some happy snaps that your missus would just love to see. If you don't get us out of this fucking mess, and quick, she's going to get the picture show of her life – 'x' certificated at that!"

"Joe, we've known each other a long time and I've always done my best for you. You know that. In fact, one of the main reasons for us going down the Swanee is that you are our biggest producer by far. Because of the deal we have and the favours we've extended, we don't make a penny's profit on any of it. I've tried to explain this to you a dozen times, but........."

"Spare me the hearts and bleeding flowers George. Just tell me the fuck how we're going to get out of this."

"I understand only too well the predicament you're in Joe, but there's nothing that I can do. This Company is insolvent and that's that. The only thing that I can suggest, is that you find yourself another Insurance Company that will take over all the business that you would have been placing with us........."

"And just where the fuck do I start looking? Christ, I've been naïve to place all my trust in you. You've had every red cent of the business that my blokes can write and this is how you pay me off! Who's going to take on our account and pay us the same rate of commission? You tell me that."

"I very much doubt whether any company will give you the same commission deal – they will have seen what's happened to us. I can, however, suggest Apex Life; they're a South African outfit just trying to get a toehold in the UK and they might be worth a try. They are desperate to get big quickly and the volume that you put through could be just what they're looking for. Their sales Director, I met him at a BIBA Meeting a few months ago, is Kevin Schmitt. Just a second, I've got his card somewhere." After a slight pause, "Ah, here we are. Kevin B Schmitt, Marketing Director, 0171 450 4500. Give him a call and the best of luck. I wish that there was more that I could do. As you can imagine, I've got my own problems sorting out where we go from here. The DTI are bastards when they get their hooks into anything like this."

"George, I don't give a fuck about your problems and I've a good mind to brighten your fucking day still further by sending a nice little present to Mrs Wellbeloved. Goodbye!"

As he slammed down the receiver, Joe's first thought was to call that 'idle sod' Tom Cummings.

"Tom," he started without preamble. "We've got a problem, a fucking monster of a problem and we're in deep shit." Joe proceeded to relate the details of his conversation with George.

"You phone that Schmitt guy now," fired back Tom, "and you make a fucking appointment to see him first thing tomorrow. I'm coming with you. And further, get your new finance, Director, what's his name?"

"Brian, Brian Enderby, a bloody good chap he is too."

"He had bloody better be. You tell him to knock up a set of management figures for the current year. Tell him to include all the commissions owing to us and to ignore completely any provision for clawbacks. That was OK when we were trying to defer tax, but now we're fighting for our lives, we need figures that are going to make us look not good, but bloody fantastic.

"Tell him also to write a budget for next year assuming that we open four more offices and that our commissions reach one point two million. As far as start-up expenses are concerned for each office, tell him to capitalise them and write them off over ten years. I want to see a paper profit of at least a quarter of a million for next year and you can help by dropping your salary to the same as mine. At that level you're probably still overpaid because it's you who has got us into this bloody mess. I want all of that by seven-thirty tomorrow morning and I want to see you and Brian in the Office then with all the answers. We'll get the early train to town, Brian should come too, and we'll see Schmitt as soon as he gets to his Office. Now is that clear?"

"Sure Tom, I'll get down to it."

"Call me back to confirm."

"Will do. Goodbye for now," Joe concluded – but the line had gone dead.

Joe called Brian in and relayed the contents of his conversations with George Wellbeloved and Tom. "What do you think?" he asked.

"I appreciate its not much help my reminding you that I always said we were always seriously exposed to have all our eggs in one basket. But there it is. I know nothing about Apex Life, but if what George says is true, it would make sense for them to want to 'buy' as much business as they possibly can in the early years.

"If we can promise them upwards of a million pounds of commission business a year, they're bound to be interested. In the early years, a Life

Assurance Company can offset its start-up costs against profits for many years to come. If they're part of an International conglomerate, they've probably given this man Schmitt an almost open cheque book to buy what he can.

"As to the figures, I'll have to work late tonight, but I can get together what Tom's asking for by first thing tomorrow. One thing to bear in mind though, and that is, all of our forecasts are based on us receiving four percent commission. I doubt if we'll get much more than two percent from anyone else. Having said that though, Apex is not going to be too bothered about our profits. Just as long as they can see that we can remain solvent, they're only going to be interested in how much premium we can sell for them. I think that I should be able to come up with a pretty interesting set of figure."

"You get on with it Brian. I'm going to call Mr Schmitt."

....

"Ah, Mr Schmitt," Joe began as soon as he was put through. "My name's Joseph Hendry. I'm the Chairman of Castle Financial Services. Perhaps you've heard of us."

"Can't say I have, Mr Hendry," came the courteous, clipped Afrikaans accent. "But what can I do for you sir?"

"I understand that you've only recently opened your UK office and that you're looking to appoint Brokers capable of producing a considerable flow of new and good quality business. If that's so, I feel that I could be of assistance."

"That's precisely the case Mr Hendry. Please go on."

"Well my Company has been established some five or six years now and we employ five or six hundred agents. We produce getting on for a million pounds of business a year and, until today, all of that was placed with a reputable British Insurance Company – the Life and Equity."

"Ya. I see where you're coming from Mr Hendry. I heard the news only an hour ago. It seems that their decline could be good news for the rest of us. It's a tough world out there. I'd like to meet you, Mr Hendry. When would you like to call in?"

"As you can imagine, we've got to act quickly and there are, of course, one or two other Insurance Companies that we are going to be talking to," lied Joe. "How about first thing tomorrow morning?"

"Nine thirty would be just fine. Can you fax me anything about yourselves before we meet, just so that I can get the picture?"

"I could, but I've got my Finance Director putting a few facts together and I think it would be best if we bring all the information with us tomorrow. I would like him to join us and I would also like to bring my fellow Director, Tom Cummings, with me."

"That's fine, Joe. I'll have my finance boys here too. If we're going to have to act fast, the more brain-power the better. By the way, I've met George what's his name, from the Life and Equity. Do you mind if I give him a call to get a little informal background?"

Joe thought for a moment. In view of the tone of their last conversation, would George give a glowing report of their relationship or would he insert the proverbial spanner in the works? The irregularity of their 'arrangement' would win them no brownie points at all with Kevin Schmitt. After a moment's pause, 'no' thought Joe. He's got too much to lose in upsetting me, he'll play it straight, he decided.

"Not at all," he answered. "George is a good chap. We think the world of him and feel very badly that he's found himself in this position. I am sure he can tell you everything you want to know about us. Give him my best wishes, and our commiserations of course, when you call. We'll see you tomorrow at nine thirty."

Joe put the phone down. He was not entirely happy, something that he could not put his finger on was troubling him, but he felt slightly less worried that he did an hour ago.

The following morning, Joe was having a very early breakfast, if the toast and coffee that Samantha had produced could be described as 'breakfast'.

Samantha, her hair in curlers with a smouldering cigarette hanging out of the corner of her mouth, was drinking her coffee watching early morning television.

Why she had the Breakfast Show on, he could never fathom since she appeared to take in absolutely nothing she watched (unless there had been a murder in one of her Soaps). As far as Joe was concerned, the fat cow that she had become seemed to spend all day gawping brainlessly at television.

"Here, listen to this Joe," she called. "There's something about your firm on the telly."

Startled, Joe rushed across the room and turned the volume full up in time to hear the Newsreader announcing,

"..........a tragic incident presumed to have been caused by the stress of the previous day's news. Mr George Wellbeloved, aged fifty nine, the Life and Equity's Marketing Director, was found dead on the pavement outside his Company's Head Office yesterday evening at seven thirty. It appears that he had jumped from the window of his fifth floor office and had died immediately. Police say that Mr Wellbeloved's secretary witnessed the tragedy and that there are no suspicious circumstances.

News was only received noon yesterday that the Department of Trade and Industry had closed the ten year old Company down, following a full investigation into its financial affairs, prompted by fears of the Company's inability to meet the solvency requirements demanded in the Life Assurance Industry.

Colleagues inform us that Mr Wellbeloved was a popular and well-respected member of the Staff and that he will be very greatly missed. There will be a full report, including comment as to how this will affect Policyholders, in our City news at ten past eight this morning, when we hope to have a statement from the Company's Chairman."

"That's sad isn't it Joe?" whined Samantha. "He was a bit of a toff but I quite liked the old chap."

"He was a total prat and I can't say that I'm sad the tosser has gone," was Joe's ungracious reply. Joe, quite unashamedly, felt a sense of relief at the news. With a DTI investigation, there was no telling what the old fool would have blurted out. The little arrangement that they had 'agreed' with George might have looked too much like blackmail had George Wellbeloved been around to blab to the Authorities. But the arrangement had died along with its principle reluctant participant. It was one more problem out of the way, as far as Joe was concerned, and he had enough problems to deal with at this particular moment.

....

At seven thirty sharp, Joe, Tom and Brian Enderby were huddled around the table in Joe's office, totally engrossed in the figures that Brian was elaborating upon.

"So there you have it," concluded Brian. "If we put the best possible gloss on our current year's trading, we could show a pre-tax profit of just over one hundred thousand pounds. Personally, I think that forty thousand will be nearer the mark, but I've done what you asked Tom.

"Looking to next year, I've forecast a profit before tax, based on your estimate of gross commissions of one point two million, of close on four hundred thousand pounds. Again, particularly taking into account the fact that we will be on, at best, two thirds of the commission rate we currently enjoy, half of that figure would be nearer the mark in practice."

"Just you answer the questions and let me do the talking when we're with Schmitt," snapped Tom. "Remember that it's what he believes now that's important, not what might happen in the future. The future can look after itself. Now, what is the likely premium income that we could give the Apex if these figures pan out? He's going to be far more interested in the premium they will get from us than the profit that we might make. You can take that from me."

"Hear bloody hear," agreed Joe, morosely.

"Again, it all depends on what rate of commission you agree. At the very best, we could be looking at a premium income next year in excess of two million pounds, but I really wouldn't bank on it."

"I'm not asking you to bank on anything. All I want is a good story to tell. The one that you're outlining is good enough for me," replied George. "I've got my driver to take us up to town. No point in risking bloody British Rail on something as important as this meeting. Let's go."

At 9.20 promptly, their driver dropped them outside the Apex head office in the City– a modern six-storey block with an imposing communal entrance hall. The security officer directed them to the lift for the sixth floor.

"Gentlemen, so very pleased to meet you," greeted Kevin Schmitt with outstretched hand as the receptionist ushered Joe, Tom and Brian into Apex Life's sumptuous boardroom. Coffee anyone?"

Kevin Schmitt was a short, stocky, archetypal Afrikaner with dark hair, slicked back from his receding hairline and a black, neatly trimmed moustache. He was immaculately dressed in a dark grey, hand-made suit, with matching blue silk tie and pocket-handkerchief. He looked the type of man he was – an efficient 'no-nonsense' modern businessman.

"Coffee for all please, Jane," he smiled to his receptionist in response to nods from his guests. Now let me introduce Bob Jennings our Group Finance Director and Mark Johnson, our head of Strategic Operations. Mark is, like me, on our Main Board and he takes a keen interest in group acquisitions and the like. Gentlemen, please be seated."

As they all shook hands, Tom said, "it's good of you to see us so soon Kevin. As you know, we have to move quickly, very quickly. We had two very nasty shocks yesterday. Firstly, the quite unexpected news that Life and Equity was about to wind up. You can take it from me, that there's no way a Company of our standing would do business with any firm that gave us the slightest cause for concern as to its financial strength. Our reputation is too important to us to take that sort of risk. Their demise came as a complete bolt from the blue. How they kept their financial position so well hidden from us is a complete mystery, but Brian here is looking in to that right now.

"Secondly, the tragic death of George Wellbeloved. He was a good friend of ours, one for whom we all had the deepest respect. He was a true professional and a great loss to our wonderful industry."

"I entirely agree," interjected Joe. "We had great faith in George and I have to say that we had a very soft spot for the guy. Yesterday was a sad day for us, very sad indeed."

"I must say that I entirely agree," added Schmitt. "It is seems macabre that, after I spoke to you yesterday Joe, I had quite a long chat with him. He gave me a great deal of information about your Company and your working relationship."

Joe paled. Had the stupid bastard told Schmitt about their 'deal'? If so, they might as well go home now. "That's good," he forced himself to say. "That should save a lot of time on your side. I take it he gave us a glowing report."

"He certainly told me how your account with them had grown over the years," replied Kevin enigmatically. "He had the Official Receiver with him at the time so could only give me the bare facts. Funny thing is, he said that he had one or two things he would like to add about 'personal relationships' and that he would phone me back later in the day, as soon as he became free."

"And did he?" queried Joe tremulously.

"Afraid not," replied Schmitt, to a greatly relieved audience. "He clearly had other matters on his mind, poor chap. It seems he jumped before he communicated with us or anybody else, for that matter. Anyway, to business. What have you got for us?"

Tom, to Joe's relief, took the lead.

"Let me say, first of all, that the company is enjoying a period of unprecedented growth. Our profits should hit the one hundred thousand mark this year and we confidently expect to quadruple this figure next year. Let me show you the figures gentlemen. Brian, perhaps you will kindly pass round copies of this year's management accounts and next year's forecasts."

Whilst the papers were being distributed, Tom added, "These figures, let me assure you, have been produced on the most conservative of assumptions. Brian is, by nature, an optimist, but we have had to restrain him. There is no way that we would want to mislead you gentlemen." Brian, for his part, wondered momentarily whether he was at the right meeting.

Whilst the three Apex men studied the figures intently, Tom and Joe lent back in their chairs and enjoyed their coffee. Joe whispered to Tom, sotto voce but loud enough for the others to hear "Shame that George did not get back to Kevin. He would have had nothing but good to say." Tom smiled affirmatively. Brian, for his part, looked the least comfortable of the three.

"A very impressive set of figures gentlemen," announced Schmitt eventually. "Bob, are there any questions that you would like to put to Brian?"

"Quite a few, actually. Perhaps it would make sense for Brian and I to pop off into my Office so that I can go through the nitty gritty with him whilst you can all get down to the wider issues."

"That's fine by me," agreed Tom hastily, not overly confident that Brian could lie as smoothly as he could himself. "But before you leave, could you just give Joe and me a flavour of the sort of information that you will be looking for."

"Fine," said Jennings. "What I need to know is, how the figures for this year compare with the equivalent periods over the last three years so that I can judge the trends and understand the reasons for dramatic changes, if any.

"I would also like a detailed analysis of just how the income and expenses have been calculated for next year and what provisions you are making for likely reductions in commission rates, clawback and the effects of the Life and Equity's demise. That sort of thing. All pretty boring for you gentlemen, but bread and butter for the likes of Brian and me."

"OK," agreed Tom, feeling less than happy about this turn of events. "Just remember Brian, give Bob every scrap of information he needs and bear in mind that these figures are the most conservative forecast we could put forward. Don't forget that we are planning to open a further ten offices next year, for which the Bank have agreed the finance."

This was news to Brian, but he nodded dutifully as he and Bob Jennings left the room.

"More coffee gentlemen," asked Schmitt as he walked around the table with the coffee pot, topping up their cups. "Which other Companies are you proposing to approach may I ask?"

"I would rather not say at this stage, if you don't mind Kevin. I can say, however, that you are our first choice and, although we will see what the others have to say, we would prefer to 'get into bed' with the Apex."

"Why do you say that?" asked Schmitt, surprisingly sharply.

Although Tom was slightly wrong-footed by his brusqueness, he was adept at thinking on his feet. "Two reasons really. Number one, your Group has enormous financial strength – so important to us and to our clients, especially after the current debacle. Number two; you wish to expand rapidly in the UK – so do we. In short, this has the makings of a perfect marriage."

"There is a third reason too" cut in Joe. "George recommended you and that's good enough for us".

"I'm very pleased to hear that. Now, if we were to grant you an Agency," Mark Johnson was contributing to the discussions for the first time, what percentage of your business would come to the Apex and what would be your estimate of the first and second year's premium income?" Turning to Joe, "perhaps you could help me Joe." Tom, in Jenning's mind, was doing too much of the talking and yet, according to his notes, he was only a non-executive Director.

Joe fielded the question. "We prefer to keep things simple. We are only looking for one agency and we would intend to give you one hundred percent of our business. That way, we would expect to negotiate the maximum rate of commission – with which to remunerate our highly skilled sales force," he quickly added.

"That's good news for us," replied Jennings, "but how can you be sure that you are offering the best possible deal to your clients if you give us all of your business. I'm sure that Kevin here would say that Apex are the best in every field, but we know that's not true, don't we?"

'Who the fuck cares about the best deal for the clients?' was the first response that came to Joe's mind. What he said, however, was, "That is a concern, of course. But our feeling is that it is hard enough to sell Life

Assurance in any event, and provided that we are offering good quality products from a reliable source, our clients will be better off with a package from us as opposed to having no cover at all – which would be the case if our salesmen were not doing their job."

"I can sympathise with that," agreed Kevin. It was not in Kevin's nature to turn away business if it was being offered to him 'on a plate'.

Schmitt then proceeded to bore Tom and Joe with a long prepared synopsis of what the Apex Group stood for, their history, their parenthood, their plans for the future and their business philosophy. They both listened politely, endeavouring to hide the 'who the fuck cares?' expressions from their faces.

"Now are there any questions about our Company that you would like to put to us?" concluded Schmitt.

"You could tell us a little about your commission structure," suggested Joe, wondering when they would get down to the really important matters.

"That's easy, gentlemen. We pay the standard two per cent on the Sum Assured. That does mean, of course, that your salesmen will earn rather more if they sell Non Profits Policies rather than With Profits policies, but I'm sure you know that."

"Two percent!" echoed Tom. "Life and Equity pay us four percent. Don't forget that we will be promising you over one million pounds of premium each and every year. You'll have to do better than that, a whole lot better."

"As I say, that is our standard rate of commission, and although we cannot change that, I should be able to negotiate an over-rider for you so that if, for example, you exceed a target of five hundred thousand pounds we will pay you an extra percentage which will increase proportionately. I'm bound to say though, that even with a million pounds, we could never exceed an effective rate of three percent. We would not want to go the same way as the Life and Equity. I'm sure you wouldn't want us to do that either."

This thought had not even crossed their minds, nor, had it done so, would it have troubled them for a moment. But they both nodded their heads vigorously in agreement.

At that point, Brian and Bob Jennings re-entered the room. Schmitt looked up and declared, "Ah, the financial geniuses have returned. How do things look Bob?"

"Not too bad," replied Jennings. "Brian is going to go away and get me a few more figures but, all in all, I think we could have the makings of a deal here."

"Excellent, excellent. Can you get the figures to Bob this afternoon, Brian?"

"I think so, Kevin. I'll go straight back to the Office now and I'll fax them to Brian before close of play tonight."

"Good. Well I presume you gentlemen have got appointments to keep with our opposition so we won't take up any more of your valuable time. When we have Brian's figures, the three of us will put our heads together and see what we can come up with. It's Tuesday today; why don't I drive down to Ashbridge on Thursday morning, take a look at your Offices and put a proposition to you?"

"That's fine by us, Kevin," affirmed Tom. "We shall look forward to seeing you then. Perhaps we could have a spot of lunch afterwards?"

"Excellent gentlemen, I shall look forward to that. Let me see you out."

In the car on the way back to Ashbridge (there being no other appointments for them to attend) Tom turned to Brian.

"What the bloody hell does that bloke Jennings want? How much more information can he need? Haven't we given them enough to be getting on with, for Christ sakes?"

"Well, not surprisingly Tom," replied Brian, "he wants to see my working papers to show how I arrived at my figures. I can't give him those, of course. On the other hand, with a bit of creative accounting, I should be able to put together another set of 'working papers' that will look reasonably convincing. As long as I'm not expected to stand by the figures if they should all go pear-shaped in the next twelve months, I'm happy with that. I'm an accountant, not a magician."

"Don't you worry about that Brian. Let me and Joe here, worry about next year. Your job is to convince the bastards now." If Tom had to look for a scapegoat in twelve month's time, it wouldn't be his problem if the axe fell on Brian Enderby.

"How do you think the meeting went Joe?" asked Tom.

"On the face of it, I thought it went pretty well. You can't be sure though. Kevin is no-one's fool and I shouldn't think that Mark Johnson would give anything away. We've got nowhere else to go and we'll just have to keep our fingers crossed till Thursday. In the meantime, I've got to think what I'm going to tell our sales force. They'll all have heard the news by now and must be worrying what the bloody hell we're doing about it."

"Send them all a fax this afternoon telling them that we're having high level discussions with the Board of Life and Equity and a number of other Insurers and call a sales conference for Friday afternoon. In the meantime, they can all have three day's unpaid leave," instructed Tom. Joe had reluctantly to accept that perhaps, after all, Tom was worth his fifty grand a year.

And so the die was cast.

Twenty-Five

Tim Harrison was at his desk early. Colin Cooper had phoned him at his home the previous evening to say that all the information that he and Roy had requested to enable them to bid for his firm had been faxed through to him only an hour previously and would be on his desk by the time he arrived for work.

He hoped that they could work quickly. Colin had expressed the concern that, if things took too long, then someone on his staff might find out and then all hell would let loose. Confidentiality was the keyword.

Tim could fully appreciate the sense in this but was left with the impression that Colin might have had some hidden agenda. Why, after all these years, was he suddenly so keen to get rid of his business?

Tim recovered the reams of paper that had spilled from his fax machine and, after sorting them into approximate order, became deeply immersed therein.

It seemed that Coopers had been a highly profitable company five years earlier, but that there had been a steady decline ever since. In 1970, the Company had shown a profit before tax of just over fifty thousand pounds but, notwithstanding the fact that the income had risen fairly steadily by about ten percent each year, the 1975 figures were showing a profit of only ten thousand pounds.

At Harrison's, Tim strove to show a ten percent return on gross income, and succeeded, whilst Coopers had dropped to a lamentable two and a half percent. Admittedly, there was a further profit of twenty thousand pounds from Coopers Life and Pensions division but this was a notoriously volatile income stream and could not be relied on in the future.

Tim was beginning to see why Colin Cooper was getting ready to bale out and why he was in a hurry.

He turned to the Balance Sheet and this did make slightly brighter reading. The amounts shown for fixtures and fittings did seem a trifle on the high side, but the picture was greatly enhanced by virtue of the fact that the Company owned its own office building entirely free from debt.

Tim heard someone moving outside his office and was surprised to see that Roy Brown had arrived.

"Bit early for you, isn't it?" Tim asked.

"That's as maybe, but I didn't think I could trust a youngster like you with all those complicated numbers. You might come up with the wrong answer and bankrupt this company by bidding too high."

"Not a chance. Grab a coffee and take a look at this lot."

One hour and three coffees later, Tim said, "Well, what do you make of it all Roy?"

"It has not come as any surprise to me to see that Cooper and Smythe's decline coincided with approximately the time that you started your company. Until then, they had virtually no competition in this area and had clearly become complacent. Unlike his father, Colin Cooper has always considered golf more important than work, and this is the inevitable consequence.

"It's good to see, though, that they have maintained a reasonable level of income. I reckon that's largely down to Chris Wright; he's their Office Manager and its Chris who takes all the flak when Colin cocks things up. He's a bloody good chap and, if all else fails, we should try to get hold of him ourselves.

"On the basis of commission income, almost four hundred thousand pounds a year, the Company could be worth getting on for three quarters of a million pounds.

"On the basis of their pre tax profits, however, the most that you could value the Company at would be two hundred thousand pounds – and that's taking a generous view of their Life and Pensions income.

"If, and it's a big if, if you want to acquire the business, it has to be on the basis of the savings that the combined company would make by kicking out Colin Cooper and saving all of his costs. We could then add to this the economies that would arise by merging the two companies under one roof, the increased brokerage we would earn through increased turnover and the advantages of eliminating a major competitor."

"And what, do you think, that all adds up to?" asked Tim.

"That's very difficult to say. Colin must cost the Company fifty thousand pounds a year, there would be a saving in accounts staff and other overheads – say fifteen thousand pounds and we could earn perhaps another five or ten thousand pounds of extra over-riding commissions.

"On balance, all that could increase the pre-tax profits to around one hundred thousand pounds and perhaps the valuation of seven hundred and fifty thousand becomes plausible. Have you thought how you might raise the money, by the way?"

"Not really," replied Tim. "I just thought that we would agree a deal and that good old Tony Fellowes at the Bank would come up with the ackers."

"It might not be as easy as that," cautioned Roy. "I think that we will have to give careful thought as to how we might structure the deal. For example, if we were to offer Colin, say six hundred grand, we could be talking about paying him three hundred 'on the nose' and the balance in two instalments at the end of each of the following two years. These payments could, however, be performance related. In other words, should the income that we are buying fail to increase by, say, ten percent a year, then there would be a reduction. Admittedly, if Colin agreed to this, he would look for some kind of additional payment if he actually exceeded these targets, but this would all be down to further negotiation.

"Furthermore, I think that we should reduce the offer price by a substantial amount in return for paying Colin a non-executive's salary for a period of three years – in this way, not only would we reduce our initial outlay, but we would bind Colin in to help us retain clients should any of them want to leave."

"Sounds good to me. What do we do next?"

"I'll take all this home with me," said Roy, "and I'll draft out a Heads of Agreement as a starting point for our meeting with Colin. I'll also work out several alternative structures as to how much we could offer and how we would intend to pay this over. I could pop back about four o'clock and let you know what I've come up with."

"Better make that nine tomorrow morning," suggested Tim. "This afternoon is our big presentation to the Board of Sunbury's. It's make or break day today. They've already had presentations from Thompsons and Christie French – two International Insurance Brokers against a little tiddler like us. It's hardly fair is it?"

"The very best of luck to you. May David defeat Goliath, or Goliaths, I should say. I'll see you tomorrow."

Tim spent the rest of the morning going through their presentation for the afternoon meeting. They redrafted their report half a dozen times until Tim finally said, "that's enough for now. If we can't get their account after all this work, then that's just tough. I reckon we've given it our best shot and now it's up to the Sunbury Board. I just hope that they've all had a good lunch!"

Chapter Twenty-Six

At precisely two thirty, Tim, Graham Wiltshier and Brian Epps were ushered into Sunbury's magnificent Board Room and were shown to three empty seats on the opposite side of the table from their would-be clients. In front of them had been placed a foolscap note-pad, a 'Sunbury' ball point pen and a glass of Perrier water.

Sir Leonard Passmore, Sunbury's avuncular, non-executive chairman rose to welcome them, saying, "Good of you to come gentlemen. I'm Len Passmore and only here to keep order. I used to be in charge here but, now that I've been put out to grass, so as to speak, they only wheel me on occasions such as this. To tell the truth, I used to take responsibility for our risk management programme but that's now really the bag of these boys sitting next to me.

"Let me introduce Bill Bates, our FD. Let me tell you," he added with a smile, "he won't let you charge a penny more that you should. He can't help it. He's a typical Scottish Accountant, tight as the proverbial. And next to me on my right is Cecil Banks, our over-worked Company Secretary. It is these gentlemen who you'll have to convince, not me. Now over to you Mr Harrison. Let's hear what you have to say."

"Many thanks Sir Leonard," began Tim. "I'm Tim Harrison and I founded this firm some six years ago. On my right is my Commercial Director, Graham Wiltshier and on my left is Graham's assistant, Brian Epps. The report that Brian is handing to you gentlemen now, is largely the work of Graham and Brian and I'm going to leave most of the talking to Graham." Tim adjudged that business-like brevity would be the best strategy for the day.

Graham took them, page by page, through the report and he and Brian answered the questions that Bates and Banks fired at them from time to time. Tim was, as always, impressed by Graham's grasp of the subject and the ease with which he responded to the 'fast balls' that were being bowled at him.

More than that, he was very pleasantly surprised by young Brian Epps' performance. After an initial appearance of nervousness, he appeared to relax and was completely unfazed by the most difficult of questions.

Tim was particularly impressed when, faced with a question that he simply could not answer (and, frankly, neither could Tim) he showed no signs of bluster and stated confidently, "That's a very interesting question, Mr Bates. I would like to make sure that I give you the fullest possible answer. Would it be alright with you if I do a little research and call you back later this afternoon?" No bullshit there, approved Tim.

After two hours, an hour longer than the meeting had been scheduled for, Sir Leonard leant forward to say, "If there are no further points Bill or Brian, I think that we have taken up quite enough of these gentlemen's time.

"I have only one question that I would like to put to you Mr Harrison, before you go, and that is this. As you know, we have been insured through Christie French, one of the UK's largest Brokers (and the world's twentieth largest they tell me), for the last ten years. We have also asked for a comparative quotation from Thompsons, the world's number three. With advisers of this size and strength available to us, just why should we place such an important element of our business management with a firm as small as yours?"

"I'm sure that I need not tell you that 'size isn't everything' and that 'big is not necessarily beautiful' but that is absolutely true in this industry," answered Tim.

"If your Insurances are currently being handled by one of the majors, I'm sure you will be in competent hands and with a firm of undoubted financial strength; but you will not have your insurances handled by the Principals of the firm – their best men, their shareholders, the ones at whose door the buck stops. "Furthermore, as I am sure you have already found, the people that you will deal with will change from year to year. Relationships are more difficult to maintain. I believe that the 'Big Boy' Brokers are for the 'Big Boy' clients – the British Petroleums, the Sainsbury's, the ICI's and the like.

"To us you would be a major client. At Harrison's I can guarantee you that you will always have ready access to the Chief Executive or any member of the Board at any time, and that the team that your people will be working with will remain in place for many years to come.

"In short, I am confident that we have proved that we can deliver on price, and you have my word that, if appointed, we will never fail to deliver on service."

With no change of expression, no hint as to whether he was impressed or otherwise, Sir Leonard formally brought proceedings to a close with, "Thank you very much for coming Gentlemen. We will let you know our decision within the next two days. Cecil will show you out."

....

As Roy walked into Tim's office at nine o'clock the next morning, his first question was, "Well, how did things go at Sunbury's? Are we in with a shout?"

"Difficult to say, Roy," replied Tim. "Graham did a marvellous job and I was more than impressed by Brian's performance. We've got a good chap there. All seemed to go well until the Chairman compared us to Thompsons and Christie French. More or less said that we were wasting our time when they could just as well go to an International firm. We can only hope that they will see the sense in being with a firm that's prepared to fight all the way. We'll know the answer within forty-eight hours. Now, what have you got for me re Coopers?"

"As promised, I've burnt the proverbial midnight oil and here," he handed Tim a thin sheaf of papers, "are my suggested Heads of Agreement and my calculations."

As Tim started browsing through the papers, Roy continued, "I think that Cooper's has been slowly dying but that, given the injection of new blood that we can deliver, we could turn it into an extremely profitable operation.

"You will see that we could argue that the open market value of Cooper's would be somewhere between four hundred and six hundred thousand

133

pounds, dependent on a number of variables – not the least being the current valuation of the property.

"I believe that we should offer Colin two hundred thousand pounds now, with further payments of twenty five percent of the annual retained brokerage at the end of years one and two. At the same time, we should offer Colin a consultancy agreement to work, as required (but no more that a day or two a month), for the next three years."

"Do you think Colin would accept that? I'm sure he thinks that his Company is worth two times income – possibly eight hundred thousand pounds," observed Tim.

"If he does, he's in cloud cuckoo land. No, I think he's desperate to sell and a reasonable chunk of cash now, combined with some income for the next three years, is as much as he can honestly hope for. His pension would click in about then. We might have to negotiate upwards a bit, but that's what I would offer him in the first instance. Have you spoken to the Bank yet, by the way?"

"Not yet. Let's give him a call now," said Tim. Dialling the bank's number.

"Mr Fellowes please.........Tim Harrison of Harrisons........thank you very much.......Ah, Tony me boy, Tim here, how are you?"

After a moment's mild joshing, Tim said, "I'm just checking how much cash you've got swilling about in those vaults of yours Tony. Only we need a bit. Say half a million or so. We have been approached by Colin Cooper, of Cooper and Smythe's, to buy their little old business. Look, I've got Roy with me. He's got all the figures. Why doesn't he pop round and see you in a few minutes and go through the whole deal with you? Good, say half an hour then. Roy will be with you then. Have your cheque book ready."

Replacing the receiver, Tim turned to Roy and said, "He seems OK. Said that it would not be up to him. It would have to go to Head Office, but he'll do everything he can to oil the wheels."

"Excellent, now what about a call to Colin to sound him out?"

"Good idea, no time like the present. I'll get him straight away," replied Tim, rifling through the file for Cooper and Smythe's number and dialling it."

"Colin, Tim here. How are you?" he said once he was through. "I've got Roy with me and I think we can come up with something quite fair all round which, I'm sure, you'll find interesting. Mind if I put you on loudspeaker so that Roy can join in?" Tim pressed the button and replaced the receiver.

"Afternoon Roy," came the metallic voice. "Tim still keeping you at it? I thought they'd put you out to grass a long while ago. Anyway, I presume you want to give me a million quid and tell me to bugger off and reduce my handicap. Have I got it about right?"

"Hello Colin. Nice to talk to you again. No, I'm not ready for the scrap heap yet, maybe next year. As Tim says, we have done quite a bit of work and I think we can put together a good package," replied Roy.

"Let's have it then, and make it good," answered Colin.

"Based on your current trading, we reckon that a fair cash price would be in the region of four hundred thousand pounds. Now....."

"Four hundred thousand!" exploded Colin, "where the hell did you get that figure from?

"I wouldn't let the business go for a penny under three-quarters of a million and that's only because I'm keen to retire. If I were a few years younger, I could build the business up to double its size and I'm damn sure that that's exactly what Tim and his people will do. Don't waste my time."

"That's just the point Colin," agreed Roy. "Your business has declined a little over the years because you're not prepared to put in the hours and the effort that you did twenty years ago. You can't expect Tim to pay for the work that he's got to put in to make your business grow in value. Anyway, what we are suggesting is that we pay you two hundred thousand now, and then two further instalments of twenty-five percent of your turnover over the next two years. That way, you will share in the business' growth."

"And, I suppose, suffer in its decline if your people foul up?" cut in Colin.

"Not necessarily," added Tim. "I think that we could build in some guarantees so that our payment did not fall below an agreed figure, anyway, there's more to come, isn't there Roy?"

"Sure," said Roy. "We would also like to offer you a position as a Consultant or as a non-executive Director for a period of three years or so, at a modest stipend, of course."

"How modest?" asked Colin.

"We had in mind something in the region of ten thousand pounds a year," replied Roy.

"You'd have to do a hell of a lot better than that, but we might have the basis of a further discussion if you're prepared to be a bit more flexible. Perhaps some share options or something like that. It's all too much to absorb over the phone. You put your proposition in writing and I'll mull it over this weekend and give you a call on Monday. How's that?"

"That's fine Colin," replied Tim. "Roy and I will formalise this conversation and I'll get something in the post later this afternoon. I presume you'd like it sent to your home address?"

"Of course. I look forward to a little light weekend reading. Goodbye for now."

Tim and Roy spent the next hour fine-tuning their offer and, when they were satisfied, Tim dictated the offer and put the wheels in motion.

Chapter Twenty-Seven

It was Thursday morning and Joe had been sweating for nearly two hours waiting for Kevin Schmitt's arrival. Schmitt had phoned last night to say that he would arrive sometime between ten and noon, dependent on when he could get away from the Office and dependent on the traffic.

Joe had been running through in his mind all the possible scenarios if they failed to tie up a deal with Apex Life. There were no alternatives. The future looked bleak. He just had to wrap up a deal, and fast. Without an Agency from Apex, Castle Finance would be history.

The afternoon before, he had called in Fred Barker to tell him the bad news. Since becoming Group Sales Manager, Fred's views were becoming more and more relevant and worth listening to. He knew precisely what made his salesmen tick and he knew what the Company had to offer to make worthwhile sales.

Fred was surprisingly philosophical. He told Joe that it was only a matter of time before the L&E folded.

"We've been screwing them for years," he pointed out. "Something had to give sometime and it's a wonder that they lasted as long as they did. Its about time that we found another Company to screw – me and the boys would have no trouble in selling someone else's policies – in fact, we could do very nicely thank you by switching them from the L & E to the new Company and earning our commission all over again."

Joe was comforted to learn that, if they pulled off a deal with Apex Life, he would have no problem in persuading the Managers and their Agents to switch Companies.

"It's just a matter of making sure that the product that they are offering is not complete rubbish and that we get a good enough commission deal to make it worth their while. Once you've done that, you can leave it to me," Fred assured Joe.

"Of course," he added, "if you can't put a deal together quickly, say one or two weeks at the most, you can kiss goodbye to the lot of them. Most of them would be able to earn as much, or even more, if they simply signed up with one of the Direct-Selling Life Assurance Companies. So, for both our sakes, I hope you get it right."

Joe's problem was that he was not at all certain that he could pull it off. He was pretty certain that, if Apex' team pulled their figures about too much, they would soon smell a rat. But there was nothing that he could do now other than sit and await developments.

After discussing it fully with Fred, Joe faxed his twenty Branch Managers with the news and informed them that, after a couple of day's well-deserved break, they could all congregate at the County Hotel, next to their Head Office, at three o'clock sharp on Friday to hear some very exciting news. They would learn how their Management had foreseen the L&E's collapse and, in accordance with their customary shrewd forward planning, had implemented a stunning contingency plan. Turning disaster into triumph was going to be no problem.

"If only," Joe prayed.

If, on the other hand, he had nothing to tell them, if Apex simply walked away, he could expect the entire sales force to drift off, as Fred had forecast, without even a fond farewell. All those that were any good would be gone within a fortnight and he could expect to be left with only the dross.

In less than one month, the business that he had worked so hard to build up, would be gone, a distant memory. It didn't bear thinking about.

The shrill of his phone jerked him from his morbid reverie. With trembling fingers, he pushed the conference button to hear Sally, their receptionist say, "I've got a Mr Schmitt from Apex Life to see you Joe. Shall I bring him up?"

"Yes, right away please Sally. And could you give Mr Cummings and Brian a call and tell them that our guest has arrived and ask them to join us. Oh, and could you ask Mr Schmitt how he likes his coffee and organise coffee for the four of us?"

A moment later, Sally opened Joe's Office door to usher Schmitt in, closely followed by Tom and Brian.

After the usual pleasantries and after Sally had handed around the coffees, Schmitt came straight to the point.

"We've been through your figures with a fine tooth comb and I have to tell you gentlemen, that you are in deep shit." No more 'Mr Nice Guy', Joe observed with a feeling of impending disaster.

"Hang on a minute Kevin," began Tom. "Just because Life and Equity......"

"Let's cut the crap Tom, shall we?" retorted Schmitt. "You've been living in a fool's paradise for years. Your salesmen have been selling pure unadulterated crap for which you've been grossly overpaid. On top of that, you've got away with keeping your commission dozens of times when it should have been clawed back - even after a policy has been cancelled. Why the hell the Life and Equity allowed this to happen, and how the hell they could afford to pay you four percent, is a complete mystery. Well, at least we now know that they could not afford to pay it!

"There is no other Company in the UK, or in the world for that matter, who would take a second look at a portfolio of business of the type that your people have been turning in, and you know it."

Joe's spirits, already low, sunk further. His worst fears were about to be realised. Where could they go from here? If they failed to strike a deal with Schmitt, and strike it today, they were lost. Tom at least had the decency to look shell-shocked. At last he realised that bullshit did not always work. Brian merely looked resigned. Schmitt took a sip of his coffee as he let his message sink in.

"The only thing that you've got going for you," continued Schmitt, and Joe's spirits lifted a tad, "is the fact that your people certainly seem to know how to sell. If they can sell the type of junk that you've been telling them to sell up to now, they should be able to do even better with a quality product.

"You might well have been very lucky indeed in calling me when you did. Our medium to long-term investment products are good, bloody good, and we've got some past performance to back it up. As it happens, because we're new to the UK, we're keen to put on turnover in the next couple of years at the fastest rate possible – even if it is relatively expensive to achieve."

"So what are you proposing Kevin?" enquired Tom. He too felt hope stirring in his breast.

"If we can harness your sales force's selling ability to market our products, they should do well. I appreciate that they are used to earning high commissions for what they sell, but they will just have to get used to earning rates of commission that are more acceptable in the market. Its time for you and your sales people to get into the real world."

"We pay them on the basis that we receive four percent," pointed out Joe. "If we halve their commission, they'll all walk out, of that I'm sure. They know that they can do better elsewhere."

"I am well aware of that Joe," said Schmitt. "I told you at our last meeting that the absolute maximum that we could ever consider, would be three percent. But, only then if you reach one million pounds in sales in the first year. What I am prepared to do, is to make an exception to this rule, and to offer you three percent from the start. This is on the understanding that all bets are off if you do not achieve at least one million pounds in sales by the end of year one. In other words, we'll be giving you one percent over-rider as an act of faith."

"That's good of you Kevin," agreed Tom. "But even then, to keep the buggers selling, we would have to give up more than half of what we earn and I'm not sure that that would give us enough to cover our overheads. Wouldn't you agree Brian?"

"Absolutely, Tom," agreed Brian. "Our margins are pretty tight now, and on this proposed basis, without a very harsh pruning of costs, we'd be making a trading loss, almost certainly."

"I am aware of that and I'm inclined to say 'tough shit' because, the way things are now, you are not going to be in business very much longer," said Schmitt. "However, there is one final part to the equation. We want to grow and we believe that, given the right circumstances, there is growth potential in your Company. We think that the actual value of your Company today is diddly squit. However, we will be prepared to purchase twenty five percent of your Company's equity for the sum of one hundred thousand pounds. There can be no negotiation. It is 'take it or leave it' time.

"Once you have this sort of money in your bank account, you should be able to make up any shortfall in your profits.

"Let me make it quite clear gentlemen, we are not a Charitable Organisation. We will not be handing you personally a cheque for one hundred grand for a quarter of your shares. If we did, you might just decide to bugger off to the Caribbean or somewhere and waste it. We would want the Company to issue additional shares, which we would acquire, so that the Company has sufficient working capital to see it through. Your own holdings will simply be diluted."

"That's one hell of a lot to consider Kevin. How long have we got?" asked Tom.

Looking at his watch, Schmitt said, "well, its twelve thirty now. Why don't I take myself off to the pub, have a quick pie and a pint, and get back here by one thirty to hear your decision?"

"That's fine by me, but we wanted to take you out for lunch ourselves," said Tom.

"No time for the niceties. Just tell me where the nearest pub is, and I'll be back within the hour."

After he had left, Tom let out a loud sigh and remarked, "Holy shit! Our Kevin is one tough bastard, make no mistake."

"Hard as fucking nails," agreed Joe.

"But a bloody good business man," contributed Brian. "It will be tough, but I think that he has solved our problem and I think that we should snatch his hand off without delay."

"That's OK for you to say," said Tom, "it's not your fucking shares that he's stealing. The way this Company's been going, our shares should be worth a million each to Joe and me in a year or so, and he wants to give us – not even us, but the fucking Company - a measly one hundred grand for twenty five percent. It's a fucking insult!"

"The way the Company's going now," observed Brian, "I'd have to agree with Kevin's current valuation – 'diddly squit'. If we don't wrap up a deal now, or in a week or so at the most, we won't even have a Company to sell. Kevin knows this and he is absolutely right. There isn't an Insurance Company anywhere in the UK that would take us on as we stand, certainly not without screwing our commission rates to the floor. At least we would be getting fifty per cent more than the norm and the hundred grand in the Bank will be enough for us to close the gap with our key salesmen."

"Those greedy buggers won't be getting one single cent of that cash," cut in Joe. "That's our money, that is. It's Tom and me who've sweated blood to make something of this Company. No you can forget what Kevin said there. As soon as the coast is clear, Tom and I will be transferring that cash to a more accessible account, don't you worry about that."

"Absolutely right, Joe. That cash will be on its way to Jersey as soon as Schmitt walks out the door," agreed Tom.

"I have to say, gentlemen, that would be extremely unwise. If you want to get full co-operation from Apex, you're going to have to go along with them for at the least the first twelve months. You do anything but invest that money in the business, and you will have Lawyers and the Official Receiver through the door before you can say 'knife'.

"At least until we've got the first million pounds premium under our belts, and they can't start asking for their one percent over-rider back, you will have no alternative but to play by their rules." Brian knew that, if he did not try at least to knock some financial sense into his bosses, he could forget any long-term career prospects at Castle Financial himself.

"Well, we can worry about that in the next few months," conceded Tom. The main thing is, do we accept, or do we try to negotiate a better deal? Why don't we tell him that we've already had a better offer and see how he takes that?"

"I wouldn't push your luck Tom," urged Brian. "I think that you've had Kevin's best offer and if you push him, he'll simply walk out and look for other fish to fry."

"I can't see any harm in trying him out a little," said Joe. "Why don't we say that we'll let him have fifteen percent of the Company for one hundred thousand, or push for a one and a half percent over-rider? I can't see that that would do any harm."

And so the discussion continued with Tom and Joe confident that they could improve the deal and Brian urging caution.

Exactly one hour after his departure, Sally opened the door to show Mr Schmitt back in the room.

"Well gentlemen, do we have a deal, or do I put my coat back on and get back to London empty-handed?" he greeted them.

"We've considered your proposition very carefully Kevin," started Tom, "and we like it in principle. We are very keen to build up a relationship with your very fine Company but we feel that your terms are, perhaps a little harsh. What we thought was that, if............"

"Well that's it gentlemen," Schmitt said, standing up and reaching for his coat, "I said 'take it or leave it' and I meant 'take it or leave it'. I wish you well with your other negotiations and I thank you for your time."

"Hold on minute Kevin, not so fast." Tom rushed to his feet putting a restraining hand on Schmitt's shoulder. "We are very pleased to go along with your terms. It's just that we had rather hoped that you would have placed a higher value on our Company – given its past success and it's huge potential."

"I told you that I had put a higher value on your Company. It's worth precisely sweet F A at the moment, and here am I valuing it at four hundred thousand pounds. If that's not a generous valuation, I don't know what is."

"Sure, sure," agreed Tom hurriedly. "Please sit down and let's see if we can fully understand your offer. I am sure that we can agree a deal that suits us all."

Three hours later, Schmitt walked out of Joe's office with a copy of the Heads of Agreement signed by himself, Joe and Tom. The deal precisely mirrored Schmitt's initial (and final) offer.

With effect from tomorrow, Friday, Castle Finance would be placing one hundred percent of its business with Apex Life. The Salesmen would be trained to sell a new brand of Life Assurance Policy and they would earn approximately two thirds of the commission that they had become accustomed to.

Apex would own twenty five percent of Castle Finance, and Castle Finance would be solvent – at least for the next twelve months.

It was agreed that Fred should travel back to London with Schmitt and collect a supply of Corporate Brochures and spend as long as it took to make himself fully conversant with Apex Life's products.

Tom felt that he had done a bloody good two-day's work. Brian agreed. Joe looked forward morosely, to losing fifty thousand pounds a year from his salary and gave up all hopes of owning a second hand Rolls Royce.

Chapter Twenty-Eight

It was Monday morning and Tim had arrived at his office in a particularly jaunty mood. Some time today he would be receiving a call from Sir Leonard Passmore of Sunbury plc telling him whether, or not, they had been successful in securing their account. For some inexplicable reason, he felt that this was to be his day.

Furthermore, he would be getting a call from Colin Cooper accepting, in principle (or otherwise) their offer for his business.

He had had a good weekend with Mary and the kids. Two days at a holiday centre where the kids swam, played and ate all day whilst he and Mary could relax, watch and, at the end of the day, enjoy romantic candle-lit dinners.

He felt refreshed and revitalised, confident that nothing was going to spoil his day. He had convinced himself that Sunbury's would have seen the advantages of appointing a keen and thrusting local firm, with local service, and that Colin Cooper will have realised that his business would be far better off in the hands of Harrison's.

He got down to his work but with only a fraction of his attention on the tasks before him. The next two significant phone calls were all that he could focus on.

His pulse raced every time the phone rang and it was as much as he could do to keep the disappointment from his voice when the caller turned out to be other than Colin Cooper or Sir Leonard Passmore.

By lunchtime, his nerves were stretched to breaking point. He decided to join Roy and Graham for a pie and a pint at the White Hart, something he very rarely did. If he wasn't being entertained by an Insurance Company for lunch, Tim always preferred to have a sandwich at his desk – selected and purchased by the ever-loyal Janet.

The conversation over lunch was stilted. All three were on edge and, eventually the "what ifs" and "supposing theys" became repetitive and tedious.

As Tim returned to his office, passing Janet's room, he asked, "any calls?"

"Afraid not," replied Janet. "At least, not the calls you're waiting for. Bob Baker of the City and Commercial has asked you to give him a call back when you have a moment, and Tony Fellowes returned your call. Said he'd be in all afternoon if you need him.

"Thanks Janet," said Tim as he wandered disconsolately into his office and sat down. "Might as well give Tony a call," he thought to himself, and dialled the number.

"We've had a look at your proposition," said Tony, "and the Bank will be pleased to help. They're not too keen on stumping up the full two hundred thousand, however, and would like to feel that you and your colleagues will come in for some of the risk capital. I should think a total of about fifty thousand from your own resources should be sufficient."

"Fifty thousand pounds! Not a chance, Tony," responded Tim. I can't ask the chaps for any cash – they're not even shareholders. As far as I personally am concerned, what with school fees and the like, I'm absolutely broke. I'm afraid that you'll have to do much better than that Tony. I can't see the problem. If we do buy Coopers, it's worth twice what we're paying so you've got all the security you need – you're only putting up half its value."

"We've only got your word for that Tim. The business is all goodwill with no concrete value, except for its freehold, and it will only be worth what you say it is, if you make it work. We're prepared to help, but we are not in the business of putting up one hundred percent of any new venture. The only way I might be able to move head office would be if you would be prepared to sign personal guarantees, but I know how much you hate those – Mary too, for that matter."

"Too right," concurred Tim. "Anyway, as of now we don't have a deal. I've been waiting all day for Cooper to call me, but not a dickie bird yet. You see what you can do to make the deal more attractive, and I'll phone you when I hear from Colin."

"Fine by me Tim, but don't raise your hopes too much. The bank will only go so far."

Tim sat back in his chair and wondered where he should turn next. The euphoria he felt this morning had completely evaporated and he began to fear the worst on both counts. Surely Colin would have phoned by now if he wanted to go ahead – he said that he was going to make up his mind over the weekend.

By four o'clock, Tim could bear the tension no longer. He picked up the phone and called Colin Cooper.

"Mr Cooper is in a meeting and cannot be disturbed," came the clipped response. "Would you like to call back later?"

That didn't sound too helpful. He would have thought that Colin would have taken the call over anything else if he was as keen to close a deal as he had seemed last week. Might as well call Sunbury's too, Tim thought, and get all the bad news over in one shot.

"Sir Leonard is in a meeting right now Mr Harrison," replied Sir Leonard's secretary, "but I am sure he will call you back as soon as he is free."

By five o'clock, he could wait no longer and he had to call Colin Cooper again. "Mr Cooper has left the office for the evening Mr Harrison. Didn't he call you back? I gave him your message. Perhaps he will call you tomorrow. Goodbye."

"I'm being given the run around," announced Tim to Graham and Roy who had now come to his office to find out what was going on. "I just can't understand it. Colin was falling over himself to sell his business when we last spoke and now he can't even find the time to return a phone call. At the very least you would expect him to call back, even if he only wanted to increase the price. I'll just have to call him again tomorrow."

The phone rang. Tim lifted the receiver, "Sir Leonard Passmore for you Tim," came his telephonist's voice.

"Sir Leonard. How nice of you to call. I've got Graham with me and we were just talking about you. What can I do for you?" Tim tried desperately to keep the tremor out of his voice.

"I thought that I would call you personally," began Sir Leonard, "and I apologise for the lateness of the hour. I and my colleagues were very impressed with the presentation that you and your colleagues gave us last week and we would, all things being equal, liked to have been in a position to have given you a chance." Tim's heart sank as he could hear the "but" loud and clear.

"We were on the point of making a decision, one which I am sure you would have found most satisfactory, when we had a call from our existing brokers. As you know, one of the strong points in your favour is that you are local – only twenty miles away – and the geography would be a significant advantage. You would be on the spot, more or less, if we should need a cover note or anything of that sort, in a hurry. Surprisingly, Thompsons, our existing Brokers, have called us to say that they think that they can overcome that hurdle.

"They were a little secretive as to what they meant, but I can only assume that they are intending to open an office in this area. If they do, I am bound to say that we would find it very difficult to transfer our account from them. They have served us fairly well for over ten years and I think you would agree that it would be somewhat churlish to cast them aside when they appear to be taking so much trouble to accommodate us.

"What they have proposed, and what my Board have accepted, is that they will extend all our Insurances for a period of one month. If, during that time, they can satisfy us that they will be able to provide the service that we are looking for, then I am afraid Mr Harrison, we shall have no alternative but to remain with Thompsons.

"If, on the other hand, they are unable to make such a commitment, then we will be free to review our decision. I am sure that sounds fair to you, does it not Mr Harrison?"

"Of course, Sir Leonard," replied Tim. "Needless to say I am, of course, disappointed that you are not in a position to appoint my firm now, but I thank you for your kind words and for your courtesy in explaining the position so fully to me. I can only hope that Thompsons decide against establishing a presence around here and that you will look kindly at our submission before the month's end."

"We shall see Mr Harrison. Goodbye and thank you for all your work to date. Goodbye."

"You got the drift of that, did you?" he asked the others. "I'm mystified. I just don't believe that a firm of Thompson's size would ever consider setting up an office in a place as small as Ashbridge. It just doesn't make sense. What do you think Roy?"

Roy looked a little pensive. "Maybe I'm being unduly pessimistic, but have you thought that they may not be setting up an Office here? Maybe they are thinking of acquiring a business here."

"You mean Coopers?" shot back Tim.

"Precisely. There's nothing secret in this business and if Thompson's got wind of the fact that Coopers was up for sale, it makes sense that they might like to have a crack at it. Especially if they can use the deal to keep one of their largest clients and, at the same time, cause us some grief. Killing two birds with one stone, as it were."

"Jesus Christ," exclaimed Tim. "That's just bloody perfect isn't it? Here was I, thinking that today would be one of our most golden days and we look like being stuffed on both accounts, and stuffed in spades."

"The only thing on our side Tim," suggested Graham, "is that we have one month to do something about it. I appreciate that things look pretty black at the moment, but in reality, can you see any logic in a firm like Thompsons acquiring a firm like Coopers?

"Thompsons are looking for major clients, far bigger than the majority of Cooper's clients. At the same time, like so many of the larger Brokers, their natural instinct is to centralise their operations, not decentralise them."

"Graham's right, Tim," agreed Roy. "The majors are being crippled by overheads and, if they were to buy Coopers, they would be stuck with a freehold office out in the sticks, a stack of tiny clients that they don't really want, and a client that might be well and truly pissed off as soon as Thompsons revert to form and shove off back to London. No, I think that this may be a knee jerk reaction and that, as soon as they have completed their due diligence, they will ditch the Cooper deal and the coast will be clear for us again."

"I wish I shared your optimism," groaned Tim. "The way I see it is that they will spin things out past the one month extension, tie Sunbury's in with a three year deal and then decide whether to buy Coopers or not. By that time, we will have missed the boat with Sunbury's for three years and I'm buggered if I would ever want to go back to contemplating a deal with Colin Cooper after the way he has treated us."

Graham added, "Well, we're only assuming that they're talking to Coopers. There's nothing we can do about anything now so I'm off home."

"Good idea chaps. Thanks Graham and thanks Roy. Let's try and get a good night's sleep – unlikely in my case – and see what the morrow brings."

With that, the unhappy band headed disconsolately on their separate ways.

Chapter Twenty-Nine

By two thirty on Friday afternoon, the atmosphere in the County Hotel's one and only conference room was one of rumour, confusion and apprehension.

Castle Financial Service's twenty Branch Managers had all arrived and, over coffee and tea, were sharing their own thoughts and forecasts as to the effects of the L&E's demise. The fax that they had all received the day before had done little to allay their fears and they all assumed that there were going to be mega-problems ahead and that they were the ones who would have to bear the brunt and try and sort things out.

They knew their Management only too well and the suggestion of 'foresight' and 'forward-planning' was, they knew from personal experience, as foreign to Messrs Cummings and Hendry as were staff welfare and generous bonuses. What they were about to learn was a complete mystery to them all but would, undoubtedly, hold some fatal fascination, nonetheless.

As Joe and Tom strode into the room, the buzz of conversation ceased and the silence was palpable. Fred Barker detached himself from a small group of Managers and joined them at the table on the small raised dais.

"Please take your seats, gentlemen," Joe called out. He waited whilst the mumblings ceased and all of them had found a seat. With no preamble, Joe cleared his throat and began.

"To set the scene gentlemen, I am going to hand the meeting over to our Chairman, Tom Cummings. Tom has some very exciting news to impart. Tom, the floor is yours."

"Thank you gentlemen for coming," began Tom, as if they had had any choice in the matter. "I know that some of you have had a long way to travel and I know that, following the news of the insolvency of the Life and Equity Insurance Company, some of you must have felt more than a little troubled.

"Let me tell you right away, Joe and I saw this coming some time ago and, as you would expect, we were already in the process of making contingency plans. Admittedly, their final collapse came rather quicker that we had anticipated, but, if we're good at anything, we're good at acting instantly; and effectively," he added for emphasis.

"The past is the past and we all have to accept that the L and E is history. What we have to do is to decide how we go on from here. How we can convert a problem into an opportunity. This is, I believe, precisely what we have achieved.

"I am sure that you have all heard of the Apex Group of Companies. They are one of the strongest financial institutions in South Africa and they are now making waves - some would say tidal waves - in the UK and, for that matter, elsewhere in Europe. Apex is committed to becoming the leading Financial Services Group in the World, be assured of that.

"I am delighted to announce that, as part of their strategy for growth, they are determined to make acquisitions of strong and forward-looking Financial Services distribution companies. In accordance with this plan, they approached your Board to see if there might be a possibility of their being able to acquire a strategic stake in this Company.

"I am equally delighted to announce that, as of yesterday, your Board agreed terms which will enable Apex Life to acquire twenty five percent of the equity of this Company for a considerable sum of money (all of which, I may add, will be re-invested in the growth and development of this Company). It will not" he added with a chuckle, "find its way into Joe's or my own trouser pockets.

"For a Company of Apex' standing to make such a bold commitment to the future, is an incontrovertible assurance as to the high regard in which they hold us. It is a clear signal that they intend to ensure that Castle Financial Services becomes the premier Life Assurance Broker in the UK.

"With Apex' backing and our own proven marketing abilities, Castle Financial Services faces a very exciting future. There will, of course, be a number of operational procedures that will have to change as a result of this merger, and I would like to hand you back to Joe who will elaborate on these. After that, Joe and I will be pleased to answer any questions that you might have."

As Tom resumed his seat, Joe again mused that, perhaps, he had not done such a bad thing in selling Tom a slice of the Company. Twenty-four hours ago, they were facing an absolute nightmare and here was Tom, for all the world, presenting it as a fucking triumph. The bloke had style; that was for sure. Even Joe was convinced as he listened to Tom's oratory. He looked around the audience and was encouraged to see that the general demeanour had changed from sullen resignation to one of interest and even enthusiasm. Their audience was impressed. He rose to his feet.

"Gentlemen," he began. "My thanks to Tom for outlining the present position. I have to say that your Chairman's assistance at this important milestone in our Company's development has been invaluable. He has been a tower of strength to both me and my team at Head Office. Thank you Tom," he bowed his head towards Tom who smiled with a self-deprecating shrug of his shoulders.

"As Tom has already told you, Apex Life is one of the most forward-looking Companies in the UK and they have a range of Investment Products that are the envy of the Insurance Industry. On the table behind you is a pack - one for each of you - with full details of all of the types of Policy that they issue. Equally importantly, there is a schedule of the commission terms that is on offer to you and your own sales team. We have asked Apex Life to send packs of Brochures to each of your offices without, of course, any reference to commission. These packs are for your sales force. In a moment, I will ask Fred Barker to explain, in a little more detail, just how attractive these products are, and how easy, in consequence, you and your sales teams will find it to sell them.

"We have decided that all new business that this Company writes is to be placed with Apex and, in consequence, we have negotiated an extremely competitive commission package. Not, as I'm sure you will appreciate, as generous as the terms we previously enjoyed with the L&E, but generous nonetheless."

At this, a groan went around the room and Joe was not surprised to observe that most of their expressions had changed back to ones of sullen acceptance. It could not be helped. He continued.

"The fact that we enjoyed extremely competitive terms from L&E is undoubtedly one of the contributory factors towards their downfall. They were, quite simply, living beyond their means. Tom and I had drawn their attention to this on many occasions, with offers of a compromise deal, but they would not listen. I am afraid, Gentlemen that they were too greedy – they were terrified that, if they were to harden the terms they offered us, we might jump ship and place our business with one of their competitors. As you can imagine, a Company of our standing had several suitors. Sadly, they did not appreciate the true depth of our concern, our integrity and our loyalty. In consequence, the inevitable has occurred – rather more quickly than we had anticipated, I must admit." Joe possessed an innate ability to string lies together with inordinate ease. He congratulated himself on having been blessed with such a talent.

"However," he continued, "although there will be a modest downgrading in the rates of commission, Tom and I confidently predict that the volumes will rise. This is because the products that you and your teams will be selling in future will be far more attractive to your Clients than those that you have been selling up to now. In short, you will sell more."

At this, Tom Fields, the Manager for Lambeth, stuck his hand in the air.

"Yes Tom, have you a question?"

"I certainly 'ave Mr 'endry. You say that you was telling L&E that they 'ad problems some time ago. If that was the case, why didn't you say anything to us? We've been selling this stuff to our punters, some of whom are personal friends, and even family in some cases. 'Ow do you think we is going to tell 'em that we what we sold them just a few months ago was a load of crap? They're going to 'ave our guts for garters when they learns that they're going to lose all their dough."

There were murmurs of assent around the room at this interjection and Joe realised that Tom had, indeed, hit a raw nerve. There were times he simply could not understand all this airy fairy concern for the punter but, clearly, not all the Managers had his own enlightened view of how modern business should be conducted.

"I'm glad you raised that point Tom," replied Joe. "As you know, we at Castle Financial Services place our Clients' welfare at the very top of our concerns. Followed closely, of course, by our concern for you, our Managers, and your sales teams.

"All those clients who took out Policies with the L&E over three years ago have nothing to worry about. The surrender value under the terms of their Policies is fully protected." (Joe saw little point in reminding those present that this 'protected' surrender value would equate to little more that fifteen percent of all of the money that they have paid in. Worry about that when the time comes, he thought).

"Alternatively, they will be able to continue paying premiums to the Company whilst in Receivership and they might eventually get back as much as they were previously entitled to, largely because of the 'Policyholders Protection Act'."

"From what I hear," chipped in Tom Fields, "that would be the thick end of bugger all. What usually 'appens in cases like this is that another Insurance

Company takes them over and milks what's there for all its worth. I can't see my punters accepting that load of baloney."

Joe was inclined to agree but this was no time for ethics. He had to get them on his side and married to Apex Life if it was the last thing he did today. The future of his Company (and his own standard of living) was dependent on that.

"That is, of course, conjecture Tom," Joe continued. "I think that it is extremely likely that another Company will take them over at some time in the future and, at that point, we can discuss the prospects with our clients. Until then, there is little point in guessing.

"As I have already said, the range of products being offered by Apex is extremely attractive. I am sure that you will be able to persuade a good many of your old clients to make their existing L&E policies 'paid-up' and convince them that they will do far better in the future by transferring to Apex than if they had stayed where they were. You will be doing them a favour, in fact. And need I say, you will be earning your commission all over again.

As this sunk in, there were no more groans and Joe could see that a good few were doing their mental arithmetic to estimate how much they could earn by switching all their clients from the L&E over to Apex.

"And what," persisted Tom Fields, "will 'appen to the punters who've taken out their Policies in the last three years? They'll lose all their dosh won't they? What do we tell them?"

"Another good point Tom," Joe reluctantly conceded. "Under the terms of their contracts with L&E they were clearly informed that the Policy they took out was a long term investment and that, if they stopped paying premiums in the first three years, all of their contributions would be absorbed by the costs of issuing the contract. It costs a great deal, as you all know, to set up an Investment Contract and they all understood this when they signed up.

"I appreciate that they might consider that they have been unfairly penalised if they had not voluntarily decided to stop payments. They could, of course, continue paying to the new Company, but I doubt that you would recommend this. This is where the deal that we have negotiated with Apex is particularly helpful. The commission terms set out in the Information Packs applies to all new Business written. However, where a client has surrendered an L&E Policy, Apex Life are paying and extra ten percent so that you, in turn, can offer this to your client as a 'sweetener' to take out the new Policy and soften the blow of writing off the premiums that he has already paid." Again, Joe did not think it relevant to point out that he and Tom had reduced the standard commission payable to their Managers to ninety percent on the basis that they expected pretty well all the business to be written in the first twelve months or so to be replacements of the L&E policies. It was a simple case of robbing Peter to pay Paul – it was a very pragmatic approach and it happened all the time.

"What sort of investment performance do Apex Life have?" asked the Manager for Leicester.

"One of the best in the market," replied Joe without hesitation. "In your packs you will find an assortment of graphs showing how their funds have performed against their competitors over the last twelve months – they come out at or near the top in every case."

"Twelve months is rather a short time to compare, isn't it?" persisted the Leicester Manager. "If we're selling long term investments, we need to tell our clients how they've done over five, ten or even twenty years. How have they done over the longer term?"

"Although Apex are very big in South Africa, they only started their business in the UK fourteen month's ago," replied Joe. "That is why the graphs only go back one year. You wouldn't expect them to lie and give figures for periods when they weren't even over here would you? The fact that they have done so well from the start is the important thing. Their UK Equity fund, for example, has grown by twelve percent in the first year. You multiply this by twenty years and you're talking big money."

"Yes, but all funds tend to start well. They are not carrying the baggage of the larger and more established funds. Can you at least tell us how they have done in South Africa?" Their Leicester manager was becoming a real pain in the arse, thought Joe.

"I do not have those figures to hand right now," said Joe. "The reason being that they would be entirely misleading. The South African economy is totally different from our own and I would not want to be held responsible for telling people how well their money is going to be invested by reference to a Country that is only now getting over the effects of Apartheid. It would be irrelevant and, in my view, an improper misuse of information." He silently cursed himself for not have checked the Parent Company's investment performance. Had it been good, Joe would have been the first to have used it to his advantage. He made a mental note to check this out with Schmitt in case it should prove useful in the future.

"Returning to my original theme, I would like you to know that we have ordered entirely new stationery, business cards and the like and we will be sending each or you an Agreement to sign appointing you and your team as 'Appointed Representatives' of Apex Life. A new relationship that I am sure you are going to enjoy and benefit from. As from Monday, you will be free to write Apex Life business and I wish you all the luck in the world. I am sure that we will all benefit very greatly indeed by our relationship with our new Partners. Now, Fred has spent a great deal of time with Apex to fully understand what it is that they are offering. I would now like to ask Fred to give a short presentation that, I am sure, you will find fascinating and well worthwhile. Fred, over to you."

"Thank you Joe," began Fred, rising and walking towards a pre-prepared flip chart. "Apex Life offer the traditional forms of Endowment and Whole of Life Contracts, but they also have a very comprehensive range of Lump Sum Investments which, I can guarantee, our Clients are going to want to buy – and buy in large numbers. To begin with..........."

Fred then spent the next thirty minutes giving a detailed resume of all the money-making opportunities on offer from Apex. Joe was, again, more than a little impressed by Fred's depth of knowledge and grasp of his subject. He had clearly taken his time at Apex Life yesterday afternoon very seriously indeed – and it showed on the faces of his audience. He had come a very long way since their first meeting so many years ago in the Lion Public House.

After he had concluded, Joe again rose and said, "I told you that you would be excited by what this Company is now offering its sales force. Something I am sure you will agree, that very few Brokers will be able to offer. We can now handle a full range of investments for the rich and the poor, the old and the young and the saver and the spendthrift. Now are there any more questions?"

To Joe's concern, several hands shot up. "Yes George?" he asked, pointing to the Manager for Basingstoke.

"This has, of course, come as a bit of a shock to us all. I feel a lot happier now that I have heard what Fred has to say, but I must admit that I had never even heard of Apex Life before today. I doubt whether any of my clients have either. Does Apex intend to run a training course so that we can get to know something about the Company and what they stand for?"

"A very good point, George," replied Joe, who hadn't until that moment, given this a thought. "In your information packs, you will find a brief history of the Company and I hope that this will be sufficient for you to be getting on with. Everything has happened rather quickly for the reasons I have already outlined. As you know, here at Castle Financial Services, we pride ourselves on the fact that our representatives are fully trained." A few eyebrows were raised at this, but Joe continued.

"Tom Cummings and I have, therefore, been giving much thought to this matter and we have, agreed with Apex, to run a series of seminars with them to enable you all to feel comfortable with them. We want to enable you to recommend this very fine company to your clients in the certain knowledge that they have the best products on the market. We will get back to you all as soon as we have made the appropriate arrangements." Another mental note and Joe hoped and prayed that Schmitt would go along with this suggestion. More to the point, he hoped that, as with the L&E, Apex would meet all the costs.

"Yes David?" he said pointing to the Manager for Brighton.

"One or two of my salesmen have been telling me that they could earn more commission if they went and worked for 'Allied Scottish' direct. They are offering two percent to all their reps and they pay for all their phone calls when they work from one of their Offices. If we are going to have to pay them less than we got from the L&E, how are we going to keep them? Whilst I'm on my feet, please explain why I shouldn't go and work for Allied Scottish myself? I am sure that I could earn approximately the same as I do now and without all the hassle of training up my salesmen."

This was the question that Joe dreaded the most. In truth, he had to admit that most of his salesmen would, indeed, do appreciably better working directly for the new breed of Insurance Company.

"Perhaps I can come in here," interjected Tom, rising from his seat, and much to Joe's relief. Was he going to pull another rabbit out of the bag?

"As I said earlier, Apex Life have recognised in this Company a degree of professionalism which is very rare indeed in our Industry. Their mission is to join with us in creating a Financial Services Company that will be the envy of the world. And you, gentlemen, are being given this unique opportunity of getting in at the ground floor.

"You are being given the opportunity of helping to create the Financial Services Company which will become the blueprint by which all modern companies will strive to model themselves upon through to the turn of this century. By working with us now, and in the years to come, you will feel justly proud to have participated in such a dynamic venture. Having helped to create the finest Financial Services Group that this country has ever seen you will, by definition, be amongst the pioneers of this great Industry of ours.

"But more than that, gentlemen, much more than that, by staying with us you will be given the opportunity to own part of this great Company. Joe has yet to explain our Share Option Plan. Details will be sent to you very shortly, but it is our intention to reward all of you for your loyalty and your labour by giving you shares in our Company. As your commissions build up over the years, so will the size and value of your shareholding. Not only will you have helped to create a major Company, but you will also have created real wealth for you and your families. We do not seek to make you the highest paid Managers in this Industry. We intend to make you rich, very rich. No Insurance Company can offer you the challenge that we are offering you. And no Insurance Company can offer you such a reward.

"Join with us in this definitive chapter of our history, and I promise you that you will never regret it. Forget the short-term 'inducements' that Insurance Companies might dangle before you and look to the future – our future, your future."

Bloody hell, thought Joe, where did all that come from? It was the first that he had ever heard of a Share Option scheme but, he had to admit, it sounded a whole lot better that seeing all his men bugger off to Allied Scottish and the like. He had his audience by the balls this time.

"Any more questions?" Joe asked.

"Only one," said the Manager from Brighton. "When do we start?"

There were "hear hears" from around the room and Joe judged that this was time to wrap things up. Quit when you're ahead, as his Father often said.

"I am delighted to repeat that, as of now, you are all eligible to start on Monday as Appointed Representatives. Just read through your packs, sign and return the Agreement, and we're off.

"On that happy note gentlemen, I will call the meeting to a close and wish you all the very best of luck for the future, the very exciting future. Now, the bar is open and the first round is on us, so let's all repair to the bar and enjoy a well-deserved drink."

Chapter Thirty

A week had gone by since Tim's 'Black Monday'; the day that he had learned that, not only was the Coopers deal off, but they were unlikely to be appointed as brokers to Sunbury plc.

Although the Firm was running smoothly and his monthly figures continued satisfactorily, Tim had to admit that that double blow had knocked much of the stuffing out of him. He had adopted a brave face to both Mary and to his colleagues, but he was only now beginning to realise just how badly he had wanted to pull off both deals. The disappointment hurt, it hurt deeply.

Roy had joined him for a coffee and they were discussing current trading and other routine matters when Roy said,

"You know Tim; I've been thinking about the possibility that Thompsons might be making a bid for Coopers and the whole thing strikes me as more and more crazy. The logic in such a deal to Thompsons is, in my view, nil. You know that I've always had a high regard for Chris Wright, Coopers General Manager."

"Yes, but he's not going to tell us anything, is he? His loyalty, however misguided, must be to Colin Cooper."

"Under normal circumstances, I would agree. Looking at our gross income, the size that we have now reached, and the number of staff we are now employing, I reckon it is about time that we had our own General Manager. It's not fair expecting Graham to oversee all the underwriting and expect him to pretty well run the office at the same time. He needs help."

"What are you getting at?" asked Tim.

"I know Chris very well – we've always been on pretty much the same wavelength. Why don't I have a word with him and see if he would be interested in applying for the position of General Manager with us? If big things are about to happen at Coopers, he will either want to get out before the redundancies start flowing, or he'll want to stay put because he can see an exciting possibility for himself. Either way, his reaction to an offer from us might give us some sort of clue as to how the wind is blowing there. Best of all, he might jump at the chance of joining us and that would be very much to our advantage – to say nothing of it being a major blow to our favourite competitor."

"Bloody good idea Roy," agreed Tim, particularly warming to the thought of causing Colin Cooper some grief. "You give him a call and buy him a beer and find out what you can."

Janet, looking as lovely as ever was particularly radiant today. She came in with fresh cups of coffee for them. She seemed to be making a particular fuss of placing the tray on Tim's desk and fiddling with the cups as if trying to get them dead centre.

"What's up with you today Janet? Why are you looking so bloody cheerful when all is doom and gloom here, and why are you making such a balls of the simple task of giving us a cup of coffee?" enquired Tim, not unkindly.

"You must both be blind," answered Janet. "Isn't the diamond on the third finger of my left hand blinding you? It's fair dazzling me for God's sake."

"Bloody hell, it's an engagement ring!" exclaimed Tim jumping up from his desk and rushing round to plant a resounding kiss on Janet's cheek. "Bloody fantastic. Congratulations! So that old bastard, Simon Crowley, has decided to make an honest woman of you at last. About bloody time. How long have you been going out together now?"

"Five years next month. Its not that he hasn't asked before, it's just that I decided to say 'yes' this time."

"That's wonderful. So when's the big day Janet?" enquired Roy.

"Saturday week," came the prompt reply.

"Saturday week!" they both shouted simultaneously. "Why such a rush?" added Tim.

Janet coloured slightly. "Oh, the usual reason. I got the results of my tests yesterday and, when I told Simon that they were positive, he threw me in the air, took me out to dinner, proposed to me and gave me this, his Mother's engagement ring. It's beautiful, don't you think?"

"It certainly is. Congratulations again, to you both. I suppose this means that you will want time off for a honeymoon and then, in about six or seven month's time you will be expecting maternity leave. The things people do to get a bit of time off!"

"In about seven month's time, actually, but don't worry; my mother's been dying for a grandchild and she's already started work on setting up her own nursery and crèche. You won't get rid of me that easily."

"Thank God for that," sighed Tim. "Get your coat. Roy and I are taking you out to lunch – to be washed down with a bottle of Moet. These are events that must be celebrated without delay. Let's go."

They spent an extremely enjoyable two hours at the Taverna after which, Janet was sent home for the afternoon. Roy disappeared to the Golf Course and Tim returned to tackle anything that the world threw at him in the office – feeling mightily refreshed.

On Wednesday, two days later, the news was not quite so good.

At ten o'clock, Tim took a call from Colin Warrington – Bill's oldest son and the one who now ran the family business since Bill had taken virtual retirement a couple of year's ago.

"Bad news, Tim, I'm afraid," began Colin. "Dad died yesterday morning."

"Oh God!" cried Tim. "I can't believe it. I was with him only a week or so ago and he seemed fit as a fiddle. Was just off for a couple of week's golf in Portugal. Couldn't wait to get there. God, I'm so sorry Colin. What happened? How's your Mum? Is there anything I can do?"

"That was the only good thing Tim. He was playing golf, playing bloody well as it happened, when, without any warning, he collapsed with a massive heart attack. They got him to hospital within half an hour, but he was dead on arrival. "It's the way he would have wanted to go. Mum's not so good. You know how close they were. They've got her under sedation for the time being but I don't know how she'll be when she comes round. It's very good of you to offer to help. I'll get back to you if there's anything that you could do and I will, of course, let you know about the funeral. Best be off now, got dozens of calls to make."

"OK Colin. Mary will be devastated and we'll be thinking of you all. I can't take it in myself – he was such a lovely man. I don't know how we will get on without him. We will all miss him terribly. Without your father I would not have started this business – I owe him so much. Thanks for letting me know so soon and the best of luck with everything."

Tim was devastated. It was true; he owed so much to Bill. Without Bill, Tim would never have got started and look what he now had – a successful business employing fifty staff, a lovely house, two well-educated children, a happy home-life and so the list went on. Bill's generosity, encouragement and moral support had contributed so much to all of this and more.

But worse was to come.

Half way through the afternoon, Janet put a call through to Tim from Colin Cooper.

"Just thought I'd let you know," began Colin without preamble, "that tight-fisted offer you tried to fob me off with the other day was a load of balls. You thought you had me against the ropes, didn't you? Well, let me tell you, I've just had an offer from Thompsons for double what you were offering me - and with no strings attached. You and Roy thought you were the 'bee's knee's' didn't you? Now you can see what real business men think of this firm."

Tim was stunned by Colin's vehemence.

"Hang on Colin. No need to get stroppy with me," complained Tim. "It was you who approached us and we simply told you what we thought your business was worth to us. If someone thinks differently, then so be it and jolly good luck to you. I presume that Thompson's can see greater value than us because they will be able to close your Office down, get rid of a few staff and absorb the entire operation in their Head Office. That way they should be able to make a greater profit than we could and I can quite see them putting a higher value on your Business that we were able."

"That's where you're quite wrong, old boy," retorted Colin, clearly enjoying himself.

"Thompsons have made it quite clear that they intend to expand operations here, in this town, and use this office as their base for a major push into UK businesses in the South East. There won't be any redundancies and you'll have to watch out as they start attacking all your clients. You've had it all too bloody easy for far too long. Now we'll see who's going to come out on top."

Tim was still startled by the bitterness of Colin's attitude. He could not understand why he should be so aggressive – Tim had never gone out of his way to 'attack' Cooper's clients. Since Colin was in a vengeful mood there seemed nothing more to be said so, with a polite "Good luck and goodbye" he rang off.

Another hour went by before Tim suffered his third blow. A call from Sir Leonard Passmore.

"Mr Harrison, Leonard Passmore here," came the cultured and courteous tones of Sunbury's chairman. "I thought that I would call you again personally. Bad news I'm afraid. You recall that Thompson's extended our covers for a month whilst they looked into the possibility of their being able to match your local service?

"Well, I've just had their Chief Executive on and they tell me that they have just completed the acquisition of a local firm. Coopers and Smythe, you may know of them."

"Very well indeed Sir Leonard," answered Tim. "As a matter of fact, we were hoping to acquire their business ourselves, but it seems that we have been pipped at the post."

"Were you indeed? That's most interesting. I must confess that I am a trifle surprised that a firm the size of Thompsons would be interested in a relative tiddler like Coopers and Smythe. Still, there it is. As I said before though, the fact that they can now offer local service nearby does make it rather difficult for us to sever our connection with them after all these years. Apparently our affairs are going to be overseen locally by a chap called Christopher Wright. You don't know him, by any chance?"

"I do indeed," repeated Tim. "He's absolutely first class. You couldn't be in better hands unless, of course, you were a client of ours."

Sir Leonard chuckled, "That's very generous of you to praise your competitor, especially at a time when I have had to be the harbinger of such unwelcome news for you. I would like to thank you and your excellent team for the very professional work you did on our behalf and I do hope that we can keep in touch. You never know, we might fall out with Thompsons one day and, if so, I would very much like to give you a call."

"That's very kind of you, Sir Leonard. I can only hope that our competitors might give us a chance in the future, in the not too distant future. Goodbye and good luck with your new arrangements."

Tim replaced his receiver and sat back in his chair, his misery complete. Sicker than the proverbial parrot he could not be.

He was still sitting there, motionless, an hour later when Janet popped in to say goodbye. He looked so totally dejected that she stood behind him and started massaging his neck and shoulders.

"You've had the mother and father of a day," she murmured. "What you need is a little TLC."

Despite himself, Tim found himself aroused. The proximity of Janet, her perfume and the gentle caress of her breasts against the back of his head as she rubbed his shoulders was having a powerful effect on his emotions. Without thinking, he put his hands on hers and drew them down his chest. As her face drew level with his, he kissed her gently on the cheek and on the neck.

Janet moved round and kissed him on the lips. It was a sensation that Tim had dreamed of many times but one, for the love of Mary, he had never given in to. His hand dropped to her waist, down her dress until he touched her legs. They were so smooth and so cool to the touch.

He couldn't stop himself from stroking her calves, her knees, her thighs, her inner thighs, revelling in the ecstasy of exploration. He felt the mound of her sex under the thin film of her silk panties.

Neither of them could avoid the sight of his straining erection.

"Tim," she whispered sensuously, "I've wanted this for so long and next Saturday will be too late. Take me home. Make love to me. Just this once. We both need it."

He knew he should say 'no', but he could not say no. He remembered that Mary would not be expecting him back early. He was due to play squash with Johnny Williams.

"You go home now Janet," he said huskily. "I'll follow you in about five minutes. We shouldn't be doing this, but after today............ I'll be at your flat in about twenty minutes."

She let her hands linger on his chest, kissed him hungrily and left. "Don't be long," she whispered as she swept out of the door.

Tim picked up the phone and called Johnny.

"Look, sorry Johnny. Something's come up here and I'm not going to be able to get away for at least an hour, or maybe even longer. Any chance we could scratch our game tonight and fix another date? Sorry it's so late – I hate to do this to you."

"I knew you couldn't take another thrashing Tim. I quite understand," came the sardonic response. "As a matter of fact, Martin is sitting in front of me and his game's been cancelled too so we could do battle together. He won't be as easy as you, but I could do with a bit of a challenge for a change. Why don't you join us for a drink when you finish there? You'll be paying of course, only fair since you've buggered us about."

"Good idea. I'll see you both later."

As he got into his car and started driving towards Janet's flat, he couldn't believe that this was really happening. It felt surreal. But then, he persuaded himself, when he got there, they'd call a halt to this nonsense. He'd have a drink and say goodbye. He half hoped that this would be the outcome; it made him feel better. He also half hoped that that would not be the outcome.

Tim pulled up in a side turning near Janet's flat, found a place to park and got out and locked his car. His hands were trembling; in fact, his whole body was trembling. He walked briskly across the road, located the flat and tremulously rang the bell. He stood close to the intercom so that Janet's voice would not be drowned out by the passing traffic.

There was a click and Janet's throaty voice. "Come straight up, Tim. Second floor, flat four, the door's unlocked."

Tim ignored the lift and took the stairs. His heart beating furiously, he pushed open the door and entered the flat. There was a small hall that opened into a good-sized living room. Tim drank in the scene – tasteful yellow and green pastel décor, comfortable rather that ostentatious furnishing and, above all of this, Janet's scent lingered everywhere.

"I'm here," he croaked. He felt like a schoolboy on his first date.

"And I'm here," whispered Janet as she pushed open the bedroom door. She was stark naked.

Tim stifled a moan. She was so beautiful. Her breasts had always been objects of his fascination. There they were, revealed at last for him to admire. Perfectly rounded and proud with tiny, erect nipples. Her slim arms framed a slender waist that tapered into the longest, smoothest and shapeliest legs that Tim had ever imagined.

She walked towards him, put her arms around his neck and kissed him lingeringly. Tim was transfixed, almost helpless.

Janet gently loosened his tie, eased off his jacket and then, as the heat rose, the slow movements became faster and, then, frantic. Tim assisted clumsily and, together, they started tearing off the rest of his clothes. In seconds he stood naked before her. His readiness was all too obvious and he pressed himself to her, kissing her feverishly, on her forehead, on her lips, on her neck, and, what bliss, he enveloped, and tasted, her nipples.

156

She slowly slid both her arms around his neck, effortlessly drew her thighs up around his waist, paused deliciously and slowly, agonisingly slowly, she lowered her thirsting sex on and around his rampant member.

"Carry me into the bedroom," she whispered and, to Tim's stunned, but uncontrolled delight, she added, "then fuck the living daylights out of me."

It was over in minutes. A brief moment of time as flailing legs and arms entwined and locked together in mindless confusion. Sated, they lay together in a state of shock, arms entwined, legs entwined, bathed in sweat and panting for breath.

"That was amazing, simply amazing," gasped Tim. "I've never experienced anything like that in my life. I'm so sorry it was so quick. Are you alright? I haven't hurt you have I?"

A wicked smile played on her lips. "You could always kiss me better – not there, but down there. As it happens, I believe that I will be able to put up with the pain when you take a little longer next time. Wait there."

Janet jumped from the bed and ran from the room. She returned only a minute later clutching a bottle of champagne and two glasses.

"If you have still got the strength, perhaps you would uncork that and fill the glasses. Mummy always told me that there's nothing like Champagne to restore one's energy."

Mummy was right. The second time was as tender as the first was fierce.

An hour later, Tim rose and with an apologetic smile, started to get dressed.

"I've loved you since the day we first met, Tim," she told him. "I've wanted to do this each and every day for the last five years. I'm so glad that we have. Don't feel any guilt, darling. I love Simon, I will love our child and I will be a faithful wife.

"We've done what we had to do and it's done. I'm so happy and I have no regrets. See yourself out and I'll see you tomorrow as if nothing has changed – but it has darling, it has."

Tim had nothing to say. It felt wonderful to have loved this glorious girl. He felt guilty to have betrayed his lovely and loyal wife, he forgave himself with the knowledge that she would never know.

He could only bend over, kiss her softly and whisper inadequately, "Thanks, you're a wonderful girl and Simon is one of the luckiest men in the world. Goodbye my darling."

He drove to the Squash Club and arrived just as Johnny and Martin were finishing their match. He decided to join them for a shower "To get rid of the heat of the day" he told them. Rather ashamedly, he admitted to himself, to get rid of the scent of a glorious girl.

In the bar afterwards, Johnny introduced Tim to his playing partner – Martin Bushell – and whilst he was getting the first round, Martin turned to Tim and said, "Johnny tells me that you're in the Life Assurance game. You must know my next-door neighbour, Joe Hendry. If you're doing as well as Joe, you must be making a fortune."

"I don't know him personally but we did take on one of his chaps a year or so ago. As I understand it, he deals in the 'bottom end' of the market. Why, what gives you the impression that he's doing so well?" Tim couldn't help feeling jealous, and even angry, if Hendry was doing well, believing as he did, that the man was a crook.

"Joe is always throwing his money around. He built a swimming pool last summer, seems to change his cars more times than I have hot dinners and his wife, a bit of a tart if you ask me, struts around in her designer clothes as if she was Jean Shrimpton – except she's more of the mutton dressed as lamb type.

"Joe tells me that he employs several hundred staff around the country and talks of millions of pounds of business as if it's nothing at all. I don't like the chap one little bit, but he clearly seems to know what he's doing. Amazing thing is that he told me last week that one of the biggest Life Assurance Companies in the country has just taken a twenty-five percent stake in his Operation. If so, someone else must be impressed by is company."

"I suppose so," admitted Tim, reluctantly. "I must find out what he's up to and see if I can emulate his success. Thanks Johnny," he added as he took the pint of beer he was being offered. "I've had some pretty bleak news today. You know old Bill Warrington. I'm afraid the dear old boy keeled over on the golf course yesterday and died – of a massive heart attack."

"What a way to go," observed Johnny.

They discussed mortality, business, politics and sport until it was time to go, not without fixing a date for their next match.

Tim arrived home as Mary was watching the news. She switched off as soon as he entered the room and rose to give him a welcoming kiss.

"Good game?" she greeted him. "Who won?"

"Didn't play after all." He replied. "I've had such a bloody day at the office I decided to work through. I called Johnny to cancel and he was able to fix up another game. I joined them both for a drink afterwards."

"How bloody, darling? While you tell me, do you want me to make you a coffee or something stronger?"

"Totally bloody, I think that we had better both have a brandy. I'm afraid that I've had the saddest and worse news possible - dear old Bill collapsed on the golf course in Portugal yesterday and died before they got him to hospital – a massive heart attack."

"Oh no! Not Bill. He's such a darling. How could that happen? He's always as fit as flea," Mary sat back in her chair. "I just can't believe it. Poor Martha. She must be devastated. I must go and see her tomorrow and comfort her, or try to comfort her. How will she cope? They did everything together and, though she was always ready to give him a tongue-lashing, she was absolutely devoted to him – literally worshipped the ground he walked on. I doubt whether Bill would have been half as successful if he hadn't had Martha behind him."

"You're probably right. Anyway, Colin will let us know what's happening about the funeral and all that. It's too early to think about at the moment, but Bill still owns twenty-five percent of the Company. I suppose the shares will pass to Martha. It would be something of a hoot to have Martha sitting at the table at our Board meetings!"

"Don't laugh, Tim, it's not funny," said Mary as she took the brandy glass that Tim had handed her. "After that awful news, what else could have happened to make your day so bad! I can't think of anything sadder than that."

"Not sadder, darling, but bloody nevertheless. You know that I was hoping to buy Colin Cooper's business. Well he's had a better offer, a far better offer and the deal is in the basket. Surprisingly, when he called me, he was so incredibly aggressive, almost spiteful. For reasons I cannot fathom, we seem to be at war with Coopers.

"Finally, Sir Leonard Passmore called to say that he was not transferring the Sunbury's account to us. To rub salt in the wound, it's staying with Thompsons who have bought Coopers so, if that's not a double whammy, I don't know what is."

"Darling, after a day like that, there's only one cure," Mary said as she kissed him gently and put her hand suggestively on his lap. "Come on, time for bed." She took him by the hand and led him upstairs.

Tim felt a moment's panic that, after his torrid session with Janet, he might fail to live up to expectations. What his excuse would be, he had no idea. He could only hope.

In the event, they made long and lingering love and, to Tim's surprise and relief, the orgasm that he reached was even more mind-blowing than those he had experienced earlier. Love, he realised, was a far greater aphrodisiac than lust.

An hour later, as he began to drift off to sleep, he counted the day's score. Bill's death was a major debit. The breakdown of communication with Coopers and his failure to secure Sunbury's business were negatives but, in truth, he was no worse off that he had been the previous day.

His insane frolic with Janet was a plus in that he had consummated an unspoken desire and it was also a minus in that he had, for the first time in his life, been unfaithful to Mary. However, Janet's confirmation that this was a first and a last time gave him great comfort and lessened his guilt – neither would renege on that commitment, he felt certain.

The news that Joe Hendry appeared to be doing so well did niggle him, but he would look into that another day.

The fact that his love for Mary was so deep and so unequivocally reciprocated was the biggest plus of all and the only one that really mattered. In comparison, everything was trivial.

As Tim finally drifted off to sleep, a small smile remained on his lips. It had not been such a bad day, after all.

Chapter Thirty-One

It had been almost a month since Joe had wrapped up his deal with Apex Life and, by and large, he had reason to be satisfied with progress so far. Of course, there had been the usual teething problems getting his salesmen to adapt to the new regime, to work for a lower commission and to try to learn something new. Most of them had stayed but about fifty had already left and gone to pastures new, to Insurance Companies or, in most cases, simply back on the dole.

On the plus side, he was much relieved that not one of his Managers had defected – yet. He was conscious, though, that Tom Cummings had not yet put together the proposed Share Option scheme. This was supposed to make most of them millionaires in short time as the Company grew and he felt that the better Managers were simply marking time until they saw how it was going to work and how it would benefit them.

The mechanics of such a scheme were a complete mystery to Joe and he sensed that Tom was already having second thoughts as to the wisdom of giving up another slice of his share of the business. However, for the time being, that was not his problem and his chief concern was to ensure that the money continued to roll in.

He was pleasantly surprised to learn how many of the L&E clients had agreed to switch to Apex, notwithstanding the loss each of them was incurring in so doing this. He attributed this, quite correctly, to his Managers' total lack of ethics. It was their smooth talking that would result in the successful pursuit of higher commissions – a philosophy he endorsed without reservation. The knack was to convince the punters that the new policy they could have with Apex would make them even more money than the original with L & E would have done. To realise this, they would have to be persuaded to forget the one hundred percent penalty they would incur for switching. Joe was proud of his salesmen's ability to deflect the punter's attention from this unpalatable fact. It was a testament to his training methods.

There was a tap on the door and in strolled the cheery cockney manager for Lambeth, Tom Fields.

"Come in Tom me old mate," he greeted him. "What brings you to the centre of the Universe on this wet and windy day?"

"Watcha Joe, I got meself a bit of an interestin' problem. 'Ave you got a moment?"

"Sure, sit down and I'll get Wendy to bring us a coffee." Whilst he organised this, Tom was rummaging though a weather-beaten brief case and pulled out an assortment of papers. He spread them out all over Joe's desk.

"It's like this Joe. You may remember that I got a mate wot runs a Nursing 'ome for old biddies."

"Sure, you mentioned it the other day. Not thinking of going in the Nursing Home business yourself are you. I'm told there's a lot of dough in it if you do it right. The State pays for everything – all you have to do is keep the old folk happy and dry and make sure that you don't knock 'em off with salmonella poisoning. Piece of cake. Beats the hell out of running a Company like this."

"No chance, mate," replied Tom, "but I got in there the other day 'an saw one of the old biddies and walked away wiv a cheque for ten grand to put in one of them Bond things wot old Schmitt was bangin' on abart. Never could understan' 'ow they worked, but as soon as 'e said that we got five percent for one of them an' only three percent for them Unit Trust things, that was good enough fer me.

"Anyway, I did me bit an' she dug into 'er bag an' fished out a cheque for ten grand, sweet as a nut, an' then she asked me 'ow much I earned for fixin' the thing up. Well, I thought I 'ad better be honest an' I told 'er five percent. 'Oh she says,' after scribblin' away in 'er notebook for five minutes, 'that's another five 'undred quid isn't it' and, before I could stop 'er, she wrote out another cheque for five 'undred smackers to Castle Finance. Look, 'ere it is," Joe added holding out two cheques and an Application for a ten thousand pound Investment Bond. "So what do I do abart that then? We got the five sobs from Apex an' another five sobs from the punter."

"So how old is this lady then, Tom? Has she any idea what she's doing?"

"No chance, Joe. She's over eighty and she don't even know what day of the week it is, let alone what she's just bought. When she signed the form, I asked 'er if there was anything, she didn't understand an' do you know what she said? She said 'I always like to keep my money in the Building Society so as I know how much I've got'. No, she ain't got the foggiest idea an' I reckon there's plenty more where that came from."

"Well, I can't see the problem Joe. If she doesn't know what she's done, we are in the clear. I'll bank the cheque and I'll add two hundred and fifty smackers to your commission this month and we won't say anything more about it." In Joe's book, if the punter does not ask, the punter does not get, and a commission for double the going rate was to be encouraged – after all, it reflected the value the client perceived their service to be worth.

"Now, you reckon that there's more where that came from? What about from the other Residents?"

"Sure, why don't you come over an' meet Bill Washington? 'Es the guy what owns the 'ome, an' I'm sure you could get 'im to introduce you to the others 'an we could make a killin'. None of 'em know what's goin' on – 'e specialises in demensher or somefin' like that. It's all a bit posh an' he doesn't 'alf charge 'em. Some of 'em are payin' three 'undred quid a week – they're loaded an' waitin' for someone like us to 'elp 'em out a bit and get rid of some."

"Bloody good idea, Tom. You give him a call and say that Castle Finance would like to offer a free Financial Seminar for his residents. Say that we know that they probably have difficulty understanding their finances and that we have a few ideas which will keep them all on the right lines. Let me know when they can do it – Wednesday or Thursday next week look good for me," said Joe, flicking through his near empty diary.

....

Half an hour later, Tom popped back to Joe's Office. "OK mate, I've been on the blower," he said. "Ten firty next Wednesday mornin'. Bill says it's no use doin' it in the afternoon cos they're all be asleep. Most of 'em are there in the mornin' cos they know they've got to be abart if they wants any dinner. 'e says 'e'll 'ave abart twenty of 'em in the lounge by that time 'an 'e'll have a cup of coffee for us all, then it's up to you."

"Fine Tom, just perfect. I'll sketch something out and I'll talk to them about investment for about half an hour. You make sure you've got twenty Brochures and Application forms and, after I've finished, we'll see each one on their own and sign them up for as much as we can. It would be a good idea if you got Bill to tell them to have their cheque books with them because I'm going to tell them about a special offer which expires on Thursday so, if they want to get in, they'll have to move fast.

"What about your pal Bill? Won't he want a cut? If he thinks he's going to get something out of it, he'll try to soften them up a bit won't he? We might as well get him working on our side."

"Bloody good idea mate. What abart givin' 'im twenty quid for every punter wot we sign up?"

"I think that we could do a bit better than that Tom. You've got them thinking that we're going to charge five percent. Why don't we tell them that, as we have a special offer and, if there's at least ten that will sign up, we'll only charge them two and a half percent and give that all to Bill? That way, he gets a real bunch of money and we still get our five percent from the Apex."

"Wiv you mate. I'll get 'im on the old dog an' tell 'im its 'is lucky day. Bill's always one to skim a few quid 'ere an' there when he can. 'e'll like this one, I'm bloody sure of that."

....

The Meadow View Retirement Home for Gentlefolk turned out to be a handsome mock Tudor Mansion standing in its own extensive grounds. Joe had to admit that he was impressed by the understated grandeur and opulence, the manicured lawns and the immaculately maintained flower beds.

On entering the main hall, Joe's first impression was in no way diminished. Everywhere he looked, he saw fine furniture and a profusion of cut flowers. A sweet scented bouquet greeted his nostrils. If first impressions were meant to count, Bill Washington had got things just about right. Joe could imagine any well-heeled son or daughter being more than happy to leave their beloved aged relatives in this gentle oasis of tranquillity to spin out their declining years - free from all filial resposiblities.

A dapper, portly but cheery Bill Washington bounded out of his Office with outstretched hand.

"Joe," he cried, "you must be Joe Hendry. Tom has told me a great deal about you and your very fine Investment Company. It's a pleasure to meet you, and it's so kind of you, the great man himself, to spare his time to meet my simple souls and spread knowledge and enlightenment about the world of high finance."

"Nor at all," smiled Joe, flattered and impressed by such a warm welcome. It was gratifying to realise that people no longer saw him simply as a

Salesman, but that they now recognised him as a pillar of the financial world – one able to explain and expound on the intricacies of the financial world to the public at large. Yes, he must devote more time to developing his new-found status. He was, after all, a true professional.

"It's a very great pleasure to be here Bill," he smiled modestly. "Tom was telling me that a number of your Residents have difficulty in managing their financial affairs. If there is any way that I can make their lives easier in this respect, then my visit will have been worthwhile. If I have any talent at all, I like to think that I am possessed of the ability to cut through the jargon that my peers seem to think so important, and to focus the layman (or lay woman) on the essence of money. To make money work for them and for them to understand what we, the professionals, can do to shift the burden of investment over to the shoulders of those that are trained to bear the burden."

"Precisely so Joe. Yes, they all have difficulty in understanding money and, for that matter, remembering anything that they've been told. Some of my residents can ask a question, listen to the answer and, only seconds later, ask the same question once again. You will have to make everything simple for them."

"That is my raison d'etre," replied Joe, recalling an expression that he had read somewhere. "I haven't been in the investment business for twenty years without being able to simplify, what is a very complex subject, for the benefit of our thousands of clients."

"Excellent, excellent," beamed Bill. "Now, Tom tells me that there might be a crust or two in it for me. Anything that I can earn to invest back into this business for the benefit of my residents, of course, is always a great comfort to me. As you can see, we keep the place in tip-top condition for the meagre dues we receive from our residents. Any additional source of revenue is always greatly appreciated."

"Absolutely, Bill. Nothing is for nothing. Well, we receive the market rate of commission from the Fund Managers with whom we place our investments but this, I am afraid, barely covers our overheads – what with research, fund analysis, compliance costs and all that sort of thing. You know only too well yourself how much is needed simply to keep a business on the road.

"We provide added value to our clients, and for that we charge a fee of five percent of the amount invested. What I have in mind is, that because you are introducing a number of clients to us at one location, and thereby minimising our marketing costs, we will be happy to assist your residents by halving our fee. This means that we will reduce our customary five percent to two and a half percent and we would have in mind transferring this entire fee to you by way of an introductory servicing fee. In short, you would earn two and a half percent on everything your residents might invest with us."

"That's extremely generous of you old man. I find your suggestion entirely satisfactory. Now, if you follow me, I'll take you along to the lounge – Tom is already there mingling with the masses. We'll all have a cup of coffee and then you can begin. Tom tells me that you would like to see them individually afterwards. You can use my office if you like and I'll get Mavis to hang around so that she can fetch each resident for you when you are ready. Now is there anything you would like me to say when I introduce you, anything that will help the cause?"

"Well yes there is," responded Joe. "The offer that I would like to extend today is, I believe, particularly attractive to the aged but it actually expires tomorrow. If they are able to let me have a cheque for this particular investment today, they will be getting an enhanced investment allocation. I'm sorry to say that this offer will expire tomorrow and there is nothing that I can do about that.

"If you could tell them that and, that if they accept my recommendation, they will do particularly well, but only if they can let me have a cheque today. If you can get them to understand the sense of acting immediately, then that will be most helpful. I hate to put your residents under any pressure – it is not my style – but a bargain like this does not come along every day. I find that a bargain always sharpens the mind – though, as I understand it, some of their minds are a little past sharpness," laughed Joe.

"Sadly so, I'm afraid," conceded Bill. "I have to give some of them a great deal of help in many ways – even in paying our bills. Leave it to me; I'll get them ready and raring to go."

As they entered the room, Joe noticed that Tom was in the middle of a group of octogenarians, all of them laughing uproariously. Joe certainly had a knack with these people he observed. Though whether they had the faintest idea what they were laughing about, Joe had his doubts.

Bill stood up and tapped his coffee cup a few times with his teaspoon.

"Ladies and Gentlemen," he began. "Will you all be so kind as to take your seats?" He paused as they tottered to their various seats, some looking bemused, others simply vacant.

"Thank you Ladies and Gentlemen. Today it is my very great pleasure to introduce to you Mr Joseph Hendry. Mr Hendry is the Chairman and Chief Executive (Tom Cummings would not have like that mused Joe) of Castle Finance. Castle Finance is a highly respected Firm specialising in Investment and Fund Management and Mr Hendry has had over twenty years experience in this Industry. We are all extremely fortunate to have a man of Mr Hendry's abilities to address us today, for he is an extremely busy man with countless calls upon his valuable time.

"I am sure that, like me, you find high finance to be both terrifying and impossible to understand. That is why we are so fortunate to have a gentleman of Mr Hendry's stature here with us today to throw some light on this extremely important subject.

"Mr Hendry, and his colleague Mr Fields, are the sort of men we can trust. I urge you to listen attentively to what they have to say and to take advantage of their expertise. They have very kindly offered to stay behind and see each one of you individually to answer any queries that you may have and to assist you to actually make an investment should that be your wish.

"Without wishing to steal any of Mr Hendry's thunder, I can let you into a little secret. He does have one particularly attractive Investment opportunity today that he will bring to your attention. (Looking around, Joe wondered just how much attention they were capable of summoning). So attractive is this opportunity that, regrettably, today is the last possible day that you will be able to take advantage of it. So, if you like what Mr Hendry has to say, please stay back to see him afterwards with your cheque books ready. If any of you need to know your current balances, Maureen, my Secretary, will be pleased to call your Banks for you. Now, with no more ado, I give you Mr Hendry. Joe, the floor is yours."

"Thank you Mr Washington. Thank you for those kind words. Ladies and Gentlemen, it is a great pleasure to address you today on this very important subject and I am most grateful to you for giving up so much of your valuable time to listen to me. I am sure that there are many useful things that you could be doing rather than sitting here listening to me droning on, so I will keep my address brief and I will endeavour to make your attention worthwhile. Now, is there anyone here who understands the Stock Market and how it can be used to increase your wealth?"

Unsurprisingly, nobody moved.

"Not to worry, is there any one who knows how Building Societies have got rich by sitting on your money? Do you appreciate that, whilst some people are making a fortune by investing wisely, others are seeing their nest eggs dwindle daily as inflation and rising costs eat away at their capital?"

Unsurprisingly, the same reaction – not a flicker.

Joe launched into the well-tried formula of running down Building Societies, highlighting their poor returns, their high charges and their arrogance. He then pointed out how investments in Stock Markets, despite their modestly increased risk, have made millionaires out of paupers. He omitted to dwell on the inconvenient fact that there were some millionaires who had become paupers in much the same process.

"I like to think of ourselves as Investment Strategists," Joe intoned. "We don't promise the earth. We simply cut out all the jargon that some fund managers try to blind their clients with. We ensure that our clients have a good mix of risk, a balanced portfolio and an adequate income stream.

"We make sure that our clients invest their hard-earned money with some of the strongest Financial Institutions in the world with a truly global mix. We also make sure that the plans we recommend are tax-efficient."

Joe was pleased to observe that his audience were truly lost. A glazed expression was apparent on each and every face and a look of worried bewilderment was beginning to appear on the faces of the frailer members of his audience. It was as if he were speaking a foreign language and leading them into a hypnotic state.

He continued in a similar vein for a further fifteen minutes, failing to utter one single word of cogent financial advice. This he reserved until the moment he thought the time had come to wind up.

"So there we have it Ladies and Gentlemen," he concluded. "I am proud to present you with the opportunity to invest in one of the most attractive Investment Bonds ever offered to the British public, and at a discount never before envisaged by our Industry. As Mr Washington mentioned in his opening address, if you make an Investment today, the bid offer spread of five percent will be reduced to a mere four percent. In this way, Castle Finance will be ensuring that your money will be working flat out for you from the very first moment. That's a gift of one percent of whatever sum you might choose to invest – entirely free of tax. Now, are there any questions? Mr Field and I will be only too pleased to help you in any way that we are able."

Joe stood before them with an expectant expression on his face and with what, he liked to believe, a caring countenance. Not one hand was raised though Joe detected a few looks of relief on the faces of his audience that the lecture had concluded. It was as if they had just woken up to the fact that their ordeal was over.

Rising from his chair, Bill Washington addressed his residents.

"Many, many thanks indeed, Mr Hendry. An illuminating lecture on a difficult subject. I am sure that all of us have greatly appreciated the erudite way in which you have bought the vagaries of the world of high finance to our humble home and, so eloquently, explained the mysteries that surround them.

"I did not expect any questions at this time as I am sure that each of us feels that his or her own financial affairs are a very personal matter and, as such, not matters that should be discussed in front of an audience. I am sure that each and every one of you Ladies and Gentlemen will wish to have a personal consultation with either Mr Hendry or Mr Fields and I have, therefore, offered to lend them my own and Maureen's offices for the rest of the day. I will allot each of you fifteen minutes of their very valuable time and one of our Nursing Staff will come and locate you to bring you to an office so that you can all take advantage of this wonderful and most generous offer. With that Ladies and Gentlemen, I thank you all for attending and I call this meeting to a close."

During the course of the afternoon, Joe and Tom saw twelve residents each and explained in, glowing terms, the advantages of entrusting substantial amounts of their cash reserves to Apex Life. Those who had portfolios of Shares were promised a further visit once Castle Finance had been able to carry out a valuation and prepare a 'conceptual' investment report.

The latter, so the Residents would learn, would be a loosely worded recommendation to sell as many 'high risk' shares as they could and to transfer these funds to 'high commission' Bonds. A laudable strategy by any standards - by any of Castle Finance standards, that is.

During the course of the afternoon, Tom Fields had an interesting discussion with a Mrs Hampshire – a relatively sprightly lady of eighty who had been a resident at Meadow View for only twelve months.

"So wot you do luv," explained Tom, "is stick as much as you can wiv a Bond. Wot you 'ave at the moment, is twenty-five grand in the National Counties Building Society an' they're givin' you a measly seven percent a year. At the same time, the value of your twenty-five grand is goin' down the plug 'ole each year. Did you know, that ten years ago, you couldv'e bought a bleedin' Roller for twenty five grand. Now it'd cost you fifty grand. So where's the sense in that?"

"Young man, I've never spent twenty five thousand pounds on anything in my life. And anyway, what is a Roller – something for doing the garden? I haven't got a garden any more."

"Na," explained Tom. "A Roller is a car, a Rolls Royce. A bleedin' expensive car an' what I'm saying is if you'd left your money in the Building Society, whereas you could've afforded one ten years ago, it wouldn't buy you half of one now. If on the other 'and, if you'd put your money in one of our Bonds, you could buy ten bleedin' Rollers by now!"

"But I don't want a Rolls Royce young man. If I go anywhere, I go by taxi unless my son or daughter-in-law pick me up. Then I go in a very nice motor car. A very nice one indeed."

Exasperated, Tom persevered. "Any road up, luv, wot Mr Washington is telling you to do is to take your money out of the Building Society where they are robbin' you blind, an' put it wiv us so that you will get richer an' richer an' you won't 'ave to worry no more."

"Well I certainly trust Mr Washington and if that is what he says, I am sure that I should. I'd rather wait until I've discussed it with my son, if you don't mind. Since my late husband died, he has looked after all my money – it's a great comfort."

"I'm sure it is luv. The problem is though, if we don't get a cheque to Apex by first thing tomorrer, we lose out on the special offer. Now Mr Washington don't want any of you to do that, does he?"

"Oh dear, I suppose not. How much do you think I should invest?"

"Well, let's see. You've got twenty-five grand in the National Counties an' there must be almost a grand of interest still to go. You say that you've got a few 'undred in the Bank an' then you've got some Stocks an' Shares, but you don't know 'ow much. I suggest that we 'ave another meetin' next week to look at that. The important thing now is to make sure you don't miss this special offer. I fink you should put in twenty-four grand plus our fee which makes a total of (Tom tapped at his calculator) ah yes, twenty-four thousand six hundred pounds. Now let's get these forms filled in and a cheque written out cos' there's some more people out there waitin' to come in an' see me. What we do is fill in this Buildin' Society withdrawal form 'ere (Tom had bought withdrawal forms for almost every Building Society in the Country) an' they'll pay the money into your Bank wivin seven days. You give me a cheque on your Bank for twenty-four thousand six 'undred pounds an' we make sure that Apex Life don't get their sticky 'ands on your money till the Bank 'as cleared your Buildin' Society account. Easy as that!"

"You really are very kind Mr Fields to take so much trouble. I'm sorry if I've been a little slow in grasping what you and Mr Hendry have been saying. I'm sure if Mr Washington says so, everything's going to be alright."

"Course it is luv. We won't let you down. You put your trust in Joe an' me an' you won't know what to do wiv all the money wer'e goin to make yer. Now, you just sign 'ere, ere an' ere." Tom indicated the dotted lines on the forms that he'd already completed whilst they were talking.

Three hours later, Tom and Joe were sitting back in Bill Washington's Office enjoying a large scotch and soda, reviewing the day's labours.

"Not a bad day's work, Bill," Joe confided. "By my reckoning, Tom and I have written over two hundred thousand pounds of business today. That means a cheque for over five grand for you Bill. Better than a slap in the face with a cold kipper by anyone's standards."

"Not half, Joe," chuckled Bill. "I don't know how you do it. They're all daft as brushes and not one of them has the faintest idea how much they're worth or how much it costs to keep them here. Between you and me, we often have to take them to the Bank to get a transfer made so that our fees are paid in full – as you can imagine, living in a place as up-market as this, there are quite a few 'extras' and we like to deal directly with our residents rather than involving their families – they can be a bloody nuisance at time, I can tell you.

"Give it about six months, and they'll all have forgotten they'd been to this meeting and you could do it all again. I'll get Maureen to get you a list of what most of them have got in the Bank and elsewhere so that you could have another crack at it. I quite like the idea of the odd five grand every now and again."

"I told you it would be a piece of piss mate," added Tom. "Like taking candy from kids. You're sitting on a bleedin' gold mine 'ere you are."

Bill topped up their glasses again and the conversation continued until the weary but contented duo decided it was time to return to their Office to complete the paper work. A boring bind, but it was one that was going to make them another ten thousand pounds in excessively generous commission, and with more to come.

"God shines on the righteous," observed Joe.

Chapter Thirty-Two

"Chris, how are you? Roy here, Roy Brown. I just thought that I'd give you a call and see how things are going in your neck of the woods. It seems that there have been some pretty exciting things happening over there at Coopers."

"Good to hear from you, Roy," came Chris Wright's cheery reply. "You can say that again. I don't know whether I am on my head or my elbow. First I thought that we – that is ourselves and Harrison's – would be joining up together. That's something that I would have looked forward to, I can tell you – then the next thing that I hear is that the whole thing is off. Colin Cooper was stomping around like a bear with a sore head – absolutely beside himself with rage.

"It's my view that he used Tim to get some idea of the value of this business and then phoned pretty well every National Broker in London to see if he could get a better deal. The next thing was that Thompsons are round us like a rash and, surprise, surprise, the bastard's sold us out to them."

"Sounds as if you're not too happy with the deal Chris," observed Roy. "I thought that it would suit you down to the ground now that you've got some people around you who really know how to grow a Company. As I understand it, you're a key player. Your job should be safe now that you've got an account like Sunbury's to look after."

"Safe! Thompson's only interest in us is to transfer all the business to their Cheltenham Office, sack all the staff here and make a bigger margin than we could ever have hoped to. I'll be lucky if I've still got a job at all in six months. Even if Thompson's offered it, there's no way I could move to Cheltenham, what with the kids being in the middle of their "O" and "A" levels."

"You surprise me Chris. Anyway, I was wondering if you would fancy a beer and a bite sometime. Just to chew the cud and compare notes. Are you likely to be free one lunchtime in the next week or so?"

"How about one o'clock today Roy?" came the immediate response. "I could do with getting out of this madhouse for an hour or so. I'm free if you're free."

"Perfect Chris. Let's say one o'clock at the Kings Head. I'll bring Tim if he's free. I'm sure he'd like to have a chat with you."

"Suits me fine Roy. See you then. Cheers for now."

Roy strolled into Tim's Office and repeated the nub of his conversation with Chris.

"The bastards," retorted Tim. "That's just what we thought. Apart from doing us out of a bloody good deal, they've stuffed us over the Sunbury account under false pretences. I've a good idea to give Sir Leonard a call and tell him that they intend to bugger off out of here as soon as the ink is dry. Yes, sure, I'll join you for lunch. It'll be good to hear what Chris has to say. We might get the better of the buggers yet.

"By the way, I met a chap last night, a fellow called Martin Bushell. It appears that he lives next door to that chap Joe Hendry. You know, the fly boy that runs the firm that Jimmy Smith used to work for. A shady outfit by all accounts, but he appears to be making a ton of money. I wonder what we've been doing wrong. I think I'll get Jimmy and Chris in to see what they know."

"Janet," he called through the open door. "See if you can rustle up Chris and Jimmy will you please, and ask them to pop in for a chat."

A few moments later, Janet appeared round the door, wearing a light yellow short-sleeved summer frock. Tim's heart missed a beat. Was it only a few hours ago that he held that beautiful, naked body in his arms? He wondered if he would ever be able to resist her if the opportunity occurred again. Reluctantly, he hoped that such an opportunity would never arise again and banished such thoughts from his mind.

"Chris's out for the day, but Jimmy will be with you in a minute. Coffee everyone?" she smiled. She acted as if nothing had happened. Perhaps he had dreamed last night, Tim thought. He knew he had not.

As she left, Jimmy bowled in.

"Wotcha mates," he greeted them. "Just signed up another two grand's worth of business. Glad to say that everything's going like a train Tim. What can I do for you gentlemen?"

Tim told him of his discussion with Martin Bushell.

"Apart from the fact that I can tell you that Hendry's a total crook. I haven't heard too much of him or Castle Finance over the last few months. I've been too busy making you a rich man Tim. I did hear that the Life and Equity had gone belly up and I did wonder how that left Joe and his men. They placed absolutely everything with the one Company and I know that they had negotiated pretty fancy terms with them. God knows how they did it. It was a disaster waiting to happen. I've still got one or two ex-buddies who work there who I could give a call and try to suss things out a bit if that's what you'd like me to do."

"I certainly would Jimmy. It sounds as if we don't want to be a part of whatever they're up to, but if a Company the size of Apex Life has taken a twenty five percent stake in them, they must be doing something right. Companies like Apex don't exactly have a name for throwing their money about. Ah thanks Janet," he said as Janet re-appeared with a tray and three cups of coffee. As she passed Tim his cup, their hands touched and Tim felt as if a thousand volts had shot up his arm. He hoped that the other's had not noticed as he fought to keep the cup upright in its saucer.

"I think you could find that the only reason Apex took a stake in Castle Finance," suggested Roy, "was so that they could keep an eye on them. If what Jimmy says is true, one of the reasons for L & E's demise could have been the quality of the business that Castle was giving them. The lapse ratio on that sort of rubbish can be horrendous and the costs, consequently, astronomical. I very much doubt that the shareholders in Castle will have got rich on the money that Apex paid out for their shares. Anyway, it will be interesting to find out. You never know, we might even find a Father Christmas who would like to make us millionaires for our shares."

"Don't you buggers sell out until I've got my options," cut in Jimmy. "I've told my missus that that's what's going to provide our pension when I'm old and grey."

"Don't worry about that, Jimmy, I'm far too young to sell out, even if there was anyone out there mad enough to want to buy this cowboy outfit. No, all I want to do is make this the biggest and the best firm in the South East and then we'll sit back and see where we go from there. Plenty of time for you to make your fortune, I promise. Let's call it a day for now and you pop back when you've found out anything interesting about Castle."

The King's Head was a typical Country Pub a couple of miles out of Ashbridge. Oak beams, oak tables and chairs and, in the winter, a blazing log fire in the Inglenook fireplace.

When Tim and Roy arrived, Chris Wright was already seated at a table by the fire, nursing a pint of bitter. As he rose to greet them, Roy introduced Tim to Chris.

"A pleasure to meet you Tim," he said. "I've heard a great deal about you and it's good to be able to put a face to the name. What will you have?"

"No, sit down," said Roy. "I'll deal with this. You two get acquainted. Leave it to me and I'll go and get a bottle of red. Is a ploughman's all round OK for you? You get to know each other and I'll be back in a minute."

"I don't know what you've heard about me," began Tim, "but if it came from Colin Cooper, not too favourable I would imagine."

"I wouldn't say that," Chris replied. "I think he has a grudging respect for you. He's certainly pissed off when you pinch one of our Clients but he seems to be on a high at the moment. I think he feels that he's got one over on you at last – but I doubt it."

"Oh, what do you mean?" asked Tim.

"Well, it's no secret that Thompsons hate Christie and French. When they found out that they were unlikely to get Sunbury's account because Sir Leonard had a bee in his bonnet that he wanted local service – I suppose that you put that idea into his head – they realised that Colin had been trying to get them to make an offer for his business and they saw this as a way of pulling a stroke over on Christie and French. That's no basis for a sound commercial acquisition, is it?"

"It certainly isn't," rejoined Roy as he returned with a bottle of wine and three glasses. Made in heaven, a deal like that certainly is not. It will end in tears, I'm sure of it. But how does that leave you Chris? Over the phone you sounded none too happy."

"To tell the truth, I'm worried. I can, for the first time in my life, see redundancy staring me in the face and it's a very uncomfortable feeling. I've got the usual commitments of wife, family and mortgage and, under no circumstances can I afford to do anything that might jeopardise the boys' education. They're bright kids and their future is dependent on getting the right grades now. No, it has all come at the wrong time and I do find the whole thing rather unsettling."

The food arrived and they carried on chatting about generalities and Tim found that he was getting to like Chris, like him a lot.

"Cutting to nub of the matter Chris, we're looking for a General Manger. Roy and I would like to offer you the job. What do you think?"

"Wow," exclaimed Chris, "how would I like it? I would like it a lot. What sort of role would that involve? Tell me more. I'm interested, very interested."

By the time Tim and Roy left the pub, they had their new General Manager. He would give one month's notice and he would be starting at Harrisons on the first of December. All three felt that it had been an illuminating and very worthwhile lunchtime meeting.

....

That afternoon, Tim had an appointment that he would normally be looking forward to greatly but, on this occasion, he faced it with trepidation. He was going to see Martha Warrington, Bill's widow, to discuss her share holding and what she wanted to do with it.

Tim had wondered whether he should offer to buy the shares from her, but at what price? He really had no idea what the Company was now worth. At the same time, he was not entirely sure that he would be able to raise the cash necessary to give Martha a fair deal. Whatever price he paid, he was absolutely committed to paying the top dollar. Bill had meant everything to him and he would insist on paying Martha every penny she wanted if she wanted to give up her shares.

Or would she want to keep them? He and Mary had giggled at the thought of Martha sitting at their boardroom table. She was big hearted and generous but with a mouth like a navvy when she wanted to make her point. To her a spade was a fucking shovel and you couldn't help loving her for it.

Or would she pass her shares to her sons and ask one of them to sit on the board? Tim would not be averse to that. They were good solid citizens, but they were not their father. They would certainly not be liabilities to the Company, but Tim felt that there was very little that they could positively contribute to the success of an ongoing business such as his.

No, he had no idea what Martha would do and he only hoped that, whatever decision she had reached, he would be able to accommodate it.

....

"Come in luv, dump yer mac on the chair an' come in the sittin' room," Martha pointed to a priceless Chesterfield and helped Tim off with his Burberry raincoat. "I've got a fire goin' there an' Mary will be in in a minute wiv a nice cuppa. Let's 'ave a look at you. You're not puttin' on enough weight an' you're beginning to loose yer 'air. You're workin' too 'ard, that's the matter wiv you," she observed appraisingly.

"Thanks a lot, Martha, you sure know how to make a chap feel good!"

Tim settled down on a vast, luxurious, stuffed settee whilst Martha took up her position opposite him on an identical perch.

"Ah thanks Mary," she said as her faithful retainer entered the room. "Dump yer tray there and I'll pour. Nip off could you, and find some cakes or biscuits for Mr Harrison 'ere. He looks as if 'e's come straight out of bleedin' Belsen."

They chatted amiably for ten minutes or so. Martha gave the appearance of having not a care in the world but, at every mention of Bill's name, Tim could see moisture in her eyes. How she had loved that man he thought. How I loved him myself he confessed.

"Well Martha, when are we going to have the pleasure of your company at a board meeting?" he finally asked. "As a twenty five percent shareholder you're entitled to come whenever you like and very welcome you would be. I think that your advice would be invaluable and you'd certainly keep us smiling."

"Gawd! Me on a Board? You must be jokin'. No, no chance there dearie. I don't know if you knew it, but Bill thought the world of you. 'E was always saying what a true gent you was an' 'ow, if ever I was in trouble, I could always rely on you."

"That's very kind of you to say, Martha. I loved Bill. I owe him so much and, true, if there is anything, anything at all that I can do, you have only to ask."

"Gawd bless you for that Tim. Anyway, I never wanted any bleedin' shares, wouldn't know what to do wiv 'em. Bill's left me more than I know what to do wiv any road up. That bein' so, until a year ago, 'e 'ad left the whole lot in 'is Will to you an' Mary. 'E said you'd built the Company up, so you should 'ave the benefit. All of it."

"I don't know what to say." Tim was truly astounded. Although he had no idea what the shares were worth, the figure would be in the hundreds of thousands. He was completely shaken by Bill's generosity.

"I said 'until a year ago'. I don't know if 'e 'ad a premonition or anythin' like that, but last year 'e made a lot of changes to 'is will. I didn't understand everythin', but when 'e explained it all, it seemed like it was for the best.

"What 'e said was, you an' Mary deserved all your success an' the best way to make sure that 'arrisons continued growin' was to reward them wot 'ad also 'elped in it's success. I'll 'ave to leave the details to the Solicitors, but the nub is that 'e wants that lovely girl Janet to 'ave five percent – she's been a brick an' no mistake. 'e also wants Roy to 'ave five percent and another five percent for Graham - I don't know 'is other name - cos he thought that they all deserved a bit. The other ten percent 'e wants to place in a Trust or somefing so that all your employees can 'ave a bit. There, wot do you think of that? I 'ope you're not disappointed 'e changed 'is mind about you an' Mary. 'e said you would like wot 'e's done an' I 'ope 'e's right."

"Martha, that's the most wonderful thing I've heard in years. I don't know what to say. Bill's been so generous, and so have you. He could have insisted that you had the shares, even if you sold some. They would have been worth a lot of money – how much, I don't know, but enough to keep you going or quite a while. Janet will be absolutely thrilled. Particularly as she is so close to getting married, as you know. It will give them both a wonderful start in Life. Roy and Graham will be absolutely delighted too and, I can assure you, absolutely dumbstruck. The employees' Trust is a brilliant idea. They don't need incentivising, but I love the idea of giving them this reward. I cannot tell you how grateful I am and how grateful all my people will be, particularly Janet."

Half an hour and two cakes later, Tim was driving back to the Office. He hoped that Janet would still be there.

....

"If you've got a moment fellow shareholder, would you step into my Office please." He asked.

"What did you call me just then?" asked Janet as she followed him into his Office. "Fellow what?"

Tim told her of his meeting with Martha Warrington. At first she was wide-eyed with disbelief. Then she cried. She sobbed uncontrollably.

"What a lovely, lovely man," she sobbed. "I'm so happy with what he's done but so sad, so very sad, that I can't thank him. I can't believe it! I will go and see Martha tomorrow and thank her. They were two in a million."

"She would love that," said Tim, taking the opportunity to put a comforting arm around her shoulder. My, how she affects me, he thought guiltily. What wouldn't I give to spread her on the settee and make mad passionate love to her? Fortunately (or was it?) common sense reigned and he let her go. He returned hurriedly to his chair, as much as to conceal any chance that Janet could see the physical effect that she had had on him.

....

By the first of December, events at Harrisons had moved on a little.

The major happening had been Janet's wedding. It had been a small gathering, only twenty guests, a short service at the Registry Office and quiet reception at a local Hotel. It had been a bitter-sweet occasion for Tim. Janet looked absolutely ravishing and he simply failed in his efforts to banish the thoughts of what the happy pair would be doing together on this their Wedding night. It was, nevertheless, a very happy day and Tim was relieved that an impenetrable barrier had now been erected to make any further rupture of his marriage vows impossible.

Back in the Office, it transpired that Jimmy had been able to find out a lot of information about Castle Finance. What Tim learned convinced him that Direct Selling of Life Assurance was a business to be avoided at all costs.

The type of tricks that Joe Hendry and his boys were getting up to gave the Industry a bad name and it saddened Tim to think that it was possible for charlatans like Hendry to make so much money from the process of giving such appalling advice. Tim was not a whistle-blower himself, but he hoped that someone in a more knowledgeable position than he, would be able to bring such practices to an end in time.

He resolved to keep an eye on Castle Finance and asked Jimmy to let him know if he found out anything more that would be of interest to Harrison's.

On another front, Tim had been intrigued to hear from his contacts within the Universal – who underwrote a large proportion of Sunbury's account - that things had not been going too smoothly there.

It appeared that, rather than renew all the covers at the date of expiry of last year's policies, Sunbury had insisted that they wanted to change the renewal date to the first of January to coincide with their financial year. Thompsons had tried to talk Sunbury into a fifteen-month period of insurance with renewal to the first of January 1985 rather than 1984, but Sunbury's were having nothing of it.

....

"Come in," called Tim as Chris Wright tapped on his door. It was his first day at Harrisons. "Come in and welcome. Let me tell you a few things about Harrisons and then I'll get Roy and Graham to introduce you around. I'm sure that you'll already know quite a few people here, and I know that you'll be made to feel very welcome by all."

After Tim had told all he felt he would want to know, he asked, "By the way, when you were last in the Office, what was the position re the Sunbury business? I hear that there have been one or two glitches."

"You can say that again Tim," replied Chris. "It's a right can of worms and I'm glad that I'm out of it. There's no way that Coopers have the expertise to handle the account and Thompson's have sent one of their own chaps down from Cheltenham to do all the technical stuff. The chap they have sent is pretty pissed off because he only gets home week-ends and they have put him up in the Winchester Arms – you know what that's like; as crappy as they come. I'm sure he's been told to get the account transferred to Cheltenham asap."

"Very interesting Chris. We'll certainly have another go at that account next year. Now, here's Graham; over to you Graham. You show Chris what he's let himself in for and where he's to sit. Have a good day Chris."

After they had left, Tim mused over recent developments. He still felt sore that he had lost out to Coopers over Sunbury's and, in the process, had seen his acquisition ambitions bite the dust.

The phone rang. "Sir Leonard Passmore for you Tim," called Janet.

"Bloody hell! Put him through Janet."

"Mr Harrison, how are you?" came the modulated tones of this very likeable gentleman. "I trust I find you well."

"Fit as a fiddle, thank you Sir Leonard. It is good to hear from you. How can I help?"

"I'm afraid to say that we have been rather badly let down. I am sure that you will think that this is a problem entirely of our own making, but I thought that I would like to discuss it with you. Do you have a moment Mr Harrison?"

Tim's spirits soared. Did he have a moment? He would willingly devote the whole day to a discussion with Sir Leonard.

"Of course, Sir Leonard. What can I do for you? And please call me Tim – everyone else does."

"That's very good of you Tim, and do please call me Len. The handle is all well and good but it does make me seem rather pompous. The truth of the matter is that by two votes to one, we did make a decision to appoint you as our Insurance Brokers a few months ago. It was only at the eleventh hour that Thompsons surprised us by saying that they would be acquiring a local firm of Insurance Brokers and, in all conscience, we did not feel that we could cast them aside at that stage.

"However, it now transpires that their plans were a trifle premature and I am not entirely certain that this acquisition will proceed. Furthermore, it is now our belief that this acquisition was merely a foil and that, far from offering a local service, they intended that we should deal with their Cheltenham Office – the Ashbridge Office would simply have been a post box.

"I feel that we have been mislead and I don't like that. I don't like that at all.

"It may be a little presumptuous of us, particularly as we have 'turned you down' once, but I was wondering whether you would like to pop over one day and discuss the possibilities of your firm acting for us. I shall, of course, quite understand if you say no. We were very impressed by your presentation and particularly by your young man, Brian Epps, contribution. Would you find it an imposition to call over one day?"

"Absolutely not Len." Tim found that he felt rather uncomfortable about the Christian name familiarity, but, if that is what the client wanted, that was OK with him. "It would be a very great pleasure to visit you again. When would be convenient?"

"How is your diary fixed for next Tuesday, say ten in the morning? We have a Board Meeting on Wednesday and it would be quite nice to be able to report on our discussions then and try to reach a decision."

"Tuesday would be fine," said Tim without even looking at his diary. "If they are free, would you mind if I bring Brian and Graham with me?"

"Not at all Tim. In fact, that would be appreciated. That's capital, Tim. We shall look forward to seeing you on Tuesday. Goodbye for now."

As soon as he put the phone down, Tim literally leapt into Janet's room to relay the glad tidings and to summon Graham, Brian, Chris and, if he was there, Roy.

Chapter Thirty-Three

At about the same time as Tim's good news, a far less happy meeting was taking place in Colin Cooper's office.

Seated at his over-large desk sat a very uncomfortable looking Colin Cooper. He was showing obvious signs of strain, a worried frown and faint beads of sweat on his upper lip were forming small rivulets.

Sitting opposite him were Thomas Baker, his Accountant for the last twenty years and Simon Armstrong, the Chairman and Chief Executive of Thompsons UK.

"So having completed our due diligence Mr Cooper," Armstrong was saying, "we seem to have come up with more than one or two minor anomalies."

"I am quite certain, Mr Armstrong, that all the figures that we have given you can be borne out by the Accounts and the management figures that we provided to your people," averred Thomas Baker. "My firm cannot, of course, accept any responsibility for any opinions or statements of intent that the Directors may have given, but I am quite sure that anything that may have been said has been said in a spirit of the utmost good faith."

"Quite so, Mr Baker, but can you explain why, within only three months of signing our Heads of Agreement, income is almost fifty percent down on Budget for the same period?"

Baker looked at Colin for an answer.

"As you know, we are experiencing a very soft market at present and rates of premium are dropping steadily. In consequence, our revenue – our commissions - has dipped by about the same percentage."

"During the period in question, rates have dropped by an average of well under five percent," responded Armstrong. "That's a great deal less than fifty percent."

"Well, of course, there have been one or two losses of business. It is just possible that some of our long-standing clients have remained with us over the years and, as soon as they have seen that we have become a 'major', they may well have looked for a smaller Broker that they might conceive, quite erroneously of course, could give them a more personal service."

"With respect Mr Cooper, that is nonsense. Throughout all of our negotiations you have been telling us how much better off your clients would be to have the backing of a Company like ours with its considerable resources – risk management, surveying, IT and the like. It is simply not good enough to change your tune at this late stage. Either your business will expand with our backing, or it will contract. Which will it be? Why the volte face?"

"That's not at all what I meant," stuttered Colin. "There is no doubt that we are a more competitive Company and a stronger Company now that we are part of your Group. I am sure that, if you give us another three months, you will see a marked improvement."

"That is highly unlikely," snapped Armstrong. "Now, let's cut to the chase. According to these figures," Armstrong brandished a sheaf of computer print-outs, "over the last three months, you have lost twenty thousand pounds of brokerage against budget. My people tell me that ten thousand of this relates to the loss of the Hoskins and Hoskins business, eight thousand to the loss of The Central Cement Company and the rest to various odds and sods. Please explain these losses to me Mr Cooper."

Hoskins and Hoskins is very easy to explain – they were acquired by James Warner plc, an international consortium - who took the view that all their Insurances would be handled by the Group's brokers, Christie and French. Absolutely no reflection on us, or any of our staff – it would have happened to whoever held the account.

"Central Cement is a little more difficult. They had rather a large claim last year, when a load of cement that they delivered was found to be of the wrong consistency - too much sand - I believe. The result was that the entire foundations of a Tower Block that they were working on had to be dug out again and replaced. The work cost thirty thousand pounds and the Contractors are suing for a further fifty thousand pounds for penalties under their 'failure to complete' Clauses.

"Central claimed under their Public Liability Policies but we found that there was no 'Products' extension under their policy and the Insurers have refused to pay. They are suing us under our Professional Liability Policy. There is no need for you to worry since we have a limit of two hundred and fifty thousand so that our only cost will be our excess – one thousand pounds. We have provided for that in our Accounts, haven't we Tom? Not surprisingly, in view of this difficulty, they decided to appoint another Broker – Harrisons, I believe."

"Of course. As you have heard Mr Armstrong, all the information that you have been given is perfectly correct and the thousand pounds is fully provided for," affirmed Baker.

"Can you tell me when you first heard that Hoskins and Hoskins were being taken over?" cut in Armstrong.

"It was quite a while ago. I remember Bill Hoskins pushing the boat out at the Golf Club, champagne all round. We thought that he had holed in one! It must have been at least five, probably six months ago. He was over the moon to have sold out."

"And when did Central Cement initiate a claim against you?"

"I would have to check, but at least a year ago. These things take ages as I am sure you know. I would imagine that it will be at least another year before we reach any sort of conclusion. Unfortunately the Directors are all tough cookies and I can't see them accepting anything but the full figure. They will fight and fight. But that is our Insurer's problem, not ours."

"So let me get this straight," continued Armstrong. "At least one year ago you had every reason to believe that Central Cement, an eight thousand pound account, would almost certainly not renew with you. About six months ago, you knew for certain that Hoskins and Hoskins also would not be renewing with you. Can you tell me why, therefore, their income remains in the Budget that you produced for us prior to our making an offer? More to the point, could you please explain why these facts were not mentioned to our Accountants when they were carrying out their Due Diligence exercise? Is this memory lapse and example of your "utmost good faith"?

The colour drained from Colin's face. In his desire to paint the best possible picture of their dismal trading record, he had admitted that his Budgets were, at best, optimistic, at worst, deliberately misleading.

"I can assure you Mr Armstrong," added Baker hastily, "my firm was entirely unaware that either of these accounts were unlikely to renew. We merely compiled the figures from the information provided by the Directors."

"I am sure you did Mr Baker," said Armstrong stonily, "but I think that your enquiries could have been a little more searching. You are, after all, the Firm's Auditors. I am sure that you do not slavishly swallow everything that your clients tell you. Were that the case, there would be little point in carrying out an audit at all, would there?"

"Please don't get me wrong Mr Armstrong. We are very thorough in everything that we do. You will recall though, that there was a considerable urgency at the time and that we were working against a very tight time schedule to get the figures to you."

"So you're telling me that haste is an excuse for professional negligence are you?"

"No. Not at all. Its just that........."

"And you, Mr Cooper," cut in Armstrong, turning to Colin, "you are telling me that there was insufficient time to tell us that two of your largest clients were cancelling their business with you and you thought that it would be simpler to present misleading figures. How many more cases are there like these two?"

"None, I can assure you. We........."

"And another thing. You told me that your Account Executive, Mr Christopher Wright, was one of your best and most loyal employees. You told us how much you valued his support and that all the major accounts were overseen by him. You even admitted that you would find it extremely difficult to replace a man of his calibre and yet, within days of our signing, he handed in his notice. How long had you known about that Mr Cooper?"

"I knew nothing of his resignation at all, I swear," spluttered Colin. "It came as a complete surprise, totally out of the blue. It was that bastard Tim Harrison. He's pinched so many of my best clients and now he's pinching my staff." Colin was on the verge of tears.

"I saw no mention in your statement for Due Diligence of a sustained attack on your Business by a fellow Insurance Broker, and a local one at that. That would have been a material fact wouldn't you say? Particularly if you were acting in 'utmost good faith', as you tell me you were," he added dryly.

"We can explain all of these anomalies I am sure," Thomas Baker said attempting to pour oil on troubled waters. "If you will just be kind enough to give us a little time, a week should be quite sufficient, I am sure that we can give you a proper response to all of the matters that you have high-lighted today."

Plaintively, Colin added, "I am sure that you know, Mr Armstrong, that just because a Client is suing you, there is no guarantee that he will take his business away. Furthermore, there was always a possibility that Hoskins would have been able to keep their Insurances out of the Corporate programme and leave them with us."

"And pigs might fly," agreed Armstrong helpfully. "No gentlemen, I am afraid that the deal is off. As I said at the beginning of our discussion this morning, there are a great number of anomalies. Mr Lampard, who has been seconded to you to look after the Sunbury account – another appalling mess if you don't mind me saying – will be returning to Cheltenham with me today.

"All the stationery and manuals must be returned to us within seven days and their contents are to remain in the strictest confidence.

"My Board will consider whether or not they will wish to make a claim against your firm for all the costs and expenses that we have needlessly incurred. In the light of the misleading information that you have so recklessly put forward, I have to tell you, they are likely to be very aggressive. I must warn you too Mr Baker, that we will consider our position so far as a claim might be made against your firm for professional negligence in view of the considerable time and expense that this exercise has involved us in – unnecessarily, as it happens.

"I am sorry that things have gone so badly awry – we had been looking forward to a long and profitable relationship with Coopers and Smythe – but we are very disappointed with the way that we have been treated."

Rising from his chair, he addressed a crestfallen Colin Cooper and a shell-shocked Thomas Baker with a final, "With that I shall wish you adieu. Please do not bother to show me out."

After he had gone, Baker turned to Colin and said, "I told you that you were a bloody fool to bum up the figures so far. There was no way that a firm of Thompson's standing would not see through that blatant 'window dressing'. Now you are in deep shit and there is no way that we are going to go down with you. We will distance ourselves completely from the misleading information and the figures that you provided my Firm with. Your best bet will be to phone Tim Harrison now and see if he can rescue you, because if you don't get a backer now, you won't be here in six month's time, and that's a fact."

"Don't be so bloody stupid Tom. If you put your name to our figures, your head's on the chopping block the same as mine. As for calling Harrison, grow up. He'd laugh his head off and tell me to go screw myself. I would in his place."

"Well there's a lesson for you. When you pull out of one deal, always leave the door open in case the second one falls flat on its face. I've had enough of it all. As of now, my firm formally resigns as your Accountants and Auditors. I'm going back to my office now and you'll receive our letter of resignation in the morning. I want as much distance between you and us as possible. If Thompsons are going to start throwing writs about, we do not want to be in the firing line. Goodbye!" he called out as he slammed the door behind him leaving a stunned and ashen-faced Colin Cooper.

Chapter Thirty-Four

It was a bleak, grey, wintry day – the middle of January 1985. Tom Cummings was lounging back on the settee in Joe Hendry's newly redecorated and refurbished office. There was a definite sign of opulence in Joe's offices these days thought Tom. Even the coffee (freshly ground) was served in bone china cups and the secretaries had improved beyond measure. They all spoke with 'Sloane' accents and all dressed in the latest fashions.

He wondered if Joe was giving that tasty little receptionist, Rebecca was her name, a going over. He would for sure if he was sitting where Joe was. On the other hand, Tom recalled, Joe was clearly terrified of that tart Samantha that he had married. The thought of an expensive divorce was Joe's recurring nightmare.

"Why did you do it Joe?" his thoughts were spoken before he realised it.

"Why did I do what Tom?" asked Joe.

"Oh, I don't know. Why did you get married? You've got a load of crumpet around here on tap. Samantha is a lovely girl, I'll give you that," he lied, "but what was the point? She's into you for every penny and I'm sure she wouldn't give you half the fuck that that little bit of totty downstairs, Rebecca, would give you. I'd bet my balls on that."

"You may be right Tom. I've made some mistakes in my life, I'll grant you that. Marrying Samantha was probably the biggest. I should divorce her. I know that. But I can't be bothered. In any case, it would cost me a bleeding fortune. No, I fancy one or two of the birds around here and I'm sure they would open their legs for the boss any time of the day or night," he boasted. "But crapping on your own doorstep? No, too risky. If Samantha found out, and some bitch here would be bound to tell her, you can bank on that, she'd have by balls on a skewer. No way. Between you and me, I get all the sex I need at the 'Health Club' I visit once or twice a week. You pay for what you get – fucking marvellous, believe me – and with no strings attached. That's good enough for me. Anyway, why have you come? I'm bloody sure it wasn't to discuss my sex life. There must be some reason for you to forsake your golf or whatever you do on a winter's day like this."

"What do you know about General Insurance?" asked Tom unexpectedly.

"Sweet fuck all; why do you ask?"

"There's a chap at the Golf Club, a bloke called Colin Cooper. Do you know him?"

"Never heard of him."

"Well this Cooper bloke is an Insurance Broker and, over the years he's made a ton of money. Always mixing with the nobs up there. Big house on the hill, drives a Mercedes and his Missus' got a Range Rover. Both his kids went to private school. He must have been coining it but just now he seems to have taken a bit of a dive. He's resigned from the Committee and I notice he never comes into the bar after a round of golf – used to be the first to push the boat out – double scotches all round, none of your lagers and bitter shandies from him.

"I heard he tried to sell his Company a few months ago. Sold it for a hell of a lot to one of the big boys. But before you could say 'wink', a wheel fell off and the whole bloody deal was in the bin. I reckon he's desperate and I'm sure we could buy the business for a song."

"Why the bloody hell would we want to do that? We're doing very nicely as we are. We're expanding daily and Apex and friend Schmitt are behaving themselves. What do we want with an Insurance Broker and, even if we did, where would we get the money from?"

"Don't you see? People who insure their cars want Life Assurance. People who insure their houses want Life Assurance. All the businesses that they insure want Life Assurance and they want Pensions as well. There's a bucket of money to be made selling big pensions schemes. If we bought Cooper's business, we'd have thousands of punters at our finger-tips. And that's thousands of punters that we could send our boys out to sell to. We could make a fucking fortune.

"As to the money. How about friend Schmitt? He'd jump at the chance of expanding our business. He could put up the money for a hundred percent of the business and cede us, or in your language, give us, say fifty percent for a "finder's fee" as well as running the bloody thing for them."

Joe sat back and thought a while. Christ, he thought, Tom might have come up trumps yet again. Not a bad idea, not a bad idea at all.

"I think that you might have come up with a goer," he smiled. "What do we do, talk to Cooper, or have a word with Schmitt first to see if he likes it?"

"No way Joe. If we give Schmitt the idea first, the bastard would get one of his chaps to take a look at it and we'd be out in the cold. No, the way we play this is to go and see this bloke Cooper and find out what sort of business he's running. If we like the look of it, we offer him a bloody silly price but tell him that we've got a major International Financial Institution backing us so, if he goes for the deal, he knows the money would be good. Then, and only then, do we go and see Peter Schmitt and tell him it's his lucky day."

Tom suggested that it was about time that he and Joe went to the pub to discuss things further and, with no persuasion necessary, the meeting was adjourned to the more hospitable environs of the Coach and Horses.

....

Back at Harrisons, business was proceeding normally.

"Tim," called Janet, "I've got Colin Cooper on the line."

Ever since Sunbury's had appointed Harrisons as their Insurance Brokers, Tim had wondered what Colin Cooper had been making of things. According to the grapevine, Colin was taking the failure of his deal with Thompsons, pretty badly. Chris Wright had told him that he was almost suicidal at the time but that he had seemed to have been improving recently. He seemed to be pulling himself together.

"Hello Colin, how are you?" greeted Tim warmly. Never one to bear a grudge, he was genuinely interested in Colin's position and rather intrigued as to why he had called him. Their last conversation had ended on an extraordinarily hostile note.

"I'll come straight to the point Tim, I've been a bloody fool. The offer that you made me about six month's ago was, on reflection, about right. In fact, under the circumstances, it was generous and I should have accepted it.

"I'm sure you realise that Thompson's offer, coming as it did rather unexpectedly, put me in an extremely difficult position and I was under an obligation to do the best by my shareholders."

Tim thought that it would be rather churlish to point out that Colin held ninety eight percent of the Company's shares and that the remaining two percent was held in equal proportions by his wife and his very aged mother. The likelihood of Colin consulting, or even worrying about his shareholders, was about as likely as the Pope inviting Satan to dinner.

"Of course, Colin, I understand that. Business is business. But how can I help now?"

"I won't beat about the bush Tim. I'm too old for this game. I want my clients to be properly looked after and I want my staff to know that they have a job, a good job, for as long as I have anything to do with the firm. I'm looking for a partner and I was wondering if you would be interested."

"A partner or as a purchaser, Colin?" Tim couldn't quite let the opportunity pass without a little twist of the knife and to enjoy the sound of Colin squirming. Why couldn't he admit that he was in trouble and needed someone to bail him out?

"Either Tim. I'm fairly relaxed. I suppose, on balance, if you were interested, it would be better from your point of view to take the whole thing over lock stock and barrel."

"You could be right Colin. I don't know though. We've got a lot on at the moment. If we did think about getting together, we would have to have a total commitment that you are serious. We couldn't go all the way to Heads of Agreement again and risk you changing your mind at the eleventh hour as you did last time. That did, I'm afraid, cost us a great deal in nervous energy, to say nothing of the abortive Legal and Accountancy fees that we piled up."

"Absolutely Tim. I give you my solemn word that, if we decide that you would like to merge our Companies (still no admission of the dreaded word "sell" Tim noticed) then I will see the deal through to completion. I promise that I would not let you down a second time."

"OK Colin. I'll tell you what I'll do. I'll have a word with Roy and Graham here and you get together the 'shopping list' of what we'll need. I'm sure that you must have everything more or less ready following your deal with Thompsons. If Roy and Graham are happy with the idea, I'll give you a call and let's fix a date for a preliminary discussion."

"Excellent. I'll start work straight away. When do you think you will be ready for a meeting?"

Tim saw no point in letting him off the hook too gently.

"As I say, we've got a lot on at the moment. I should be able to get together with the others by the end of this week. I will try to give you a call on Monday, say Tuesday at the latest. Will that be alright with you?"

"Thank you, that will be just fine," not quite disguising a note of bitter disappointment that this meeting did not appear to be as much a priority as he would like it to be. "I'll look forward to hearing from you. Goodbye."

....

"If I remember aright," Roy was saying, "we had in mind offering Colin two hundred thousand pounds plus another two instalments of one hundred each over two years if he performed to target."

"In my view," commented Chris Wright, "that would have been on the high side then and would be far too excessive now. As I told you when I joined you, we had already lost a couple of our largest clients and there were one or two others that looked a little dodgy. I don't know whether the on-off deal with Thompsons had any adverse effect, but it certainly would have unsettled some of our older clients. They're not keen on change. We would have to bear in mind, also, that a change to Harrisons could cause a further disruption, though with me here, we should be able to limit any further damage. I don't know too much about valuing a business, but I reckon you should get it for its net asset value plus a reasonable income for Colin – a Pension or something like that. He's scared rigid of not being able to maintain his current standard of living. Appearances are everything to Colin and, as for his wife, well........."

"That's more or less what you had in mind, wasn't it Roy? Give him enough to live on," said Tim.

"Precisely Tim. Apart from anything else, if we can pay for the business out of revenue, it will lessen the need for us to go to the Bank. I'm sure that Tony Fellowes will give us all the support we need, but if we can avoid borrowings, then so much the better."

"How about we get the Building valued and pay him the full value of the building itself up front? We could then keep him on as a Consultant for another five years – he says he will be sixty next year. We could then shove some money in his Pension Fund and then say goodbye when he's sixty five. If he invests the cash from the sale of the Office wisely – and Tony Abbott could help him with that - he should be able to make his income up to more or less where it is today. What do you think?"

"Actually, gentlemen," interjected Chris, "it will more than make up his income. Though he won't admit it, profits have been dropping so steadily that Colin is within an ace of having to cut his salary by quite a chunk anyway. I do know for sure, that he hasn't been able to pay out any dividend on his shares for at least the last three years."

"Well that's it then chaps. I'll give Colin a call tomorrow and arrange to meet him on Monday. Are you free after lunch Roy? Don't take offence Chris, but I think that it might be more diplomatic if just Roy and I deal with this – you could be a red rag to a bull in Colin's eyes."

Chris agreed totally. "I would be too embarrassed having a conversation like this having been his employee for over ten years. No, I'd much rather leave it to you and I wish you both the very best of luck. Though his business is in decline, there are still some very good clients there and, properly managed, there could be some substantial organic growth. Don't forget also, his Life and Pensions business is miniscule compared with ours. You let Chris and Tony loose in there and you could make a fortune just by doing the job properly."

"Saying that reminds me that I rather like Colin's Office. At the rate we're expanding, it would make sense keeping that and putting, say our Life and

Pensions and our Accounts staff there, and leaving more room here for our General staff," said Tim.

"My thoughts precisely. Let's see what we can do. Yes, Monday afternoon suits me fine. You don't get much free time here being a non-executive Director it seems," laughed Roy.

"Yeah, but think of the value of your shares. You'll be laughing all the way to the Bank when we do eventually kick you out to grass you miserable old bugger," Tim pointed out, not unreasonably.

....

Colin's office building had once been a handsome, rambling Georgian Mansion sitting on the edge of Ashbridge. As the town had expanded, so the building had become swallowed up by the urban sprawl, so that it now occupied a relatively spacious site pretty well in the dead centre of town.

It boasted adequate parking space and, to other Employers' envy, an attractive garden where the staff, in summer months, could sit out, relax and eat their sandwiches.

Tim felt a tingle of excitement as he entered the building to the think that, one day soon, this could all be his. He was determined to make the deal work this time.

"Nice to see you again Colin," he said as his host ushered him into his Office.

"Good to see you too Tim. How are you Roy? Long time no see." Colin was trying hard to be the gracious host but it was plain to see that, in reality, he felt like the lamb inviting the wolf in for tea.

"Fine Colin thanks. I had hoped to have retired by now but this young bugger keeps me working. Don't know why I put up with it. At my age I should be playing bowls, mowing the lawn and watching the flowers grow. If he has his way, I'll be pushing up the daisies whilst I'm still in harness."

"You love it and you know it," rejoined Tim. "The truth is, Colin, he won't take the hint. I've been trying to get rid of him for ages but he just keeps coming back. I think the real truth is that Margaret can't stand the thought of him getting under her feet all day, so she dumps him on me. Anyway, to business. We've given your proposition a lot of thought and I'm pleased to say that we are interested."

"Did you get all the bumph that I asked my new Accountants to send you? You should have everything that you need there. There are no secrets in this organisation. If we are to do a deal, I want don't want you complaining that I haven't told you this or I haven't told you that. Let's have everything open and above board – that's my motto."

"Great. Yes we've had a chance to skim through everything and Gordon, my FD, is going through it all with a fine toothcomb. So far, he has not said to me that he has found any surprises."

"We think," Tim continued, "that your business has, for several reasons, reduced a little in value since we last spoke. As you know, we're in a soft market at the moment and we think that premiums and rates of commission will continue to drop slightly for the foreseeable future. Furthermore, we believe that you may have lost one or two clients recently."

"What's Wright been telling you? I hope he hasn't been betraying any confidences He's still bound by his covenants with us you know," shot back Colin, noticeably aggressively.

"Not at all, though he did say that Thompsons may have pulled out because they thought that the future profits might prove to be less than those that you enjoyed in the past. Anyway, that's beside the point. It is virtually impossible to value your business at this moment because of the relative state of flux you have found yourself in. What we need to do is to find a formula which will allow us to pay what we can afford, and give you what you could reasonably expect. That way, we should have a deal. Roy, would you like to take it from here?"

Two hours later, they had struck a deal. Roy brought the negotiations to a close by saying, "What I would like to suggest Colin, is that we ask your secretary to pop in so that we can dictate the principle headings that we have agreed, and that we all initial it here and now. That way there can be no future misunderstanding as to what our intentions were today. It would all, of course, be 'subject to contract' so there would be nothing binding – more a Gentlemen's agreement if you like."

"That's fine by me," agreed Colin, picking up his phone. "Stephanie, would you come in a moment?" No 'please' noted Tim. There would have to be changes made here, he thought.

A further hour passed by until Roy and Tim were able to wish their host farewell and climb back into Tim's car. In his briefcase Tim had the piece of paper affirming their intention to buy the business of Cooper and Smythe Ltd for the sum of fifty thousand pounds, plus the Freehold of the premises at valuation. Furthermore, Colin would act as a Consultant, working one day a week, for a period of five years in return for a salary of fifteen thousand pounds a year plus a Pension contribution of five thousand pounds a year. In addition, Colin would receive a small commission in respect of any new business that he might be able to introduce to the firm.

Colin had been resolute in his insistence that the business was worth more than double what they were offering. The 'clincher' came at the end when Roy had suggested that the new business should be known as "Harrison Cooper".

"That was a brilliant suggestion," Tim told Roy. "We seemed to be getting nowhere, just going round and round in circles over the same old ground over and over again. I reckon the thought that his name would continue on the note-paper has cost him the thick end of a hundred grand. To get the deal done, I would certainly have gone another fifty thousand, probably more."

Just shows you that, old as I may be, I'm still worth my weight in gold to you. Just you remember that young man. Anyway, from Colin's point of view, it's a fair enough deal. He gets just about enough to live on comfortably and he retains his status. That more than anything, is what he wants. The thought of having to eat 'humble pie' and admit that he is almost broke would have finished him off. The way things are now, he'll be able to tell all his chums that he's pulled off a coup. He'll be telling everyone that he's merged his Company with ours and that we feel he's so valuable that we have persuaded him to help us out for another five years."

"Still," agreed Tim, "what does all that matter? We've bought a solid business that we can develop for an amount that we can easily service from our annual revenue. Our only borrowings will be a Mortgage on the property which, we need in any case, and which won't be a bad investment at all on its own merits. No, not a bad day's work at all Roy. Many thanks – you probably are worth the enormous fees we pay you now."

"Ta very much, you ungrateful swine," was the considered response.

Chapter Thirty-Five

A week had gone by since Tom Cummings had suggested that they might consider trying to buy Cooper and Smythe. He had been busy sorting out a few personal affairs, but he now found himself at the office and at a loose end. Might as well give it a go he thought to himself and asked Rebecca to get Colin Cooper on the phone.

"Colin," he announced, "This is Tom Cummings. We have met at the golf club once or twice. Never actually played with you but I have seen you about from time to time."

"Yes, Tom, I remember you," replied Colin uncertainly. "What can I do for you? If you're looking for a game, I'm afraid I'm not playing much at the moment. Pressure of work and all that sort of thing – I'm inundated. You know how it is."

"Sure do, never a dull moment here. No it is nothing to do with Golf. I couldn't help overhearing the other day that you were thinking of selling your business. I was just wondering, if that were true, whether we might be able to have a chat. I'm in a similar line of business myself, or pretty well the same – Castle Finance – you may have heard of us. I happen to be the Chairman and we are pretty acquisitive at the moment. I've got some very strong backers and they're very keen to see us expand, and fast. They are a Multinational Institution with unlimited funds. They look upon us as candidates for a flotation in the not too distant future and the sooner we can double our size, the better. Would you be interested in a meeting, entirely without any commitment, of course?"

Damn it thought Colin. If only this conversation had taken place a fortnight before – before he had agreed to do a deal with Harrison. Still, no harm in hearing what this man has to say. After all, he hadn't signed anything legally enforceable yet – only a bit of paper agreeing to take things further.

"Well, I would be interested but, unfortunately, I have already had a very attractive offer from another party and I'm afraid that it might be too late now."

"Sorry to hear that, but good for you. How far advanced are your discussions? Is there any room for manoeuvre? My people are very keen to take things further and there would certainly be no trouble in finding the cash."

"We are pretty far advanced, but no money has changed hands so far so I don't see why we could not at least have a chat. Nothing is ever completed in this world until the cash is in the Bank, I always say. When would you have in mind?"

"How about this afternoon, Colin? No point in letting the grass grow under our feet."

Colin found the thought of trying to get a higher offer for his business infinitely more appealing than anything else he had scheduled for the afternoon. Tim was robbing him blind anyway, so perhaps this conversation would give him the opportunity to screw a little more out of the tight-fisted bastard.

"This afternoon would be fine. I'll cancel my three o'clock, how about three-thirty here at my office?"

"That would be just fine Colin. I'll bring Joe Hendry, my MD, with me and we will see what can be done. Look forward to seeing you then."

Tom gave his accountants a call and instructed them to find out anything that they could about the financial health of Cooper and Smythe Ltd and told them that he would call round in an hour to pick up anything that they had got.

By the time he arrived at his Accountants, they had faxed copies of Cooper's last three years' Accounts and they were able to advise him that, in their opinion, this Company was solvent, but heading gradually South.

"If I were you, I wouldn't touch it with a barge pole," George Chalmers told him, "unless, of course, you were interested in buying their freehold cheap – wouldn't mind those offices myself."

"We could do with the space, but the real reason for my interest is that they have a lot of well-heeled punters that my boys could get stuck into. As I hear it, he's desperate to sell and if we can pull one over on Harrison's who have already made him an offer, nothing would please us more. They pinched one of my best chaps a few years ago and, every now and then, as soon as we've got a really good producer, Jimmy Smith tries to get his hooks into them too. Costs me a fortune in increased bonuses just to keep them."

"Best of luck then, Tom. You know your business, but if there's anything I can do, just give me a call."

At three-thirty precisely, Tom and Joe walked into Colin Cooper's office. They were mildly impressed by what they saw but struck by the faded splendour of the décor and the well-worn furnishings. This used to be a profitable business, thought Tom, but in recent years things had evidently not been so good.

"Good to meet you again Colin, let me introduce you to Joe Hendry. Joe's been running Castle Finance since we started – must be fifteen years now, isn't it Joe?"

"Almost to the day Tom," concurred Joe. "Nice to meet you Colin."

After the ritual cups of coffee were served, Colin got down to business.

"I do hope that this will not be a wasted journey for you gentlemen. Until recently, I had no intention of selling the business when, out of the blue, I received the proverbial deal that I could not refuse. One of the largest Insurance Brokers in the land had obviously been keeping an eye on us down here and clearly liked what they saw.

"Entirely without any warning, they bowled in here and offered me a very substantial sum for the Company.

"I must confess that I was rather flattered by their attention and, in the heat of the moment, I was completely won over by them.

"It was only when I realised that the offer would not have been in the best interests of my staff – they always come first and foremost in my consideration, as I am sure you will appreciate – that I began to have second thoughts.

"It became apparent that they would be expecting my key staff to move to Cheltenham and those that refused would have been given the heave-ho. As soon as this became evident, I had no alternative but to pull out – at a great personal cost to myself I have to say - as I am sure you will appreciate. Still, one has to live with oneself and I have always acknowledged my responsibilities."

"I can see that we cut are from the same mould," confirmed Joe gravely. "Our most valuable asset is our staff. There is nothing that I would do to jeopardise their security and well-being. So, tell me, why have you been considering another offer?"

Tom was impressed. He could almost believe this pious nonsense.

"Again gentlemen, this also was entirely unexpected. I was sitting here quietly one day when I received a call from Tim Harrison. I know he has always envied our operation here and he's young and keen to grow – he would like to be able to mirror this operation himself if he could (which I seriously doubt he would ever be capable of). It would seem that he is not without his own problems and he felt that a merger with Cooper and Smythe would increase his credibility in the market place – which, of course, it assuredly would. We are pretty highly regarded in our particular market place.

"He also made me a very generous offer though, of course, one of his main stipulations is that I should remain on board for a minimum of five years. In that way, he would be bound to learn how to run a successful and well-respected broking house. It would also mean, of course, that I would be able to protect my own staff for a period of five years. In my opinion, my staff would soon see his staff out of the door, such is their quality – they are like chalk and cheese in comparison. In fact, I had been trying to get rid of one of my real duffers for years, a chap called Wright. I only kept him on out of loyalty and, lo and behold, one day he told me that Harrisons had offered him a job at an increased salary. It was as much as I could do to keep a straight face.

"Anyway, that's where we are at the moment. They have made me an offer and, since I'm now sixty and would like a little more time to myself – you can't keep up a seven day a week job for ever - I am inclined to accept."

"Would you care to tell me how much they have offered, Colin?" asked Tom innocently.

"Afraid I can't do that old man. I wouldn't betray another firm's confidence, even though, at this moment, they are the opposition. It is a matter of professional ethics. I can say, however, that I did turn down the thick end of three-quarters of a million about three months ago."

Like hell you did, thought Tom.

"You will appreciate Colin, that we've only had the sketchiest information about your Company so far," he said. "We would like to see a full set of accounts, current management information and all that sort of thing before we could make a firm offer. Our main interest in your Company is the potential to develop your Life and Pensions business. We have some pretty cute salesmen and, given the opportunity, they should be able to make a mint if given a chance to get amongst some of your wealthier clients. Do you think that there is any potential there?"

"An absolute gold mine old boy," replied Colin without hesitation. "I've been keeping on to my chaps for years that they don't do enough in that division. We've got millionaires, we've got Company Directors, we've got Doctors, we've got Solicitors, you name them, we've got them – clients who have been with us over twenty years. Do our chaps sell enough to them? Do they hell. If I were younger, I'd be in there day and night making sure that they've got pensions coming out of their ears. The one thing you learn in this business is that you can't do everything yourself. No, there are rich pickings out there for the right sort of men. I've been too soft with my people – I have never put them under enough pressure. But with a company like yours involved, well the world is your oyster."

"That's encouraging Colin. If you can get the information to me that we will need, Joe and I will have a think and a chat to our backers and see if we can come up with an interesting proposition."

"I've got it all here," said Colin hastily. "Having gone through this exercise twice in recent months, I've got everything that you'll need right here." He handed them a folder bulging with three year's bound copies of their Accounts, computer print outs, sample brochures and draft staff service contracts.

"I think you will find the lot here – in the strictest confidence of course. I don't know about your time-table, but please appreciate that Harrison's have made me an offer and I think that they are expecting to wrap everything up in days rather than weeks. Having met you both, I must say that I have a feeling that a merger with your very fine firm might prove a more attractive proposition, all other things being equal. I am, of course, thinking of my staffs' welfare."

"Of course," concurred Joe. "Our thoughts precisely. I can't see why Tom and I shouldn't be able to get back to you before the end of the week."

"Splendid, let me show you out and I very much look forward to our next meeting."

In the car on the way back, Tom turned to Joe, "he's a lying little prat, is our Mr Cooper. He's desperate to sell and, as to an offer of three-quarters of a million pounds, what planet does he think we've come from?"

"What do you think the business is worth then," asked Joe.

Rifling through the data on his lap, Tom opined, "I'd say, looking at this pile of information, I would think that a fiver should cover it. He's been going backwards for years. If he got half that figure, he would be bloody lucky. Still, that's not our problem. If we buy the business, we won't be paying for it, Apex Life will."

....

"Kevin, nice of you to spare the time," said Tom as he entered Schmitt's impressive office the following morning. "As I said yesterday, I've got an interesting proposition here that you might like to think about.

"As you know, Joe and I have been thinking of expanding into General Insurance to build up a client bank that our blokes can have a crack at.

"There's a friend of mine at the Golf Club, a Colin Cooper, who's got a fantastic business but he's decided that he would like to retire. The trouble is that another firm, Harrison's, have already made him an offer – about three-quarters of a million – but, because I know the bloke well and I get on with him, I think that, given the backing, we could steal it from under their noses.

"What I had in mind was a proposition that, if Apex would like to put up say half a million, we could buy it in Castle Finance's name. Colin will only deal with me personally. That would mean that Apex would get seventy five percent of the business for a paltry five hundred grand and Joe and me would get twenty five percent of the equity for setting the deal up and for running the show."

"That seems a lot of dough to make you two a present of twenty five percent of a Company," retorted Schmitt brusquely.

"Hardly a 'present' Peter. It would be part finder's fee and part our commitment to run it for you. By the time we get going on Coopers, you'd be making a fortune in dividends to say nothing of the increased business that Apex would be getting from all their clients."

"I'm not so sure that we want to fanny around with General Insurance. Our people in South Africa do, but we're strictly Life and Pensions only in the UK. Still, I'll take a look at all this stuff, get our Accounts people to run a rule over it, and get back to you. OK?"

"Sure Peter. How long do you think that will take?"

"What's the hurry? A week or two at the most."

"I'm afraid there is a rush. Harrisons have made their offer and unless Colin thinks I'm serious, he'll go for their deal. I don't think he'll risk losing that deal."

"You tell him that it's in the hands of one of the largest financial conglomerates in the world. If that doesn't hold his attention, then he's a bigger prat than you thought. If we don't like it and Harrisons take it, that's not our problem."

Somewhat irritated, Tom had to leave it at that. He never did like dealing with South Africans and this one was no exception. Schmitt never had time for other people's views and seemed totally devoid of any social graces. However, Schmitt held the purse strings and if Tom wanted to get at the cash, he'd have to play along with him. You do not have to be in love with your business partners, he reminded himself.

....

Only two days later, Schmitt summoned Tom and Joe back to his Office.

"Tom, Joe" he said, "meet Bill Capaldi, the CEO of CFA – the Combined Financial of America. CFA are, as I am sure you know, one of the largest Casualty Insurers in the States. They represent our interests over there and they're in the process of joining together with us over here. We've got quite a few projects on the boil together haven't we Bill?"

"That we have Peter. Gentlemen," Capaldi said, turning to Tom and Joe, "We at CFA find ourselves in more or less the same position that Apex were in here five years ago. We are, at this point in time, in a position that we can do a great deal of regular premium business and get some pretty useful tax breaks whilst Peter here has about used all of his tax breaks up. In other words, we're keen to take on as much regular premium business as we can whilst Peter wants to concentrate on the single premium business end – bonds and that sort of thing.

"At the same time, unlike Apex, we're into general Insurance business too and we could find an investment in Cooper and Smythe an interesting proposition, subject of course to all the usual checks and balances.

"You told Peter that you reckon that the business could be taken for about five hundred grand, give or take a dime. The idea that Peter and I have hatched up is that we buy twenty five percent of your Company for five hundred grand and your company uses the cash to buy Coopers. That way, we have enhanced the value of your holding by creating a stake in another business, diversification if you like, and we and Apex have a meaningful stake in the whole operation."

"Hang on a minute," exclaimed Tom, "you seriously think that Joe and I would dilute our stake to fifty percent? No way. We've taken years building this business up and we're not about to see our shareholdings halved."

"But they're not being halved Tom," cut in Schmitt. "Under this deal, you and Joe will have an asset worth over five hundred thousand pounds – probably a great deal more when you look at the overall package. This is a clear case where the whole is worth very much more than the sum of the parts."

"You might see it that way Peter, but I don't. What alternatives have you to suggest?"

"Actually, none." Schmitt was unmoved by Tom's distress. "Its 'take it or leave it' time again. If you don't want to go along, that's fine and dandy by us. We'll go ahead on our own and buy Coopers ourselves and we'll put a team into manage it. At the same time, we'll stop taking on your new regular premium business, there's too little profit in it for us now, and you can find another Company to support you."

"Are you seriously saying if we don't go along with you, we're stuffed?" Joe spoke for the first time.

"Got it in one," affirmed Capaldi. "Anyone for another cup of tea?"

They continued discussing all the possibilities that they could think of but, before long, Tom realised that they had been shafted and that they had nowhere else to go except with these bastards. At least, Tom comforted himself, none of his money was on the table. In fact, twelve and a half percent of the enlarged Company probably was worth more than twenty five percent of Castle Finance on its own. Furthermore, all their eggs were no longer in the same basket.

"Alright gentlemen, we will go along with your suggestion," he accepted, as if he had any choice in the matter. "I'll give Cooper a call tomorrow and wrap up a deal where we'll pay two hundred and fifty grand now and a similar sum at the end of twenty four months provided that the business has performed to target. That should do it; I know that he'd give his right bollock to be able to hold up his head again at the Golf Club."

....

It was Friday and Tim gave Colin Cooper a call. "Glad to say that my Solicitor has called and confirmed that everything's done and dusted now and that we can exchange contracts exactly as per our heads of Agreement. I know that you're in a hurry to get things finalised, and so are we, so how about us getting together at five this evening to sign all the papers and then perhaps you and Eileen would care to join Mary and I for Dinner tonight? It would be good to celebrate. The champagne will be on Harrison's of course."

"Very kind of you Tim but, er, I've got quite a lot on this evening. Today would be a bit tricky. I would rather make it one day next week. Thursday looks pretty good."

"Thursday?" echoed Tim. "That's a long way down the line. You're not cooling off the idea are you?" he laughed.

"No. Of course not. Very keen still. It's just that we're very busy at the moment and I want to get everything up straight. I could make Wednesday, I suppose. Yes, let's go for Wednesday. I could be at your Solicitors at five and, if the offer's still on, we'd love to join you somewhere for Dinner."

Tim felt the first twinges of uncertainty. Surely he wasn't going to renege on a deal for a second time? No, perhaps he is telling the truth, it must be hard to give up one's business after all these years. Yes, perhaps he should proceed slowly for Colin's sake.

"OK Colin, I'll give George a call and tell him to have the Champagne on ice for five o'clock on Wednesday. Let me know if anything crops up in the meantime."

....

The next call that Colin Cooper took was from Tom Cummings.

"Good news Colin. I've just come from my people and they've agreed the finance. We're going to offer you two hundred and fifty grand on the nose and another two and a half after two years. When do you want to meet to wrap things up? My people won't hold out the finance for ever, so the sooner the better."

"Oh. I thought that we were looking at six hundred and that it would all be up front. You didn't say anything about waiting. I'm not sure I could go along with a deal like that."

"Fair enough," said Tom. "I understand. We'll call it a day then and I wish you luck with your other negotiations. It's been good talking with you."

"Hold on, hold on. I didn't say that I couldn't do the deal in two parts. It's just that I would have preferred to wrap it all up in one go. What do we have to do to guarantee the second payment?"

Tom smiled. He knew he had his man by his short and curlies and he could now give them a little squeeze to see how far he could go.

"Easy Colin, you just make your brokerage increase by ten percent each year, and you get the lot. Any shortfall, and the payment will be reduced pro rata."

"Ten percent a year! You know I can't guarantee that. Anyway, what if I should do more than ten percent, I presume the second payment is increased pro rata?"

"No way sunshine," said Tom cheerily. "You know that five hundred grand is a bloody good figure. You won't get anything like that anywhere else. It's just that your business fits into our strategy at this point in time and that we can afford to be a little generous. I tell you what. That's the deal, but let's meet and talk and if there is anyway that I can relax the terms for the second payment, I'll see what I can do. It's Saturday tomorrow. Why not come to my house at about ten and we'll have an informal chat?"

"I'd love to. Will there be any one else there or will it be just you and me?" Colin, quite rightly, had picked up that there may be a hidden agenda lurking somewhere.

"No just the two of us. You know where I live. I'll see you at ten."

....

As Colin drew into the drive of Aspley House, he could not help but be impressed. A wide entrance gave way to a tree-lined turning area flanked by beautifully manicured lawns. The garden, in superb condition, must be at least three acres he estimated. The imposing Georgian-style house would have at least seven bedrooms and three reception rooms. Tom lived in some style, more so than he, thought Colin ruefully.

Tom strolled out to greet him as Colin slammed his car door. "Let's go round to the pool house," he suggested. "I've got a bar there and we can talk in peace."

After they were settled and Colin was well into his first scotch and soda, Tom announced, "I've been giving our deal a lot of thought and I want to make things as easy as possible. My backers are rolling in money but they are tough bastards and they are completely inflexible.

"I told them that you kicked at the ten percent stipulation (as it happened, he hadn't spoken to them for forty eight hours) and their first reaction was to pull the deal. However, I told them that we wanted your complete co-operation and backing and that we should relax a little.

"It was tough going, I can tell you, but they eventually left it to me to negotiate whatever I think is viable.

"Now, I don't take much out of Castle – all my shares are held in a family trust in Jersey – so it's really only a hobby. However, as you can see – he waved his hands around expansively - I've got certain out-goings. What I am going to suggest is that, provided you can keep your turnover at no less than ninety per cent of its current level over the next two years, and that shouldn't be too hard, what with inflation at its current level, we will pay you the full two hundred and fifty grand.

"Of course, there has to be a price for this concession. For me to get their agreement to this, you give me a fee of ten grand now and another ten grand in two year's time – paid into my Jersey account, of course."

"Twenty thousand pounds? That's a bit steep isn't it?"

"Not if the alternative is that you lose sixty thousand – or more – from your final payment. Have another scotch?"

Colin had the feeling that he was being lead by the nose. He was between the proverbial rock and a hard place but, but to jeopardise this deal was unthinkable.

By midday, the deal was done and Colin had signed an irrevocable promissory note promising ten thousand pounds to Yaycee Ltd in the Channel Islands and a further ten thousand in September 1987. Failure to pay would trigger an interest charge at the rate of five percent over base rate per year. Tom Cummings left little to chance.

....

On Monday morning, Tim took a call from Colin Cooper.

"I've been thinking about your offer all weekend and you know what you can do with it?" he began malevolently. "You can stick it up your back side, that's what you can do with it. I'm sick and tired of being ripped off by you and your type and I'm going to dictate my own terms and deal with gentlemen, not sodding crooks like you and Brown."

Tim was shaken rigid. What had happened to bring about this complete change? Only last week, they were talking amicably about a 'done deal' and now this.

"What's the matter Colin? What's come over you? I thought that the deal that we had put together was precisely what you wanted. You came to me, remember, not the other way around. All I have done is put a proposition to you as close as possible to what you wanted. What's happened to make you change your mind?"

"I should have known better than to talk to you. All you've ever wanted to do was to screw my Company and me. Well, it's just not going to happen. I've had an offer for what the Company is really worth so goodbye." Tim's ear rang to the sound of the receiver being slammed down at the other end.

After a moment to collect himself, he called Roy and Chris in to tell them of the latest development.

"The fellow's completely of his rocker," concluded Roy. "We're better off without him. That's the second time and, thank God, the last."

"He's not so bloody stupid as to throw away what we were offering him," added Chris. "I know the bloke and I know his financial position. There's no way he would do this if he hasn't had a better offer and one that he knows will go through. I wonder who the hell it could be with?"

They found out a few days later. There was a half page spread in the Sussex Messenger under the headline 'Local Business Acquired by Multi National' with a smaller heading 'More jobs for local people'.

The article went on;

Local businessman, Colin Cooper, Chairman of Cooper and Smythe, is delighted to announce that, in a complex four-way deal, the mighty Combined Financial of America, alongside the equally impressive Apex Financial Services Group of South Africa, had acquired majority holdings in both Cooper and Smythe and Castle Financial Services.

The combined group would be employing some five hundred people and would bring greater security to those employees currently working in the Ashbridge area.

Commenting on the announcement to the Stock Exchange today, Mr Cooper said that it was encouraging to note how two of the finest Financial Institutions from different Continents, had recognised the quality of service and personnel found in his own and in Castle's firms. The deal would bring considerable added prosperity to Ashbridge, he added.

"Bloody hell," exclaimed Tim. "It's Castle again. Just what do Insurance Companies like Apex and CFA see in a shower like that?"

"I've said it before Tim," counselled Roy. "It will all end in tears. You see if it doesn't. Castle is just about OK all the time it is taking on new Agents. When the problems will appear is when they start losing more Agents that they are taking on. There are so many Companies out there with their own direct-selling sales forces that the competition will get to them soon. As for Coopers, God knows what CFA can see in them. If they think that they can get all their clients to switch from their current Insurers to themselves, they'll soon be bitterly disappointed. If they pick up fifteen percent of Cooper's business they'll have done well. When the novelty wears off, they'll want out, of that I am sure."

"I hope you're right, Roy, it really bugs me to be pissed about like this. I've got a good mind to sue the bastard for our costs. We've spent a small fortune on Legal and Accountancy costs. We've got a signed agreement. Let's make it stick."

"Good idea," agreed Roy. "I'll give Tony a call and tell him to issue a writ for recovery of our costs. If he thinks that we have more than a fifty, fifty chance of winning, let's go for it."

Chapter Thirty-Six

Tom Fields had a problem. He had just spent a very painful thirty minutes on the phone listening to a tirade of abuse from a very eloquent Solicitor, Keith Hampshire, son of Mrs Eileen Hampshire, currently resident at the Meadow View Nursing home.

It seemed that his Mother had not informed him of the investment she had made of virtually her entire bank balance. Nor had she informed him that the investment was made into an inflexible and entirely unsuitable Investment Bond. The fact that she had built up an overdraft of over three thousand pounds as a result of the lack of funds which had been deposited to cover her monthly Nursing Home fees made matters worse.

Tom Fields was explaining his difficulty to a less than sympathetic Joe Hendry and concluded, "He more or less told me, that if we didn't get 'is mother's fuckin' money back' he'd have my fucking guts fer garters. He said that we 'ad no right connin' the old bird into somefing she don't understand."

"I can see that Tom," accepted Joe, "but under the new rules and regulations you have to be sure that the Client fully understands the contract. You should have given her all the crap that Apex gives you to hand out to the punters. Even if the punter can't understand a word of it, you cover yourself by proving that the old biddy had a chance to find out all about it."

Tom went on to explain the embarrassing fact that the original investment of twenty five thousand pounds had now declined in value to just under twenty thousand pounds and that an exit penalty of one thousand nine hundred and forty pounds would reduce her funds still further. A twenty five percent loss of his mother's capital in less than three months had made Mr Hampshire a very cross man, very cross indeed.

Mr Hampshire was insisting on a meeting with the Managing Director and that meeting had to occur tomorrow at nine am sharp. When he heard that the MD's name was Joe Hendry, he seemed to recall that he had met a Joe Hendry before. He wasn't the Joe Hendry that used to be in double glazing was he, by any chance?

"Dunno mate," was all that Tom could offer at the time, but he did undertake to arrange the meeting if that was at all possible. The sooner that Tom could get out from under this one and drop it on Joe's lap, the better as far as he was concerned.

"Do you know this geezer Hampshire, Joe?" Tom enquired. "'e seems to know you mate and is he on the fuckin' war path or ain't he? Wot we goin' to do mate?"

"God knows. You'd better tell him to come in and I'll make sure that Tom Cumming is here. He'll know what to do."

Now it was Joe's turn to be worried. If the figures were right, Mr Hampshire had reason to be annoyed. What the fuck was Apex up to, losing five grand of a punter's money in only three months? The fact that Castle had had two thousand pounds of it in commission, and then there was the 'skim' to Bill Washington, had nothing to do with it. They had to be paid and it was up to the Apex to make up the difference.

He apprised Tom Cummings of the position.

"What the fucking hell have you done now you stupid bastard?" came the encouraging response. "I remember that Hampshire bastard. Don't you remember him? It was him who caused us all that grief when his Mum got pissed off about our windows. We had to close the Company down because of him. With Apex and CFA around our necks, we can't afford to let this get out of hand now. I'll be there tomorrow at nine but, in the meantime, you get on to Schmitt and ask him what the fuck they're doing with the punter's money. They're meant to be investing it to make a profit, not pissing it up against the wall! You make sure he sends someone down tomorrow to take the flak. We are not taking the can on this one."

Feeling slightly relieved that there was probably someone else who would bear the brunt, Joe called Schmitt to put the problem before him.

After he had explained the current position, he was not a little taken aback to be told, "You're on own there sonny. We issue Investment Bonds for all grades of risk. If you've got a thirty year-old whiz kid earning a fortune, put him in our Speculative Funds. If you've got a comfortably off, married couple, put them in our Balanced Funds. If you've got a doddery, eighty-year old lady suffering from senile dementia, put her in the Cautious Funds. Just what the fuck do you think you're doing putting her in a Speculative Fund? And where do you think your fucking commission comes from, Father Christmas?

"No Mr Hendry, we provide the product, you provide the advice. That's what you're paid for. You just see Mr Hampshire and you sort it out. It's your problem, not mine, Goodbye."

Joe was not a happy man.

....

Tom duly arrived before nine the following morning and Joe brought him up to date with the uncompromising stance being adopted by Schmitt. Consequently they kept Mr Hampshire waiting downstairs for five minutes whilst they digested this unsavoury information.

"Christ knows what we do now," was Tom's considered response.

Keith Hampshire stormed into Joe's Office crimson with rage, all but removing the door from its hinges in the process.

"It is you Hendry. I might have known it. You were the shyster who sold my mother duff double glazing and then had the gall to fiddle her out of her nest egg. You were a crook when you were in double glazing and you're a crook now. God only knows what qualifications you have to be in the investment business. What the hell do you mean by robbing senile old people of their assets? You will pay for this, and you will pay heavily, be sure of that!

"There are two ways we can deal with this," he continued. "One. My mother handed over twenty five thousand pounds. Today it's worth twenty thousand pounds. You give me a cheque now for twenty six thousand pounds to include interest and my time and I'll give you the Policy and a signed discharge making the surrender value payable to your Company – I have my mother's power of attorney.

"Or, two; you get ready to receive a writ for professional negligence and mis-selling, seeking damages in excess of seventy thousand pounds to include the special damages for the appallingly retrogressive effect this has all had on my mother's health. Furthermore, I will make it my job to ensure that your Professional Body, whichever it is, strikes you off and I will make it my personal commitment to see that you both go to jail for fraud. Now, which is it to be?"

Not surprisingly, neither alternative appealed to either Joe or Tom.

Joe was the first to speak. "Mr Hampshire, I realise that you're upset and concerned that your mother's investment has performed poorly, but you must realise that it is the nature of stock market investments that they may rise or fall in value. It is unfortunate that, in this case.........."

"Spare me the homily. You know and I know that my mother was in no fit condition to make any investment decision, let alone one as risky and inappropriate as this one. I repeat, which is it to be, a cheque or the Police?"

"I am truly sorry Mr Hampshire," contributed Tom. "I happen to know the salesman who advised your mother, very well indeed. Though something of a 'rough diamond' Tom Fields is one of our most experienced Managers and I am absolutely certain that he would have appraised your Mother fully of the potential risks and rewards of such an investment. We go to inordinate lengths to see that all of our Consultants are fully trained and you may rest assured that there is no way that he would have advised your Mother to proceed had he the slightest doubts that she would not have fully appreciated the terms of the contract. The Stock Markets have been a little nervous of late and I am sure that, if the investment is allowed to mature, the picture will look considerably brighter. If you will just allow.........."

"For the last time, a cheque or the Police?"

Tom knew when he was beaten.

"Please may we have a little time to consider our position? I am sure that you will appreciate that we are as disappointed as you about your mother's Bond's performance and the last thing that we want is a disappointed Client. I would like.........."

"I will give you until nine am tomorrow. Here's my card. You turn up at my Office tomorrow morning with a cheque for twenty six thousand pounds and that will be the end of it. Fail to turn up with the cheque, and that will be the end of you. I give you my word."

After he had gone, Tom turned to Joe and asked, "Just what the bloody hell was Tom Fields playing at? Surely he could see that the old biddy needed her cash to meet the Nursing Home's Fees. Sticking it all in a Bond was a recipe for disaster.

"This one is bad enough, but how many more cases are there like this? If there are any more, we're on the road to ruin and I can't see Messrs Schmitt or Capaldi riding to the rescue. Do we have any Professional Indemnity Insurance for chrissakes?"

"God, I forgot about that," exclaimed Joe. "Yes, we do. We took out a policy last year. We're covered for a quarter of a million but we have to pay the first bit – the first two and a half grand, I think."

"Well, you give the Brokers a call and you make bloody sure that we're covered and that at least those bastards will pay for all of this."

Two hours later, Joe had confirmed that they were indeed covered for a quarter of a million and that they had to pay the first two thousand five hundred pounds themselves. The problem was, that they must, under no circumstances, make any admission of liability and no offer of payment. To do so would invalidate any claim.

Joe explained to their Insurance Brokers that their failure to pay Hampshire's demand by 9.00 am the following morning would have the most serious consequences. Their Brokers advised Joe that they were on very thin ice indeed. They could play it the way they wanted, but there would be no guarantee that the Underwriter's would honour the claim if they did not play it strictly by the book.

In short, by paying up tomorrow, they would invalidate their Insurance. By not paying up tomorrow, they would risk going to jail. They were, once again, firmly placed between a rock and a hard place.

"Perhaps we can get Hampshire to give us a little more time, suggested Joe when explaining the current position to Tom.

"Perhaps pigs will fucking fly," responded his Chairman. "No, we'll go and see him at his office at nine tomorrow and see what we can do. If we have to pay, I'll deal with our Insurers personally and I'll soon make fucking certain that they pay up. What do they think we pay all these premiums for?"

Joe felt rather less sanguine and resigned himself to not sleeping well this night.

....

At just before nine the following morning, a disconsolate Joe Hendry and an out of breath Tom Cummings, emerged from their taxi in Fetters Lane outside a typical modern high rise glass office block.

"You pay the cabbie," was Tom's the first comment he had made in the last five minutes. He strode into the impressive foyer and marched up to the uniformed security man sitting at the twenty-foot long natural oak reception desk. "Mr Hampshire of Hampshire Jacobs and Partners," he barked gracelessly.

"Please sign here gentlemen," the guard asked, indicating a book full of tear off slips. "And who may I say is calling?"

"Cummings and Hendry," snapped Tom.

As the guard folded the slips into their plastic wallets and handed them back, he dialled a number and waited patiently whilst Tom's blood pressure continued its upward spiral. Joe experienced the usual palpitations he always suffered at times like these.

"Mary. Bob here. I have two gentlemen (with heavy emphasis on the word 'gentlemen') here to see Mr Hampshire. "Yes," he laughed to the unheard comment, "you could say that. Shall I ask them up? OK, they will be with you in two ticks."

Bob replaced the handset and turned to Tom, "Mr Hampshire's secretary will meet you outside the lift. Take any of the lifts over there and proceed to the sixth floor. A pleasure to assist gentlemen," he added unnecessarily, to their departing backs.

"This way gentlemen," said Mary as she escorted them briskly down the corridor and into a small meeting room. Mr Hampshire will be with you in a couple of minutes. He's just finishing off a long distance phone call."

No mention of a cup of coffee or even a query or comment about the weather, noted Joe. This was not going to be a social meeting.

"Like hell he's on a long-distance call," muttered Tom after she had left. "The bugger's just making us sweat. Well I'm damned if I'm going to give in to the bastard. He almost ruined me once and he's not going to get away with it for a second time."

Ten minutes later, the door opened and in strode Keith Hampshire, grim faced and unwelcoming.

"Got my cheque?" he opened.

"Well, Mr Hampshire," began Tom. "We would like to see if we could come to an amicable conclusion. We are as distressed as you that Apex' fund managers have not been able to enhance your mother's investment. We............"

"Cut the crap Cummings," interjected Hampshire, "I've given you the alternatives. It's either twenty six thousand pounds on the table now, today, or it's the Police. Which is it to be?"

"I fully appreciate your position Mr Hampshire." It was Joe's turn to make a contribution. "We are a substantial, very well established and respected Company. We are backed by two of the world's foremost financial institutions. I am sure you will realise that we have procedures to adopt, just as I am sure you have here at you own firm.

"On the face of it, I agree that it would appear that your mother has been badly advised. But we do have to be absolutely certain. We have already called Mr Fields, the Consultant involved in your mother's case, to a disciplinary hearing this afternoon. At this meeting, he will have to give a full account of what he perceived was your mother's financial position and why he made the recommendations that he did. Not only do we have to be fair to our clients – your mother in this case – but we have to be fair to our staff. Innocent until proven guilty and all that sort of thing, but I shouldn't be teaching my grandmother to suck eggs, if you'll excuse the expression.

"Then we have to satisfy ourselves that we have complied with the exacting requirements placed upon us by the Financial Services Authority. Finally, Mr Hampshire," added Joe, warming to his theme, "Finally we have to bear in mind that this could, and I emphasise the word 'could', lead to a claim under our Professional Indemnity Insurance. As I am sure you will understand, we are quite unable to make any statements at a meeting such as this, that might prejudice our Insurer's position without reference to them in the first instance. As you know, any admission of liability on our part would render our cover inoperative, and if we are unable to make a claim, we might be unable to make a payment."

Tom was impressed. Perhaps Joe did understand this business after all. He, himself, was convinced. Perhaps now, they could expect a rather more conciliatory response from Hampshire. He was to be disappointed.

"Your problems Mr Hendry are of your own making. They do not concern me one iota. Your firm ripped my mother off about twenty years ago and it would seem that you have not learned your lesson yet. You might like the idea of getting fat on elderly persons' limited knowledge and cash resources, but I'm not having any of it. You give me a cheque for twenty six thousand pounds now and I'll be letting you off far more lightly than you deserve.

"You will get the Policy back with a signed discharge and, whatever you are able to cash it for, you keep. If your Insurers won't pay, that's tough. You will have lost five or six thousand pounds and I'd say that is a cheap and much needed lesson. It should help to teach you how to run a business properly and ethically. I take it that you have brought your cheque book?"

As before, Tom knew when he was beaten. "Mr Hampshire, you're a hard man. I'll give you your cheque, but only as a gesture of good will and because we want to keep our good name – a name that has taken us years to create."

"Spare me the hearts and flowers, Cummings, just write it out – to my mother. You have her full name."

So saying, Hampshire produced the Policy document and a letter and some papers. "Here's the Policy; I wish I'd never seen the bloody thing, and here's the letter signed by me authorising the Apex to pay the full surrender value of the Policy to your firm. Finally, here's a certified copy of my mother's power of attorney."

Taking the cheque and standing up to declare the meeting over, he said, "Goodbye. I take it you can see your own way out.

"Oh, by the way, it is possible that we may be meeting again. My mother tells me that your friend Mr Fields has sold several similar investments to other residents at Meadow View. I have asked her to check with each and every one of them as to whether they are happy with the Investments that they have made. If they are happy, then all well and good. If not, I have told my mother that I will be happy to represent them in any claim they may wish to make against your good selves on a 'pro bono' basis. Goodbye," he repeated as he disappeared back into his own office.

"Jesus Christ," moaned Joe. "We're in deep shit. Tom's sold dozens of those policies to the inmates and he's been cutting that thieving bastard that runs the place in on the deal. What the bloody hell's 'pro bono'?"

"It means," Joe, that we're in it up to the neck and more. He's not going to charge the punters a dime to work for them. We know that these bloody bonds won't show a profit for years. They've got to be going at least three years before there's any chance of the old biddies making any profit at all. Sure, we send them a valuation each year showing that they've made a bob or two provided that they don't ask for the money there and then. But if they do cancel, then they lose a grand or two. Knowing old Tom Fields, he didn't tell them that bit."

"Be fair Tom, how could anyone sell those Bonds if they told them all the details? They've got to trust someone. We know that, if they keep them a long time, or better still until they die, (when they can't argue), they'll be all right. No, you can't blame Tom. It's the fucking Apex' fault for not making them grow faster. If they got their act in order, there'd be none of this trouble. Any way, I sold some of them myself."

And so the two masters of financial services debated the merits of their products and how tough it was to make a living in this cruel world.

As they travelled back, reality began to dawn.

"Will our Professional Indemnity Insurers cough up?" asked Tom.

"I can't say," replied Joe. "Gordon, our Broker, was pretty adamant that we should make no admission of liability, and what have we done? We've actually handed over the cheque. If that's not an admission, I don't know what the fuck is."

"I'll speak to them when I get back," said Tom. He didn't want Joe dropping them in even deeper shit.

"How many other Policies like this has that bloody fool Fields sold? How many did you sell? How many more claims can we expect? Once that bastard Hampshire gets his teeth stuck in, he's not going to let go."

"I don't know," replied Joe, "but there must be at least twenty of them. The one's I 'sold' I left to Tom to wrap up since he was the one who was getting the commission. He earned a ton of commission from that Nursing Home, I do know that. They weren't all that size but, if this one has cost us six grand, we must be looking at something in excess of a hundred grand. Of course, if our insurers pay up, we'll only have to pay two thousand five hundred each, but that could still mean that we'd still be looking at fifty grand down the tubes."

"Jesus Christ," stuttered Tom. "And here was I thinking that you knew how to run this bloody company when, all the time, we've been sitting on a time bomb, and the bloody thing is about to go off. At least we've pulled off a fucking good deal in buying Coopers. With all the extra commission coming in from there, we should be able to hide this little problem from our friends in Apex and CFA."

Joe kept quiet. He did not feel quite so confident. There were storm clouds on the horizon there as well, but now was not the time to burden his Chairman with, what had every promise of becoming, a deeper and seemingly insoluble problem.

Chapter Thirty-Seven

Being possessed of a broadly optimistic and resilient nature, Tim soon overcame his disappointment in having lost out on the Coopers deal. At the time it had been a bitter blow, but he comforted himself that he was no worse off than he had been before the prospect of a deal had even been raised. With this behind him, he threw himself wholeheartedly back to work, determined to make Harrisons the foremost Insurance Brokerage in the South East, if not still further afield.

Although not overtly vengeful by nature, he did feel that there would be much sport to be enjoyed in 'attacking' Cooper's client bank and seeing how many could he could persuade to change loyalties. If he could cause Colin Cooper a little grief in the process of building up his own company, then that would be a small bonus.

He reasoned that clients generally appointed Insurance Brokers to get independent advice. If that Broker were to be part owned by an Insurance Company, how could that advice be wholly impartial? Surely, CFA would want their pound of flesh?

Surely, they would want to 'cherry pick'? In short, he would expect CFA to demand that Coopers should offer all their most profitable business to them, whilst leaving the dross to the rest of the market.

He made two decisions. Firstly, he called Chris Wright in and asked him to make a list, from memory, of all of Cooper's clients who would be paying premiums in excess of two thousand five thousand pounds.

In the event, that proved to be quite an extensive list – about twenty-five Companies. The total estimated premium turned out to exceed three hundred thousand pounds. If he could persuade even half of these to become clients of Harrisons, it would be an extremely lucrative and worthwhile exercise. Furthermore, it would be a very damaging experience for his public enemy number one – his rivals and competitors.

Secondly, he phoned the local Inspectors of the three Companies that his own firm placed most of their business with – the Universal, the Accident and General and the Mutual Combined Underwriters. He suggested a working lunch at his offices in three day's time.

Intrigued, all three accepted with alacrity.

....

On the appointed morning, the group forgathered in Tim's boardroom and he put forward his plan.

"You will all know," he began, "that Roy and I were committed to acquiring Coopers and that, on two occasions, we were thwarted. However, as you all know, Coopers still have quite a few clients that we would prefer to see as clients of this firm, rather than theirs.

"I do not believe that their clients necessarily want their existing policies cancelled – many being placed with your good selves – simply to feather the respective nests of Coopers and the CFA. We have the capacity, we have the expertise, and we have the drive. We also have the motive for being rather more aggressive than usual."

There were murmurings of agreement from his guests as they helped themselves to the sandwiches and sparkling water laid before them.

"Now, as I have said, Coopers have been taken over by CFA and you don't need me to tell you that they will be sniffing around all the worthwhile business that Coopers handle and switching it from Companies such as your own to themselves as soon as anything falls due for renewal."

"Too right," confirmed Ron Green of the A&G. "We've already estimated that we stand to lose between one hundred and one hundred and fifty thousand pounds of business in this year alone. That's going to be bloody hard to replace. God knows what's going to happen to my figures this year."

"Same here," agreed Dave Watson of the Universal. "Between these four walls, we're looking at a loss of over quarter of a million."

"I'm not so badly placed," added Clive Jones of the Mutual Combined. "We only started an account with Coopers a couple of year's ago. We've probably only got about fifty to sixty thousand at risk."

"So," summed up Tim, "that looks like about four hundred and fifty thousand pounds of your premium income that could go down the tubes from your points of view. At our average rate of about fourteen percent, that would be worth about sixty five thousand pounds of commission to us – well worth having.

"Now, I've asked you three gentlemen here today because, between you, your three firms get the lion's share of our business – over seventy percent, I would estimate. What I would like to propose is that the three of you form and informal consortium and co-insure any business that we can successfully transfer from Coopers, if it is under attack from CFA. It should be placed on a third, third, third basis so that each of you gets a fair share.

"At the same time, I would expect you to agree to take every client's business that we offer you and that you would put it on your books at precisely the same terms as before. In other words, you would take the rough with the smooth and without any further argument as to burglary precautions, risk surveys and all that red tape. More than that, you would offer all clients a fifteen percent reduction in their current premium."

"Fifteen percent!" exclaimed Ron Green. "We can't knock fifteen percent off for business that might already be on our books, let alone new clients. That's impossible, my head office will never agree."

"I'm not asking you to give fifteen percent. We'll chip in too. We'll agree to knock five percent off our commission on all the business thus transferred so, in effect, you will only be losing ten per cent. A small price, I'd say, to retain hundreds of thousands of pounds worth of business between you. There would be one other thing though. To do the thing properly, we would have to get the message out and I think that a co-ordinated advertising campaign would be essential. I am sure you could each squeeze your PR departments for a modest contribution of, say, one thousand pounds for a campaign. You do that, and we'll throw in another thousand ourselves.

"If you go along with my plan, not only will you have hung on to all the business you stand to lose, but you will have picked up more, probably much more, and you will have reduced your individual exposures to one third on each risk. You just can't lose," added Tim.

They continued debating the project, raising objections and developing their own solutions until they felt that they had all established a workable basis. By two o'clock, they had all agreed that the idea had huge potential and they would each go away to endeavour to persuade their Branch Managers and their Head Offices that they should all go along with the project.

Later that afternoon, Tim phoned the local newspaper and offered to write them a series of articles on the Insurance Industry today as it affected their particular region. Always hungry for copy, the assistant editor leapt at the suggestion and promised to hold two one thousand word slots for next, and the following week's, editions.

Tim also phoned the Editor of 'Sussex Today', the monthly county Business Magazine, with a similar offer. Again, it was accepted with alacrity.

Two days later, Tim had sent out draft articles to both organs, outlining the risks of failing to obtain proper insurance protection and extolling the virtues of seeking independent advice at all times. The articles touched on the concerns of the coming practice of Insurance Companies acquiring Shares in Insurance Brokerages, which would, inevitably, lead to a conflict of interest. It stood to reason, the articles explained, that if an Insurance Broker were owned by an Insurance Company, who was there to argue on the Client's side in the event of a contentious claim?

Needless to say, the three Inspectors from the Universal, the A&G and the Mutual Combined, cut these articles out and forwarded them to their Head Offices as added ammunition to promote the virtues of participation in the consortium.

As it happened, none of this additional 'insurance' proved necessary. Within three weeks, all three Inspectors had called Tim to say that their Head Offices had agreed and that they were 'on'. Without further delay, Tim called a meeting to finalise the modus operandi.

Within four weeks of promulgating the plan, Harrisons sent out thirty letters to clients of Coopers. They began:

You may have noticed in the Press recently that certain Insurance Companies – commonly overseas Companies – have embarked upon the practice of acquiring Equity in Insurance Broking Houses.

Whereas such purchases may represent excellent investment opportunities for the Companies themselves, we at Harrisons are rather disturbed by this development. We feel that it removes one of the central tenets of our business. That is, our independence.

We believe that the relationship between the Broker and the Underwriter should be one of mutual respect but one where either party may feel free to take up the cudgels on behalf of their clients or principals without fear or favour.

If you should find that this development has occurred in the case of the Insurance Brokers that your firm currently employs, then perhaps it would be worth seeking an independent review.

Harrison's have the expertise and resource to meet your most demanding requirements and, if you would appreciate a second opinion, we would be very happy to hear from you – entirely without obligation, of course.

Over the next three months, Tim had had twenty replies and, over the next twelve months, the consortium was handling just over three hundred and fifty thousand pounds of new business.

In June 1987, at the Company's seventeenth Annual General Meeting, Tim was happy to report that, after only twelve months from the inception of the scheme, Harrisons had generated a further thirty thousand pounds of net revenue and rising. Furthermore, the Universal had intimated that they might now be able to waive the 5% concession that Tim had offered, and restore their commission rates to the previous levels. If the other two Insurers would agree, then it would have a major impact on their bottom line. It looked like 1987 was going to be good year, a very good year.

In reviewing the last seventeen years or so, Tim was acutely aware of his relative good fortune. Of course, he had had his share of knocks and disappointments but, on balance, more things had gone his way than had gone against him. "You make your own luck in this life" his grandfather had often told him and Tim had just cause to believe him.

Apart from the bitter disappointment of being unable to wrap up the Cooper's deal, Tim felt that the last year or so had been particularly good for both he and Mary.

He told himself that his luck could not continue forever and, sooner or later, another setback would arise to wipe the smile off his face.

He was right. The next knock was on its way.

....

"Have you got a minute Tim?" called Chris Wright, waking him from his reverie. "If you're busy, it can wait, I'll come back later."

"No, come in Chris. I was just reflecting on our recent triumphs and wondering what would turn up next. What can I do for you?"

"I'll come straight to the point," said Chris, sliding into the chair opposite Tim. "As you know, I've been extremely happy working here with you and Roy and the others. The last twelve months or so has been particularly exciting, what with most of my old clients from Coopers coming back to roost.

"The thing is; I've been head hunted."

"You've been what?" cried out Tim. "I suppose I should say congratulations but you've taken the wind out of my sails. Whose approached you? What have they offered you? Are you interested?"

"Slow down Tim," smiled Chris. "I didn't say that I had accepted anything. Last week, a chap by the name of Sir Stanley Noble, representing a City firm called the Huntingdon Partnership phoned me and asked me if I would like to consider a job in the City. Of course, I said 'no thanks' but he did apply a little pressure and, to be honest, I suppose I was flattered.

"Anyway, I eventually agreed that I would see him and, as you know, I took last Thursday afternoon off. I went up to their offices – very swish I must say – and listened to what he had to say.

"It seems that there is one of the 'Big Five' Brokers who is looking for an MD to head up their UK operation. Apparently, they heard of me via the CFA who had been bemoaning the fact that they had missed out on a great deal of business that they had been anticipating and, rightly or wrongly, they have the impression that I had something to do with it."

"Rightly," conceded Tim. "You've been invaluable to me and to the entire firm. I have to say that, without you, we wouldn't have done half as well as we have since you joined us. That's reflected, of course, by the fact that we were delighted to offer you a Directorship last year. Anyway, what are your thoughts about this offer?"

"There's no offer as such at the moment Tim, but they have outlined the likely package. I have to say that I would hate to work in London, that Jane is totally opposed to my moving from Harrisons and the very last thing that I want to do is to say goodbye to my friends and clients here, and most of all, to you."

"I'm relieved to hear that, but," interjected Tim, "there is a 'but' isn't there?"

"I am afraid there is. I have been perfectly happy with my salary here. Thirty thousand a year in Ashbridge is pretty good and Jane and I can live well enough on that – particularly with her occasional locum work. However, they have suggested a figure of fifty thousand pounds a year, plus a car, plus a non-contributory Pension and all the other bells and whistles that a firm like theirs takes for granted.

"As I say Tim, I would hate to leave, but you can see that I can't say no to a package like that without the most serious consideration. I know that there is absolutely no way in which Harrisons could match that and, to be fair, I wouldn't expect you to."

"Bloody hell Chris. That is an offer and a half. As you are only too well aware, I need you desperately here but there is no way I could get anywhere near that figure. I could go a few thousand or so more and I had, to be honest, been thinking that it is about time that the firm provided you with a car – a 'pool' car is no way for you to deal with your clients. I don't know what to say. Do you have to make up your mind quickly, or can I have a day or two to think about this?"

"Of course, Tim. I'm not going to make any hasty decisions. I want to mull things over with Jane this weekend so, if we can have another chat on Monday, I would be most grateful."

"Thanks Chris. Well done, you deserve this sort of recognition. I only wish I could match it somehow. I'll see you on Monday."

Tim resumed his reverie, but this time, beneath dark clouds. No one is indispensable, he assured himself but the loss of Chris, particularly at this point in time, would be devastating.

As had so often been the case in the past, he would have a meeting with Roy. Despite his advancing years, Roy was a huge asset at times like these. So often he spotted a solution that would not have occurred to Tim. But this time, he could not see one. Even if he could find another twenty thousand a year for Chris, and a car, it would wreak havoc with his differentials – his entire staff would expect uplifts too. Much as he would love to oblige, it could not be done. Perhaps he would have to grasp the nettle and consider life without the invaluable Chris Wright.

Chapter Thirty-Eight

Joe Hendry was having a bad day. He was sitting in front of Tom Fields who had confessed to the full extent of the business that he had written at the Meadow View Nursing Home.

"They were all bloody gaga," he was claiming in his defence. "There was no way they would have understood a bleedin' word I said to them even if I had bovered. I told 'em that their dough was wiv a bleedin' great Company an' that they knew a bloody sight more about 'ow to 'andle cash than them an' I would ever know. What more did they need to 'ear?"

"I 'anded them all the paper work and got them to sign something to say that they had read and understood it all -- even if they 'adn't the foggiest. We've now got that bastard 'Ampshire breathing down our necks and he's going for us in spades, make no bones about that."

"You'll have to give back all your commission on these cases, you realise that, don't you?" pointed out Joe helpfully.

"Over my dead fuckin' body," replied Tom. "I earned that dough by me own blood, sweat an' tears. There's no way you theivin' bastards is goin' to 'ave it off me, no way."

"Under the terms of your contract Tom........."

"Stuff yer fuckin' contract. I'm off. I was fair pissed off anyway an' I've been offered a bloody sight better job wiv the National and Provincial, so you can 'ave me notice now. I'm leavin', goodbye!"

With that, Tom Fields rose from his chair, which fell backwards with a deafening thud, exited and slammed the door, leaving a stunned and dazed Joe Hendry wondering just what the hell had gone wrong. Joe realised, with a sense of rising panic, that he had just lost one of his most prolific salesmen, that he'd gone to one of the Insurance Companies' own 'Direct Sales' forces, and that he, Joe Hendry, was left holding the baby. This happened to be a baby that was turning into a towering monster by the minute and he realised that he had no one to help him sort it out. Time to phone Tom Cummings.

"After listening to Joe's diatribe for ten minutes, Tom Cummings asked, "And what did our Professional Indemnity Insurers say? Are they going to pick up the tab?"

"Christ," replied Joe. "I had completely forgotten about them. I'll get onto Gordon White straight away. Hang on a minute, didn't you say that you would deal with that side?"

"No, of course I bloody didn't. You're the flaming Managing Director. It's your job. You get on to it now and phone me tomorrow morning latest to tell me what the are going to do about it."

Half an hour later, "You did what?" exclaimed a startled Gordon White when he had listened incredulously to Joe's story. "You actually handed the third party a cheque? You actually admitted liability without speaking to us? I don't believe it; I really don't believe you could have been so incredibly naive. You've wiped the floor of any chance at all of the Insurance Company convincing your Client that she ahs no claim against you. No, I'm sorry Joe, you're on your own this time; the Insurers will tell you to take a running jump."

"The fact that we gave Hampshire a cheque doesn't make a blind bit of difference to you or the Insurers, Gordon," whined Joe. "We were as guilty as hell and the Insurers would have had no alternative but to do exactly the same thing. We've just seen to it that, by acting quickly, we've stopped things from getting out of hand, of going from bad to worse. If we had not paid up there and then, we would be looking at a claim for the thick end of a hundred grand, including costs."

"That's what you think," retorted White. "Professional Indemnity Insurers are masters at wriggling out of claims. They would have a hundred and one ways of establishing that your Mr Fields had acted quite properly, and that Mrs Hampshire had no valid claim against your company."

"They will pay, though, won't they?" asked Joe, a note of panic creeping into his voice. "They won't penalise us for sorting things out on their behalf, will they?"

"Too bloody right they will," came the prompt reply. "Not a cat's chance in hell. We'll do everything we can, of course, to protect your interests. I'll want a full report and I suggest that you ask Mr Fields to call in my Office tomorrow and give me his own statement. Can you get him in to me tomorrow, I don't want to waste any more time?"

"Afraid that's going to be difficult.   Tom walked out this afternoon. Handed in his notice on the spot. He'd already got himself another job, the bastard, and the mood he was in, he's not going to be too co-operative."

"Jesus. Well he's just got to come in. From what you tell me, Hampshire might still decide to sue and then he'd be subpoenaed anyway. Give me his home address and telephone number and I'll speak to him myself. Perhaps I will be able to persuade him to see reason. He won't get far with his new firm if I report his reluctance to sort out a ball's up of this magnitude. No new Employer would want to take the risk of having one of their newest salesmen in court – with all its attendant bad publicity. Now is there anything more you are holding back from me Joe?"

"There is, I'm afraid. There could be another thirty claims exactly like this one.   I don't know what he was up to, but it seems that Tom has sold Investment Bonds to pretty well every one of the inmates there, and it is more likely than not that they are all in a similar position to Mrs Hampshire.

"In other words, they need to get their hands on their money now and not wait the next three to five years. We train our staff thoroughly Gordon, believe me we do. Under no circumstances are they allowed to 'oversell' – we take a very tough view if we see it happening. Somehow or other, Tom escaped the net and, completely off his own bat, broke pretty well every rule in our book," he continued lying desperately.

"Jesus H Christ!" stuttered Gordon. "I've never heard anything like it. I'm coming over tomorrow morning myself and I'm going through this whole bloody debacle with you. God only knows what we will find. Just bear in mind that your Insurers are not a Charitable Institution and if they can find a way not to pay, they will find it. Is nine thirty tomorrow OK with you?"

"Yes, fine Gordon," replied Joe weakly. "I'll see if Tom Cummings can be here too."

....

The following morning, the meeting went badly, very badly.

By the time that Gordon left them, some two hours later, Tom and Joe were looking at a potential claim well in excess of one hundred thousand pounds with the likelihood of any help from their Insurers at virtually nil. Gordon had explained to them, in very colourful language, that they had broken pretty well every rule in the Professional Indemnity book and that their Insurers had absolutely no obligation to contribute a single solitary penny to their imminent losses.

"Give me some good news Joe," said Tom Cummings when he had got his breath back. "At least tell me that we're still producing a ton of commissions from our other salesmen and that we're making a bucket more from Cooper's clients."

Joe hesitated. He'd been worried for some months now about the worsening position at Coopers, but had hoped that something would turn up. It hadn't and now was the time to find someone to blame.

"When you came up with the idea of buying Coopers in the first place Tom, you may recall that I had some reservations. I told you that I knew sweet FA about general insurance and, in consequence, I would have to leave most of the running of that division to the existing staff.

"Well, it appears that we've taken on a whole load of wankers and tossers. If you ask me, they couldn't run a piss-up in a brewery, not one of them. The big trouble is, I don't know enough about the business to decide who to put in charge and, if I find someone who does not perform, I don't know where to look for someone who could replace him."

"What are you telling me Joe?" asked Tom menacingly. "Are you telling me that you've fucked up on this one too? For Christ's sake, I engineer a deal whereby I get someone else to buy the Company for you – a Company making a healthy profit – and all you have to do is keep the bloody thing ticking over whilst our boys crawl all over the customers and flog 'em Pensions and Investments. What could be simpler?"

"It's not quite like that Tom. General Insurance is a completely different game to the one we're in. If the bloody fool who was running it had half a brain, we'd be OK. As it is, that prat has allowed those thieving bastards at Harrisons to pinch half our bloody clients. They're crucifying the business Tom and I don't know what to do about it. Furthermore, since all the clients are buggering off, there's very little for our boys to get their teeth into. In fact, I don't like to say it, but I think that one phone call from one of our salesman actually encourages the client to make up his mind to transfer his business away. Anyway, that's the way it's looking to me."

"So what are the new business figures looking like now for Chrissake? Are we making a profit, a loss or are we breaking even?"

"At the moment, we're still ahead of the game, but only just. Some of our boys have done bloody well and the good one's are covering for the hopeless cases. My only worry is, that one of our best salesmen was Tom Fields and he's buggered off leaving us with one almighty headache. I reckon that half of his cases are going to lapse and we will then be faced with having to pay most of his commission back to CFA and Apex."

"You'll get all that back from Fields though, won't you?" demanded Cummings.

"Contractually yes, but in practice, not a chance. What do we do if he won't cough up?"

"Sue the bastard, that's what," affirmed Tom Cummings. "Before that, I'll get our old friend 'Twister' Evans, to pay him a friendly visit and ask him nicely for a cheque. That will sort it. Just get a letter off to him today telling him how much he owes and I'll see to the rest."

Joe, greatly relieved, was even more relieved not to be in Tom Field's shoes. He'd visited a former Castle Windows salesman in the local Accident and Emergency ward after one of 'Twister's' visits. It was not a pretty sight.

In a mood of deepening gloom, Tom and Joe continued to review the current and future trading prospects of Castle Finance plc.

....

At about the same time, Peter Schmitt was entertaining his friend, Ray Capaldi' to lunch at Borrello's – one of the City's more salubrious restaurants. They had already enjoyed a couple of gin and tonics and were now starting on a bottle of South African Chardonnay accompanying their Melon and Port.

"Just what the hell did you get me into Peter?" Ray was saying. "On the face of it, this Castle Finance deal looked bloody good. In practice, it is turning into a total nightmare. My people are telling me that they've pretty well lost all the worthwhile general business at Cooper's. We were expecting to take on at least four hundred thousand pounds of new premium income and, to date, after over one year, we have barely reached fifty thousand.

"On top of that, the regular premium life and investment income has been pathetic. If things don't buck up soon, I reckon we'll be down a couple of hundred grand with sweet bugger all to show for it. What do you suggest we do about it for God's sake?"

"I know how you feel Ray. The lump sum business we were expecting has gone down the tubes as well. I can't see us making a penny's profit out of the goddamn deal for years – if ever.

"I have to admit, I've never liked Hendry – too bloody sharp. But, he did seem to know how to sell and how to build up a sales force that could sell too. The problem now is that he's completely out of his depth. I think that we should dump him, and dump him fast. Furthermore, whilst we are about it, we should get rid of that shifty bastard Cummings. I wouldn't trust him further than I could throw him, and that's not very far. Let's have another bottle."

Whilst the wine waiter was dealing with the order, Ray took himself off to the toilet, partly to relieve his bladder, and partly to give himself some thinking time. They were both in difficulties with this one and Ray had no illusions that Peter Schmitt would dump the whole problem at CFA's door if he got the opportunity. He had to be careful.

"I've been thinking, Peter," he said as he returned to his seat and appreciatively took up his refreshed glass, "We are both in this together and we need to find a way out that benefits both of us. I do not relish the thought of telling my Board that we've fucked up on this and I don't suppose you do either."

"Couldn't agree more. What have you got in mind?"

"In my view, direct sales of Life Assurance and the like are the coming thing but I just don't know why we need to be paying tons of money to second rate 'Brokers' just to distribute our products. Allied Finance and the Old Mutual are just two examples of Life Assurance Companies who have built up their own sales forces. That way, they are in full control of their salesman and they can make absolutely sure that they are selling what the Company wants them to sell, not just whatever gives the broker the biggest commission."

"We've looked at that concept ourselves from time to time but, up to now, we've been quite happy for the Castle Finance's of this world to do the selling for us. What are you suggesting Ray?"

"The costs of setting up a direct sales force are considerable. So are the costs of setting up a new Insurance Company. We both know, however, that a new Company gives us some pretty useful tax breaks.

"What I would like to consider is the thought that both your Company and mine should set up a brand new Company between us to do nothing but direct sales and cut out the middleman completely.

"We both have good names in the market, well known to Joe Public, and so we would have no trouble with clients being 'frightened ' off by a new name.

"We could simply 'steal' Castles four or five hundred salesmen to form the nucleus of our business and tell our friends, Cummings and Hendry to go take a hike. The money we'd save would give us a head start and I can see us both making a mint.

"What's more, Castle's salesmen have as much loyalty to Hendry as David had to Goliath and they would love to ditch 'em and know that their commission would be safe coming from someone like us rather than that couple.

"Instead of telling our Boards that we may have dropped a goolie, we'd be telling them that this has been the learning curve to enable us to set up a new and very profitable enterprise. Promote it as an invaluable exercise in getting us into the direct sales market. What do you think, Peter?"

"I like it. I like it a lot. Let's have another bottle. Fillet mignon without a good South African red is an opportunity missed. Anyway, we deserve it."

As this was being served, a thought occurred to Schmitt.

"That's all well and good, but what do we do with the general insurance business that we took over from Coopers. There may not be much of it left, but we would have to do something with it. No way could we make a profit just keeping it on as it is."

"Simple," replied Ray. "We still owe a hundred grand or so to Cooper as our final payment. We tell him to fuck off since he's done bugger all to keep the business afloat. I'm sure our contract covers that but, if not we just tell him to sue us – he's got no cash and would never dare to take us on. Then we sell what's left to Harrisons – they seem keen enough to take the clients over so we might as well make it easy for them. If they won't pay, we give it to them and we look for a route to get back at them some other way. No trouble."

"Good. That seems all fine and dandy to me," agreed Schmitt.

And, in this way, the seeds were sewn for the formation of Apex Combined – a Life Assurance Company that was set to become one of the largest direct sellers of Life Assurance, Pensions and Investments business in the UK.

A company that could do very well without Castle Finance and their grasping directors, but, a Company that would provide ample opportunity for the Messrs Schmitt and Capaldi to feather their own nests very satisfactorily.

Chapter Thirty-Nine

Tim and Roy were huddled together over their morning coffees, the door to Tim's office uncharacteristically closed.

"We just can't afford to lose Chris, Roy," repeated Tim. "He has been largely instrumental in pulling over dozens of new clients from Coopers and almost all of them look to Chris to provide them with the type of service that we have promised. If Chris were to leave, I'd bet a pound to a penny that most of them would want to follow him to his new firm.

"I'm sure that we could rely on Chris to honour his covenants, but if a client wants to move, he will move, and there's nothing much we can do about it. I'd love to be able to match the fifty thousand he's been offered. It would be worth all of that to keep him and we would still be making a healthy profit. The trouble is, of course, if we do that, then what about Graham's salaries and everyone else's come to that? It would be unfair to do for one that we can't afford for the other."

"More than that, Tim," pointed out Roy, "no matter how good a man is, once you've given into 'blackmail', there's no end to it. I know that's a bit strong in Chris's case, but that's how the others would see it. Everyone would think that they would only have to threaten to leave and you will give them a rise. No, you can't do that."

"Chris is not blackmailing us Roy. He's not even been given a firm offer. He's been honest enough to keep me informed, that's all."

"I know that Tim. He's a bloody good chap and I am sure that he would hate to leave us. Having said that, if we were to roll over and cough up an increase of that order, we would only be making a rod for your own back."

"What do we do then?" asked Tim despairingly.

"Equity, that's the answer," replied Roy. "Thanks to dear old Bill Warrington, Janet, Graham and I own fifteen five percent of the Company and the staff that were employed at the time of Bill's death own another ten percent. You and Mary own the balance. What's our turnover now, about a million pounds a year?"

"About that," agreed Tim. "With any luck, we should be on about one point two by the of the year."

"I'm not too up to date with valuations of brokerages nowadays, but I would think that, if you could find a willing buyer, this Company would be worth something in the region of one and a half to two times turnover − say one and a half million pounds to be on the safe side. That means, that if someone wanted to buy, say, five per cent of the Company, they'd have to write out a cheque for seventy five thousand pounds.

"Why not issue a few more shares and give Chris five percent of the Company. I'm sure that Janet and Graham would not object to their shares being diluted by five percent. After all, as you have said yourself, Chris has added a hell of a lot of value to the Company – he has earned it. If Chris had five percent, 'a' he would be so grateful that he would stay and 'b', he would want to continue working his balls off to increase the value of his holding.

"Give him the shares and give him the car – you said that you were thinking of doing that anyway – and I think that by giving him some wheels and the shares, you would have a very happy bunny indeed. To say nothing of a happy Mrs Bunny," he added.

"You're right Roy. What a bloody good idea. As long as I've got over fifty percent of the Company, I'm happy. What about the others though? There would bound to be some jealousy if this got out."

"Not at all," replied Roy. "If you put it across well, you would say that you are rewarding Chris for something over and above the call of duty. In other words, you would be recognising the fact that he had brought us a bundle of Cooper's clients – you would normally have to have paid for a block of business like that and you've had it almost for on a plate, thanks to Chris. Good as they are, none of the others have brought that sort of business with them. No, he's been the one that brought home the bacon."

"Not forgetting my brilliant deal with the panel of Insurers to make the whole thing possible," reminded Tim, not wishing to miss the opportunity of scoring a point or two for himself.

"Fair enough, Tim. Whilst we are on the subject, though, I think that this would be the ideal time to go one stage further. You are right in thinking that several of our staff would like to hold shares in the Company. Why not set up a share option scheme for them? In this way, not only do you increase their loyalty to the firm, but you give them an opportunity to directly benefit from the Company's success – by paying them dividends out of profit."

"Bloody good idea. How do we go about it?"

Their meeting took them through lunch, by which time the Harrisons Share Option Scheme had been born. Tim looked forward to his Monday morning meeting with Chris Wright with considerably more relish than when Chris had first announced his discussions with a headhunter.

Janet poked her head around the door, "Got a moment O Lord and Master?"

"For you, Mrs Brown, any time. Come in. Sit on my lap. No, on second thoughts, you'd better not, I might do something I'd regret." Tim could never completely forget his moment of passion with Janet, but since that day, they had rarely referred to the subject again, and then, only obliquely. It was as if each enjoyed a silent pact that these had been moments sacred and secret only to each other. He never, for a moment, regretted his 'fling' and, not infrequently, fantasised about a repeat performance.

"What's up?" he asked, putting his carnal thoughts behind him.

"The duff, I suppose," she replied happily. "I am now able to pronounce that I am on the verge of increasing the world's population by one."

"That's fantastic!" cried Tim, jumping around his desk and enveloping her in a bear-like hug (which still resulted in the old familiar stirring, he realised). "When is it due? How long have you known? Does anyone else know?"

"Approximately six months, approximately two and a half hours and only my family and you – in that order."

"Marvellous and oh bugger, in that order," replied Tim. "Wonderful news, but I suppose that means that you'll need a day or two off when the time comes. What am I going to do without you?"

"Actually," she said, "I'll be taking my full six month's maternity leave when the time comes. I want to spend time to bond with my baby. Whilst I'm about it, perhaps I should warn you that I might not even come back. I will miss it terribly, of course, but Colin keeps making noises about me not being around enough. He's doing particularly well at the moment and it's not as if we need the income. I do feel rather guilty at times, slaving over a hot desk all day and then feeling too knackered to get him his supper."

"I realise that Janet, but bugger Colin – he can cook his own supper can't he?" Tim, observed, not unreasonably he thought. "There's a time for everything. You've been the backbone of this Company from the day you started. I really could not have done it without you. You're absolutely irreplaceable, and now, I suppose, I'll have to find some second best who might be able to keep things ticking over. The important thing is for you to have your baby, get used to the idea of another mouth to feed and keep an open mind – and then come back. You never know, life as a housewife might bore you to death and you'll come back on your bended knees begging for me to take you back."

"Highly unlikely Tim, but we will see. By all means keep the door open, but I've got a feeling that my days of bonded slavery are drawing to an end. I'll see you on Monday, have a good weekend."

Tim sat back, emotionally drained. First he was on the verge of losing Chris Wright and, thanks to Roy, they may have saved that day. Second, he would almost certainly be losing Janet. He was delighted that she was about to become a mother and he knew that Mary would be thrilled for her, but life without Janet's exuberance, her unfailing good humour and her efficiency? It did not bear thinking about.

Chapter Forty

Joe Hendry had been surprised to receive a peremptory call from Peter Schmitt demanding that he get to London at ten the following morning to attend a meeting with he and Ray Capaldi. Even more so since he had insisted that Tom Cummings should attend also. Normally, for routine matters, they dealt with him alone and Tom had not been involved in any meetings with either of them since Apex and CFA had taken a controlling interest in the Company. Why should they wish to see the two of them?

He had called Tom who had cussed and sworn at the imposition. Bang went his regular Tuesday morning Stableford. Neither of them could figure what the meeting was likely to be about. Their shareholders could not possibly have heard off the problem with Hampshire yet and the threat of serious litigation. Joe and Tom had enough problems dealing with this disaster without having that pair breathing down their necks.

Neither could Apex or CFA be too fussed about the figures right now. Only Tom and Joe knew that much of the commission recently earned was about to be clawed back. They would have to have a good story to cover that one, but it seemed a bit premature to go on the defensive just yet. In this business, things had a habit of 'turning up'.

Of course, they knew that the general business had been disastrous but they could hardly blame Joe for that. He had admitted all along that he knew nothing about the business. It was Capaldi's own fault for not putting a good man in to run the Company. Penny pinching at the start would only lead to tears later – that was to be Joe's message.

"Perhaps," suggested Joe, "they want to make another acquisition and want to see if you will be happy to invest alongside of them. There are hundreds of firms like us – not as large as us of course – up for sale at the moment. They're all running scared of the Direct Insurers. Perhaps they acknowledge my skills, our skills," he corrected himself, "and want me to run another operation in parallel with this one."

"*Perhaps pigs might fly,*" responded Tom. "*In my personal view, they don't hold you in particularly high regard at this moment. The purchase of our shares hasn't exactly turned out to be the bargain of the year for them. We'll just have to wait and see, but I have a feeling you could be in for a rough ride and, frankly, I want no part in that.*"

They arrived at Apex' sumptuous Offices and were shown upstairs by an elegant dark-suited secretary.

"Sit down gentlemen," invited Schmitt as they entered Apex' Board room. Without any of the usual pleasantries, he began, "Ray here, and I have been doing some serious thinking on the subject of Castle Finance and Coopers. In short, we're not happy."

"Let me explain..............." began Tom, but was allowed to go no further.

"In fact," Schmitt continued, "we're so unhappy that we're going to pull the plug."

"You're going to do what?" shouted Tom and Joe simultaneously. "You can't," continued Tom. "We've got a bloody fine business going there and, despite a few teething problems since the merger, we're making real headway."

"Teething!" echoed Capaldi. "More like a complete set of fucking dentures if you'll pardon the expression. Your operation has been a complete bloody disaster. I'll admit that you have got a very substantial sales-force and, properly trained, they could bring in a ton of profitable business. As it is, there are a few pockets of productive activity and many pockets of sweet fuck-all. There's no co-ordination and, more to the point, the opportunities that you have been offered by access to the Coopers' client bank have completely failed to materialise. No, we've got a far better idea. Peter, you tell them."

"The days of paying firms like yours for selling our products are over. We don't need you any more. In fact, I often wonder why we ever thought that we did. We will be far better off employing our own people direct, controlling them, training them and exploiting them. As of next month, we are launching a new Life Assurance Company and winding up Castle Finance."

"Winding up our Company? Not so bloody likely. We'll sue your bollocks off if you try anything like that." Tom now had a full head of steam now, and it showed. The gloves were off and no one was going to push Tom Cummings around.

"That's your privilege, Mr Cummings, but that's what we are going to do. The decision has been made and there will be no turning back. We have given you both every opportunity to make a success of our Company and, quite frankly, you've blown it," replied Schmitt icily.

"What about my sale-force?" cried Joe. "There are almost five hundred of them. You can't just tell them to fuck off!"

"We have no intention of doing that," interjected Capaldi smoothly. "Apex Combined will be recruiting a new sales force and, if your people wish too apply to join us, most of them will be made very welcome, very welcome indeed.

"With the cash we save by not having to pay for your operation, we will be able to offer our own Salesmen far better terms and incentives than most of them currently enjoy. I rather think that the majority, if not all of them, will be only too happy to come across."

"You thieving, twisting, devious bastards. You won't get away with this. I'll see you in court if it's the last thing I do. You'll regret this day you slimy bastards."

"If that's all you have to say, Mr Cummings, I will call this meeting to a close. I will just remind you that, as holders of seventy five percent of the shares of Castle Finance, there is very little that we can or cannot do with our Company. Just remember Mr Cummings; it is the Piper who calls the tune. Good day gentlemen. I believe you know the way out."

With that, Schmitt and Capaldi stood up and ushered the shell-shocked duo out of the door.

As they hit the road, Tom, quivering with rage, too stunned to talk, stormed off on his own leaving a disconsolate, shaken and dejected Joe Hendry standing alone.

He decided to take himself to the nearest coffee shop and do some serious thinking. He could not believe that, today he tom owned 25% of a substantial company whilst tomorrow they would own 25% of nothing. Not only that, but the team that he had created would walk away from him without a single qualm. Here had to be a way out of this one.

. . . .

Meanwhile, Tim was having a much better day. He had proposed Roy's suggestion to Chris of giving him five percent of the Company and Chris had been over the moon. Chris had suggested that, out of courtesy, he should still attend the meeting that the head-hunters had arranged, if only to find out what it was all about. He was intrigued to learn what they had in mind.

Tim had no alternative but to agree but could not help feeling slightly concerned that even now, at a face to face meeting there might be an offer too attractive for Chris to turn down, notwithstanding his acceptance of Tim's Share deal.

Still, he reasoned, far better to have an employee that has turned down a good offer elsewhere than an employee who spent his time wondering whether he had missed the opportunity of a lifetime. Tim would just have to wait and see and remain patient until Chris 'debriefed' him after his meeting.

. . . .

Tim only had to wait four days. Chris strolled into his Office to enlighten him as to his headhunter discussions.

"It turned out that the firm that the head hunters were acting for was none other than Christie and French," Chris began. "I guessed it might have been. Christies have been concentrating on their overseas expansion, largely in the States, over the last five years and have been rather neglecting their UK activities, it seems. They are probably number three in the world but only number seven in the UK.

"They want to rectify that position and they have published a mission statement that indicates that they will get to number three in the UK within three to five years. That means acquisitions, of course, but they are also very keen to grow organically.

"What they had in mind for me, was that I should head up their UK new business team. It seems that they have heard from the market that I have been something of a producer for Harrisons and they thought that I might be able to do the same for them. They were very flattering and, you will be pleased to hear that they said some very nice things about you too.

"They didn't actually make me an offer there and then but they said that, if I were interested, they had in mind a 'package' worth seventy five thousand and a seat on the main board within five years subject to my meeting their targets."

"So what did you tell them?" With a seventy five grand package on offer, Tim was still not quite sure whether Chris was leading up to dropping a bombshell or not.

220

"I said, 'thanks very much, I'll take it'," then, seeing the colour drain from Tim's face, continued, "of course I didn't. I told them that I was extremely flattered to have been considered and that I thought that it was a challenge that I would be able to meet. However, I told them, I was very happy where I was, that this firm is expanding like topsy and that you had offered me a slice of the Equity.

"They were very professional and accepted that they could meet any reasonable requirements that I might have requested, except the last. If you work for Christies, you can earn well, but you cannot create capital.

"What they did add, however, was that they were very impressed with our operation down here and that they felt that there would be ways in which they could be of help to us. They have access, of course, to markets that we can't get to because of our comparative size. They have re-insurance facilities that we can only access indirectly. They have risk management techniques that we cannot afford. In short, they suggested a 'strategic alliance' whereby we could take advantage of these facilities on a commission-sharing or joint venture basis. They are a very professional bunch of people Tim, and I reckon that we should take them up on their offer. It can only be to our advantage."

"I entirely agree," replied Tim. "Well done. It looks as if you have done us a big favour by getting to meet them. The main thing, of course, is that you have decided to stay. For that I am very relieved, very relieved indeed. Now, have you given any thought to the choice of car you would like?"

....

As soon as Chris left his office, Tim picked up his phone and called Roy.

"Bloody good news, Roy. Chris loved your suggestion of shares and he's definitely staying. A big relief, I can tell you. Thanks for the suggestion, it really saved the day this time."

"A pleasure, replied Roy." I find that the older I get, the cannier I get. I shall have to demand a raise in my paltry Director's fees, I'm clearly only paid a fraction of my actual worth. By the way, who was it that was offering Chris his crock of gold? Anyone we know?"

"Yes, as a matter of fact, it was our old friends Christie and French. It seems that they are rather keen to start concentrating on the UK market again – according to Chris they have let things slide in that department, and now want to get as big here as they are in the States. Interestingly, they have offered us a 'Strategic Alliance' so that we can buy risk management services and that sort of thing through them. They are even offering us access to some of their markets. Chris clearly impressed them and it looks as if a lot of good could come out of this. The head hunters might have done us a favour after all."

"That's all well and good," observed Roy, "but it sounds to me more likely that they have eyed you up as a takeover opportunity. You watch those buggers. They'll soften you up and then make you the proverbial offer you can't refuse and all those years of work building the business up will go down the plughole. Mind you, you might have a few bob in the bank as a result."

"Not a chance, Roy. They wouldn't be interested in a firm of our size; we're far too small for them. Anyway, I'm only forty-four and there's no way I'm going out to grass at my tender age. I shan't be looking for a quiet life for another sixteen years at least."

"Don't you be so sure of that Tim. You mark my words. By all means use Christies as much as you can, but you keep an eye on them. They'd swallow you up tomorrow, given half a chance."

Tim was sure that, on this occasion, Roy had got it wrong. Tim would be more interested in buying another Company than selling his own. No, there would be no 'hidden agenda' with Christies, of that he was absolutely certain.

....

At about the same time, in the City cafe, Joe was sipping his coffee thoughtfully. His situation was desperate. He knew that with the pending litigation from Hampshire, the claw back of commissions and the dubious chances of being able to recruit and retain his salesmen, the prospects for Castle Finance were grim.

If he had to put a value on the Company at the moment, it would be sweet bugger all. He could not blame Schmitt for wanting to wind the Company up and walk away from its liabilities. He had no illusions about Apex being the type of Company that would hang around and pick up the pieces. It would not be their style to pay off creditors, honour commission agreements and the like. They would wind up the company and cut and run as fast as their sharp-nosed, well-heeled lawyers would allow.

Tom's threat to sue was an idle threat. You simply did not bother to sue bastards like Schmitt and Capaldi, particularly with their virtually unlimited financial resources and their ready use of the expensive lawyers.

There was only one man that he had to look after on this occasion (as on most occasions). There was one man who had to be protected from this calamity. That man was Joe Hendry. He picked up his mobile and phoned Apex Life.

"Could I please speak to Mr Schmitt please?"

"I'm sorry, he's in conference. Would you like to call back later?"

"I know he's in conference, I was in that conference just ten minutes ago. Could you please tell Mr Schmitt that it is Mr Hendry and that it is very urgent?"

Joe's heart was racing. If Schmitt refused to take his call, he was finished. Suddenly, his line clicked. "Schmitt here, what the bloody hell do you want Hendry? We're busy here, as you well know. Thanks to you and Cummings we've got one hell of a mess to sort out," came the unpromising opener.

"Sure Peter, I know that and I want to help. There's something I think you should know, something I think you will find very interesting. If you and Ray would be so kind as to give me five minutes – I'm only round the corner in Emilio's – I think that it would be worth your while."

He could hear Schmitt talking to Capaldi, muffled by his hand over the mouthpiece, but eventually, "OK, come round now. You've got five minutes and only five minutes, and it had better be good."

Joe dropped a couple of pound coins on the table and ran out of the coffee house, ran to the office and, panting, signed his name in the visitor's book for the second time that day.

"As I said Hendry, this had better be good, bloody good," came Schmitt's uncompromising welcome as Joe, again, seated himself at the boardroom table.

"I didn't feel able to betray a confidence at our meeting this morning, but I have been worried about Tom Cumming's activities for some time now," began Joe. "I am sure that you did not know it, but when you completed the deal with Coopers, Tom cut himself in on a private deal with Cooper so that he would get a slice of the action. As always, he arranged for a 'commission' to be paid into his Jersey account – Tom has always had an offshore account to assist in landing some of his shadier deals. I only found out about it recently or I would, of course, have brought it to your attention earlier."

"The thieving bastard," shouted Schmitt, paradoxically echoing Tom's very own view of Schmitt. "Can you prove this?"

"Yes, I certainly can. And I could enlarge on one or two other of his little indiscretions too. My main concern, however, has been the adverse effect that he has been having on the company over recent months and how an untimely exposure could have made things worse.

"He has, for example, been undermining my authority in a most serious way. As you know, I have personally interviewed and taken on every single one of our salesmen. Without me, they would never have joined. I set the rules by which they must operate and, of course, set my own very high ethical standards. Despite this, Tom Cummings has been going around behind my back telling them that they must sell, sell, and sell totally regardless of the client's requirements and ability to pay.

"I have tried my best to keep him in the background, but you know yourselves, what sort of a bombastic man he is. He is just not capable of leaving things to the professionals and can't stop himself from sticking his nose in when he thinks that our turnover should be increased at any cost.

"This goes directly against all my professional instincts. I know as you know, if you oversell, then you run the risk of being faced with lapses that, in turn, will lead to a claw back of commissions. Worse still, there is the threat of Professional Indemnity claims if the salesman has stepped over the line.

"Unfortunately, Tom's interference is now having some most worrying consequences. Tom has taken one of our top salesmen directly under his wing – Tom Fields. The result of this unholy alliance is that Tom Fields has been selling a number of inappropriate investments to the residents of a nursing home – entirely with Cumming's support, approval and encouragement. In consequence, it now looks as if we are going to be faced with a number of claims against us. They will be claims for having sold too much to clients who do not fully understand what they are being sold. In fact, half of them are gaga.

"Of course, as soon as I found out what was happening, I sacked Fields on the spot. I also banned Tom Cummings from having any further contact with my sales force. As you know, he's an extremely difficult man, but I think that he has, at last, got the message."

"That's all fine and dandy," commented Capaldi, "but we seem to have solved the problem by agreeing to wind the Company up and chuck you and Cummings to the wolves."

"Very possibly," agreed Joe, "and I think, if I may say, that on the face of it you have taken precisely the right action. I only wish that I had had the resource to have got rid of Cummings myself some years ago. I have always had my doubts about Tom's ethics and practices and now my worst doubts have been realised. However, with your current plans, that's history. On the other hand, there is one other consideration I that would like to put to you."

223

"Oh, and what is that?" asked Schmitt, belligerently.

"My sales force. You say that you will offer them a more attractive deal and that most will accept and come over to you. Maybe they will. But what if they like the look of the terms being offered by your competitors even more? If one goes elsewhere, to St Christopher's for example, they'll all get the same idea and you could lose the lot – the good ones at least. St Christopher's are offering some pretty fancy deals at the moment. The important thing about me on the other hand, is that I know them all. I employed them. I trained them. They trust me."

"So what are you suggesting, Joe?" asked Schmitt.

Joe's hopes rose. He took note that the 'Hendry' had been dropped.

"I am suggesting that you should do exactly as you have said you will do. You should wind up Castle Finance. You should dump Cummings. You should dump any Professional Indemnity claims that you can. You should offer a contract to all my salesmen but you should let me front it.

"If they know that I am, for example, the Chief Executive of the new Company and endorsing that Company, they will feel more comfortable about coming across – better the devil they know and all that. If they know that I am involved, they will be far more likely to stay. And from your point of view, you would not have to find and appoint a new Chief Executive. I will cost you nothing since I will be on a percentage of what my men bring in. I am, gentlemen, suggesting a way that will guarantee that your new Company will get off to a racing start."

"Just stay where you are Joe. Ray and I are going into my office for a brief chat. We'll be back shortly, help yourself to another coffee."

Joe's spirits soared. It looked as if they had bitten. He might just have saved his own neck.

Ten nervous minutes passed as Joe tried to guess the outcome of their deliberations. His hands shook as he poured himself another coffee. When, after what seemed a lifetime, the door opened and they returned, Peter was smiling and stretched out his hand to shake Joe's.

"Congratulations on your appointment as Apex Combined's first Chief Executive, Joe. You start on Monday. Your first job will be to tell Cummings to fuck off and your second will be to ensure that all Castle's salesmen that are any good at all will be contracted to us within one month. How does that seem to you?"

Joe could not believe his luck. One moment he was totally washed up, no job, no prospects; and the next moment he had landed one of the most exciting opportunities in the business. Chief Executive of a brand new Company with all the financial backing he could ever need. All this and he would have the added, sadistic pleasure of grinding Tom's sanctimonious nose in the dirt. And about time, he told himself – Tom had lived off his efforts for far too long.

"I thank you for your confidence in me gentlemen, and I will not let you down. I now have a great deal to do so I will get back to my office without delay and start work. I shall look forward to seeing you both on Monday. I will, of course need quite a lot of support from you both – new contracts for the men, new agreements, training facilities and all that sort of thing. Who shall I report to on Monday to get things started?"

"You get here on Monday, eight thirty sharp, and Bill Wiseman will be here to greet you. He'll have everything you need. You rely on Bill and everything will be fine," replied Schmitt. "Goodbye for now."

They all shook hands and Joe walked out, floating on air. He could not wait to tell Tom and watch his reaction.

Joe might have been a little less sanguine if he had heard Capaldi and Schmitt's comments once the door had closed behind him.

Capaldi had said, "I agree that he has a point, Peter. He must have a better rapport with his men than we would have, but I just don't like the man. In my view he's a twisting crook and he'd sell his grandmother for a tenner. Look at the way he shat on Cummings. How can you trust a slippery bastard like him?"

"I entirely agree Joe," acknowledged Schmitt. "The sooner we're rid of him the better. We'll let him get his salesmen over to us and, as soon as that's done, we'll shoot him out the door. We should be shot of him within six months at the latest. In the meantime, let's use the bastard. Are you with me if we make that our target?"

"Absolutely Peter," agreed Capaldi. "Let's go."

And on that basis, Joe's future job security had been defined.

Chapter Forty-One

Joe decided that, on reflection, he would leave it a couple of days before apprising Tom of current developments. He realised that his vicarious pleasure might be countered by Tom's undoubted rage. He decided to give him a call on Sunday morning. Tom was not one to appreciate a dagger in his back.

"Tom, how are things?" Joe began, diffidently. "We had a pretty rough time with Capaldi and Schmitt didn't we? I did want to talk things through with you but you rather rushed off and I didn't get the chance.

"I don't know if either of them got through to you after we left," he lied, " but I was very surprised that, about half an hour later, they called me on my mobile and asked me back for another meeting. It seems that they realised that they had been a little heavy handed and, possibly short-sighted in their original plans and they......"

"Heavy handed, short-sighted!" exploded Tom. "The bastards are intent on ruining us both and, at the same time, stealing the Company from under our feet. I can tell you, I spent most of the day with my Solicitors and I'm going to sue them for everything they've got, fucking millions, that's what this is going to cost them. They're not going to get away with this.

"I didn't like that bastard Schmitt the moment I set eyes on him and, as for that fucking Dago, Capaldi, I'll run fucking rings round him. You just watch. You'd better come round tomorrow and we'll start working on all that angles that will nail the bastards. You can bet your sweet life that they will fight dirty but you can bet your sweet arse, nowhere near as dirty as me. How about nine thirty tomorrow and let's get down to work?"

"Well actually Tom, I'm afraid I won't be able to help much. I wish you all the luck in the world, of course, but they called me up and asked me if I would like to be MD of their new Company. They recognise that they can't operate a sales force without someone like me who really knows what he's doing. They want......"

"They've done fucking what?" screamed Tom, causing Joe to hold the receiver a foot from his ear. "The bastards have offered you a fucking job? You've told them where they can stick it, of course?"

"Actually no, Tom. It's alright for you. You've got all the dough you need. I'm fucking skint and I have got a wife that spends more in a week that most people earn in a year. No, they've made me a fair offer and I had no alternative but to accept. I'm sorry you feel the way you do Tom, and I wish there was something I could do to help. But, you know how it is."

Joe was enjoying this. For the first time in his life, he had scored one over on Tom Cummings and the sound of him squirming and then wasting a fortune on costly but pointless litigation was giving him quite a high.

"You take that fucking job, and you'll be getting a visit from Twister, and that's a promise, you scheming, two-faced bastard," shouted Tom as he slammed the receiver down.

In one second, Joe's ebullience evaporated, completely. It was if a balloon had been burst. The one thing that terrified Joe more than anything was the damage that Twister Evans could do to a body. That it was his body that was likely to be the next target was something that Joe could not have imagined, not in his wildest dreams. A threat like that from his old mate Tom Cummings was the last thing that he could have anticipated.

Joe spent the rest of his Sunday in a blue funk. There was no one he could talk to. He ruefully admitted that the one person he could turn to in times of trouble had been Tom Cummings. Samantha was a complete dead loss. At best she would not believe that that 'nice Tom Cummings' would be capable of anything so violent and at worst, she would laugh. "Serve you right for being such a prat," she would say.

Joe considered putting the matter to Capaldi and Schmitt, but the more he thought about that idea, the less he liked it. Any thought of violence, which could drag them into the fray, would lead to a flat refusal to take him on as MD. He would be sacked before he even started work.

His only hope would be the Police. He could ask for protection. But what could he tell them? They could hardly be expected to react to what was simply a threat.

To gain their ear, he would have to explain just how real the threat would be. To admit to that knowledge, he would have to admit that he had previous experience of Twister's techniques, and to admit to that would be to open a bottomless can of worms.

The more he thought about it, the more desperate his position became.

On the other hand, he reasoned, what would Tom have to gain by having him beaten into a pulp? Revenge, certainly, but what good would that do him? It could, quite easily, land him with a prison sentence for aiding and abetting GBH.

Tom was looking at a cripplingly expensive lawsuit and, without Joe's assistance and with a bit of inside knowledge, he stood no chance at all of winning. If Joe were able to give him a few pointers, then perhaps his chances would be more realistic.

To give Tom a hand in suing his new Employers, however, would be an exceedingly dangerous game to play. But, if nothing else, Joe was a past master at playing both ends against the middle. He was a great believer in never committing himself personally until he knew for sure which side would win. Anything that could get Joe Hendry out of a tight spot was anything worth doing.

Yes, that was it. He would write to Tom explaining that he had no alternative but to take the job – and, thereby secure the future of his sales force. But Tom could rest assured that, behind the scenes, Joe would be working to ensure that Tom got all the aces in his hand when he took Apex to court.

Tom was a reasonable man; Joe tried to convince himself. He would see the sense in that. He would forget about Twister Evans and concentrate on winning his lawsuit – made so much easier by virtue of a great deal of help and guidance from his old friend Joe was now on the 'inside'.

With that decided, he felt a great deal better and he settled down to compose his letter of peace. In it, he wrote:

"I know that you were as surprised as I that Apex called me back to put this proposition to me. My first reaction was, of course, to tell them where they could stick it.

On further reflection, however, I realised that, without me, our loyal team of salesmen would be left high and dry. For this reason, and this reason only, I decided to accept the position but, believe me, as soon as their positions are safe, I will leave Apex to their own devices, to sink or swim.

In the meantime, please rest assured that I value our friendship more than anything in the world and you may rely on me one hundred percent to assist you in whatever course of action that you may decide to pursue.......etc."

By the time he turned in for the night, Joe was relaxed once more, content and very pleased with himself. He had solved his problem with his customary diplomatic flair. There were no flies on Joe Hendry when he had his own skin to save, he congratulated himself.

....

At eight thirty on Monday morning, Joe strode into Apex House attired in his charcoal grey Gucci suit, Church's black calf's leather shoes and black leather briefcase in hand. Apex Combined was going to be impressed with their new Managing Director.

He favoured the receptionist with his best proprietorial smile, "Mr Wiseman, if you will be so kind."

"Certainly sir. And who shall I say wishes to see him?" she asked.

"Hendry. Joe Hendry. And by the way my dear, I am the Managing Director of your latest subsidiary – Apex Combined. I am sure we shall be seeing a great deal of each other in the coming months."

"Congratulations and welcome sir," she smiled as she dialled Bill Wiseman's extension. After only a few seconds, "Mr Wiseman will see you right away. Take the lift to the third floor and he will be waiting for you."

Joe emerged from the lift to be greeted by a worried-looking little man. Bill Wiseman was a slightly built man in his late fifties or early sixties. He wore a shabby grey suit with worn cuffs, his tie was at half-mast and his wire-framed spectacles seemed in danger of falling off his beak nose at any moment.

"Pleased to meet you Mr Hendry. Come along, follow me. I have only had a very brief conversation with Mr Schmitt and Mr Capaldi. I think I know what they want, but I must admit, that there are quite a few details that I will need clarification on. Quite a few blanks I am afraid. Perhaps you will be able to enlighten me. Ah, here we are. Step this way. I apologise for the muddle."

Joe looked about him with some surprise. Compared to the pristine appearance and efficiency of the rest of the building, Bill Wiseman operated from a rabbit warren.

His tiny office was accessed via two secretary's desks placed outside its door and, behind his desk, was another door that opened into a general office containing some half a dozen desks – all but one were now manned even though it was only eight thirty five.

There were bulging files wherever he looked and reams of computer printouts on desks, chairs and even the floor.

"Don't worry, Mr Hendry," said Wiseman as if reading his thoughts. "I know where everything is and I do know exactly what we are doing. I am of the school that says that, as soon as you file papers away, you will need them immediately. For that reason, everything that I might want during the next working week is in sight. Now, a cup of coffee?"

So far, Joe had not uttered a word. "Yes, yes please. A coffee, white with two sugars would be perfect. Now where do we start? Where do I sit?"

"Sit? Oh dear, I hadn't given that a thought. Here, Julia," he called as his Secretary was about to depart in the direction of the coffee machine, can you find me a chair please? I think that we had better base Mr Hendry in my office for the time being."

Joe was appalled at the thought of having to squeeze into this dog kennel of an office, but he restrained himself for the time being. 'Doesn't this stupid old fart know who I am?' he asked himself. 'I'm the fucking Managing Director and he expects me to squat in his pigsty whilst I try to turn around a multi-million pound business,' he reminded to himself.

"OK," he said. "That is probably a good idea for today, so that we can sort things out and you can get to understand how I shall be running Apex Combined."

"Running the Company?" repeated Wiseman. "Mr Schmitt didn't say anything about that. He said that I was to run the Company – I am in charge of all of our subsidiaries, you know – and that your job was simply to employ our new field force. I will, of course, give you all the help and assistance I can to make your job as easy as possible. Now, let us begin."

Joe decided to 'bite his tongue' for the time being. There was no need to disillusion this loser now – he might prove useful. He would soon realise who would be in charge here, thought Joe.

With that, Wiseman drew out a sheaf of neatly typed papers from somewhere under one of the numerous folders on his desk.

"I have enumerated our principle aims here and made a list of the tasks that I would like you complete during your first week. I have to say that I worked into the early hours last night and this morning to complete this, but I think I have everything we need.

"Firstly, I want you to telephone the Financial Services Authority, inform them of your own qualifications and complete the registration process to get the Company admitted as a Direct Selling Insurer. At the same time, I would like you to draft a letter to all your salesman advising them that you have taken up a position here and would like to welcome them to an inaugural conference to be held at our Training College in Barnstaple in ten day's time. I take it that you have brought a disk with all their names and addresses on?"

By the end of the first day, Joe was a beaten man. Never in his whole life had he been confronted with such a mountain of bureaucracy, regulation and pure unadulterated tedium. Never in his whole life had he been treated like a serf, a man whose own ideas counted for nothing in the face of the machine that was Apex Life.

In Bill Wiseman, Joe found, Apex did not just have an employee, they had a computerised robot capable of doing fifteen things at the same time and carrying out four different conversations simultaneously. Joe would not last long in Bill Wiseman's office; that was for certain. He needed to get out into his own lair where he cold work at his own pace and do only the things he understood and was good at. That was what he was to be paid for, wasn't it?

By the end of the week, Joe looked back in disbelief. They had contacted all his Agents. There would be a conference the week after next. There would be at least three hundred attendees. They would all be offered shiny news contracts – considerably more attractive than those Castle Finance had got away with. There would be a complete range of contracts for them to sell.

As Joe drove home, he had to admit that Peter Schmitt knew what he was doing when had taken Bill Wiseman on. The man worked miracles and then went on to sort out everyone else's problems. He had learned a lot and, he had to admit, he was a better man for it.

As he pulled up in his drive tired after a full week's work, his first thought was that he could murder a gin and tonic. His second was that, perhaps he should take Sam out for a decent dinner tonight. With the hours he had been working, he had not seen much of her during the last week – a fact that he had rather enjoyed. Now, however, with the week's work behind him, perhaps he should show her a little thoughtfulness. It wouldn't hurt. Yes, he would take her out tonight; he had earned a little relaxation.

He was just pressing the remote on his key lock when he heard, or rather felt, movement behind. He swung round.

"'Allo Mr 'endry. Nice to see yer again." Joe was looking into the toothless, grinning, broken-nosed, pugilistic face of Twister Evans. His blood ran cold.

....

Tim was wrapping up to go home. It had been a long day and he couldn't wait to get home, hug Mary, hug the kids and settle down to a well-earned glass or two of wine whilst the domestic machine ran smoothly around him.

Just as he was rising from his desk, the phone rang. It was his direct line. With a mumbled 'oh bugger it', he lifted the receiver and announced his presence.

"Mr Harrison?" asked the caller in a clipped South African accent. " You probably don't know me. My name is Peter Schmitt. I am the CEO of Apex Life. As you may know, Apex is a South African Company based in Jo'burg. I run the UK operations."

Tim's interest was immediately awakened. He recalled that Apex was the firm that had got together with CFA and beaten him to the post when he had hoped to wrap up the Coopers deal.

"That's right, Mr Schmitt," he said. "I don't think that we have had the pleasure of meeting, but I do, of course, know your Company very well. How can I help?"

"If you know us Mr Harrison, then I am sure that you know that we dipped our toe into the water with General Insurance when we formed a consortium with the CFA and took a stake in a little Insurance Brokerage not far from you – Coopers and Smythe – I am sure you must have heard of them."

Tim laughed. "I am sure you know of our interest in Coopers Mr Schmitt, just as I am sure you know that, if you will excuse the expression, we were somewhat pissed off by your intervention. Now what can I do for you?"

Schmitt chuckled. "All fair in love and war what? No hard feelings? Actually, I've called to do you a favour. Can we meet sometime soon? I've got a proposition that I would like to put to you."

"Certainly Mr Schmitt. I would like to hear what you have to say. I hope that you're not asking for your clients back. We've made a number of them very welcome here, as I presume you know."

This time Schmitt's reply was a wry laugh. "Touché Mr Harrison. It is about that very subject that Jim Capaldi and I would like to meet with you. How about tomorrow here at my office about noon? If we find that we have some common ground, perhaps we could adjourn next door for lunch. By the way, please call me Peter."

"I would like that very much Peter." Without looking at his diary he added, "I do have a two o'clock meeting here but I am sure that I could cancel or postpone it. Good, I shall look forward to seeing you tomorrow at noon. It is Apex house, isn't it? And do, please, call me Tim."

"Sure is, Tim. Until tomorrow, then."

Tim felt that his wine would taste even better after that call. Surely, for them to call him, he had them on the run?

....

Joe could feel his bowels churning. He prayed that he could control himself. With a bravado he did not feel, he managed to croak, "Hello Twister. Long time no see. What brings you to this neck of the woods?"

With what passed as a smile on Twister's battered features, he leered at Joe and announced, "Mr Cummin's told me that he'd 'ad a little problem wiv yer and he asked me to clear it up for 'im. Nothin' personal, of course, but I was wondrin' if yer would like ter step in ter yer back gardin for a minit. I've got somethin' to show yer."

With that, Twister took hold of Joe's right arm and forced him past the garage into his rear garden. Any thought of resistance was rendered useless by Twister's sheer size and unbelievable strength.

It was a small garden but privacy was ensured with it being bordered by a six foot high hedge. The privacy thus afforded was now something that Joe deeply regretted.

As they entered the rear garden, Twister told Joe in a chillingly normal tone of voice, "Now yer mustn't get too upset Joe. Mr Cummin's told me that he was pleased that yer gave 'im a call an' I was only to 'urt yer a little bit so that yer wouldn't ferget yer promise to 'elp 'im art wiv 'is bit of bovver wiv that Insurance Company. Don't worry, it'll soon be over."

With that, to Joe's horror, Twister pulled Joe's right arm behind his back, forcing his wrist up to his right shoulder, dislocating his shoulder instantly with a sickening 'pop'. He then coolly gripped Joe's forearm between both his hands with the strength of a power vice, slowly but mechanically twisted one against the other until, with a gut-wrenching 'crack' both radius and ulna snapped apart.

Joe, too stunned to cry out, simply fainted and thereby missed Twister's words of comfort. "There, that weren't too bad, were it? Jest 'member wot Mr Cummin's said an' I won't be back fer more. Goodbye Mr H."

Half an hour later, Joe, wracked with pain, regained consciousness. The agony was unbearable, relentless and mind numbing. The horror of the moment that Twister had lived up to his macabre nickname was still starkly etched in his brain.

Joe dragged himself up and, painfully and slowly staggered to the kitchen door, whereupon he again collapsed. Samantha, disturbed from her favourite soap, petulantly opened the door.

"What the bloody hell do you think you're doing Joe? Bloody drunk again. Well you can just piss off till you're sober you miserable bastard. I'm busy."

She was just about to slam the door when she noticed that Joe, white-faced as he was, was lying in a peculiar position. His arm looked wrong. On closer inspection, she let out a scream, "Bloody hell Joe. What's the matter with you? Has someone worked you over? For Christ's sakes, get up and get in here. I'll call the Ambulance. What the bloody hell have you been up to this time?" Her wifely concern was quite touching, Joe felt.

Four hours later, Joe woke up in a clean bed with clean sheets and with a nurse standing over him.

"I'd guess that someone doesn't like you Mr Hendry," she was saying. "I've never seen injuries quite like yours. I'm afraid you won't be playing golf for sometime yet."

"Never liked the game anyway," Joe attempted a feeble joke.

"How long have I been here? When will I be getting out?"

"Four hours and several days, in that order, if you ask me."

"Christ! That's no good. I've got a job to do. I've got to get to the Office by Monday, latest."

"All in good time, Mr Hendry. All in good time." And with that she was gone leaving Joe in considerable discomfort, both physically and mentally.

The next morning his day was not much brightened by the visit of his nearest and dearest, Samantha. At least she was sympathetic and she had brought a large basket of fruit.

"Thanks love," he smiled. "I don't feel much like eating now but they look good – it was kind of you to buy it."

"No, them's not from me. That nice Mr Cummings sent the basket round. God knows how he knew you had been duffed up, but he seemed very concerned and asked me to tell you that he was very sorry that it had happened and that you could rely on him to do everything that he could to make sure that it would never happen again. God knows what Tom could do about it, but it was a nice thought, wasn't it?"

"Bloody marvellous," thought Joe. "I'll get even with that bastard one day."

"Yes love," is what he said, "Tom's one of a kind. You can always rely on Tom. Now, what I want you to do is to phone this number." Joe passed Samantha a business card, "and speak to Bill Wiseman. Tell him that I've been involved in a motor accident and that I am very sorry that I will not be able to get in for a day or two. Tell him that I'm working on the project, even as I lie in my hospital bed, and that, one way or another; I will get to the Conference on Thursday. Have you got that?"

Samantha repeated the message and, by the time she left the Hospital, Joe was reasonably sure that the message would get through

....

Not knowing it at the time, the following day Tim followed in precisely the same footsteps as had Joseph Hendry as he walked into Apex' board room and introduced himself to Messrs Schmitt and Capaldi.

"Now let's get down to business, Tim," Schmitt suggested as the secretary departed, having poured out the obligatory coffees.

"We will not beat about the bush. The fact is that you seem to have devastated Coopers' general account and left us with the relative dross and too many staff to handle what we are left with on anything like an economical basis. Jim, and I have given thought to two possible strategies.

"One. We take on a new MD and fight you all the way and do our damndest to get back all the accounts you've stolen from us."

"Hang on Peter," Tim interrupted. "We've stolen nothing. We've been very active, that I admit, but its all been fair and square and above board........"

"I know, I know," laughed Schmitt. "A figure of speech. Jim and I admire the way you've done it. We don't much like what you've done, but we would have done the same to you if we had been able to, don't you worry about that. Now where was I? Oh, yes, that's option number one. Option number two is to see if you would like to buy what's left of the business. We are Underwriters, not Brokers and Jim and I recognise that. Now, would you be interested in making us an offer for the business?"

Tim had to admit that he would. There was still the thick end of a million pounds worth of business there plus one or two members of staff that he would have no objections to employing himself. He decided to 'test the water'.

"If you had asked me that question a year ago, my answer would have been a decisive 'yes'. However, as you have admitted yourselves, we find that we are able to attract many of Cooper's clients to us in any case. Why would I want to pay for something that I can probably get for free?"

"Quite so, Tim," contributed Jim Capaldi for the first time. "I can see your point, but let's be honest. Most of the remaining clients are relatively happy where they are. You would have to work pretty hard to dislodge them and that would cost money, a great deal of money. Even then, a competitive approach from you might well make these clients sit up and think that now would be as good a time as any to seek a quotation from an entirely different source. In that case, we could both end up as losers and waste a great deal of time and money in the process.

"We are seeking a method whereby we can both end up as winners. You get the business with the minimum of effort and we receive some compensation for our costs to date. Furthermore, to be brutally honest, the clients will probably be in better hands with you and the staff that you retain will have a brighter future with you than with us. All in all, a win, win situation. What do you say?"

"I have to admit that there's a lot in what you say," conceded Tim. "Its just that, with our recent rapid expansion, we've eaten into our cash resources and now is not a good time to be laying out capital for what could still prove to be a speculative venture."

Schmitt looked at Capaldi, who nodded.

"I'll tell you what we will do Tim. We would quite like you to take over the running of the general account. You would like to have it but you don't want to pay for it. How about you take over the whole shooting match and, instead of writing out a cheque up front, you pay us seventy five percent of your commission for the first five years? That way, you get the business and we get a few bob for our bottom line. How does that grab you?"

"Make it twenty five percent for the first three years and you've got a deal," replied Tim without hesitation.

Both Schmitt and Capaldi burst out laughing. They knew that they would get a deal of some sort. "Come on, Tim, let's go out and get some lunch."

Two and a half hours later the three of them left the restaurant, all well pleased with their day's work.

Harrisons would take over the management of Coopers with immediate effect. They would keep all the staff for a period of six months and, if any redundancies were required thereafter, Apex and CFA would pick up the tab. In the first year, Harrisons would pay Apex Combined a management fee of fifty percent of all commissions retained, reducing to thirty five percent in year two and a final payment of twenty five percent in year three.

In addition, arrangements would be made for Mr Joe Hendry to meet with Harrison's Tony Abbott to see if there was any way in which the two Company's life assurance selling operations could work together.

Apart from the latter proviso, Tim was entirely satisfied with the Agreement that the parties had reached.

Chapter Forty-Two

New year's day 1990 dawned cold and bright, a faint sunlight glistening on the frost. In short, a perfect climate to recover from the excesses of the night before. Tim and Mary had always enjoyed New Year's Eve and had regularly made it a special occasion – in their early years with their family, but latterly with a close circle of friends.

It seemed to Tim, and all of their friends, that the dawning of a new decade warranted an extra effort, and an extra effort they had made. They had invited a dozen couples to their home to dine, dance and play childish games and the revelry had continued until three or four in the morning. It was now ten thirty and both he and Mary were ruefully studying the chaos that remained. There were streamers, burst balloons, empty bottles, the occasional broken glass and a kitchen sink overflowing with dirty crockery.

"Still," Tim observed, "it was worth it. I think everyone had a good time. God knows what Bill is going to think when Sheila tells him that he was trying to fit a doughnut on his old man. He was completely gone."

"I'm glad I didn't see it," remarked Mary rather primly. "He's old enough to know better. Anyway, from what I'm told, he could have done just as well with a polo mint."

"That's a bit unfair," laughed Tim. "I think I'll give him a call and apprise him of your rather pithy observation."

"Don't you dare! Anyway, what I want to know is have you any intention of keeping your New Year's resolution? I must say that I quite like the idea."

"What resolution?" asked Tim. "I can't remember making any resolutions. I'm damn sure I wouldn't have been so bloody stupid as to make any commitments in front of that crowd."

"*You said that you would definitely retire at the age of fifty. You were telling Susannah Childs that you reckoned that you had made enough dosh, and had enough in your pension, to pack up in two years time and enjoy the fruits of your labours. Surely you remember that? I think it's a damn good idea.*"

"Ridiculous. I never said that. If I did, I was only joking. Even if I did, what would I do all day? I'm far too young to be put out to grass at this time in my life."

"You must have been drunk, but yes you did. You definitely said that, by age fifty, you would pack up. There's no way I want you around the house all day but, at your age, you could start something else. You've often said that you need a new challenge; that work is becoming a bit of a bind.

"Why don't you try something different? Open a restaurant, start a dry cleaning business or go to University and learn something completely new? I don't know; there are hundreds of things that you could try. The only thing stopping you now is time. The kids don't need you now – except as a banker.

Becky finishes University this year and I wouldn't be surprised if Tom marries Georgie this year. Its about time, they've been living together for three years now."

"You may be right. I'll think about it," promised Tim half-heartedly.

....

Tim was sitting at his desk, sipping his second cup of coffee, half way through the morning of the second of January – his first day back after the New Year's Eve celebrations – when his mind drifted back to yesterday's conversation with Mary.

He had to agree that there was something in what she had said. He had gone through the morning's post and delegated pretty well all of it to his staff.

He lent back in his chair, stretching his arms and gripping his hands behind his head in a reflective mood. He had to admit that his job had become rather repetitive, that there was virtually nothing to challenge him. Business rolled in and occasionally, very occasionally, a client decided to go elsewhere. All in all, his turnover increased year on year and there seemed very little that he could do personally either to materially increase the rate of growth or, indeed, slow it down.

Roy Brown had eventually retired last year. Tim still missed his wise counsel. Sadly, Jenny had never returned after the birth of her baby, but Sheila, her successor was equally as good.

Tim had reluctantly donned the mantle of Chairman following Roy's departure and Graham had become Managing Director. Tim should have handed him this responsibility earlier, he accepted – it had been the making of him and he ran the Company with spectacular efficiency. Brian Epps was a first class 'second lieutenant' to Graham.

Chris Johnson, Tony Abbott and Jimmy Smith ran the financial services division with flair and panache and now employed over thirty staff themselves.

All in all, Harrisons had a payroll of over seventy people and an annual profit hovering around the three hundred thousand pound mark – a very far cry from his humble beginnings some twenty years ago. If Tim were honest, he would never have anticipated running a Company the size it had become today. Not that he was complaining, of course, but events had seemed to have taken on a character of their own.

Perhaps it was time to plan the future rather more determinedly. Perhaps he should start taking events into his own hands and working out a three-year strategy – a process he had hitherto always regarded as a pretty pointless exercise.

He drew out a sheet of paper and started jotting down a few notes. 1991, anticipated brokerage, anticipated profit, anticipated growth rate, anticipated boredom factor. No, it was no use. He couldn't be bothered. He would call James and suggest a game of golf instead.

His direct line rang, shaking him out of his reverie. Rather guiltily, as if he had been caught out with his finger in the till, he answered, "Tim Harrison, how can I help?"

"Morning Tim. Happy New Year, Its Len here," announced Lord Passmore, the erstwhile Sir Leonard Passmore and still current chairman of Sunbury International plc.

"I suppose you're still nursing a thick head. How's the gorgeous Mary? I trust you're looking after her well. You slip up and stop looking after her the way she deserves, and I'll be round myself to give you a going over, despite my advancing years. (Lord Passmore would never see sixty five again, but he still turned up at the Office every day – the Stock Market would mark the share price down several ticks the day Len decided to hang up his boots).

"Yes to all of that Len," laughed Tim. "How are you? They haven't got rid of you yet I see. I'm not so sure I'd still be turning up every day if I ever get to your great age."

"Enough of that! I'm only a kid compared with some of the old duffers I have to deal with. Anyway, its what keeps one young. You would be bored stiff if you packed up and I can't see you doing that for many a moon. You enjoy it too much."

"I suppose you're right Len," he conceded. "Anyway, to what do I owe the pleasure? What can I do for my most important and revered client?"

"It would seem that a couple of my chaps have come up with a wheeze that they rather like. Believe it or not, they think that we should go into Financial Services ourselves. You know, Insurance, Pensions, Investment and all that sort of thing."

Tim tried to disguise his alarm. The thought of his largest client becoming a competitor was almost too ghastly to comprehend.

"Why on earth would they want to do that?" he asked (a little too shrilly for his liking). "You know, there's no money in this game. You work twenty four hours a day for sweet bugger all."

"Sure, I fully understand that. Your Mercedes and Mary's BMW, to say nothing of your delightful 'mansion' bear that out. You have my every sympathy. But no, let me put you out of your misery. Bob Manners and Colin Crawford have said that they would like Sunbury International to buy your business. Apparently they feel that there is a vast amount of business from our suppliers and our customers that we could funnel into a Financial Services operation if we had one in-house."

"Great, but it's not for sale!" cried Tim. "I'm delighted that Bob and Colin can see that they could make a mint in this business but, I'm sorry, they can't do it by buying us. That's just not on."

"I told them that that would be your reaction. Their view is that everything is for sale – it's just a question of agreeing a price. Personally, I don't go along with that philosophy, but there it is; it seems to be the modern way of doing things. All I'm suggesting Tim, is that you come along for a meeting with them. Hear what they have to say, and then make your own judgement. There's no harm in that is there? Now, are you free tomorrow afternoon, say at three o'clock?"

"As it happens, I am. I was to have been playing golf but it's a bit cold out there and perhaps a friendly cup of coffee in your magnificent Board Room would be a more comfortable option. OK, I'll come, but please tell your colleagues I'm not interested. I'm only being polite."

"I'll tell them that Tim. Mark my words though, they've both got skins as thick as rhinoceros hides and tongues as smooth as velvet."

"I'll remember that," chuckled Tim. "Thanks for the advice. I'll see you tomorrow."

....

Sitting alone in his tiny office in Apex House, little larger than a broom cupboard, Joe Hendry was also in a reflective mood. In his case, his recollections led to him reviewing a catalogue of disasters, missed opportunities and bitter disappointments. Furthermore, he had grave concerns as to the future, his future.

It had been over two years since he had been appointed Managing Director of Apex Combined and, during that time, he had seen his status gradually eroded. Firstly he was demoted to Marketing Director after only six months then, some three months later, to Divisional Marketing Director. To his considerable indignation, just three months ago, he had to swallow the bitter pill of being reassigned as a lowly Agency Manager. Particularly to one such as he who enjoyed grand-sounding titles, this had been an extremely bitter pill to stomach.

He had to admit, however, with the animosity between himself and Messrs Schmitt and Capaldi (entirely of their making – he was entirely blameless himself) he had reason to feel grateful that he even had a job at all.

The only good thing that had come out of his series of demotions was that Samantha could not accept their declining social position and the reduction in her ability to spend as freely as she had become accustomed to on clothes, hair, beauty products and life's other essentials.

In consequence, she had discovered a young thrusting Insurance Salesman and had fled the family nest to move in with him. At least, to Joe, domestic life had become bearable once again.

He turned in his chair and winced as he caught his shoulder on the threadbare headrest. He had been left with a permanent weakness in his right shoulder ever since his brush with Twister Evans and, as the years passed by, the onset of arthritis was not improving matters.

He reflected on the relative fortunes as between himself and his erstwhile business partner Tom Cummings. At least Joe was employed and earning a reasonable living. Tom had embarked on an extremely costly legal action against Apex and CFA, which he had lost. He went on to appeal and lost again. Not to be beaten, he decided to pursue separate actions against Schmitt and Capaldi personally for libel and, again, was defeated – this time with no right to appeal. All in all, Tom had mortgaged everything he owned to fight these actions and was now, so far as Joe could make out, virtually bankrupt. But with Tom, you could never be too sure.

Of course, Joe had kept his promise and given Tom moral support together with the occasional 'behind the scenes' snippet of information that might have helped Tom if he had ever had even the slightest chance of victory. In the event, the only purpose that this information served was to keep Twister Evans away from paying Joe a second visit. In this regard alone, Joe's support had been worthwhile - thought to Tom Cummings, it had been worthless.

With Tom Cummings' customary brash self-confidence in his own abilities, he had even suggested to Joe that they should tell Apex to go to hell and start up their own Direct Selling operation again. They would really show 'those wankers' how to run a business. In the event, Joe courteously declined his offer and, in the process, saved himself from even greater financial hardship than was currently his unhappy lot.

So far as Joe's business activities had been concerned, as had been forecast, almost seventy five percent of Castle's salesmen had agreed to come over to the new Company. In the early month's Joe's stock in the Apex Combined had risen high.

However, as more and more Insurance Companies saw easy pickings and entered the Direct Selling market, an increasing number of his salesmen had drifted away. Joe was under no misapprehension that, at the current rate of attrition, there would be no more than twenty or thirty of the original salesmen left by the time 1990 ended. It was time for Joe to think through his options before the Company's options were thrust upon him.

He also reflected on the way that Tim Harrison had seemed to dog his life over recent years. Being a vengeful person by nature, he sorely wanted to find some way of causing that 'bastard' Harrison as much grief as possible. He had always seemed to be around when Joe's luck was turning for the worse and he would never forgive Harrison and his people for the degrading and dismissive way that they had treated him back in 1987 when Schmitt and Capaldi had suggested that he should find some way of bringing the two companies together to 'their mutual advantage'.

At their request, he had attended a meeting at Harrison's offices, accompanied by the redoubtable Bill Wiseman. Tim had explained to Bill that he could never understand the commercial ethic held by some, that the only way to make money in this game was to get as many people to sell whatever paid the highest commission and as fast as they could. Bill Wiseman, to Joe's acute chagrin, clearly got the message – that in the eyes of their peer group, Joe Hendry and his ilk were a pretty shameful bunch.

Having lectured Bill on the drive over to their offices on his ideas as to the techniques of how to run a successful entrepreneurial business, Joe was further deeply galled to suffer the indignity of listening to that ungrateful little tyke, Jimmy Smith, telling him how Joe's methods were old hat and would never work in the modern world.

To Joe's acute distaste, Bill appeared more impressed by Jimmy's management capabilities than he was by Joe's.

At least, in the event, he had proved himself right on that score. In the first few months, Apex Combined had grown from strength to strength under his guidance. He had no idea what profit the Company might be making but he did know that the sales figures had been on a rising curve since day one. Unbeknown to Joe, after two and a half years, Bill Wiseman was currently reporting to his directors that he was extremely worried about Joe's methods and that they should have listened to the ideas expounded by Harrisons.

Oblivious to this, Joe decided that he had to concentrate on finding a method whereby his undoubted talent of building up a sales team could be harnessed to his own advantage rather than that to the sole advantage of Apex. He could see little virtue in watching them grow rich as a result of his own blood, sweat and tears. At the same time, whilst he remained with Apex Combined, there seemed little that he could do to do damage to Harrisons. There must be a way to achieve both ends, he was sure.

....

At three o'clock precisely, as arranged, Tim was ushered into Sunbury's Boardroom. Lord Passmore was seated at the head of the table engrossed in conversation with Bill Bates, the Finance Director and two men who Tim did not recognise.

Lord Passmore rose from his chair with a broad smile on his face and hand outstretched.

"Good to see you Tim", he said. "You know Bill, of course. Let me introduce you to Bob Manners and Colin Crawford, our two 'young Turks."

The introductions were completed and they all sat down, Tim with an expectant look on his face. He was intrigued but he showed no signs of his interest as he sat there with his mind firmly closed. No one was going to persuade him to part with his Company at this stage in his life.

"I will let Bob and Colin do the talking, but I should explain that their presence on our board marks a considerable departure from the way we have done things in the past. Bob comes from a Merchant Banking background whilst Colin is what I would describe as a hard nosed Accountant – though you haven't looked at a set of books in the last dozen years have you Colin?"

"Not in that way Len," Colin smiled. "But not a day goes by when I haven't been taking a pretty keen look at other people's books – our 'target' Companies that is to say. Bob and I," he continued, turning to Tim, "have, in fact, been browsing through your most recent Report and Accounts – pretty good reading they make too, congratulations."

Tim nodded his thanks.

"Let me explain, Tim. Sunbury's, under Len's stewardship, has grown steadily year on year and is now the leader in almost every sphere of its core activities. More to the point, the Company has accumulated a considerable pile of cash – a cash mountain, in fact.

"The Board have been considering for some time now, how they should best deploy these considerable funds. The core businesses are all self-supporting, all generate a positive cash flow, and there is absolutely no need for additional liquidity to expand these businesses – a very happy scenario indeed, and one for which Len should feel justifiably proud. What to do with the cash, though? That is the question.

"The answer to this dilemma can be summed up in one word – 'diversification'. To develop the Company at the current, or still better, a faster rate up to the end of this century, the Company must diversify. It must use its vast cash resources to get into the businesses of the future.

"There are some incredibly exciting opportunities in the new technologies. You might find it difficult to believe, but the fax machine will be redundant by the end of the century, computers no larger than your wallet will be capable of processing information in a hundredth of the time that a main frame takes today. We at Sunbury's need to be a part of those businesses. I tell you, the opportunities are limitless and we are going to make sure that Sunbury's are in on the action.

"Now, why are we telling you this? Let me explain.

"Everything we do has to be insured, but we are paying too much for our Insurance." He waved Tim's precipitate interruption aside. "We are now big enough to have our own Captive Insurance Company – Bob and I have both worked with Captives in our previous commercial lives.

"Every Company we acquire will need Insurance – we should earn something out of arranging the insurances for each of our acquisitions.

"Every new technology we become involved in will have a function that could be applied to Financial Services. We want to be the front-runners in Information Technology for the Financial Services Industry.

"Now you don't need me to tell you that, with all Sunbury's resources, we couldn't simply set up our own Financial Services division. Why should we need to pass all this gold to Harrisons?"

Noting Tim's rather crestfallen expression, Len intervened by inviting Bob to contribute.

"I agree, of course, with everything that Colin has said. In fact, I would go further. A high percentage of our activities are carried out abroad. Currently, as I understand it, you sub-contract all our overseas Insurances to local Companies. Why are we seeing commissions ceded overseas when we could be keeping them all to ourselves and, almost certainly, saving ourselves a fortune by the judicious use of our own Captive Insurance Company?

"Many of my City friends are slavering at the mouth to set up joint-venture operations with us to work on this Cassandra's box of opportunity. But, we don't want a fifty-fifty arrangement; we want to own it all.

"However, and it is a very large 'however', Len is a very loyal business man. Len has stressed the way that, over the years, nothing has been too much trouble for your firm. You have looked after all our requirements – both risk management and employee benefits – impeccably. In a nutshell, Len has completely banned Colin and I from even talking to anyone else until we have had this conversation with you. Can you see where we are coming from, Tim?"

"I surely can Bob," replied Tim. "I am extremely grateful to you gentlemen, particularly you Len, for outlining your current thinking. What I believe that you are saying is that you want to buy my Company."

"Got it in one," affirmed Colin. All four looked at him expectantly. Tim was flattered to have been considered worthy of being part of a team of the strength and size of Sunbury, but his mind was in turmoil. On the one hand he could see a great future for the Company as part of this group, on the other, he would be trading his independence for a crock of silver or, very possibly, a crock of gold.

"As you can imagine, gentlemen, this has come as something of a bolt from the blue," he began. "True, Len intimated that you might be interested in making a bid for my company but, frankly, I considered ourselves to be far too small to be of any real interest to you and that, after today's meeting we would all carry on as before.

"Having outlined your plans, however, I do see that this could present a great opportunity, not only for myself, but for my staff too. After all, you would not be interested in bringing my Company into your Group if you did not value my team and their abilities, and if you did not want to make it grow."

"Precisely so Tim," put in Lord Passmore. "I would not have suggested that this meeting should even take place unless I felt that it could be a two way deal – in other words, your expertise combined with our opportunities should create what, I believe, they now call a 'win win' situation."

"Not wishing to sound too vulgar," said Tim turning to Colin Crawford. "What valuation would you place on my Company?"

"Nothing remotely vulgar about discussing pricing," replied Colin smoothly. "Its my job. I'm doing it every day of the week. Well, according to the figures we've seen so far, I would guess that you will turn over approximately one point five mill this year and make a profit before tax of close on three hundred thousand. Am I about right?"

"Close enough, but we're hoping to rise to about five hundred thousand pre-tax next year."

"Not if you lost the Sunbury account," countered Colin. Tim took note that, when he got down to the serious matter of negotiating, the gloves were off with Colin. No more 'Mr Nice Guy'. "But setting that aside – we can only deal with facts and not forecasts – I would value a Company such as yours at somewhere between one point eight and two million pounds."

"That's a bit tight isn't it?" exclaimed Tim. "It was not too long ago when brokerages like mine were changing hands at between two and three times the commission income."

"I don't think so," chipped in Bob Manners. Tim got the feeling that he was now beginning to be held firmly in a pincer movement – these two clearly operated as a pair.

"When interest rates were under five percent, that might have been the case," explained Bob. Nowadays we have to look at the cost of money. If it would cost us three hundred thousand a year to service a loan to buy your Company, we can hardly pat ourselves on the backs if that is barely covered by the profit that we are hoping to generate. Where's the point in that?"

"Two points," responded Tim immediately. "One, you will not be borrowing the money – you have already told me that you've got a whole pile of it simply burning a hole in your pockets. Two, this year's profit is irrelevant – you would buy us to use us as a foundation to make increasing profits, substantially increasing, by the sound of it, from all the plans that you have just outlined. No, even if I were interested in a deal, your starting point is far too low."

"It always is," chuckled Lord Passmore. "These two wouldn't pay a fiver for a bottle of wine if they could get it around the corner for four pounds ninety. What I suggest we do is call this meeting to a close now. You've got a lot to ponder and I think my friends here would like to spend a little more time on thinking about the deal itself. Would you mind, in the strictest confidence of course, letting us have a look at your latest management accounts – just so we can all get a better idea of what we might be talking about?"

"I've no objection to that, Len. If you don't mind, though, I would like you to sign a confidentiality agreement. I'll get Graham to fax you an Agreement and, if that's OK with you, we'll fax over the last three month's figures. I am not saying, I must emphasise, that in so doing I am making any commitments at all at this stage."

"Absolutely not," agreed Lord Passmore. "Perhaps you would care to give me a call in a day or two and let me know what you are thinking?"

With that, they all shook hands and Tim withdrew, his head in a spin. He would need to talk this over with, in the first instance, Mary and he thought that, despite his retirement, a few words with Roy Brown may prove time well spent.

Chapter Forty-Three

Joe arrived at is office on Monday morning feeling terrible. Whilst innocently strolling down the High Street on Saturday morning, he had bumped into Samantha who had proceeded to berate him in front of dozens of shoppers in a voice capable of cracking a plate glass window at fifty paces. The shoppers had observed the spectacle with increasing interest and enjoyment. Joe had no alternative but to stand there, completely stunned, whilst she heaped vitriolic abuse on him with a shattering intensity; and all because he had cancelled his monthly bankers order to her.

Why the hell should he be paying the bitch five hundred quid a week when the bastard that she was living with earned a damn sight more than he did, he reasoned? It seemed, however, that her lawyer did not agree with Joe's interpretation of how matrimonial finances should be run and that he could expect to be hearing a great deal more from him in the very near future.

Money was tight enough at present and now he was terrified that he would be even shorter of the stuff, if Samantha were to get her way.

The day hardly improved when he decided to take an old flame of his – justifiably accepted as a bit of a 'scrubber' – out for dinner. It happened that Tom Cummings and his temporarily estranged wife were seated at the adjoining table and he was treated to a short-tempered harangue from Tom throughout the entire evening. Even Mrs Cummings had much to add and it was clear that, in the eyes of Mr and Mrs Cummings, Joe Hendry was the prime cause of all their own current financial woes (and that he was public enemy number one).

Unsurprisingly, Mandy Spinks, his date for the evening, was unimpressed and she walked out as soon as the bill appeared. Joe had assumed that she had merely gone to the toilet but, in fact, she had gone home for fear that Joe would be expecting her to go 'dutch'. Much as Joe would have appreciated such a supportive gesture, his only aim was to get Ms Spinks into his bed, preferably with the lights out so as to avoid too close and inspection. All he wanted was a one-night stand to relieve his pent up frustrations. In the event, he had a sleepless night, a boring Sunday and now had a splitting headache recovering from the solace that he had sought that night at the Nag's Head.

The day was starting badly. It was going to get worse.

His phone rang. It was Schmitt's secretary.

"Mr Schmitt would like to see you in his Office. Right now, please," she announced peremptorily.

"What the hell does he want now?" thought Joe.

He knocked back the dregs of his black coffee, threw his plastic cup in the basket and made his way done to Schmitt's office.

"He'll see you now," spat the guard dog.

"Come in," called Schmitt. "Take a chair. I won't beat about the bush, Joe. These figures are fucking awful and getting worse. We can't go on this way. We are going to have to let you go."

"What!" reeled Joe, thunderstruck at the news. "Let me go? What the fuck are you talking about? I've got about a hundred salesmen working for you at the moment – all of them piling in the business. What are you talking about? Its that bastard Wiseman, isn't it? He's been whingeing about me behind my back hasn't he? I don't know what it is, Peter, but that bloke is always on my back. The trouble is, he's got no fucking idea about how to run a business like mine. He's the cause of the trouble, isn't he?"

"Not at all. On the contrary, Bill knows *precisely* how your business should be run. The Board have total confidence in him. Furthermore, they are not *your* salesmen. They are *our* salesmen, and we have come to the conclusion that we do not need you to stand between them and us. We can run the operation very well without you and that is what we are going to do. Thank you for your past assistance – it has been appreciated – but it is now time for us, and you, to move on."

"You can't do that!" shouted Joe. "I'll sue you bastards."

"I'm sorry you feel that way, but we can do that and, should you wish to sue us, that is, of course your prerogative. I would remind you, however," he added coldly, "that we would resist any action that you might take, vigorously, and that our lawyers have, of course, already been advised of our intended course of action. They have entirely approved it. It just remains for me to say goodbye. Mr Foster, our security officer, will escort you to your desk where you can collect your personal belongings and he will then escort you to the front door. Miss Marples will be writing to you with the formal closure of your contract of employment and, of course, enclosing a cheque for every penny that is due to you."

Joe turned to see the uniformed Mr Foster standing in the doorway, ready to carry out his instructions. In a daze, Joe had no alternative but to follow him out of the offices – for the very last time. The indignity cut deep.

....

Tim and Mary were holding hands across a restaurant table. Tim had decided that the best place to discuss news as momentous as this was away from the distractions of domestic life. He had returned home, told Mary to get her coat and, half an hour later, they were sitting in the Taverna, each with a glass of champagne before them.

"OK give," demanded Mary in a mock American gangster voice. "You've won the pools, or you've been sacked or you've decided to retire or you've had a hole in one. What is it? Why are we here and why are we drinking champagne? Not that I'm complaining, we should do it more often."

"None of the above, darling," confided Tim. "I've had an offer for the Company. That's what this is about."

"How exciting. Does that mean that I get my mink coat, or have you got a house in Monte Carlo in mind? Or an executive jet, perhaps? I wouldn't mind that. Its such a bore having to queue up at Heathrow with the riff raff."

"Well, I suppose we might be able to afford a pair of mink mittens, a caravan or a new Ford Sierra. Let's be serious though."

Over their starters, Tim explained precisely what Bob Manners and Colin Crawford had outlined and, by the time they had finished their main courses, they were both beginning to appreciate all the implications that such a dramatic step entailed.

Always one with a tidy mind, Mary asked Luigi for a piece of paper and then said, "Let's make a list of all the plusses and all the minuses that we can think of, and then see if we can decide what would be best. If the advantages outweigh the disadvantages, then we will have no problem in reaching the right decision.

"On the plus side, there's the money, lots of it. I like that. Then there's your work – being part of a bigger company, you should not have to work so hard. Then there's your retirement," she continued writing. "You'll be able to retire much earlier. There's your staff – they'll have greater security and, from what you tell me, more opportunity. So now let's look at the minuses."

After a few moments, she added, "I've still got a blank piece of paper. That's it; the 'ayes' have it. It's a done deal."

"Not so fast, Mrs Harrison. You're forgetting the biggest stumbling block of all. My independence. I built this Company up from nothing. It's mine. If I do this deal, I'll be back to being an employee again. A well paid one, admittedly, but I would not be able to make major decisions myself – not if they conflicted with the Board's wishes. After all these years, I would find that very difficult, if not impossible."

The debate drifted backwards and forwards throughout their sweet course, their coffees and continued on their drive home.

"Let's sleep on it," suggested Mary. "It will seem much clearer in the morning."

"I'm not tired enough to go to sleep. I've got a better idea," whispered Tim huskily, pulling Mary towards him. He proceeded to put his 'better idea' idea into practice. Fortunately, Mary being a willing participant, they eventually drifted into a long and deeply satisfying sleep.

. . . .

Joe's bender lasted a week. He had been unceremoniously marched out of the office by the security guard with undignified haste and, effectively, dumped on the doorstep – not that there was anyone there that he wanted to say his goodbyes to. In a shell-shocked state he had drifted into the City Pub over the road for a coffee. It was only ten in the morning.

"What the hell," he thought and ordered a brandy to liven his coffee. Two minutes later, he was mildly surprised to be looking at an empty glass and an empty coffee cup. So he ordered another round, but without the coffee.

By midday, he was completely oblivious to the world about him but something told him that he should go home. After much thought, he eventually remembered where he had parked his car and staggered painfully to the multi-storey car park in an endeavour to locate it.

After stumbling up three floors, hacking his shins remorselessly and aimlessly wandering around all the cars he could see, he eventually reached his own and set about the tricky task of inserting the key in the lock.

The journey home remained a complete blur, and he might have travelled via The Lion, but he later recalled that, as he staggered through his front door, the long case clock in the hall was striking five am.

He awoke some hours later to find himself on the dining room floor, face down in a pool of his own vomit. Appalled, with faltering steps, he dragged himself up to his bathroom, fell into the shower stall and managed to immerse himself, fully clothed, in a shower of ice-cold water.

By seven o'clock, he realised that he should have something to eat so, dragging on the nearest clothes he could find, he made himself as presentable as possible and walked, or rather stumbled, to the Nag's Head.

By midnight, the landlord had the good sense to call him a taxi, give the cabbie a fiver and Joe's address and pass on his responsibilities to one more experienced in dealing with these matters.

By Sunday, Joe was reduced to a tottering Zombie, unshaven, unkempt and barely recognisable as a human being. In all that time, he had not left the house but had consumed every bottle of wine, gin and vodka that he could find in the kitchen, the lounge and behind the imitation bar in the dining room. He had also consumed one stale loaf of bread, three cans of baked beans and half a packet of biscuits.

It was the realisation that there was no more alcohol left in the house that gradually began to penetrate Joe's consciousness and begin to bring him to his senses. His last drink had been somewhere in the middle of Saturday night and, by noon on Sunday, Joe started to realise that he could not go on like this any longer.

He glanced in the mirror and started in shock to see the apparition that confronted him - a total stranger. Bearded, gaunt and lifeless.

He headed for the shower and luxuriated in the cold spray as sensation began to return to his hands, his feet and, finally and most painfully, to his head. He had the mother of all hangovers.

He made himself a black coffee and swallowed a handful of aspirin. After sitting perfectly still for half an hour, he found that he could move his head without too much pain. He decided to shave.

He then got dressed in casual slacks, and open neck shirt and a pullover and for the first time in a week, he began to feel almost human. He realised with a feeling of deep shock that he had been within inches of committing suicide. As he tried to rationalise his position, one thing was abundantly clear – he did not want to die; he definitely wanted to go on living.

Life had dealt him some devastating knocks over the years, but none more so than being given the sack by a bastard that he had despised from the moment that they had first met. As he sat reviewing his circumstances, he determined that he would rise again, he would get even with those bastards at Apex and the CFA and he would also settle scores with that other bastard, Tim Harrison. He was not sure why, but he attributed almost all of his recent setbacks and disasters to that particular self-satisfied, stuck-up prig.

He began to work out a strategy. In his favour was the fact that he had built up a successful sales force and it mattered not whether they sold double-glazing, insurance or coals to Newcastle. Some of his erstwhile agents would, he felt sure, back him if he started up another business.

Despite their recent fall-out and the coolness of their current relationship, he also had a powerful 'ally' in Tom Cummings. Tom, even though he was currently 'down' could never be counted 'out'. Like him, he shared a hatred for both Apex and Harrison. Together, he was certain, they could again pose a formidable team and take on the World. He would, he decided, set up a meeting with Tom Cummings.

He had a plan and, if Tom bit, he would be the man to help him put it into practice.

....

Tim was thoroughly enjoying his lunch with Roy Brown. It felt so much like old times.

Tim ran through the entire story of how Sunbury's had approached him and how Mary seemed to think that he should accept the deal. Roy listened silently throughout, smiling broadly from time to time and enjoying, both the story, the wine and the excellent filet mignon.

"So what would you do, if you were in my shoes Roy?" Tim finally concluded.

"If I understand you aright," replied Roy, "you are quite happy to be part of the Sunbury team, you are quite happy to accept an obscene amount of money for your worthless little venture and you are quite happy for your staff to row in with you. You are only hesitating because you do not want to lose your independence."

"That's precisely it, Roy. I've worked for over twenty years as my own boss and I do not simply want to give it all away."

"I would hardly describe the receipt of some two million pounds, after satisfying us humble minority interests, as 'giving' it away," observed Roy wryly. "Let me ask you, though, what is the 'independence' you currently enjoy? You say that you are 'independent', but you would not make any major decisions without at least consulting your fellow Directors. You would not conclude this deal without, at least referring it to your fellow shareholders (of which, very happily, I remain one) and I doubt if you would move at all if Mary preferred you not to do so. In other words, any 'independence' you may feel you have, is purely illusory. If you accept this deal, you are simply substituting this interdependence with another form of interdependence.

"From everything that you tell me, this deal is good for the Company, good for your shareholders, good for Sunbury's and, what's more, good for you.

"If I were you Tim, I would accept, but, with one important caveat."

"Which is?" prompted Tim.

"I would not sell one hundred percent all at once. Sunbury's will, of course, want at least fifty one per cent – as a Public Company, they must have a controlling interest. In fact, it is a virtual certainty that they will require seventy five per cent since they will not be able to consolidate your profits if they hold anything less. My advice to you is to go back and agree a deal but subject to the remaining shareholders retaining twenty five per cent of the equity. I would be very surprised if they would not go along with that, especially if you are prepared to enter into a buy-out deal (which I would recommend) to sell them the remaining twenty five percent after, say, five years."

"As always, Roy, I am glad we had this chat. It has been more than helpful and you may rest assured that I will return to the negotiating table with my fellow shareholder's interests foremost I my mind."

"I'll drink to that, and so, by the way, will Janet. With three kids now, I am sure she could do with the cash," laughed Roy.

....

Joe's initial call to Tom met with little enthusiasm but after a few minutes persuasion, Tom agreed to a meeting and it was arranged that Joe would call round at ten the following morning.

Joe was pleasantly surprised to see that, despite the rumours of Tom's financial downfall, he still maintained an appearance of splendid opulence.

"Good to see you again Tom. Long time no see," Joe greeted Tom at his opened door. "How are things now? You look fit and prosperous. Things can't be so bad."

"No thanks to you, you bastard," replied Tom, but Joe was relieved to note that this was not said with any obvious malice. "Come in the pool room and you can tell me what's been happening."

After about half an hour, Joe had given Tom a complete resume of how he had developed the business for Apex Combined – 'working his balls off twenty four hours a day'.

"The problem with that bunch of creeps is, Tom, they couldn't run a piss-up in a Brewery. I've taught them all they know – they've lived off my connections and my know-how – and now the ungrateful bastards have turned round and told me that they can do very well without me."

"And I suppose they can," observed Tom shrewdly, but with feeling. "So what's this meeting all about? Apex and CFA have given you the push and you want me to give you a job, is that it? My last experience with you was not exactly profitable. If I hadn't had my Jersey bank accounts, I would have been in deep shit, just like you."

"That's it Tom. You've always been the businessman; I've always been the grafter. I was just thinking that, together we were a bloody good team and I reckon that, together, we could do it all over again. We would show those bastards – and Harrison for that matter – exactly where they all get off."

"I would certainly like to get even with those bastards Schmitt and Capaldi but I never could understand your problem with Harrison. He seems pretty harmless to me."

"You might think so, Tom, but whenever something goes wrong with my business, I'll bet you a pound to a penny that that bastard Harrison is behind it somewhere. I just know he is."

"That's as maybe. Personally, I think that you are being a little paranoid. But what have you got in mind?"

"Home Income plans, Tom. That's the latest big money spinner. You go along to an old biddy with a house worth, say a hundred grand, and you tell them that, without it costing them a penny, you can increase their tax-free income by anything up to five grand a year. They love it. I tell you, there's a fucking fortune to be made out there."

"Hang on, you can't just give them an income because they own a house. There's got to be something more in it than that."

"There is," replied Joe, cutting to the nub of the project. "Three grand in commission for us, that's what's 'more'. What we do is, we get them a mortgage for seventy grand from a source that only wants interest payments – there are dozens of them out there and they are happy to wait for the punter to die. Then they sell the house and get their money back. They charge a higher rate than they would for a straightforward repayment mortgage but who cares?

"Then we take the seventy grand and invest it in an Annuity. Let's say that the interest costs the punter five grand a year, we can get over seven and a half grand a year from the Annuity. That way, the punter is about two and a half grand a year better off than he was before. Of course, the kids miss out since, when the old bloke (or his Missus) peg out, the house is only worth thirty grand to them instead of a hundred. But fuck them I say, it's not their bleeding money anyway."

"That sounds OK Joe, but you said they would be *five* grand better off, why is it now only half that?"

"Oh, that's the best bit. On an Annuity, we would only get one to two percent commission – only one thousand four hundred pounds. What we tell the punter is that we can do better than the Annuity; we sell them a Bond. We can show them figures that will prove that, over the last five years, the Bond would have earned over ten grand a year rather than a measly seven. The great thing is that, for a Bond, we can earn double the commission – sometimes more. That's much more like it."

"I see that Joe," agreed Tom. "But what if the Bond fails to perform as well as it did in the before? What if the Stock Market goes down? Wouldn't the punter be worse off? He could possibly find that the income from the Bond would not even cover his interest payments. Then where would he be?"

"Who the fuck cares?" rejoined Joe, surprised at the irrelevance and naivety of such a question.

"We sell them a bloody good idea. We get our commission. If it goes wrong, what's that got to do with us? We're long gone by then."

"Christ Joe, I hate to say it, but I think you've got a bloody good idea there this time. How much is it going to cost to set this operation up?"

By six o'clock that evening, the groundwork had been covered and the preliminary plans had been finalised. Future Security plc, a financial services company to advise the aged, had been conceived.

Chapter Forty-Four

Tim was seated opposite Bob Manners' in his spacious office chatting idly whilst waiting for Colin Crawford to join them. Tim found that he was beginning to warm towards Bob who seemed genuinely concerned to put together a deal that would be in both of their best interests – Sunbury's and Harrison's. Colin Crawford, he judged, wanted a deal that was one hundred percent to the advantage of Sunbury plc and only marginally good enough from the vendor's viewpoint – just enough to make him 'bite'.

Eventually Colin breezed in. "Sorry I'm late," he apologised without any apparent concern. "We are OK with Jenkins Compucentre, Bob. That crafty old bugger Jenkins has caved in. I told you that we'd get it for a mill. I was right after all."

"Well done Colin," congratulated Bob. "I only hope that you haven't screwed him down so hard that he feels de-motivated. That deal is only going to work if we have Tom's undiminished and unwavering effort for at least the next three years. We'll never get it up to scratch for an 'AIM' flotation if he loses interest."

"Don't worry about that, I've got him by the balls – the golden balls. If he doesn't meet my budget by month twenty-four, he loses *all* of his second payment. I think we can rely on the old bugger to fight for that. Anyway," he said, turning to Tim. "I'm sorry about all that. However, do we have a deal or do we have a deal?"

"At the moment," Tim replied, "I'm waiting to hear what sort of deal you have in mind."

"Simple," said Colin, "as we said before, we give you one point eight million, half up front and the rest spread over three years, and we take you over, lock stock and barrel. You run it, of course, Bob and I know sweet FA about insurance, but we'll shovel all that lovely new business your way. We'd leave it to you and Bill Bates to sort out your service agreement, but I shouldn't think that will pose any problems."

"Don't forget, Tim," added Bob, we would also want you to set up the Captive Insurance Company for the Group. You would be able to charge a fee for that too."

"True," agreed Tim, "but the fee would be nowhere as much as the commission we're already earning that we'd be giving up by not handling your insurances in the traditional way. We would have to allow for that in assessing our revised bottom line.

"However, more to the point. In principle, and having slept on it, I do like the idea of 'getting into bed' with Sunbury's. My problem remains, however, that I am too young to give up my independence completely at this stage in my life.

"My suggestion is that you give me one million for fifty one percent of the Company now, and I sell you the remaining forty nine percent on and agreed buy-out basis over the next five years, subject to an absolute minimum of another one million pounds. I would be happy to take the bulk of my payment in Sunbury shares – although some of the minority shareholders would probably prefer cash – so we would not be a burden to your cash flow."

"Jesus H Christ!" responded Colin, causing Bob to blanch. "What do you think this is? A bloody charity? I want to do a deal with you Tim, I think it would be good for both of us but, do get real. Harrisons is a good Company maybe, but not bloody gold-plated. Anyway, we only buy one hundred percent of anything we acquire."

"In principle you're right Colin, but with a deal like this where we are buying people rather than bricks and mortar, plant and machinery or intellectual property, I rather like the idea of Tim and his colleagues continuing to own some of the equity. It will keep them committed. We would, however, have to own a minimum of seventy five percent Tim or we would not be able to consolidate the profits."

"I realise that Bob, and I might be prepared to go along with that. That's not a deal breaker. However, I'm afraid that we are a mile adrift on the shape of the deal that you are proposing at present."

"What do you think your Company is worth now, then?" asked Colin belligerently.

"Ten million pounds, but I'd settle for less," replied Tim. They all laughed, the tension was relieved and they settled down to a rational, good-humoured debate.

Some three hours later, Tim emerged from their meeting with Heads of Agreement signed by all three of them. In principle, Harrison Sunbury Financial Services Ltd would be formed; to be known as HS Financial Services. Sunbury's would acquire seventy five percent of Tim's Company. Tim would be the Chief Executive and would be offered a seat on the Board of Sunbury Financial plc, a new holding Company that would control all of the Group's current and future activities in the financial services field.

He would receive one hundred and twenty thousand shares in Sunbury plc – currently worth just over one million pounds – for his three quarter share of the seventy five percent of Harrisons being purchased. His fellow shareholders would be offered cash or shares for their twenty five percent on an equivalent basis. After three years, dependent upon performance in line with a budget to be mutually agreed (which Tim was confident would be readily achievable), Tim and his fellow shareholders could expect an identical payment for their remaining twenty five percent. Tim and his senior directors would also be able to participate in Sunbury's attractive share option scheme.

Three months later to the day, H S Financial Services started trading.

....

Around about the same time, in Tom Cummings' garden house a hive of activity was taking place. The garden house was currently the head office of Future Security plc.

Joe had written to every single man and woman that had ever been an agent of Castle Financial Services Ltd, advising them of a spectacular opportunity that now existed in a relatively un-exploited area of Financial Services. The new service would be irresistible to tens of thousands of men and women in their sixties, seventies and eighties.

The rewards for providing this service would far surpass anything that they could currently expect to earn in the field of 'traditional' financial services.

They were cordially invited to a Seminar to be held in the conference hall of a top London hotel in three week's time.

Joe had hesitantly booked one hundred seats for the event but Tom had told him to 'think big'. It appeared that Tom did, much to Joe's surprise and relief, seem to have relatively unlimited funds with which to finance such an undertaking.

Joe called the Chief Executives of three of the smaller and newer Life Assurance Companies. He knew from past experience that, to achieve the highest rates of commission (the cornerstone of Joe's strategy) it was pointless to approach the major well-established Companies. He needed a lean and hungry Company that was prepared to take a chance and one that would not be too fussy about the 'quality' of the business that they would be asked to write.

In the end, he selected the Investor's Mutual of South Africa, a three-year old Company based in Johannesburg that had just started a London operation. In view of the rapidly declining value of the South African rand, this company was desperate to increase its overseas earnings - at almost *any* cost. The IMS, as the Company was known, had agreed to write annuities within five percent of the top rates currently achievable in the open market but with a commission rate of double that which was currently available in the market.

At the same time, IMS agreed to issue a 'Future Security Managed Bond', linked to one of the 'big five' Bank's Unit Trusts - at a commission rate of double that which was currently available elsewhere.

Gordon Gibbons, IMS' Chief Executive did have the decency to point out that this was a relatively expensive contract since the client would be paying IMS his one percent annual management charge on top of the Bank's one percent. He indicated that, even in times of rising Stock Markets, the client might not be able to see any profit on his investment until, at the earliest, year three.

Since Joe's Company would be receiving double the normal commission straightaway, this downbeat assessment of the client's likely return, was entirely irrelevant.

Joe also called several of the smaller Building Societies to endeavour to agree terms that would enable the mortgages that his firm offered to them to be accepted at reasonable rates and with virtually no formality. Joe did not trust his Agents to be too discerning in ascertaining their punters' financial position or requirements when completing a bunch of Mortgage Application forms. But, why should they? They were not being paid to arrange the mortgage, only for arranging a Bond or the Annuity.

Joe had to admit that he had only met with modest success and he felt that the Societies, old fashioned and blind to new opportunities that he was offering them, may well refuse a high percentage of the applications that they would be presenting to them. Since, without the mortgage in place, they would not be able to earn their commission on the annuity or the investment bond, this could be a major stumbling block. Joe's inability to find a suitable market was a cause of increasing concern to him.

The big break-through came when Tom popped into Joe's 'office' to announce that he had just had a call from his old mate, Brian Campbell, the Managing Director of the United Bank of Jersey.

It seemed that the Bank had just obtained its UK Banking Licences and it was bursting to find secured borrowers in the UK who would pay 'over the odds' rates of interest. The Bank had a very large number of wealthy off shore depositors who were expecting higher rates of return on their cash deposits than were currently achievable through the recognised channels.

When Tom had explained their company strategy to him, Brian had jumped at the opportunity.

"I tell you, Joe," Tom explained, " not only is this fucking Bank going to say 'yes' to every mortgage that we put to them (provided it is no more than seventy five percent of valuation) but they will pay us a half percent finder's fee for every one we give them. It's a fucking gold mine!"

And so it proved to be. Joe had three hundred acceptances from the six hundred invitations to would-be salesmen that he had sent out. The hotel was, fortunately, able to switch the function to their sister hotel which could accommodate the increased numbers.

Joe had bullied the printers to work over-time to produce attractive, eye-catching folders containing full details of the 'Future Security Home Income Investment Plan', the IMS Annuity, the IMS Future Secured Investment Bond' and the United Bank of Jersey Open-ended Mortgage Plan." On every page there appeared a picture of one or more happy, smiling, carefree Pensioners enjoying his or her increased affluence as a result of having taken out one of their Plans.

He had had slides prepared professionally showing how the plan worked, complete with graphs and tables showing how to calculate the client's increased earning potential and, more significantly, how much commission each sale would generate.

By the first of June Nineteen Ninety, the Company's first trading day, there were two hundred and fifty 'Associates' ready to transact Future Security business throughout the length and breadth of the country.

Joe had the perfect set of circumstances for his style of business – an Investment company paying double the commission, a Bank that did not ask too many questions and a group of hungry salesmen with little or no ethics.

By the thirty first of May Nineteen Ninety One, Joe and Tom were able to see that the turnover of the Company in its first year had exceeded their wildest expectations. It had just topped one million pounds.

....

Tim and Mary had been delighted to accept the invitation to Lord Passmore's retirement party. It was a relatively small affair with only fifty-five couples invited to Connery's in the West End.

Tim was particularly flattered to see that he had been seated between Lord and Lady Passmore whilst Mary was seated on his Lordship's right. During dinner, Tim enjoyed a particularly animated conversation with Sheila Passmore who grudgingly admitted that she had no idea what she would do with him all day. She did confess, possibly as a result of a modest excess of good wine, that Len was not as unhappy to be leaving as he thought he might have been.

He had told her that, although the 'young Turks' probably knew what they were doing, he felt that he must be too old for their 'modern ways'. He could never get used to the idea that nowadays you bought a Company for prices based on what people *thought* they would achieve in the future as opposed to what they could demonstrate by their own past performance and abilities.

After Sunbury's Chief Executive had risen to propose a most eloquent and enthusiastically acclaimed toast to Lord and Lady Passmore, Leonard rose from his chair with a broad smile on his face.

"Sheila and I are deeply grateful to you all, our closest friends, for sparing the time to join us here this evening. I know that most of you are here to make absolutely sure that, this time, I really do go and that you have got rid of me at last."

And so he continued in his gentle self-deprecating manner until, as he neared the end of his speech, he said, "I wish, from the bottom of my heart, the good ship Sunbury plc every success in the future. When, thirty years ago, I joined this excellent Company, it was knocking on the door of the FTSE 100 Companies. Now, we are well in the top fifty and long may our upward progress continue.

"If I may, however, I would just like to offer one word of caution. One word of fatherly, or should I say grandfatherly, advice. Please do not run before you can walk. Sunbury's is now expanding at an *incredible* rate – into fields of activity that did not even exist only three or four years ago. I accept that the Stock Markets love it but I only hope that we are not going just a little too fast."

On the back seat of the taxi on the drive home, Mary leaned into Tim, kissed him and said, "What a lovely chap Len is. I know that they were so different in so many ways, but he does remind me so much of dear old Bill Warrington. What would Bill think if he saw Harrisons now?"

Ignoring the driver's rear view mirror, Tim responded with a long and passionate kiss. He marvelled at how, after all these years, Mary could still arouse him so totally with just the slightest of touches. How fortunate he had been in his choice of bride, he congratulated himself for the thousandth time.

"I know exactly what you mean, darling. Both of them where as honest and as straightforward as the day is long. Both of them worked hard, respected and encouraged that in others and were deeply suspicious of anyone they saw as charlatans or chancers. Not that I would describe Bob Manners or Colin Crawford as either of those, but I was rather surprised to see that neither of them were at the Dinner. They virtually control the Board at Sunbury's now. If Bob or Colin has not had a hand in a deal, then that deal does not happen. I have to admit that they have been good for my part of the business. Hardly a month goes by when they don't acquire another Company and then they hand me a new client in consequence. The only thing is, none of these Companies appear to have any assets and none of them appear to make any profits. What they all have in common though, is that they all promise that they will be making huge profits sometime in the dim an distant future."

"Len was saying something along those to me over dinner," said Mary. "He very rarely discusses business with me. Much too much of a gentleman. But he did say that he was surprised to see the direction and the speed that the

Company is moving. 'Unstoppable' he called it. I think that's why he's happy to take his retirement – he say's he must now be too old for it now, though I can't see any signs of him not being up to the job."

"Couldn't agree more. Len is as sharp as a razor. Perhaps I could ask him to become non-executive Chairman of my division. I don't see why the Board could object to that and it would give him and interest. More to the point, it would be another shoulder for me to lean on in times of stress – there are times that I really do miss the chats I used to have with old Bill and with Roy Brown."

"Providing you're not too stressed, I have a shoulder that you can lean on," suggested Mary seductively. "We're almost home now."

....

On the same day, Joe Hendry and Tom Cummings were celebrating the fifth anniversary of Future Security plc at, coincidentally, Connery's. They were being entertained to a very expensive lunch by a rotund and jovial Brian Campbell who had now risen to the dizzy heights of Chairman and Chief Executive of the United Bank of Jersey.

As the sommelier poured a glass of their second bottle of Krug for Brian to taste he raised his glass and said, "To you Gentlemen, for making all this possible." He nodded at the sommelier to fill his guest's glasses.

"You may think, gentlemen, that I called this gathering merely to thank you for the vast amount of business that your people are channelling through us day in, day out. Last year, the one that has just ended, the mortgages placed through us by your company exceeded fifty million pounds. I will refrain from telling you how much profit the Bank has made from these transactions – that would be contrary to the Bank's confidentiality regulations," he laughed.

"But, I am now able to inform you – and you are the first of our Customers to hear this – we have been acquired by one of the UK's largest Public Companies. Strictly between you and I, they have made us a bid that I simply cannot decline and, as from next month, we will be the wholly owned subsidiary of one of the most highly respected household named companies in the Country. And, I have to say, that it is largely due to the business that you have placed with us that has made us the target of this most progressive Company."

"Congratulations Brian. You've deserved it," Tom raised his glass. "I suppose this means that we've made you a millionaire and that you want to share some of this with us."

"Actually, Tom, you are not far off. They want the Bank to put forward take-over targets themselves. They are extremely acquisitive; seem to be loaded with money that they can't get rid of fast enough, and they want to expand their existing financial services division as a priority.

"How would you like to sell out? I have already taken the liberty of mentioning your operation, not by name of course and I have outlined to them, in the most glowing terms, the level of profits that you are making and the rate at which you are expanding. Do you know what they said to me? They simply said 'do it'."

"The point is," he continued, "they are like kids with a money box. They are delighted to have bought their first Bank and they want to 'look good' in my

255

eyes. Frankly, if you would like to sell and I can put up a deal that makes half-reasonable financial sense, you can take it that it would be a 'done deal'."

"So who is this fairy god-mother," asked Joe. "I have to say that, despite our success, I am getting pretty pissed off with the business and wouldn't mind flogging it off. As I have told Tom, not a day seems to go by without some petty-fogging new regulation designed to make our business a pain in the arse. We have to fill in so many fucking forms it's more like running the Post Office than selling finance. What sort of price would they pay?"

"I am afraid that I can't divulge who the company is at this stage. I am subject to a confidentiality agreement. So far as price is concerned, am I right in saying that you will have made about one million profit last year?"

"That depends whether we are sellers or tax-payers," chipped in Tom. If we're selling, then we *could* certainly show a one million pound profit."

"Well, in that case, I think that I could recommend to the Board a purchase price of ten million pounds. How does that seem?"

"Christ all fucking mighty!" exclaimed Joe. "That would mean two and a fucking quarter million pounds to me. Are you serious?"

"Deadly serious," replied Brian. "What's more, I don't think that the Board would reject my recommendation, especially as this would be my very first recommendation."

"I have to say," said Tom happily, "this does warrant further consideration. Come on Brian, we need to know who the purchaser is. For all we know, we might all go off on a fucking wild goose chase with lawyers fees, accountant's fees and Christ knows what else, and then find out the bastards haven't got the money. Come on Brian, we have to know."

"If you treat this in the strictest confidence, and I mean the strictest confidence," after his sixth glass of wine, his words were slurred, "I will tell you".

They both nodded sagely.

"It is Sunbury International plc," confided Brian. "Now you can't get any bluer chip than that can you? Are you happy now?"

"Isn't that the Company that bought Harrisons?" asked Joe.

"I do believe it is," replied Brian. "They do have an Insurance and risk management division called H S Financial. I am fairly sure that the 'H' does stand for Harrison. Why do you ask?"

"Well, my vote would be to do the deal but on one condition only," Joe said. "And that would be?"

"That nothing is mentioned to Tim Harrison until after the deal is done, don't you agree Tom?"

"I do Joe," agreed Tom. "If you can get us ten million and keep it quiet from Harrison, then, as far as I am concerned, it is a 'done deal'".

"I can see no problem with that. Harrison would only be a minor cog in the wheel – merely a Divisional Director. I am dealing with two of the main board Directors, Manners and Crawford. If I tell them not to let a minion know until the ink is dry, then that's the way it will be. Gentlemen, let us drink to the future."

They raised their glasses, "To the future," they chorused. Both Joe and Tom were finding it difficult to suppress triumphant smiles.

11 Oct.

Fred. Olsen Cruise Lines

Fred. Olsen House, White House Road, Ipswich, Suffolk IP1 5LL
Telephone: 01473 292200 Fax: 01473 292217
www.fredolsencruises.co.uk

Chapter Forty-Five

Tim and Graham Wiltshier were engrossed in a discussion that had been called by Bill Bates, Sunbury's Finance Director.

"It seems to me," Bill was saying, "that you have kept your overheads pretty much to budget, but your income appears to have fallen well short. I must confess that I have been getting a little pressure from the board to see what can be done to turn things around. Is there any way that you can trim your costs a little more, can we let some of your staff go, for example?"

"Absolutely not," replied Tim vehemently. "Graham will confirm that everyone is working under enormous pressure. There is simply no way that we can reduce head count, in fact, we are advertising for two more account executives. We need them badly, don't we Graham?"

"We certainly do," affirmed Graham. "The real problem with is the budget itself; the target income was unrealistic in the first place. No allowance seems to have been made for the fact that we are doing almost all of the work for Sunbury itself at a fee level that doesn't even cover our costs. We will have to put in for an increase in our fees. A five percent uplift would, by itself, put us back on budget."

"I am afraid that there is no way in which the Board would sanction either an increase in your staffing levels or an increase in your fees. That would only be robbing Peter to pay Paul. Colin Crawford, and I now report to him by the way, has put in place a very strict cost-cutting regime. He and Bob Manners are powering ahead with their acquisition strategy but are insisting that everything already in the Company must perform at 110% efficiency and we must look for a year on year increase in turnover of ten to fifteen percent."

"But that's bloody stupid, if you will pardon my French Bill," argued Tim. "If they are asking us to work for next to nothing, how the hell can they expect us to increase our turnover? It seems that that duo, Manners and Crawford, expect the Group companies to work miracles whilst all their acquisitions simply burn up cash. For the first time ever, I am now beginning to have some regrets at ever having come on board this Company. There is absolutely no way that we can expect a ten percent increase in our income when our largest client, Sunbury, is taking up twenty-five percent of our resource and paying us diddly squit for it all. Things were different when Len was in charge."

"Don't tell anyone I said so, Tim, but I couldn't agree more," agreed Bill. "They seem to be buying Companies with no track record for millions of pounds and then affecting surprise when they only show us losses. However, this is the world we are living in. What are we going to do about it? You budgeted a profit of seven hundred thousand before tax. It is looking to me that you may not quite make five hundred. Do you agree?"

"I do agree, Bill, but please bear in mind that I didn't write the Budget. We gave you our overhead figures, and they are about right. You imposed an income forecast, or if you did not, someone else did. I suggest that you explain that we had assumed that our inter-group fee should have been five hundred thousand pounds and, that as we have only received, or are likely to receive, half of that, we are precisely that amount behind. In other words, the Group has had a cash benefit from my division of two hundred and fifty thousand pounds and they should show this in their figures accordingly."

"Whereas I agree with your logic, Tim, I know that the Board will find it unpalatable. I will, however, pass your comments on and I will probably be seeing you shortly to discuss next year's budget."

"I can hardly wait," commented Tim dryly.

....

At the same time, Brian Campbell was engaged in intense and meaningful discussions with Bob Manners and Colin Crawford.

"I am delighted that we have sorted out the final details of our merger gentlemen," Brian was saying. "Now, I have an item of 'any other business' that I would like to air with you.

"You will recall that you asked me to keep an eye out for any likely acquisition targets in the financial services sector. Well, I think that I have something that will really make your mouths water and something that meets our synergistic aims one hundred percent.

"I am sure you remember me telling you that one of my Bank's principle sources of *mortgage* business – a particularly profitable segment of our portfolio – arises from a specialist Independent Financial Adviser known as Future Security plc.

"The company is chaired by a solid business man by the name of Tom Cummings – an extremely able and talented man with quite a track record. The chief executive is a real live wire called Joe Hendry. What Joe does not know about selling, is not worth knowing. Between them, they have built up the largest company of its type in the UK with profits approaching one million a year and rising."

"Sounds like the sort of company we are interested in, doesn't it Bob?" said Colin. "In my view, our present Financial Services division could do with a bit of a kick up the butt."

"I wouldn't go that far," pointed out Bob. "They're doing a bloody good job and, if you're honest, we are screwing them down on fees. Tim's a good chap and, given time. I am sure we'll see some very positive progress there."

"I hope you're right Bob. In the meantime, if we can lay our hands on a million pounds profit we could just do with that right now. It will go some way to masking the shortfall on one or two of the other deals we have completed recently."

Turning to Brian, he added, "Don't quote me on that. It's just that we've been buying up some fantastic companies recently in the High Tech field. They show bugger-all profit in the early days but they will show absolute fortunes in a year or two's time. We do sometimes have a little difficulty in persuading some of our less progressive fellow board members to keep the faith. It could be that Future Security will balance things up nicely. At the same time, maybe Messrs Cummings and Hendry could teach our people a thing or two. What's the deal?"

"Well, Tom Cummings has a fixed idea that his Company is worth upwards of twenty million pounds – a PE of about twenty on next year's forecast profits. I know them both well. In fact I have been spoon-feeding them for the last five years. I reckon that I could wrap up a deal for no more than ten million. Plus, of course, a three percent commission for the Bank."

Colin looked at Bob who nodded and then said, "Right, you're on, Brian. We'll leave this one entirely to you – one to cut your teeth on so as to speak. You get it done for ten mill – that is five mill down and the balance in two instalments after year's one and two – and we will give the Bank a finder's fee of one per cent."

"You are a tight bastard, I said twenty million plus a *fair* commission," laughed Brian good-naturedly. "But, since it is our first deal, I am happy to go along with that as a guide price. There is just one thing more, though."

"Which is?" enquired Colin.

"For some reason, Tom Cummings and Joe Hendry have asked that no one in H S Financial should be made aware of these discussions until we have completed the deal. Is that OK with you? They have insisted on total confidentiality."

"No trouble at all," replied Colin. "In fact, I would be pleased to give Tim Harrison a bit of a wake up call. It might make him a bit more competitive – shake his ideas up and all that sort of thing. In fact, if this chap Hendry is half as good as you say he is, with a million pounds profit under his belt, - you can offer him a fucking seat on the Board – it might give all the other old fuddy duddies a shot in the arm. Just the sort of thing we need right now."

....

The following week, Joe was seated opposite Tom in his spacious, new and beautifully appointed office.

"I must say that the complaints we are receiving from disgruntled clients are becoming a complete fucking nuisance Tom. I've got two blokes and three secretaries doing nothing but answering calls from whingeing old farts who think that they've lost their houses and half their fucking money. We've now had several letters from the PIA – whoever they are – saying that they want to come and see us. On top of that, almost every Sunday Newspaper seems to have it in for us."

"They would print anything for a bit of a story. What seems to be the problem?" asked Tom.

"The sort of thing that happens," explained Joe, "is that we get a punter a mortgage for seventy grand on a house worth a hundred. He still owns thirty percent of it, so he shouldn't complain. The trouble is though, we invest the cash in one of Investors Mutual's Bonds and tell them to draw ten percent a year to give them the money to pay the interest and the balance for them to spend on themselves.

"All that would be OK if Investors Mutual were any bloody good. The fact is, instead of their bonds growing by ten percent a year, they have actually been falling in value. The result is that some of these old biddies have less than they started with, and they don't like it."

"I'm not surprised," replied Tom. "But it's Investor's Mutual that have been letting them down, not us. What the fuck has it got to do with us?"

"I agree Tom. But we are the one's who are first in the firing line. It's us that they are complaining to and if it keeps going on like this, my boys are going to find it bloody difficult to sell much more.

"For Christ's sake, the one thing we've got to do then," announced Tom decisively, "is to make damn sure that we wrap up this deal with Brian Campbell before things go too far. Let's not fuck about. If Sunbury's get wind of all this aggro *before* we do the deal, you can kiss goodbye to your two and a half long ones."

....

The following day, Tom and Joe met with Brian Campbell at Tom's solicitor's offices.

"Thank you for coming over Brian," welcomed Tom. "I hope you don't mind the change of venue but we are all busy men and, if we can agree a deal, then it would be nice to get something formal in writing so that we all know where we are. Keith here," Tom indicated his Solicitor, "will make sure that everything is kosher and above board, won't you Keith."

"Certainly Brian. Nice to meet you. Now let's get down to business. I understand from our earlier conversation that you have complete authority from the board of Sunbury International plc to agree and commit to a deal here today subject, of course, to all parties being able to agree terms."

"Absolutely correct, Keith," confirmed Brian pompously. "As the in-house Banker to the Group and, as someone who has known and respected these two gentlemen for a very long time, the Board has asked that we waste no time and endeavour to conclude a deal with the minimum of delay – today suits me fine," he added with a casual smile.

Five hours later, Keith Blenkinsopp happily ushered Brian from his Office holding, in his brief case, a formal agreement for Sunbury International plc to acquire the whole of the issued share capital of Jaycee Ltd, a holding Company registered in the Channel Islands whose sole asset was the entire share capital of Future Security plc. It was for the sum of ten million pounds payable in three annual instalments.

Furthermore, it was agreed that Tom Cummings and Joe Hendry would enter into five-year service agreements on the same terms as their current (extremely generous) packages. Finally, after a period of three months, Joe Hendry would be offered a seat on the main board of Sunbury International plc. Brian could not wait to tell Colin Crawford the good news.

....

"That's good Brian, well done," said Colin Crawford on the phone the following morning once Brian had briefed him on he terms that he had agreed. I like three equal instalments – it reduces the strain on cash flow a little in year one. When will the due diligence be carried out and who will you get to do it?"

"Due diligence?" echoed Brian, feeling a stab of concern. "I didn't think you would want to go through all that. After all, I've known these people for five years. Done millions of pounds of business with them. I would trust them with my own life. There is no point in wasting a fortune on fees when I know what the answers will be."

"No due diligence!" exploded Colin. "We're a Public Company for Christ sakes. We can't go round buying up Companies without knowing what we're getting. We'd be the laughing stock of the City to say nothing of what our shareholders would do to us at an AGM."

"Well, I'm very sorry," said a contrite Brian Campbell, "but I am afraid that we are going to have to live with it. I have committed the Company – on your personal authority. You told me to go ahead and I have gone ahead. I am sorry, but I did not appreciate the formalities. Anyway," he added brightly, "You will never regret it. It's a bloody good Company and you'll make a fortune out of it. Oh, and furthermore, I've told Joe Hendry that you will give him a seat on the main board within three months. You will find him a great asset, I am sure."

"You've done what?" exploded Colin for the second time, and then, having counted to ten said, "just come in to the Office and see Bob and me tomorrow at nine o'clock sharp. Bring your bloody agreement with you and we will see what you have let us in for."

....

That evening, over supper, Tim was uncharacteristically silent.

"What's the matter darling," asked Mary. "You've been getting moodier and moodier every night this week. It's not like you. Something's bothering you."

"Nothing really," mumbled Tim. "I suppose it's just that I don't fit into a big organisation, but that's where I am. I've made my bed and now I will have to lie in it."

Tim then went on to explain to Mary how everything seemed to have so completely changed at Sunbury's since Len's retirement.

No one seems to bother any more about a job well done. It is now just a matter of setting a budget, the more unachievable the better they liked it, and then putting everyone under impossible pressure to bring in more business or to take on more work.

"I've got people working eight or nine hours a day simply to keep up with the workload," Tim complained. "I've got account executives, bloody good people, who bring in more business that any other brokers that I know and, as soon as they reach their targets, bloody Colin Crawford sets them a still higher one for the next year. If they do not achieve that, bang go their over-riding bonuses. Young Colin Chappell produced seventy thousand pounds of new business (and still serviced his existing clients) last year and received a paltry five thousand bonus. This year he is expected to produce one hundred thousand before he will get the same again. It is simply not the way to run a company. I wish I had never sold in the first place."

"Why don't you buy it back then?" asked Mary not unreasonably. "I notice that, since Manners and Crawford have been in control, Sunbury's share price has shot up. They must be doing something right. I saw that the price had just topped ten pounds. Doesn't that mean that our shares are now worth over one point two million?"

"You've been checking. Yes that's true, but I am under an agreement not to sell any shares for another three years. It's a nice idea to buy it back, but there are too many complications," sighed Tim. "First there's the money;

where would I find that amount particularly as I can't sell my shares yet? Then there are the rules and regulations and compliance involved in setting up a new company; that's not so easy these days. Then there's the little matter of my service agreement; quite a knotty one that."

But the seed was sown.

....

"I don't like it Colin. I don't like it all." Bob Manners was sharing a coffee with Colin Crawford in the latter's office. It was a grey day and this appropriately reflected the sombre mood of Sunbury's two brightest young Directors.

"We really know sweet fuck all about Future Security and to have this fellow Hendry on our Board before we have even met him is preposterous. I know you were only joking when you threw that one out, but that bloody fool Campbell has taken you literally. We are going to have a hell of a job persuading our dear brethren about that one. You must have been having a complete brainstorm when you suggested that little snippet to Campbell."

"I suppose you're right," conceded Colin. "I was only trying to make Brian feel important, let him know that we rated him. I had no idea the bloody fool would go this far. I cannot believe that he would commit us to a deal without going through the full due diligence procedure. The man's a fucking idiot."

"That he might be, but remember it's us who got him here. If there's any egg sticking to any faces, it's you and me who are in the stocks. I reckon Bill Bates and Cecil Banks will lap this one up. They've been getting far too critical of some of our deals of late. I am bloody certain that nothing would please them more than for them to see us to be hoisted by our own petards. Some of the others are also becoming real pains in the arse. They have no vision. They just can't seem to see that the future is in High Tech and in Financial Services. Manufacturing and trading were all well and good in their day, but that day has passed.

"My sentiments entirely, Bob," agreed Colin. "Thankfully, at only ten million, this is a Class Four transaction and we will not have to go to the shareholders. We're going to play this one with the Board in two ways.

"In the first place, we will tell them that the deal is virtually inevitable since we had already acquired the Bank – they did agree to that one. We will then tell them that, without the Bank's major business provider coming on board simultaneously, the whole thing could have been a flop. It will be difficult persuading some of the old farts to come round, but there's nothing like a fait accompli to quash any argument.

"Secondly, we'll dish the dirt on Tim Harrison. He's been getting far too uppity for my liking, of late. He can't make his budgets and he's had the effrontery to try to lay the blame on you and me! The line we'll take is that we are worried by his performance and we have decided to put a proverbial bullet up his backside by promoting a real go-getter, a man with a proven record in selling, over his head. If he doesn't like it, we will tell the Board that he's not up to the job and we'll have to 'let him go', toute de suite."

"That might be a little harsh Colin, but I agree, it will get us off the hook and in the clear. Yes, that's the way we'll play it. Now, let's turn to the small matter of Laser Technologies. I am afraid to say we've got some explaining to do there too. If they carry on at their current rate, they're going to need a Rights Issue about three years earlier than we had originally anticipated."

The two financial geniuses continued to review their rapidly expanding portfolio of under-performing companies.

Chapter Forty-Six

Bob Manners had called a Board Meeting for the Directors of H S Financial Services Ltd. Present were Bob Manners, Colin Crawford, Bill Bates, Cecil Banks, Graham Wiltshier, Chris Johnson and Tim.

Welcoming everyone to the meeting, Bob announced, "We've got a lot to get through today gentlemen and there is one other item under 'any other business' to which I would like to devote some additional time. Colin, Bill and Cecil know all about it but I have not had time to involve the rest of you in it so let's beetle through the routine business and reserve as much time as possible for the final item."

Intrigued, Tim and his colleagues were quite happy to rip through the usual boring routine at a canter so that, only half an hour later, Bob was able to say.

"Right gentlemen, item six. It may come as a surprise to you, but Colin and I have been particularly keen to acquire our own Bank. What I like about Banks is that one hell of a lot of money passes through its hands, and as it does so, some of it always sticks – a licence to print money, you might say.

"Only recently, an opportunity has arisen that was just too good to miss. As of yesterday, we became the proud owners of the United Bank of Jersey – a fine old Institution dating back over one hundred years. Much of their business has been based on the advantages of Jersey as a tax haven but, recently, they have been expanding their activities quite considerably onto the mainland. At this they have been remarkably successful."

Bob passed round a folder for each director and waited whilst they perused the contents. Each folder contained a selection of the Banks' promotional literature, a summary of the services that they offered, and a shortened version of their last three years Reports and Accounts.

After they had briefly digested these Ben opened the discussion as to the merits of owning their own Bank and the opportunities that it might present to their own Financial Services Division. It was clear to all that this was a major step forward and one that offered a great number of interesting possibilities for further expansion.

"I should say right away," said Colin, turning to Tim, " that we do not see the Bank as a part of your particular division. It will, in fact, be a 'stand alone' activity though the opportunities for synergy are obvious. I am sure that the Bank will be able to generate leads for your own people from their extensive client base. In the same way, I am sure that you will be able to offer the Bank's services to many of your own clients.

"What Bob has not said, however, is we have also secured something of a 'golden apple' with this acquisition. It happens that the Bank's most active business producer is a very progressive national firm of financial advisers which generates some fifty million pounds of business a year for them. The

Company, itself, generates a profit before tax of over one million pounds a year.

"Bob and I were slightly concerned that the change in ownership of the Bank might jeopardise the very close relationship between it and its main business partner and, naturally, we were quick to spot the danger. More significantly, we also spotted the opportunity that this offered.

"I am delighted to say that, in the space of only forty eight hours, we have been able to acquire that Company too. Golden opportunities such as these occur only rarely and, if they are not grasped immediately, the chance could very easily pass us by forever.

"Furthermore, I have to say that the man who has built up this most impressive business is one of the most highly regarded in his profession and we have been extremely fortunate in having persuaded him, not only to join us but, within three months if all goes as we trust and hope it will, to accept a seat on our Board."

Turning to Bill and Cecil, he added, "Our colleagues have already met this gentlemen and I know that they are excited to have the opportunity to work with him – I am sure that we will all learn something from him and, if a little of his success can rub off on all of us, then we will all gain."

Tim noted that the expressions on Bill's and Cecil's faces, far from showing wild enthusiasm, bore the signs of resigned acceptance; and, possibly, concern.

"So who," asked Tim, "is this firm and it's illustrious star? Do we know them?"

"I am sure that you will have heard of them, Tim," answered Colin. "The Company is Future Security plc and it is their Chief Executive, Joe Hendry, who will be joining us, eventually with a seat on our Board."

"Joe Hendry!" exploded Tim, Graham and Chris in unison.

"You cannot be serious!" exclaimed Tim. "The man's a fraud, a crook, a charlatan and a complete bloody disgrace to our profession."

"Steady on," counselled Bob. "That's no way to speak of a man of his standing and a man, may I remind you, who could shortly become your immediate superior. Perhaps we should have told you a little more about our plans before we got this far, but we have had to move fast. We just had to get on with it before the opportunity slipped away. I can understand your chagrin in not being invited to participate in the discussions leading up to completion of this deal, and I regret that. You should not, however, let that affect your professional judgement. But the deed is done, the dye is cast, and we will now all have to work together to our mutual advantage. I am sure that we will all benefit enormously in the long run."

"Over my dead body," shouted Tim. He was incandescent with rage. "I tell you now, and I tell you straight, there is no way that I am going to work in the same company as a crook like Hendry and I very much doubt whether any of my colleagues will either. You must be off your effing heads to have bought that shower of shits."

"Steady, steady on Tim," it was Bill Bates turn to try to pour oil on troubled waters. "I can see how upset you are, but that's no way to talk. I suggest that we adjourn this meeting for now and that we all get together tomorrow morning, when we have had a chance to sleep on it, and then see where we all go from here."

"That's OK with me," said Tim, recognising that he had probably gone too far. "I apologise for my language but, I have to say quite categorically, I will not work in the same Company as that man. There is *nothing* that will persuade me otherwise."

....

Back at the offices of Future Security plc, Joe Hendry was not having a good day. He had had an exceptionally tiresome meeting with his Insurance Broker.

Bob Chambers, of their Lloyds Brokers Tompkins and Harding, had proved, to Joe's incredulous surprise, that they had notified their Professional Indemnity Insurers of over one hundred and fifty possible claims over the last three years and that the rate of these notifications was rising.

To date, the Insurers had not actually paid out a single penny in compensation but they were making reserves in the millions. In consequence, Bob had explained, the Underwriters were declining to offer any renewal terms at all in respect of next year's cover – only one month away.

"They can't fucking do that," was Joe's predictable reply. "They've taken our fucking money for years and now they want to run away just because they might have to pay out a few bob. What's fucking insurance for if they all act like this?" he demanded to know.

Bob went to some pains to point out that he had told Joe's company secretary, on numerous occasions, that if they did not do something drastic to stem the flood of claims, this would be the inevitable consequence.

"Please rest assured, Mr Hendry," he assured Joe, "we have used our very best endeavours to get a stay of execution, but I am afraid that they remain resolute in their decision. We are, of course, endeavouring to find an alternative Underwriter who will accept your risk and I am not entirely without hope that we will succeed. I have to warn you however, that if we do secure alternative cover, then it will be at a substantially increased premium and, almost certainly, you will have to bear a very significant amount of each loss."

"What's that in plain English?" asked Joe. What's it likely to cost us then?"

"I can only guess, but as an educated guess, I would think that your current premium of twenty five thousand pounds a year could quadruple and your current excess of one thousand pounds per claim could be increased to something in the region of twenty thousand pounds in respect of each and every claim."

"You must be joking!" cried Joe. "You just fuck off and come up with something far better than that or you can just piss off and we will find someone else."

"I'm sorry you feel like that, Mr Hendry. That is, of course, entirely your prerogative. Please rest assured that I will do my best and I will call you as soon as I have something to report."

....

His next visitor was George Chalmers. George had been Tom Cumming's accountant for many years, but when Future Security began to lift off four year's ago, he had jumped ship and taken on the job as Finance Director.

George wore a troubled frown – nothing new there thought Joe since he was a born pessimist and could always be relied upon to spot the problems before he saw the opportunities.

He told Joe, "I've been putting off a visit from the PIA for month's – kept telling them that we were up to our necks in end of year accounts and all that sort of thing. However, they are not prepared to be buggered about any more and they are coming here to carry out a review on Friday next week."

"What does that involve?" queried Joe. "Can't they mind their own bloody business and let us get on with ours?"

"I am afraid not. They are coming and that's that. They can, if they wish, turn this place upside down. They are ten times worse than having the Auditors in. If they find anything that they don't like, they can bollock us, or they can fine us, or they can even shut us down."

"Christ almighty, that's all we need," groaned Joe. "You'd better be there and watch what they get up to like a vulture. Can we take out, or even shred, any files that you think might cause us grief?"

"I've already got rid of as much as I can but if they find too many files missing, they'll only get more suspicious and get even more aggressive. I've seen them at work and, believe you me; they are not nice to know when they get stuck in. Leave it to me. I'll do what I can to keep them as happy as possible but it's going to be tough."

....

The follow-up meeting of the Board of H S Financial did not take place. Tim had had a troubled night and there was no way that he was prepared to attend a Board meeting where he would arrive in a totally intransigent mind – it would be a complete waste of everyone's time. Tim had always recognised the advantage of attending a meeting with, albeit his own views fairly well fixed but, nevertheless, with sufficient flexibility to listen to the other person's side. It was always possible that the other side could produce an argument that had not occurred to him.

He was always prepared to be persuaded against his initial view if presented with another view that was sufficiently cogent to make reconsideration a virtue.

As to the matter of working alongside, let alone under, Joe Hendry, there was not the slightest room for argument. It simply would not happen.

He resolved, therefore, to see Colin Crawford before the meeting in the hope that he could persuade him as to the folly of this acquisition. Surely, he argued, the Board of Sunbury's could not be so blind as to employ a man of Joe Hendry's ilk once they knew the full story.

He tapped on Colin's door and walked in. Colin was poring over a mass of computer printouts and looked up with obvious irritation.

"You're a bit early Tim," he said. "The meeting's not for another half hour and I've got a mountain of work to get through. It's bad enough having to go through things twice without having to waste even more time beforehand," he added bluntly, clearly irritated that yesterday's meeting had been so inconclusive.

"I appreciate that Colin, but I think that it would be worth a brief discussion now before we all sit down together. I think it will be time well spent," said Tim forcefully; helping himself to a chair without being invited so to do.

"Very well," sighed Colin with an air of resignation, "what seems to be the problem?"

"I have known of Joe Hendry for about twenty years. He started as a rather shady double-glazing salesman, graduated to the mass selling of virtually worthless investment plans – and went bust. He then metamorphosed into the rather shadowy business of ripping off the aged and coercing them into wholly unsuitable financial arrangements that could prove completely disastrous to them."

"Before you go on Tim, I have to tell you that the decision to buy this business and to employ Joe Hendry is absolutely irreversible. What you are telling me seems more like 'sour grapes'. Hendry is pulling in business hand over fist whereas you, it seems, are simply treading water. The way I see it is that you are jealous of Hendry's success and frightened that, once he is on board, he and his team will show you up."

"You really believe that?" exclaimed an exasperated Tim Harrison. "Let me tell you that I am intensely proud of the professionalism of my company and of all my staff. Similarly, I absolutely abhor the techniques and ethics of people like Hendry. There is no way that I would wish to breathe the same air as him and there is no way that I would work in the same Company. If you take him on, I resign!"

"I'm sorry that you feel that way, Tim, but if that's the way you feel. I accept your resignation with immediate effect. I think that you have made a great mistake, but that is your decision. I will buzz Bill Bates and he will see to the formalities. Goodbye," Colin said standing up and offering to shake hands, "and good luck".

Notwithstanding the fact that Tim had intended to make it a 'take it or leave it' issue, he felt as if he had been pole-axed. To think that a company of the size and status of Sunbury International could prefer an out and out crook like Hendry to him was, simply, unthinkable. Yet it had happened.

Tim could not face Bill Bates or, for that matter, anyone else. He was stunned, felt ashamed, mystified, incredulous and, worst of all, impotent. Everything that he had built up had been taken away from him – not for any justifiable reason, but because people who did not know how to run a company had been given the power and authority to make insane decisions.

He drove home but as, half an hour later, he negotiated his drive, he could not remember how he had got there. The journey had been a complete blur.

He entered his house and called out for Mary.

"Home already, darling," she greeted him with a kiss, drying her hands from some kitchen chore. "What a lovely surprise. Have they given you the push, or something?"

"Well actually, yes. I've been fired!"

He proceeded to relate the whole unhappy saga as Mary fussed around making coffee. When he had finished, Mary sat down opposite him at the kitchen table and smiled,

"I know it has been a terrible shock, darling, but look on the bright side. You've been thinking for months, now that you have got bored with the business, that you should be doing something else. You may not have actually have planned this latest development, but look on it as a golden opportunity – a chance to do something completely different. We've got the money to take a chance. Let's do nothing for a month and then see how you feel. Let's take a damn good holiday, a cruise or something, and get away from it all and give yourself space and time to think."

"We've got the money alright," confirmed Tim. "And I shall make sure that we get a damn sight more. They can't heave me out the door without adequate compensation. I never thought I would ever feel like this about Sunbury's, but I intend to go for them for every penny that I can screw out of them."

"That's the spirit darling. Now what about having a bath and taking me out somewhere nice for lunch to celebrate?"

....

One week later, Joe Hendry had an eventful day. At ten thirty precisely, Bob Manners ushered him into Sunbury's boardroom. Seated there already was the entire board of Sunbury International plc, complete with the four non-executive directors.

Despite his delight at being projected so rapidly into the upper echelons of Public Company life, Joe had never felt more out of place in his life. His heartbeat, he could feel, was approaching one hundred, he was sweating profusely and his stomach was performing cartwheels.

His first impression of the board was that, as distinguished as they looked, they all wore expressions of grim resignation. It was as if they had all been the recipients of bad news, very bad news. Joe hoped that it was not the thought of meeting him that resulted in such grave countenances.

"Joe Hendry, gentlemen," announced Bob, drawing Joe by his arm towards the seated assembly. I will introduce you to each of these gentlemen and then we will have a five-minute spot to discuss the implications of this, our most recent acquisition."

Bob took him around the table whilst each director rose and shook Joe by the hand. After fifteen 'pleased to meet you's' the thin smile on Joe's face had grown weaker still and it came as a welcome relief when he was finally asked to be seated in the one vacant chair.

"We are all aware that, at this point in time, we have only reached an *agreement* to acquire Mr Hendry's Company. We are still going through the formalities and the small print and, until that process has been completed, no money has changed hands. Furthermore, our decision to invite Mr Hendry on to this board is not due to take place until a further three months trading has elapsed; trading that must be satisfactory, I should add. However, Colin and I felt that it was very important that Joe should have the opportunity of meeting the board and for the board to put any questions to him that they feel particularly relevant," continued Bob.

"As you know, we were to have reserved half an hour for this part of our Agenda, but we have had one or two rather urgent, and unexpected, matters to discuss – routine management problems, of course," he confided to Joe, "and we will, very regretfully, have to keep this part of our meeting fairly short. Now gentlemen, are there any urgent points that you would like to put to Mr Hendry?"

Sir Crispin de Courcey, a retired Banker, had been brought in on Lord Passmore's retirement to act as a stopgap non-executive Chairman. He was steeped in 'old money' and 'old school tie' charm and performed superbly in conveying the company's image to the shareholders, the City and the media. He had certainly not been employed for his financial acuity or for his knowledge of the cut and thrust of business life.

Sir Crispin was the first to speak. "Tell me Mr Hendry, I understand that you are an Independent Financial Adviser. What does that entail and what qualifications do you have to have to be able to purvey your business."

Joe realised that to say "God knows and bugger all respectively" would not endear him to this gathering.

"As an Independent Financial Adviser," he answered, "I and my staff are approached by a vast number of people who have financial problems and it is our job, and our pleasure, to solve these for them. We have an outstanding record of helping people, largely the elderly, to ensure that they have a greater income in their retirement than would otherwise have been the case. As to qualifications, I have over twenty years experience in the business, helping all sorts of people from all walks of life. We have over one thousand clients on our books at this point in time. You could say that I acquired my qualifications in the University of Life." Joe tried to smile at this, but his facial muscles had taken on a life of their own and what appeared on his face was a rather unbecoming leer. He noticed with increasing embarrassment that no one else was smiling with him.

"And how do you do that Mr Hendry? I mean, how do you increase their income?" asked Bill Bates.

"Well, all the clients that we deal with own their own homes. We raise a Mortgage for them and, with the money that we raise, we arrange an investment that is more than sufficient to meet the loan repayments and leave them with a surplus income."

"But what if the investment does not perform well and, or, interest rates on their mortgages rise?" persisted Bill Bates. "Surely there would be a risk that they could be left with a reduced income. And what about the equity in their home? Could not that disappear too?"

Joe's sweat problem was becoming greater with every passing minute. His shirt was sticking to his chest and he dared not lift his arms for fear of releasing an overwhelming blast of body odour. He replied, "It is our job to ensure that we choose Fund Managers with a proven track record. In our case we use a highly respected Company – the Investors' Mutual of South Africa." He neglected to tell them that their current investment performance was appalling.

He went on, "As to the equity in their houses, that becomes a loss to the client's estate, not to the clients themselves. They may continue to live in their homes without let or hindrance. It would be against our principles to put a client's primary asset – his house – at risk."

"Tell me Mr Hendry, as soon as Mr Harrison, the Chief Executive of HS Financial Services, and a man for whom I have a great deal of respect, heard that it was intended that we should purchase your company and that you could become a director on our main board, he became particularly agitated and even threatened to resign. Why do you think that was?"

Joe could not believe what he had just heard. He had pulled one over on that stuck up wanker once and for all. The bastard had actually thrown in the towel. He couldn't resist a slight but triumphant smile. He could hardly wait to tell Tom Cummings. With all the shit flying around at present, this was one piece of news that would bring them both great joy.

With some difficulty, he pulled himself together and answered, "That is news to me Mr Bates. I hardly know Mr Harrison, but I have been aware for some time that he has been a little jealous of my company's success. As I understand it, Mr Harrison runs a very fine Insurance Brokerage but he only *dabbles* in the field of Financial Services – independent advice, that is. It may be that he has watched the rate at which our company has grown and, not surprisingly, he is envious. Perhaps he has decided that he would not wish his Company to be compared too closely with ours."

"Perhaps so, Mr Hendry, but would you not agree that Harrisons offer a wider breadth of expertise than your own Company?"

Colin Crawford could see that further questioning would only unearth more weaknesses (he could happily strangle Brian Campbell for landing them with this slippery bastard, but the damage was done and they would just have to do their best).

"Well gentlemen," he intervened, "I think that there are a great many questions that we would like to put to Joe, but he is a busy man and we must let him get on. You go on and make us even more profit," he said, smilingly, turning to Joe.

"We have a great deal to discuss this morning so I suggest that we let Joe go and then I am sure that he will have no objections should you wish to call him direct with any further questions that you might like to raise. Thank you very much for coming Joe and welcome to Sunbury's."

Joe's relief to be let off the hook was palpable. He could not wait to get into his car and back to his office.

....

On his return, he was greeted by a very distraught George Chalmers.

"Bad news Joe, I am afraid. In fact, bloody awful news about our Professional Indemnity Insurance. I've had Bob Chambers on and he tells me that every bloody company he has been to have refused to offer any terms at all for our cover. Without it, we will have to stop trading with immediate effect – a condition laid down by the Financial Services Authority. Without insurance, we will have to wind up the Company – now."

"What is that wanker up to?" shouted Joe. "I've just about had enough of that bastard. He's had years of screwing us for God knows how much and then, as soon as there's a problem, he can't fucking help. Surely we can get another Broker to get the cover for us? There are thousands of the bastards out there."

"I'm afraid not Joe. I have phoned around but, as soon as I tell them that our present Insurers have refused to renew, they say that there's nothing they can do."

"Well don't fucking tell them, you prat!"

"Now cut that out Joe, or you can get stuffed and stand in and take my job this minute. I am doing my best, for Christ sakes. What I have managed to negotiate is that our existing Insurers have agreed to extend our present cover by one month. In other words, we've now got five weeks to find some one else."

"Thank God for that. I'm sorry; I've had a bloody awful morning and now all this. It's just got on top of me."

"I hate to add to your woes Joe, but I've got even worse news. The PIA Inspector was in all day yesterday and he's still here. We had a chat first thing this morning and he tells me that he is very unhappy about a lot of things that he has found. He's still checking, but he reckons that some of the 'offences' he has discovered are so serious that *they* may even close us down. As I couldn't get you, I gave Tom a call and he's coming over after lunch to see you and me and, as he says, to 'find out what the fuck is happening'."

"That's all I fucking need," groaned Joe. "I'm off to the pub."

Chapter Forty-Seven

Three weeks later, Tim and Mary returned from a magical Mediterranean Cruise. Tim was refreshed and ready for battle with anyone.

As they opened the front door a veritable mountain of post confronted them. They also found that the voice mail was overloaded and, on switching on his computer, Tim found that he had fifty-three emails in his inbox awaiting his attention.

He was deeply touched to see so many messages from staff and clients alike, expressing shock, outrage and even sympathy; and sheer surprise that he had left so suddenly without any prior notice. Not one message suggested anything other than that Tim must have been shabbily treated and that Harrisons would never be the same without him.

The three most interesting messages were from Lord Passmore, inviting him to lunch at his London Club at 'his very earliest convenience', one from Graham Wiltshier asking him to contact him 'without delay' and one from Tony Abbott to the same effect.

It was Monday afternoon and he called Lord Passmore first.

"Good to hear from you Tim," his Lordship greeted him. "Look, got someone with me at the moment – a lot of things going on, as you know. I'll be in town on Wednesday. How about lunch at one o'clock in my Club? You know where it is."

"Sure Len. I'll look forward to that. Goodbye till then." Intrigued, he replaced the receiver and called Graham Wiltshier.

"Am I glad to hear from you Tim," said Graham. "As you know, all hell's let loose here. We have to speak. What are you doing tomorrow morning?"

"I didn't know that all hell has let loose, Graham. I only got back from holiday half an hour ago. Anyway, as you know, I'm one of the world's unemployed at the moment so I have got all the time in the world. What time and where?"

"Oh Christ, I'm sorry. What with everything going on here I forgot. Did you have a good time?"

"Wonderful," laughed Tim. "You should try not working, I'm getting into the swing of it. Notwithstanding the pleasures of an idle life, I'll get to your office tomorrow at about ten. Is that OK?"

"That's fine. I'll book the meeting room so we can talk undisturbed. I'll also book a table at Georgio's. No reason why you shouldn't get some benefit out of your visit."

"Great. I'll see you tomorrow." Tim then rang Tony Abbott.

"Glad you called, Tim. Christ, that Joe Hendry is a load of bullshit, isn't he? How the hell did they sink so low as to offer him a job? They must be completely off their trolleys. I must see you about it all, Tim, and soon."

"That's fine Tony. I will be in the office tomorrow seeing Graham at about ten. We're then going to Georgio's for lunch. Why don't you join us?"

"That would be perfect. I'll give Graham a buzz and get him to add one to his booking. Looking forward to seeing you tomorrow Tim. Looking forward very much indeed," he emphasised.

....

Graham's first words, as Tim strolled into his office, were, "I simply could not believe that they told you to leave there and then. What in the name of God has got into them? No man is indispensable but, believe me, without you around, the problems are just piling up. We've got three major clients threatening to go elsewhere unless we can explain what's going on. Two members of staff have already handed in their notice – abandoning ship, they say, before it sinks.

"As for bringing in that devious bastard Joe Hendry! That's the last straw; the whole bloody world has gone mad. Come on Tim, spill the beans, what's going on?"

Tim explained precisely what had happened at his meeting with Colin Crawford and that, to his own utter astonishment, Colin had sided with Hendry against him.

"I don't know why Crawford and Manners have got sucked into believing that Hendry and his gang are God's gift to the Insurance world, but they have and there is nothing that I can do about it. My only hope is that Len Passmore will be able to throw some light on to it – I have lunch with him tomorrow and, to say that I am intrigued would be an understatement. I will let you know what happens."

Tim and Graham then spent the next hour reviewing the problems that had arisen since Tim's departure on a client by client basis. Eventually Graham said, "Well thanks a million Tim. That's a great help. At least I know what to say to these people now, but I can tell you, if they think that you will never be coming back, I am pretty damn sure that most of them will become ex clients by next renewal. Anyway, I'll give Tony a call and tell him that we're ready for lunch."

Over the lunch table, Georgio fussed over them as usual but, as soon as the orders had been placed and the wine poured, Chris got down to the business in hand.

"As you know, we are all completely dumbfounded that Sunbury's would give Joe Hendry even the time of day, let alone a leading role. That decision must be just about the craziest folly that the Company has *ever* committed.

"Apart from everything we know about Hendry's operation and, as you can imagine, Jimmy Smith has kept a pretty close eye on what's going on, I am led to believe that the firm has some serious problems with the PIA. Rumour has it that, if that is the case, they will be struck off before the year is out. If so, that would have serious consequences for us too. As you can imagine, if a 'sister' company of ours is severely disciplined, then that will rub off on H S Financial Services. No amount of PR can dissuade the public from thinking that there is 'no smoke without fire'. If a Company with which we are closely associated goes down the tubes, then we will be following very shortly unless we are very nimble on our feet.

"I have tried on dozens of occasions to arrange an appointment with either Bob Manners or Colin Crawford to let them know just how serious the problem has become, but they keep fobbing me off. What do you suggest I do Tim?"

"As of now, it's not for me to say Chris. No one could be more surprised than me that the Board appear to have been so utterly stupid. Look where it got me though. I voted with my feet and here I am, unemployed and probably unemployable. Our financial circumstances are rather different, though, and I would urge you not too do anything too precipitately. As I said to Graham, I am lunching with Len Passmore tomorrow. Why not hold everything in abeyance for the time being and let me get back to you after that meeting?"

With the main problems now out in the open, the three of them continued to enjoy their lunch and discuss what might have been.

As Tim left the restaurant and bade his farewells, he could not help feeling the pain of watching his friends return to their office – his office – to go about their daily labours *without* him. For the first time in three weeks, he yearned to be back at the tiller.

....

"Good to see you Tim my boy," greeted Lord Passmore rising from his table as the club steward brought Tim over to him. "How are you keeping and how's the delectable Mary?"

The banter continued for a while as they ordered their drinks and their club lunches until Len leant back with a sigh, "Damned if I know what goes on these days Tim. I left Sunbury's with over five hundred million in cash reserves, profits in excess of two hundred million a year and a share price of nine pounds.

"I thought that the 'young Turks' were going to make everything grow – the cash pile, the profits and the share price but, just look at it now.

"Sunbury's has spent close on one billion pounds in acquisitions in the last three years and, as a result, instead of a surplus we now have a quarter of a billion pounds of debt, and the Company will show a loss of close on three hundred million pounds this year.

"Bill Bates has asked me if I will come back. Old Crispin is running around like a fart in a colander with no idea at all as to what's going on around him and those two young buggers, Manners and Crawford, are slowly strangling the Company to death. They've bought a complete load of junk - dot coms, high techs, communications and even a dodgy bank – you name it, they've bought it. They keep talking about a fortune to be made 'just around the corner', but I can't see it, I really can't. As you know, the share price dipped below five pounds today for the first time in twenty years and it is still heading south. What do you make of it all Tim?"

"Well, as you know, Len, I have come out of the debacle as badly as anyone. Not only have I lost a packet on my own shares since I have been 'locked in', but I've lost my job as well."

"Of course, I'm sorry Tim. There I am bemoaning the fate of all and sundry and completely overlooking the fact that the buggers, if you will pardon the expression, have been so bloody crass as to ditch you in favour of some shifty low-life by the name of Hendry. I'm sorry – too wrapped up in my own affairs to remember the one thing that really matters. Do forgive me – another senior moment."

"Not at all, Len," we would have got around to it sooner or later. "The one thing that cheered me up in all of this is that you have just said that you might consider coming back to the Company yourself. In my view, that is the only thing that can turn around the present situation. We need you at the helm – at least until we have everything back on an even keel – and we need Manners and Crawford out of the door, fast. At the same time, we must do everything possible to ensure that Hendry and Cummings never get through that door."

They continued discussing all the options and, by the time Lord Passmore's driver had arrived, the prospects for Sunbury's looked considerably brighter. At the same time, Tim's immediate employment prospects were looking up. Lord Passmore had virtually made up his mind to return to Sunbury's and had even intimated that a proposal for a seat on the board for Tim would meet with his full support.

Notwithstanding that, Tim noticed in the Evening Standard that the share price had dropped fifty pence on the day and now stood at four pounds fifty. The market was only too well aware that things were not right at Sunbury's.

....

Tom Cummings was in a foul mood as he arrived for his meeting with Joe Hendry and George Chalmers.

"Now let's get this right," he began, chomping furiously on his cigar as he spoke. "I am about to sell Future Security for ten million pounds – of which you, you undeserving prat, will get a quarter – and you are telling me that the company has serious problems. Deal-busting problems. Is that what you're telling me?"

George Chalmers shuffled through his papers and drew out a typed sheet.

"According to the PIA Inspector's preliminary findings, we are in breech of twenty four regulations, three of which are deemed very serious. If we cannot put in a justifiable defence in respect each and every one of these points, he has assured me that he will close us down."

"How long can we *hide* these 'breeches', for God's sake," asked Tom. "Our deal should be through within ten to fourteen days. Can't we bury everything for a fucking fortnight for Chrissake?"

"I very much doubt it Tom," answered George. "In any event, surely Sunbury's are going to put their own Accountant's in to check that they are buying what they think they are? If that happens, we're dead in the water."

"Normally that would be the case, but you forget that I was not dealing with Sunbury's. I was dealing with the idiot Brian Campbell and the Bank and he is still wet behind the ears. He's like a kid with a new toy now that he has got a hold of the Company's chequebook. Between these three walls, I promised to slip him a hundred grand if he could get the deal through without any due diligence check up. That did the trick. He promised to act the innocent when the request for due diligence came up and tell them that they could trust his judgement because he's done business with us for so many years. And do you know what? The suckers bought it. That's why it's essential we get the PIA off our backs now."

"We can try Tom," chipped in Joe, "but we've got another problem that is almost as bad."

"What the fuck's that?" stormed Tom. "With ten million pounds in the balance, we cannot afford to have any more problems. What have you done now, for God's sake?"

"It's nothing I have done," said Joe defensively. "It's our Professional Indemnity insurance. By law we have to have it or we have to stop trading *immediately*. As we stand, our present Insurers have given us a one month extension and, in twenty nine days from now, we are finished."

"Well that's alright then," replied Tom with a sigh. "In twenty nine day's time, we will have banked our cheques and they can all go to hell."

George intervened. "I don't think it's quite that simple Tom. It would be the suppression of a very material fact. If you have accepted the cheques knowing that the Company would have to cease trading within a week or two, the whole deal would be null and void. You might even find yourselves with a prison sentence hanging over you for fraud. I must also point out, that I don't like your cosy deal with Brian Campbell either. If that got out, you would be in deep trouble, very deep trouble – that would be a very clear cut case of fraud – or bribery and corruption. I want nothing to do with this deal from now on."

"For a hundred grand, Brian will keep his mouth shut, don't you worry about that," Tom emphasised. "What the hell are we going to do about this Insurance problem? There must be another Broker or Underwriter around who would come up with something. You leave it to me. I know a few people. I'll make a few calls and you can bet your sweet life that I will come up with a deal. Let's meet tomorrow morning, here at nine o'clock sharp, and see where we have got to."

As Tom was leaving, George whispered to Tom, "Have you got a moment? I am having some grief with the Tax Inspector over the returns for Jaycee Ltd. I would like to run through a few queries with you."

"Oh fuck that for the time being. That's your job to sort that out – that's what I pay you for. I've got enough problems of my own to sort out without having to get involved in piddling little matters like that."

And so the matter was left - for the time being.

....

Over the next few days, the news circulating about Sunbury's got steadily worse. With each day that passed, further information came to light in the Press about one or another of the Company's that they had acquired during the last three years – all of it was negative.

Sunbury's were forced to issue a profits warning and announce that they would be considering a Rights Issue in the foreseeable future. Investors who had held the shares for a decade or more were becoming more and more vociferous in their complaints.

This once proud bluest of blue chip companies, with it's mighty 'war chest' was in dire danger of slipping out of the FTSE 100 altogether. This was a company to which widows and orphans had flocked as a safe haven for their nest eggs. A company noted for financial probity, steady growth and healthy dividends.

The share price had now dropped from a high of around eleven pounds fifty to just under two pounds and no one knew where the slide would stop – if ever.

On Monday of the following week, Sunbury's issued a Press Release, signed by Sir Crispin de Courcey. It read:

In recent years, your Company embarked on an exciting programme of diversification. Your Board, although proud of it's traditional strengths felt, that as we moved towards the twenty first Century, we should embrace the new Technologies and Financial Services that promised to be at the cutting edge of the British economy.

Whereas the Board fully supported this programme, we have to face the commercial reality that some of these plans were ill advised. As has become apparent from recent statements, the Board has decided to radically review this strategy, which, in some instances, will mean that we will liquidate some of our acquisitions. Furthermore, a number of acquisitions currently 'in the pipeline' will be aborted.

In consequence, there will be a number of important Board changes.

In the first instance, as of today, I shall be standing down as Chairman, though I will be remaining as a non-executive Director for as long as my services are required.

I am delighted to say that Lord Passmore, to whom this Company has owed such a deep debt of gratitude for over twenty years, has accepted the Board's invitation to return in his former capacity, as Chairman. We are extremely grateful that we will, once again, reap the benefits of Lord Passmore's exhaustive knowledge of our Company, his wise counsel and the steadying hand with which he will again steer us into the future.

At the same time, the Board has accepted the resignations of Mr Bob Manners and Mr Colin Crawford who will be leaving us without compensation. I would like to thank them both for their past contribution.

It is likely that there will be one or two further Board Announcements in the near future and Lord Passmore will be issuing a Press Release shortly.

Last week, we issued a profits warning. Shortly, we hope to be in a position to be able to announce that adequate provisions have been made in respect of all those of our recent Acquisitions that have failed to perform to our expectations.

Comment has been noted in the Press as to the need for us to make a Rights Issue. Although nothing is ruled out, Lord Passmore has asked me to state that, at this early stage, he is of the view that such a strategy will not be necessary.

Tim received a faxed copy of the Press Release. He could not have been more delighted.

So was the City. By the end of the day, the Share Price had doubled to just over four pounds. The recovery was under way.

....

The following morning, Tom was reading the Daily Telegraph over his breakfast table when a headline in the City section caught his eye.

Lord Passmore returns. Sunbury's shares leap one hundred percent in the day.

Tom Cummings felt, as he read on, as if a Mule had kicked him in the guts. He could not believe what he was reading.

"Ten million pounds," he groaned. "Ten million pounds down the drain just because that useless bastard Hendry can't run a fucking company to save his fucking life. Why did I leave him to run it? I must have been fucking mad."

"What dear?" asked is wife disinterestedly from behind her copy of *Hello*. "Something wrong?"

"Something wrong?" echoed Tom as he launched into a tirade of abuse against Joe Hendry in particular and the world in general. The bit about losing ten million pounds did, however, catch her attention.

Having let off steam, he called Joe Hendry to make his feelings clear beyond all reasonable doubt. Fortunately for Joe, he was out and he had thrown his mobile phone in the river. He had even contemplated following it in.

Tom decided to vent his spleen on George Chalmers.

"Ah Tom," greeted George when he had got through. "I've been trying to contact you. I am afraid that I have some rather bad news for you."

"Bad news," shrieked Tom. "You've got bad news for me? I've just lost ten million pounds and you tell me you've got bad news for me? What the fuck can be worse? Go on, make my day. Tell me I've just won the lottery but you've lost the fucking ticket. Is that it?"

"Ten million pounds?" queried Tom. "No it's nothing like that, though that would come as something of a blow. No, I was trying to reach you because, as you know, the Inland Revenue have been rather unhappy about the accounts for Jaycee Ltd. They called yesterday evening to say that they are coming to this Office at ten o'clock today and they want you to be there then. I have to have all the books and Management Accounts for the last fifteen years. I am afraid that it's going to be tough going Tom, when these bastards get stuck in, they want blood."

If Tom had had a gun in his hand, he would have used it, there and then.

....

On Tuesday, Lord Passmore sat down in his familiar chair at the head of the boardroom table.

He looked around with a broad smile on his face and said, "I have to say, gentlemen, that I never thought that I would be sitting here again, but it is good to be back."

Surprisingly, and rather emotionally, this statement was greeted by a round of applause from this otherwise austere and expressionless group of men.

"Thank you for that, gentlemen. Much appreciated. Now, before we go on, and we have a very great deal to discuss, I have asked Cecil Banks to allow a couple of minutes for one additional item of business. As you know, we have been saved from the folly of having a representative from the Financial Services Industry parachuted onto our Board. One of the areas that I intend that we should continue expanding, and rapidly at that, is the field of Insurance Broking, Risk Management and Independent Financial Advice. We are fortunate to have, as Chief Executive of our Harrison Sunbury Financial Services Division, a man for whom I have a great deal of respect.

"Tim Harrison is a man of considerable integrity, has a sound knowledge of his Industry and is a consummate business-man. For all of these reasons, I would appreciate his presence on this Board.

"I realise that the appointment of a Director is a weighty matter and one which should, under normal circumstances, take a little while to process. However, these are not normal circumstances. We are re-building our Company and I, for one, would like to have Tim Harrison alongside us whilst we are achieving this. I believe that you all know Tim and I hope you feel, as I do, that he is a man of the calibre that we need. In short, I would like, from the chair, to propose Tim as a Director of this Board. Do I have a seconder?"

Three hands shot up immediately. They belonged to Sir Crispin de Courcey, Bill Bates and Cecil Banks.

"Thank you Crispin," smiled Leonard Passmore. "I have a proposer and a seconder. Any discussion?" He looked around and saw nothing but nods and confirmatory comments.

"Excellent. Then the motion is carried unanimously. Now I have taken the liberty of asking Tim to wait in my office in case he should be needed. Does any one have any objections to Tim joining us straight away?"

There was a ripple of laughter around the Board and comments such as, "Good to have you back Len", "you haven't changed a bit" and "bring the young man in, the sooner the better".

Five minutes later, Tim walked into the Sunbury Board room as the equal of his peers. His head held high and his chest fully puffed. It had been a bumpy ride he told himself, many knocks on the way, but it had been worth it.

Epilogue

The Sunbury share price, under Lord Passmore's prudent stewardship, stayed around the four to five pound mark for about two years and then, as the market realised that the excesses of the mid-nineties were behind them, it steadily rose. By the beginning of the twenty first century, the price had reached twenty pounds. A ten for one issue brought the price down to a more manageable two pounds a share, but it then continued it's steady rise until, by the end of the year two thousand, it had reached a comfortable and sustainable two pounds twenty.

Sunbury International was now firmly re-established in the top half of the FTSE 100 list of companies. The Company traded and manufactured in thirty-three Countries around the World and was an extremely valuable dollar earner for the UK.

During the year two thousand and one, Lord Passmore decided to retire - for the last time – and to live quietly in the country with is wife of over fifty years. He now devotes a considerable amount of his free time to his work in the House of Lords and is currently the Opposition's leading voice in the matter of the reform and regulation of the Financial Services Industry. With his earthy commonsense, his infectious humour, and his considerable first-hand knowledge of the Industry, his views are widely sought and respected on both sides of the House.

Bob Manners and Colin Crawford faced a City investigation as to their practices whilst involved in the rapid diversification of Sunbury International. The findings were inconclusive but both were barred for life from holding Directorships in any UK Public Companies. Both men had managed to sell a large proportion of their shares at seven pounds fifty – again, another cause for concern in the eyes of the City Watchdogs – but they were allowed to hold on to their gains – ill gotten, though many observers felt.

Bob Manners retired to Bournemouth where he helped is son build up a small and moderately successful car hire business. Colin Crawford settled in Formby, where he opened up a very small Tax Consultancy specialising in helping small businesses complete their tax returns.

Future Security plc was placed in Receivership within three weeks of the aborted Sunbury bid. The majority of it's Agents managed to get jobs with other Companies within the first three months, though the staff, including George Chalmers, found future employment rather more difficult. Many of the unfortunate Investors were faced with financial ruin though, happily, the Investors' Compensation Scheme stepped in and most received ninety percent of their original investment.

The *Future Security Action Group* was formed to assist Investors extricate themselves from the convoluted mortgage arrangements that they were saddled with. To this day, the work goes on and many Investors will die before they see any light at the end of their particular tunnels.

Tom Cummings faced an uncertain future. He was the subject of several minor charges for breaches of the Financial Services Act and he was severely reprimanded on all counts. He was banned from ever working in the Industry again, a penalty that had little effect since nothing could have induced him to have a third attempt in that particular line of business.

More seriously, the Inland Revenue proceeded with their prosecution for Tax Evasion (shrouded in the mystery of numerous Channel Island Bank Accounts) over a period of fourteen years. He was found guilty on all counts, ordered to pay one million pounds in back taxes plus a penalty of the same amount. He was also sentenced to three years in prison – where he currently resides – albeit in the relative comfort of Ford Open Prison. He is also, currently, in the middle of divorce proceedings.

Joe Hendry fared rather better. After a yearlong enquiry, Joe was found guilty of twenty breaches of the Financial Services Act, all deemed to be of a serious or, very serious, nature.

He was banned for life from holding any position at all in the Financial Services Industry. To the shock of his peers, the dismay of his ex-employees and the fury of his Investors, he was sentenced to one hundred and twenty day's community service. This 'penalty' was interpreted as a licence for any rogue or ne'er-do-well to set up in business selling dubious financial products with a complete disregard for financial probity. The 'sentence' remains a disgrace to this day.

Joe, seemingly untroubled by his experience, enjoyed the pleasure of finalising his ties with Samantha whilst in a state of near bankruptcy. He derived considerable satisfaction from ensuring that she did not even receive any benefit from the family home – that had to be sold to pay off his numerous creditors.

Joe 'emigrated' to the balmy sunshine of the Costa Brava where, to this day, he is re-building his fortune by selling inappropriate time-shares to the unsuspecting and unwary public.

Janet remains happily married with three daughters and a son. The sale of her Sunbury shares, gifted to her by the late Bill Warrington in the form of shares in Harrison's, enabled Janet and her husband to live in relative prosperity, even after privately educating all four children.

Tim Harrison thoroughly enjoyed his time as a Director of Sunbury International and, during that period, expanded the financial services division to become one of the top ten Insurance Brokers in the UK and one of the top fifty firms of Independent Financial Advisers.

After Lord Passmore's retirement, Tim reviewed his own circumstances. With the increase in the Sunbury Share price, his own holdings, together with his share options, he found himself to be a relatively wealthy man.

Before he reached the age of sixty, he and Mary thought that the time had come to take life much more easily and to travel the world. Accordingly, Tim also resigned, but remained for a further three years as a non-executive director on the Sunbury board.

With the additional time Tim found available to him, he resolved to fulfil a life-long ambition and to write a novel.

His first novel was a story based on the knocks and the triumphs and the interaction between two people of entirely opposing characters. It was called 'Knock for Knock'.

Printed in the United Kingdom
by Lightning Source UK Ltd.
117128UKS00001B/142-342

9 781846 854873